Library of Shakespearean Biography and Criticism

I. PRIMARY REFERENCE WORKS ON SHAKESPEARE

II. CRITICISM AND INTERPRETATION

   A. Textual Treatises, Commentaries
   B. Treatment of Specal Subjects
   C. Dramatic and Literary Art in Shakespeare

III. SHAKESPEARE AND HIS TIME

   A. General Treatises. Biography
   B. The Age of Shakespeare
   C. Authorship

Library of Shakespearean Biography and Criticism

Series II, Part A

STRATFORD TO DOGBERRY

Library of Shakespearean Biography and Criticism

STRATFORD TO DOGBERRY

❁

STUDIES IN SHAKESPEARE'S

EARLIER PLAYS

BY

John W. Draper

BOOKS FOR LIBRARIES PRESS
FREEPORT, NEW YORK

Copyright © 1961 by the University of Pittsburgh Press.

Reprinted 1970 by arrangement.

STANDARD BOOK NUMBER:

8369-5255-3

LIBRARY OF CONGRESS CATALOG CARD NUMBER:

71-109646

4/71

PRINTED IN THE UNITED STATES OF AMERICA

Contents

v

61646

Preface

Of the thirty papers collected in the present volume, many are revised from previous publication during the past twenty-five years.
Since most of these have been widely scattered in philological and
other periodicals in this country and in Europe, general convenience
and the requests of sundry readers suggest that they be collected in
a single volume. They treat a dozen of Shakespeare's earlier plays,
before the composition of *Twelfth Night* and of *Hamlet,* on both
of which the present critic has elsewhere had his say. The first six
studies are general, and the rest chiefly concern *The Merchant of
Venice, Romeo and Juliet,* the Falstaff trilogy, *As You Like It,* and
Much Ado.

The aspects discussed are rather diverse—such time-honored
themes as source and date, and newer approaches that aim more
directly at interpretation, for interpretation is the chief object of
the scholar's task. Some of these newer approaches relate to Elizabethan social and economic life: the disintegration of feudalism and
the feudal army, and the changing status of servants, children, and
younger brothers. Some are scientific: astronomy is used to date a
play, or astrology and Galenic medicine to interrelate and explain
details of character, physique, or speech-tempo. These and other
determinants make the plays what they are, and answer the basic
questions: why did Shakespeare choose these subjects, just what significance did he mean to give them, and why did he treat them as he
did?

The ideal interpretative critic should be master of every pertinent background—if such an ambition lie within human scope—and should at will be able to transform his attitude on any matter to that of an Elizabethan of any social class. These studies are but a few steps toward this main purpose. They present a miscellany of backgrounds applied to various plays, a modest supplement to the labors of former scholars, and, one hopes, an aid to future readers, critics, and actors.

Grateful thanks are due my wife for assistance with the proofs, to the officers of the University of Pittsburgh Press, and to E. J. Stahr Esq., President of West Virginia University, now on leave as Secretary of the Army, whose good offices have helped to make this publication possible.

John W. Draper

I

Country and Court in Shakespeare's Plays

> . . . those that are good manners at the court are as ridiculous
> in the country as the behavior of the country is most mockable
> at the court.
>
> —*As You Like It,* III, ii, 41 ff.

Elizabethan life gave Shakespeare infinite realistic details, as editors know who must explain them to those unfamiliar with the age, scholars who use them to date the plays, and more recently those who see in them Shakespeare's effort to give old characters contemporary realism, old stories a timely significance of theme and a clue to Shakespeare's purpose in a given play. His dramatic form he took largely from the current conventions based on the conditions of the Elizabethan stage and illustrated in the work of his immediate predecessors; and, even late in his career, he would snatch a grace from Jonson [1] or from Fletcher.[2] But the content of his plays is essentially Shakespeare's own—not the outline of the plots, for most of these came from well-known sources—but the nice adjustment of character to plot and the timely interpretation of theme by which he gave these sources a fresh and piquant vigor. What little we know of his life suggests that he had experienced amply the hard knocks of actuality, and so might well reflect it in his work; and, as Elizabethan criticism gave to "the Romantic drama . . . no scholarly justification" [3] Shakespeare's deepening of realistic significance would accord with the dramatic theory of his time. In short, despite those critics who see in his work only a tissue of stage convention, his contribution to Elizabethan drama was an intense and immediate reality,[4] the making of art a mirror to very nature. This explains both the current popularity and the universal value of his work. Many clever playwrights have manipulated mere conventions into successful pieces for the stage, but Shakespeare used conventions, not for themselves, but for more significant purposes.

Some critics have insisted on Shakespeare's essential truth to life, but they have done little to show that truth to the specific life that he and his audience knew; and even the general themes of the plays have usually been interpreted in terms of modern, or of Victorian, morality: did Cordelia deserve her death? did Desdemona lie, and had she therefore "tragic guilt?" The study of contemporary realism in the plays, however, has placed first the characterization and then the plot and theme in a truer perspective. We understand why the maltreated Shylock and the much abused Malvolio were portrayed as hated characters, and why the naïve Orlando and the soured and cynical Timon were sympathetically portrayed. They are contemporary types and as such aroused in drama the same sense of disgust or of approval that griping money-lenders and presuming stewards, that dauntless younger sons and free-handed noblemen, aroused in the common mind. The realism of these characters was generally Shakespeare's own improvement of his sources; and thus he contributed new types to the contemporary stage: he transformed the shadowy constables of early Elizabethan drama, first into Dull in *Love's Labour's,* and later into the incisive realism of Dogberry and of Elbow;[5] he developed the clownish man-servant into the gilded rusticity of Launcelot Gobbo; and he vivified the old convention of the *miles gloriosus* into the inimitable Falstaff. This greater truth of character, appropriately expressing itself in the related actions of the plot, produced greater truth and significance of theme; for realistic people behaving realistically, reacting to varied situations and creating new situations, illustrate the basic principles that govern actual human relationships. Thus reality of theme is a corollary to reality of plot and character; and the recent study of character-realism in Shakespearean plays leads to the discovery that these timely themes must have constituted the meaning of the plays to contemporary audiences. This in turn reveals the evolution in Shakespeare of the theme, and his attitude, changing or constant, toward a given problem; and it shows the growth of a social concept in his mind, its increasing vividness and detail, and its accumulating scope and depth of meaning.

The complex changes called the Renaissance that swept over England in the sixteenth century affected first of all the court and urban centres, and left the great rural population still in the Middle Ages. The resultant contrast between court and country—apparent in all periods, but accentuated then—entered into almost every phase of life, from religion and economics to the detail of manners and social convention. It must have been apparent even to the stupidest country bumpkin that came up to London,[6] and must have struck Shakespeare at every turn. In religion, the more purely rural sections, which were shortly to espouse the cause of the Stuarts against the Roundheads, were High Church Anglican, or even Roman Catholic, at heart; whereas the towns traded with the Calvinists of Holland, read the Mar-prelate tracts, and grew increasingly Puritan. In economics, the rural landlords and their dependents clung to the feudal system and opposed the growth of capitalism, by which the merchants and usurers took advantage of the rise in prices to force landlords to mortgage their estates,[7] and so to lose them. The contrast in manners appears in the dramatists, in such a pamphleteer as Lupton;[8] and the character-writers of the age find it necessary to specify "A Country Widdow," "A Country Alewife,"[9] a "Country Gentleman,"[10] "A Plaine Country Fellow."[11] Earle, Overbury, and Breton,[12] though they usually prefer the country to the city, all admit the boorish manners of the rural districts; and the observing author of Cyuile and Vncyuile Life, with the archetypes of Petruchio in his eye, notes the "rusticitie of their houses and garments" and their "barbarous behauiour and vndecent dooings."[13] In 1617, Minsheu defines "uplandish" as rude and clownish, for "the people that dwell in the mountains are severed from the civilite of cities";[14] and, in Twelfth Night, Shakespeare himself, though he usually preferred rural simplicity to the extravagance of an Osric, echoed these sentiments:

> Ungracious wretch,
> Fit for the mountains and the barbarous caves,
> Where manners ne'er were preach'd.

This contrast between city and country must have been obvious to the Elizabethans; and one might expect it to be reflected in contemporary drama.

Curiously enough, however, the Elizabethan drama before Shakespeare and the dramatic traditions on which it was founded have little or nothing of this theme. Although Latin non-dramatic authors such as Horace and Virgil, under the influence partly of pastoral poetry and partly of the Epicurean ideal, are full of conventional praise of country life as against city life, yet Latin drama, aside from an occasional bit, such as in Plautus' *Mostellaria*,[15] was too urban and sophisticated to take the country into serious account. Mediæval drama, moreover, although contemporary poetry such as *Piers Ploughman* reflects the contrast vividly, was too much engaged with religious and moralistic subjects to express the more purely social theme. The drama of the early and middle sixteenth century was centered on ethical platitudes or on theological controversy; and even such comedies as *Ralph Roister Doister* and *Gammer Gurton's Needle* and such a satire as Skelton's *Magnificence* do not express this contrast. The Italian and the French dramatic traditions were too far removed from popular life to bring such themes into England; and, in the pseudo-Classical plays, the nearest approach is perhaps the "flouting" of Hodge and Rusticus in the first scene of Edwardes' *Horestes*. John Heywood, often crudely realistic, depicts sometimes courtly, sometimes distinctly rural, types: but there is no effort at contrast, and indeed no apparent sense of fundamental difference. Shakespeare's immediate predecessors belonged to the universities, to the court, and to the Bohemian life of London rather than to the country, and so rarely turned to rural themes, which would hardly consort with the tragic styles of Kyd or Marlowe or with the jingo chronicle plays of the Armada period. Even Lyly, who suggests in the *Euphues* something of the contrast of court and country life,[16] neglects the opportunity to develop it in his *Midas;* and it remained for Shakespeare to express this theme in the Lylian style in *Love's Labour's Lost*. Of all Shakespeare's early contemporaries, Greene seems to have been most conscious of this social disparity: his coney-catching tracts show the raw countryman lost in the intricacies of London, and that he was not without real appreciation of rural life.[17] In his plays, he exhibits some merely conventional pastoralism, perhaps satiric, in the *Orlando Furioso;* but more significant is his *Friar Bacon* (c. 1590), the theme of which is the marriage of a noble to a milkmaid.[18] Greene, however, is not very consistently realistic in the speech and actions of his characters; and the final wedding between the lovers belongs to Arcadia rather than to contemporary England. A better example is *The Taming of A Shrew,* in which the old story inherently implies a contrast between city life and the life at the tamer's country house, and shows clearly that the older play influenced Shakespeare.

The theme in Shakespeare developed parallel to the scenes of low comedy usually supplied by country clowns. The early histories use but little of this contrasting comic relief; and the best examples of rural portraiture, the crudely overdrawn Jack Cade in *Henry VI, Part II,* and the Gardiner in *Richard II,* are neither of them realistic enough to breathe of the country. The early tragedies, *Romeo and Juliet* and *Julius Caesar,* are not rural plays; for lofty tragic themes generally required a setting in courts and cities. It is in the comedies, especially of his first and second periods, that Shakespeare gradually developed this theme of the two contrasting Elizabethan cultures; and his development of it, like his development of constables and of the *miles gloriosus,* passes through several stages in which by degrees it emerges with increasing clarity and dramatic point.

The *Comedy of Errors,* built on the Classical tradition, has little of realism and nothing of country life. In his first plays, indeed, Shakespeare, like his immediate predecessors, usually put his low-life passages into verse; but, even as early as Goodman Dull in *Love's Labour's,* he begins to contrast them realistically with the more courtly scenes by putting them into prose. *Love's Labour's* is a play of fashionable life seen by an outsider; and that outsider, being lately come up from the shires, gave the play such reality as he was able to get by contrasting his "London wits" with a group of "country bumpkins." [19] The main theme of the comedy is learning *vs.* love; but the theme of love at court is paralleled by the rustic dalliance of Costard and Jacquenetta, very much as later in *As You Like It* the courtly wooing of Rosalind is paralleled by the country love-making of Touchstone and Audrey; but, in *Love's Labour's,* the contrast is implied rather than obvious; it has no great significance in the play; and it is not even carried through consistently; for Costard himself occasionally speaks with a learned wit quite out of character, and he is, strangely enough, perhaps the cleverest of the mockers in discomforting Don Armado. The best drawn rural figure is "tharborough" Dull, and he is but pale beside Dogberry and Elbow, who were to come. The great social contrast of the age, therefore, though clearly reflected in *Love's Labour's,* is not integrated into the main plot, is not always consistently developed in character and style, is implied only faintly in the setting, and so constitutes a minor theme.

In *Two Gentlemen* the language of Launce and of Speed shows considerable progress toward realism; and the country love affair of Launce contrasts, as in *Love's Labour's,* with the more aristocratic major plot. Although the theme of court *vs.* country may not be quite as evident as in the former play, it is more significantly used. Verona appears as a provincial town, from which the two young gentlemen with their servants go to the Emperor's court to "be in the eye of every exercise" that belongs to their "youth and nobleness of birth" [20]—advantages that rural Verona apparently did not possess. Proteus, in his new role as a fashionable lover, finds it necessary to substitute for his "foolish lout" of a servant, Launce, the accomplished and elegant Sebastian; and this change brings about the comic dénouement. Thus the contrast between court and country is made to play an integral part in the major plot. The characterization, moreover, of Launce and Speed is fuller, the style, more consistent, and the main theme of the play would seem to be the effect of court life upon two young gentlemen recently come under its influence, the same theme more effectively expressed by the career of Orlando in *As You Like It.*

Throughout Shakespeare's second period, this theme appears and reappears. In *A Midsummer Night's Dream* it is implicit in the contrast between the high life love affairs and the low life antics of Bottom and his fellows, which, with the associated fairy lore, forms a sort of antimasque; and this comic relief actually usurps the main interest in the play. In *The Taming of the Shrew* the theme of city *vs.* country life provides the resolution of the plot. Katherine, spoiled by easy urban ways, is tamed by the hard conditions, purposely augmented by Petruchio, that went with Elizabethan travel and rural housekeeping. Shakespeare reinforced the realism of his source in order to accentuate these trials,[21] especially the homeward journey and Petruchio's contempt for fine clothes, or even reasonable decorum in dress. The servant Grumio "throughout smacks of the stable." [22] In an incidental way *The Merchant of Venice* also illustrates this theme in the figures of Launcelot Gobbo and his father, the one with his fine citified airs, the other a humble country-man who cannot bring himself to address his son as "Master." Shallow's contrast of his gay youth at court and his old age in the country brings somethi_g of this theme even into the history plays; and, in *Merry Wives*, as in *The Taming of the Shrew*, the country triumphs over the court, and two citizens' wives of a small provincial town put down a "gentleman," a knight raised in the household of the very Howards, a former intimate of the Prince of Wales—and Mistress Page and Mistress Ford heap repeated indignities upon the poor gull Sir John Falstaff. Even in the latter '90's did Shake-speare still think of himself rather as a countryman than as a fol-lower of the court? Or perhaps, even in London, the predominantly rural life of England swayed the sympathies of the audience: the rural preferences of Overbury, Earle, and Breton suggest as much. In *Twelfth Night* also, Shakespeare sympathizes with the free and easy country ways of Sir Toby rather than with the more efficient and up-to-date arrangements of Olivia's officious steward.

In *As You Like It,* perhaps most clearly, this theme appears. Orlando's career and final marriage to the future duchess illustrate the struggles of a youth raised "rustically at home" to gain recog-nition and a place at court. The action of the play shows his su-periority both in manly exercises and in loving dalliance, and the dialogue reiterates this contrast of country *vs.* court. Orlando notes that Rosalind speaks too well for a countrybred woman. Touchstone tells Corin that if he hasn't been to court, he's "damn'd," [23] and in the following dialogue Corin replies: ". . . those that are good man-ners at the Court, are as ridiculous in the Countrey, as the behauiour of the Countrie is most mockeable at the Court." Country life, as in the earlier plays, seems to win the debate. The melancholy Jaques also does not favor life at court; and, at the end of the play, Touch-stone, by marrying Audrey, seems to decide in favor of the country, at least as far as women are concerned. Indeed, the whole *urbs in rure* in the forest of Arden is an ironic parody of sophisticated court life. The country appears in the play at its best and gayest; whereas, in the corruption that surrounds the reigning Duke, not even the patent merits of a champion wrestler can win their just re-

wards. The theme of usurpation in the play and the growing seriousness of tone underlying even the comic relief of Touchstone and
of Jaques point to the tragedies and bitter comedies that were to
follow.

In Shakespeare's later plays, perhaps because more serious themes
were engaging his attention, he confined his characters more to the
aristocracy and their followers; or perhaps his years in London and
his growing association with the court impressed this point of view
upon him; or perhaps Kemp's leaving the company of actors obliged
him to avoid such characters as Dogberry and Gobbo, and so made
rural realism less possible in his later plays. In *Hamlet* the grave-
diggers have little or no importance in the plot; in *Lear,* the picture
of the country seems remote both from the Arcadian felicities of
Arden and from the realities of the English countryside. In *All's
Well,* to be sure, Helena, a feminine Orlando, comes up to court,
cures the King, and at last wins her marked-down husband; but her
rural origins are not important in the play. Mariana and Timon
retire into the country to solace their disappointments; but Mariana
is only a minor character in *Measure for Measure,* and Timon's life
as a hermit has neither the bucolic charm of *As You Like It* nor the
realism of Petruchio's household in *The Shrew.* Country life no
longer appears as superior to the court; and, as in *Lear,* Shakespeare
seems to use rural setting, when he uses it at all, merely as a background for the tempestuous passions of characters to whom such a
setting in no respect belongs. Perhaps he thought this theme of
court and country so outworn that in his third period he preferred
to ignore its possibilities, even where his plots suggested it.

In Shakespeare's late romances this theme returns. In *Cymbeline*
he adds to his source the story of Belarius and his foster sons living
in refuge in the mountain wilds, and so contrasts their honest hardships in this "rude place" with the luxurious evils of court life, very
much as the good Duke does in *As You Like It.* Imogen sums up the
situation in an aside:

> These are kind creatures. Gods, what lies I have Heard!
> Our Courtiers say all's savage but at court:
> Experience, O, thou disprov'st report.

In *The Tempest,* also, the theme returns, but idealized beyond the
pale of reality; and, in the end, Miranda having won her lover, and

Prospero broken his staff, they both happily return to the realities of Renaissance court life. The play has no realistic rural characters; and the exquisite descriptions in the text, like so many landscape backgrounds in the paintings of the Renaissance, have a conventional fragility, against which, as in a masque, the courtly figures move and bow and have their say. Indeed, Shakespeare's interest in the social contrast of court and country seems to fade out after his second period; and the country, if it appears at all, appears, not in character and theme, but merely as an occasional bit of setting.

The theme does not disappear from Elizabethan drama, however. Early in his career, Ben Jonson, in *Every Man in His Humour,* illustrates it in Master Stephen, the country gull that comes to town. The ruin of country gentlemen by the dissipations of the town is the theme initially announced in Middleton's *Trick to Catch the Old One* and in Massinger's *New Way to Pay Old Debts;* and *The Drinking Academy* depicts a sort of masculine school for scandal to instruct the uninitiate in the pleasures of the town.[24] Though these examples may well owe something to Shakespeare's second period, the attitude is generally reversed, and the town appears as better, or at least as cleverer and more desirable, than the country.

Rural *vs.* courtly life seems to be the first social theme that Shakespeare developed to the full, and it constitutes perhaps his first important legacy to his fellow-dramatists. It grew under his hand from suggestions, perhaps in Greene and in *The Taming of A Shrew,* but chiefly from the life he saw around him. Thus in *Love's Labour's* came studies in the *genre* in contrast to the courtly characters. In *Two Gentlemen* it entered into the main action, and in *A Midsummer Night's Dream* it over-shadowed the high-life plot. In most of the comedies of the second period, it is at least a minor theme; and it dominates *The Taming of the Shrew,* perhaps *Twelfth Night,*[25] and certainly *As You Like It.* The contrast is apparent in love-making, in education, in travel, in servants and household management, and above all in the greater native candor of the unsophisticated country types. Recent studies of these comedies would lead me to propose a fundamental change in classifying Shakespeare's second period: it seems dominated, not strictly by romantic comedy in which the story runs forward to its happy end purely for its own inherent merriment, but rather by comedy of manners, *The Shrew, The Merchant, Twelfth Night,* and perhaps *As You Like It,* which are largely a reflection and a comment on contemporary life—so deeply was realism penetrating into Shakespeare's art. Thus, in the second period he was exploiting the widest and most obvious of themes for the general London stage. In the third, however, as dramatist of the King's Men, he turned to weightier matters of government: civil commotion as in *Coriolanus*,[26] regicide as in *Hamlet*[27] and *Macbeth*,[28] abdication as in *King Lear*,[29] and the ruin of the great nobility as in *Timon of Athens*.[30] Thus, by learning how to express in dramatic form the truism of the two contrasting cultures of his day, Shakespeare made the stage more vividly reflect society, and prepared himself to treat the most fundamental social and political themes. His art acquired an intense reality both wider and more profound than that of his fellow-dramatists; and so, looking into his surroundings with this deepening perspective, he became one of those few, as Matthew Arnold said of Sophocles, "who saw life steadily and saw it whole."

II

Shakespeare's Rustic Servants

The cheapness of labor, the lack of convenient machines, and the inherited custom of feudal times when personal safety had to be preserved by armed retainers made the Elizabethan nobles maintain a host of household servants and of personal attendants. The household servants were low born fellows like Gobbo in *The Merchant of Venice,* and were supposed to do menial tasks. But the personal attendants were "servingmen," the children of the nobleman's immediate feudal vassals, such as knights' younger sons, well-born pages who had grown up to no better inheritance than the amusement and companionship of their overlord, such figures as Valentine and Fabyan in *Twelfth Night.* In Shakespeare's time, to the horror of the servingmen, the two classes were becoming confused. But this study is concerned mainly with the servants, most of whom were recruited from the country, and showed their rusticity. These servants, indeed, made possible such leisure as the leisure classes possessed and were a necessary accompaniment to their almost every action. In the more realistic plays, therefore, especially in the comedies of manners, servants of various sorts inevitably fill in the plot and setting; for, in drama as in life, persons of rank must have "attendants," "servingmen," or "others," as the *dramatis personæ* sometimes vaguely calls them, who listen to their confidences, run their errands, amuse their idle moments, make comment like a chorus, or merely stand and wait. As England was overwhelmingly rural, many of these servants, even in London, were country-bred upon their lords' demesnes, and so reflected the rough and ready countryside that still clung to the Middle Ages, rather than the new refinements of the Renaissance court and town. So, in Shakespeare's earlier work, when he was only learning to depict the intricacies of urban life, the portrayal of such rural characters, well-known to him from Stratford days, gave him, even in plays of urban setting, the opportunity for a realism that he thoroughly understood; and thus, in the Dromios, Launce and Speed, Sampson and Gregory, Grumio, Launcelot Gobbo, Adam and the rest, he portrayed with an increasing artistry the outstanding servant types and the contemporary social and economic problems of their class. Most of them are comic; Launce is something sentimental; and Adam is a tragic figure; but these motives are all keyed to life below stairs, and the detail of the dialogue has often an authentic rural tang.

Shakespeare's rustic servants are strictly Shakespeare's own; the sources of his plays rarely give even a suggestion of them as part of the play. Plautus's Messenio, the single prototype for Shakespeare's two Dromios in *A Comedy of Errors,* is didactic rather than comic in speech, is the merest type rather than an individual, and seems to reflect very little of contemporary Roman local color. The courtly page Fabius in Montemayor's *Felismena* is at the social antipodes from Launce and Speed in Shakespeare's *Two Gentlemen;* and neither Brooke nor Painter give a hint for Sampson and Gregory in *Romeo and Juliet* or for the illiterate servant who bids Romeo to his master's feast. In *The Taming of the Shrew* Shakespeare has given to Grumio and his fellows a realism far beyond that of the old play. Shylock's Launcelot and Shallow's Davy have no prototypes in the sources; Adam in *As You Like It* hardly resembles in thought, word, or deed the steward in Lodge's *Rosalynde;* and the aspiring Malvolio is altogether Shakespeare's own. The addition of these figures, for various purposes of plot, atmosphere, or theme, cannot have been accident. Shakespeare clearly regarded the type as dramatically useful and important; and a study of its origins and its growth under his hands is significant.

That the Shakespearean rustic servant may owe something to earlier drama is quite possible. The late Mediæval Vice,[1] the voluble

Ragau in *Jacob and Esau,* and above all Hodge in *Gammer Gurton's Needle,* show such a type in native dramatic literature. The influence of Plautus, moreover, appears in Palæstrio,[2] in Stephano,[3] and in Jenkin Careaway.[4] But these are only partly Anglicized; and even the thievish Will and Jack in *Jacke Jugeler,* though much more English, hardly suggest the actual countryside. The rhyming couplets, furthermore, of these early plays destroy much of their realism, and such realism as they have is a matter purely of superficial detail. The "University Wits," to whom Shakespeare's art shows a more unquestionable indebtedness, rarely depict the Elizabethan countryside and rarely the lower classes. Their servants appear, usually without names, in the miscellaneous list at the end of the *dramatis personæ.* In Lyly's *Campaspe,* Manes, Granichus, and Psyllus speak to characterize their masters rather than themselves. If Corebus in Peele's *Old Wives Tale* falls under our category at all, he is clearly not realistic. Marlowe's servants are urban, if not courtly. Young Spencer and Baldock in *Edward II,* and the ostler in *Faustus* and Ithamore, who had been an ostler, in *The Jew of Malta,* have no suggestion of this vocation. Even in the realistic *Arden of Feversham* neither Michael nor Mosbie, the "steward" of low birth, who like Malvolio is making love above his station, has any touch of rural realism. In *George-a-Greene* the clown Jenkin has something of the sort, but he is not a servant. In *James IV* Greene shows masterless men posting their "billes" in Paul's in hopes of employment, and even gives a satiric example of such an advertisement; but Slipper, as his name implies, is much too sophisticated to be a countryman. In *Friar Bacon* Thomas and Richard are both described as "farmers' sons" and "clowns"; but they have little or nothing to say, and no essential part in the plot. The rustic servant had apparently died out from the dramatic tradition on which Shakespeare built. That he knew the Classical roots of this tradition, however, is quite certain, for he used Plautus in *A Comedy of Errors.* Perhaps he also borrowed hints, especially for Launce and Speed, from performances in London of the *commedia dell'arte;*[5] but unless one claims an Italian influence on the Dromios, or dates *Two Gentlemen* before *A Comedy of Errors,* Shakespeare must already have started his vivifying and Anglicizing of this type before he used Italian comedy. Furthermore, Launce and Speed and the rest are essentially English characters; and, though the *commedia dell'arte* might show the dramatic and comic values of a realistic treatment of the type, yet the actual realism in Shakespeare, being essentially English,[6] could have been suggested only in general by a foreign source.[7] Thus a study of Shakespeare's rustic servants leads one to a consideration of their background in Elizabethan life. Rustic clowns had already been used as court fools: why not employ them as merrymakers also on the stage?

Every age with some reason has complained that servants are inefficient, careless, and even intentionally tricky; and many an Elizabethan servant, like Launcelot Gobbo, might truly have been called "an vnthriftie knaue." [8] Earle and Rowlands [9] accuse the servant of their day of imitating his master's vices; James I says that nobles were enclined "to maintain their servants and defenders in any wrong"; [10] and Overbury in his *Characters* suggests a link between the vices of the two in his description of a "Servingman":

> His neatness consists much in his haire and outward linnen. His courting language, visible bawdy jests; and against his matter faile, he is always ready furnished with a song. His inheritance is the chambermaid, by reason of opportunity, or for want of better; he alwayes cuckolds himself, and never marries but his own widdow. His master being appeased, he becomes a retainer, and entailes himself and his posterity upon his heire-males for ever.

These irregularities extended from carelessness about the fires at night to thievery,[11] which was punishable by hanging if the amount exceeded 40 s.[12] A social system still largely paternalistic, kept alive, as in the case of Adam, the ancient feudal loyalties: a servant, indeed, might kill in defence of his master and be absolved from murder; [13] and this perhaps explains the bravery of the Capulet and the Montague underlings, who would gladly fight provided they could "have the law of our sides." A servant who killed his master, however, was executed for the high crime of "petty treason." [14] Masters were permitted to employ "moderate castigation," [15] which might be rather immoderate, as in the *Comedy of Errors* and *The Taming of the Shrew*. Unless formally bound prentices, servants were hired, as Bassanio hired Launcelot, merely upon "parol," and might be as readily dismissed; but a master might take legal action against another who enticed his servant away or against a servant who left without just cause.[16] Thus Launce on a moment's notice might be cashiered to give place to the more refined Sebastian;[17] Launcelot must have Shylock's consent before he dare change masters;[18] and the clown in *Twelfth Night* may off-hand be "turned away" merely for being absent. Servants were so numerous that the Elizabethans could not but be conscious of their problems and their varied status; and writers of the age are not silent on the matter.[19]

A survey of Shakespeare's servants in the early plays shows both their increasing realism and their importance. They may owe something to Latin and to Italian comedy, but the amorous *contre-temps* of Dromio of Syracuse with Nell, the fat, greasy kitchen-wench,[20] is thoroughly Elizabethan, though Dromio's description of the encounter is perhaps too spiced with wit to be a perfect study of the *genre*. Dromio of Ephesus also is at times vividly Elizabethan, but his end-stopped blank verse and the similarity of his diction to that of the other characters lessen his realism. Both are deeply woven into the plot, but are quite subordinated to the main intrigue of mistaken identity. The present study passes over such more courtly figures as the page Moth in *Love's Labour's* and Fabyan in *Twelfth Night*, for they are neither rustics nor quite servants. *Two Gentlemen*, however, supplies Launce and Speed. In their malapropisms and their word-catching, they suggest the *commedia dell'arte*, somewhat Anglicized; but Launce's description of his dog—told in comic retrospect like Dromio's *affaire* with Nell, but much more important in the general plot—is a compound of authentic Elizabethan detail. This weaving in of realism to motivate and move the plot along is even more apparent in *Romeo and Juliet*.[21] Sampson and Gregory are skilfully employed to impress upon the audience the feud that is the cause and background of the tragedy. Somewhat later, the lovers are brought together by the illiterate stupidity of another servant, who tells Romeo of the feast and even invites him to it. The vignette of the bustling domestics introduces the festivities; and the meetings of the lovers are watched over by the Nurse, coarse, garrulous, loyal, worldly-wise, and, like a Franz Hals, painted in high colors. Shakespeare had come to realize how much the hand and voice of the aristocracy were its servants, whose doings and mis-doings made for their betters weal or woe. Indeed, as Basse declares:

> Respect your servant as your servant is
> The instrument of every great affaire,
> The necessarie vicar of your good. . . .[22]

Perhaps this growing sense of their importance led Shakespeare to a deeper study of their lot; and in *The Taming of the Shrew* he starts to contrast more clearly the country and the city types. The Induction strikes this key-note of contrast in the play, but the realism of these huntsmen and servants is pale beside that of Grumio and his fellows, those "logger-headed and unpolished grooms," who are so different from the citified Tranio and Biondello. Grumio in some respects is like his Shakespearean forebears: the dialogues with Curtis suggest the comic pairs, the Dromios, Launce and Speed, and Sampson and Gregory; he has the malapropisms, the word-play, and the comic stupidity of these earlier rustic servants; but, also like them, he has some mother wit, and so can understand Petruchio's motives in looking for a wife—the usual financial motives of an Elizabethan youth bent on marriage [23]—and can explain them in downright countryman's language. He voices the Elizabethan's horror of a "curst" woman; he foretells the outcome of the wooing; and indeed, he is a very chorus to Petruchio's marital arrangements. The journey homeward, which is not in Shakespeare's sources, is presented through his eyes; he appears as the tamer's arch-assistant; and, in the end, he helps to point the moral of the piece by summoning Kate to come at the order of her lord. Petruchio's part is both fuller and more significant than that in Shakespeare's source; and his repeated comment makes us see the action from a countryman's point of view, as the audience must be made to see it if they are to give full sympathy to Petruchio's endeavors. Thus Grumio is made essential to plot, to characterization, to setting, and to theme. He is a study of the rustic servant who sojourned in the town but was not of it. Rough, unmannerly, but loyal to a fault, a striking contrast to the refinements of the son of Gobbo, he willingly returns to simple country ways.

Shakespeare, however, as he realized more and more the social changes in the London life around him, began in his second period not only to reflect the striking surface detail that he had mastered in his first, but also to analyze the underlying problems that confronted different social groups. In *The Merchant of Venice* he depicts usury, the crying problem of commercial life; in the Falstaff plays, and later in *Othello,* he lays bare the problems of a soldier's livelihood [24] and of a soldier's honor; [25] in *As You Like It,* he treats the careers of younger brothers, one of the chief concerns of contemporary noble houses. During this same period, in a series of vivid characters, he illustrates the problem of adjustment or extermination that faced the members of the servant class. Launce touches on it when he ironically asks how many masters would do as much for a servant as he did for his dog; and Launcelot in *The Merchant of Venice* does indeed "continue the story which Launce began." [26] Such a relationship is no mere literary theory, but has a basis in contemporary life. Launcelot is a Launce who makes his way in town, takes to its fine sophistications, and hopes to rise in the world; and Malvolio is but little better than a Launcelot who has risen in the world most hopefully and still aspires to even higher things: they illustrate the servant class adapting itself to change, a change that must be explained before this adaptation and its reflection in Shakespeare can be grasped.

Servants were in transition from a feudal to a modern basis, and this transition was far more advanced in London than in the provinces. The Mediæval retainer had been above all the loyal follower of his lord in battle—and the more of them the better in those distressful times. With the greater safety of the Renaissance, however, this system by degrees decayed.[27] Servants were employed more strictly for utility,[28] or, in a few cases, for elegant display,[29] and the rising cost of living and the narrower limits of town houses materially decreased their number.[30] Thus a servant must either rise to a new eminence like Launcelot, or sink to new depths like Adam in *As You Like It*. Wishing to be rid of extra mouths to feed, masters grew unreasonable.[31] Many retainers were turned off, and on the highways roamed "great swarms of idle servingmen"; [32] the profession seemed "predestinate to want"; [33] servants were "set at liberty without comfort" when they grew old; [34] and the saying was all too apt: "A young Servingman, an olde Begger." [35] Those who were still strong turned to thievery,[36] and so were finally hanged; and those that remained at home were reduced to "slavish" servitude.[37] For all but a few who could make the re-adjustment, England had indeed become the "Purgatory of Servants." The bourgeoisie, enriched by the rise of prices at the expense of the landed nobles, were no friends to the retainer class, and as they bought up the great estates near London, turned off great numbers of such men as valueless and lazy.[38] Service sank to such a low esteem [39] that the commonest farmer's son, like Launcelot, aspired to a position in a gentleman's household; [40] and yet "every dunghill clowne" thought he might ridicule the servingman [41] who by birth was his better, so that the latter no longer rested "contented with his vocation." [42] Basse laments the situation bitterly and condemns two common sorts of servants: "Those that through baseness of condition swarve Into all odious luxure and delight," and "Those that in place of Serving-men doe stand Yet scorne the title of a Serving-man." [43] The former is Launcelot, the latter perhaps Malvolio. In drama as in life, this revolution most obviously manifested itself in servants' dress. The Dromios doubtless wore the traditional blue-coat garb; [44] but the newer sort "will needes be lapt in Lyuerie," [45] and some took up the career merely for love of the fine clothes, which got them only envy and dislike.[46] It was the "rare new liveries" that brought Launcelot into Bassanio's service. Even the staid Malvolio harbored a hankering for such gauds and allowed his mind to play upon his hopes of a "branched velvet gown." These changes in the servant life of Shakespeare's age must have been obvious, and their outward expression, especially in dress, must have been very effective on the stage.

A brief review of the servants of Shakespeare's second period shows not only how acutely he depicted the major phases of this change, but also the importance that he gave it in his plays. Except for Adam, his servants show increasing adaptation to court and town. Launce does not understand the new requirements, and is cashiered. Grumio is less severely tested, but seems glad to get back home with only a few beatings. Launcelot Gobbo has actually experienced the change, has achieved some measure of success, and hopes for more. Sir Sidney Lee and other laudators of Shylock would see young Gobbo as deceitful and quite worthless. To Fisher he is a "whimsically nonsensical" creature of the Romantic imagination no nearer human life than Ariel or Caliban, and yet he is *il gobbo,* the handyman about the Venetian household.[47] I find him above all an English realistic figure who illustrates the practical manipulations of the day by which a silk purse might be fashioned out of a sow's ear. He has the usual faults of servants: he is lazy and careless, though "kind enough." He is perhaps the least loyal of Shakespeare's earlier servants, but he shows good faith to Christians and to Jessica who is to become one. On the whole, he has progressed beyond the malapropisms of the Dromios, and when he mistakes the meaning of his interlocutor, his error is more usually intentional than naïve. Like Malvolio, he is a below-stairs social climber, but on a humbler plane. As a good countryman, he complains of the Jew's stingy table; but really his mind is bent on higher things—on the title of "Master" and on the splendor of gilt braid, an ambition that Bassanio senses without being told. He does nothing for the major and little for the minor plot, and yet he is a detailed portrait of the servant-in-transition. He has little respect for his father and the country ways he represents, and, like Malvolio, who planned to read "politic authors," he is tasting of the tree of Knowledge, and elegantly refers to "the Fates and Destinies and such odd sayings, the Sisters Three and such branches of learning."

With purer realism and even slighter overlay of wit, Shallow's Davy depicts still another variant of the servant-type. He is entirely of the country, but hopes "to see London" ere he dies; and, had he chosen a career there, one feels no doubt of his success. He is an artist at managing his master. Shallow calls him to order pigeons for the dinner of his guest; but Davy, before he takes a step toward fulfilling this command, finds out just how the headland is to be sown with wheat, presents the blacksmith's bill, demands "a new link to bucket," learns that William's wages shall be stopped for the sack he lost at Hinkley Fair, and finally persuades his master, in his position as a Justice, to side with the "knave" William Visor in his lawsuit against Clement Perkes. Davy is a Grumio with Launcelot Gobbo's scheming mother wit, but without the longed-for opportunities of the town.

Near the end of his second period, Shakespeare, in two striking figures, contrasts success and failure in the servant type. The cardinal virtue of an Elizabethan servant was loyalty to his lord. Despite the unpleasing descriptions in contemporary pamphlets, and despite such well-known facts as the peculations of Lord Bacon's steward, practically all of Shakespeare's servants have this virtue, perhaps because his long study of this class made him feel that it was more sinned against than sinning. Certainly, of all his servants, the most admirable is Adam in *As You Like It,* who shares his modest savings with his master, forsakes home and shelter for him, and finally sinks exhausted by his wanderings: Adam is a pleasing commentary both on the character of his master and on the virtues of the servant class. Here Shakespeare gives expression to the tragic possibilities of an old retainer's role, tragic possibilities that he later used again in *Lear*. Much less sympathetic is his picture of Malvolio. In *Twelfth Night* he develops not a single servant but a whole great household in transition—the usual genteel hangers-on and a steward "sick of self-love," who aspires even to the hand of his noble mistress. At his first appearance, Malvolio has the assurance to criticize the taste of his betters and, by implication, of Olivia herself for bandying wit with the jester. Later he undertakes to rebuke Sir Toby and the rest for taking full advantage in their revelry of traditional hospitality. If he should become their lord, he will certainly put down their riot with austerity, so they all unite to fool Malvolio to the top of his bent, and the comedy runs merrily on. Like young Gobbo, Malvolio is an aspiring mind below stairs, but, having started from a trifle higher in the social scale, he is more serious and hopes to rise far beyond the modest plane of Launcelot. To modern eyes Shakespeare's rebuke of him seems much too great; the Renaissance, however, had not our democratic pre-conceptions. This class-struggle really dominates in the play. A major theme is Malvolio's effort to achieve gentility, and thus *Twelfth Night,* in the strictest sense, becomes a comedy of manners. In the face of changing times, Adam succumbs; but Malvolio aspires even to new heights.

Thus in his second period, Shakespeare expressed the outstanding types of servant and every major stage in the domestic transition of his time.

In his third period, just as his interest in the contrast of court and country life declined, so his studies of rustic servants and servants of rural origin disappear. Kemp's withdrawl from the company had perhaps obliged him to change the nature of this role, even as early as *As You Like It;* for, in the third period, the "clowns" become sophisticated court jesters, and the servants mere dramatic conveniences to bear a message or to summon their betters on or off the stage. As in Shakespeare's predecessors, they have often no speaking part; they stand in the background like so much scenery and are mentioned at entrances and exits merely as "and others." Most of them, like Paris' man in *Troilus* and the clown in *The Winter's Tale,* have nothing of the country; and certainly Boult in *Pericles* and Pompey in *Measure for Measure,* who serve in bawdy houses, are blessed with all the sophistications of the town. The drunken porter in *Macbeth* and Trinculo in *The Tempest* merely personify a vice that was common to all classes. Timon's servants are but duns, whose only realistic touch is their loyalty to their master, and the contrast in the ingratitude of his flatterers and their dismay when at his ruin they are "cast off" and so "undone." Even the honest steward Flavius is only a simple type, for in problem plays character must be kept in subjection to the problem. Loyalty as in Pisanio in *Cymbeline,* is still an outstanding trait of Shakespeare's servants, but it is no longer universal among them: Oswald in *King Lear* is "duteous" only "to the vices of his mistress," and Buckingham's "Surveyor" in *Henry VIII* is anything but loyal to his master. Most of all among the later plays—perhaps because it was first written earlier—*All's Well* reflects the life of service. The "honest Steward" suggests the second period; and the "foul mouthed and calumnious knave" may be a court fool, but he is full of country metaphors, and, like Touchstone, can ridicule the court. Once more Shakespeare touches on the economics of his place when he declares that "Service is no heritage." Thus, in his later plays Shakespeare rarely develops his servants for themselves.

The playwright competitors, moreover, of Shakespeare's latter years, though on occasion they borrow his realistic constable and his Anglicizing of the *miles gloriosus,* borrow but superficially of his rustic servants—merely a touch of his concrete detail, without the insight into their lives and fortunes that he showed. These playwrights seem to have had a narrower social outlook. Moreover, there was no Will Kemp to exploit the clownish roles. Ben Jonson uses Wellbred's servant in *Every Man in His Humour* merely to deliver a letter, and the waiting-women in *Volpone* are little more than convenient mutes. In Dekker's *Shoemakers' Holiday* Dodger is likewise a mere accessory to the plot, and even talks blank verse. In character and action, Sybil, however, suggests the Nurse in *Romeo and Juliet;* and the nameless "Servingman" who comes to get his mistress' shoes, though only a casual study, is truly realistic. In *The Honest Whore* George, like the Dromios, suffers from a "curst mistress," and Roger is a counterpart of Shakespeare's Boult and Pompey. The servants of Heywood's *Woman Killed,* like Grumio in *The Taming of the Shrew,* only supply a Greek chorus of running comment, and Nicholas lapses into blank verse and even into rhyme; but the servants' dance in the yard in front of Frank-ford's house must on the stage have been a vivid depiction of such festivities. Rustic servants were beneath the notice of Fletcherian romance. Even *The Duchess of Malfi,* though at first glance it seems to be a tragic counterpart of *Twelfth Night,* is really on a higher social plane, for the lady is an exalted duchess and the steward whom she marries seems clearly to be a "gentleman"; and it is she who urges him, not he who tries to rise above his station. Thus, in Shakespeare's successors the servant class drops back to its former place of mere auxiliary to plot and setting. The playwrights seem to see it only from outside, or rather from above as a social group to be exploited in drama, as in life. As men and dramatists, they had not Shakespeare's depth and breadth of understanding.

The servant problem of Elizabethan times was how to rid oneself of servants; and Shakespeare's comedies of the second period re-flect not only the dramatic uses of this class, which he transmutes to vividly Elizabethan terms, but also the cruces of its change from a feudal to a modern basis. Surely these rustic servants are more than a sop to "popularity by employing an old popular form"; [48] and surely the evolution of this type under Shakespeare's hands shows him no mere slave of convention, as Professors Stoll and Schücking would sometimes seem to think. Are Launcelot and Malvolio and Adam—and even Davy, who can turn his master to his will so pat—are these mere borrowings from the early English stage, from Plautus, or from *commedia dell'arte?* And where in dramatic con-vention did Shakespeare get the changing status of the servant class that they reflect? The present study, if it shows anything, shows Shakespeare in the act of following out a social movement from its inception in Launce, who comes to town and fails, Grumio, who re-turns safely home, Davy, who would like to go but does not, Launcelot, who goes and wins his way, Malvolio, who is balked only at his highest hopes, and Adam, who comes to court only to sacrifice his old age to his young lord's career. Few possibilities of comedy or tragedy remained; but, in his third period, although Shakespeare, in Boult and Pompey, gave another servant-type, yet he has no more to say of servants as a changing social class. And the dramatists who followed him had nothing of significance to add. The evolu-tion of this type in his plays is more complex than that of his con-stables, and it grew more gradually than did the type of boastful soldier, which, almost at a stroke, attained complete dramatic form in Falstaff. As early as *A Comedy of Errors,* when Dromio urges his master to return home to Syracuse, this theme of the servant away from his original *milieu* leads into the servant adapting himself to the newer scheme of things that are re-shaping court and city life. The early servants, like Plautus' Messenio, are static types. They grow at once more Elizabethan and more complex in Launce and Grumio, but the new environment they enter as yet leaves no mark upon them. But in Launcelot Gobbo the exultant transition to city ways cries out in every sentence of the dialogue with his father. Malvolio has few traces of the country left. Adam's effort to effect the change is the supreme test of his loyalty. Thus, in a series of swiftly painted portraits, Shakespeare depicts environment in the very act of governing men's lives. He shows men reacting to each other, not as mere conventional puppets but in a whole great social scheme, the whole social scheme of actual Elizabethan life.

III

Antecedent Action in Shakespeare's Earlier Plays

Since life is a continuum of episodes, fundamentally bound together by cause and effect, a drama that aims at the life-like significance of true comedy or tragedy must grow from a matrix of former causes and effects. This matrix may include not only a given situation and a group of given characters, each with peculiar traits and prejudices and his own social status and hopes and purposes, but also definite events that have already started the action on its course and perhaps even, as in the case of Hamlet's melancholy at his father's death, character-change that results from these events in the antecedent action. Thus a drama is a segment extricated from the flow of life which reaches back behind it; it is a seminal growth from the past like plants from seed; and, the more coherent and significant the action of the plot, the greater is likely to be the impact of these fundamental precedent forces, some of them objective in the society of the time, some subjective in the individual, forces that provide the clash of tragedy or the complication of comic elements. Indeed, the principles that govern men and societies can hardly be expressed in a few hours' traffic of the stage without at least some precurse of fierce events that motivates the swelling scene and is prologue or omen for the action coming on.

The beginning of a drama is perhaps the most difficult part to write. The author must determine just where to dive into the flow of action: whether to tell his story almost *ab initio* as in *Macbeth*, to commence early in the succession of episodes as in *Twelfth Night* and *Hamlet*, or to concentrate upon the final event as in Greek tragedy and in *Timon* and *Love's Labour's*. The later the start, the more the antecedent material to be expressed; and, even if the curtain rises early on the course of the plot, the author has before him the problem of portraying, somehow or other, at least some antecedent material—situation and character, if not actual events and their reactions on one or more of the main figures. This may consume the whole first act, and perhaps a prologue. The quickest and often the clearest way to put this across the footlights is a bald expository statement by some choral figure, like the ubiquitous parlor maid of Victorian comedy; but this method lacks probability and vividness, and is too dull to hold the flighty attention of an audience; and, sometimes moreover, no one figure in the piece, unless it be a Prologue, would presumably have the omniscience to tell all. Dialogue, as used in *The Merchant of Venice*, is more effective, and in *Othello* is combined with soliloquy. But even dialogue is not as effective as action, the third and most characteristic vehicle of the dramatic art. Action is the most interesting of the three means of exposition, but, unfortunately, it is also the least easily understood: without the Prologue in *Romeo and Juliet* and the talk of Sampson and Gregory, the street brawl between the Montagues and the Capulets would be mere sound and fury signifying nothing. Thus a finished dramatist is likely to combine two or more means to reveal his antecedent action; and the choice and arrangement of these devices constitutes an essential of his art. He must express both clearly and vividly the given elements in the initial equation that the drama is to solve; and the present paper proposes to trace the growth of Shakespeare's mastery in meeting this complex problem: where in the course of the plot he should raise the curtain, and how he should inform the audience of such antecedent action as took place before the curtain rose.

In the Mediæval conception of narrative and drama, the Classical technique of starting *in medias res* found little place: the romances both metrical and prose, the fabliaux and the numerous types of story exemplified in Chaucer start *ab ovo* or as nearly so as conditions would allow. The miracle and the mystery plays and the full-scope moralities portray every important incident visually on the stage; and, even in the moralities such as *Everyman,* that confine themselves to the last acts of their hero's life, his earlier deeds are not individually significant.

This tradition, despite the force of Classical example, seems to have made Shakespeare's early contemporaries avoid starting their plays in the midst of the events. Indeed, neither their comedy nor their tragedy has much of antecedent action; and such little as they have is likely to be baldly and rapidly dispatched either in a Prologue or in the first lines of the play. In *Arden of Feversham* the wife's unfaithfulness is told at once. In Lyly's *Endymion* the hero's love for Cynthia appears in the opening scene, but the disapproval of Tellus and the other two love affairs come to light later. Peele's *David and Bethsabe* has practically no pre-play; and, in the *Old Wives Tale* each character at his entrance somewhat naïvely tells his past. Greene's *Friar Bacon* announces at once that Prince Edward has fallen in love with the charming milkmaid. Tudor tragedy, strangely enough, was no better furnished with antecedent action than was comedy. *Gorboduc* has no pre-play. In Kyd's *Spanish Tragedy* the Ghost tells the earlier events in an Induction; and there is little effort to interpolate them in the unfolding of the plot. In Marlowe what little antecedent action there is generally appears to the reader either in a Prologue as in *Faustus* or in the opening lines of the tragedy as in *Edward II.* In short, Shakespeare's predecessors, excepting Lyly, start their plays as early as possible in the course of the episodes, briefly tell what little went before, and make slight effort either to express it in action or even in the give-and-take of dialogue, or to float it on the current of events throughout the play.

The comedies of Shakespeare's earliest period show at once a tendency to imitate his contemporaries and his sources and a tendency to try experiments. *Love's Labour's Lost,* written in the tradition of Lyly, plunges, as he does, into the midst of the story: indeed, the complication of the main plot has already taken place before the curtain rises. The King's "late edict" and the circumstances leading up to it are in the antecedent action; the "little Academe" given over to celibacy and learning has already been established; and the gay young courtiers have already sworn their pretty oaths to abjure women and to study for three years. Further-

more, even the resolution of the plot is under way; for, early in
the first scene, Biron reminds the King that the Princess of France
is coming thither on an embassy; and so the oaths cannot be kept:
thus the conclusion of the comedy is in sight at the very start. Truly,
the structure of this plot out-Lylys Lyly; and the curtain rises as
late in the chain of episodes as it does in the *Œdipus Tyrannus*.
The minor plot is an even more extreme example. To supply lively
"recreation" by reciting Spanish romances "In high-born words,"
the King has admitted to his courtly fellowship a certain Don
Armado, "a refined traveller of Spain." Even at the outset, the
Don is smitten with the charms of the not-too-virtuous Jaquenetta,
who has already consummated her desires with the lumpish Costard: thus the "late edict," even before the play began, has been
broken in both thought and deed; and Biron may well declare at
the end of the first scene, "These oaths and laws will prove an idle
scorn." Shortly, the King himself, by "mere necessity" of state,
breaks his own law; the courtiers fall in love with the Princess'
ladies-in-waiting; and this slight action constitutes the plot. The
antecedent material, the promulgation of the edict, appears in a
short initial speech delivered by the King: there is little effort to
make it realistic and probable, and no effort to dramatize it vividly
in action. The affairs of Jaquenetta, which constitute the minor
plot, are somewhat better told in dialogue, and they are more
inherently probable. Indeed, the introduction to *Love's Labour's*,
both in arrangement and in method, is quite in the style of Lyly's
Endymion in which the love affairs, which started before the play
began, are briefly set forth early in the dialogue.

Shakespeare's extension of the pre-play to include so much more
than Lyly's may arise from the usual exaggeration of an imitator;
or it may arise from the difficulty of giving verisimilitude to the
King's rather sophomoric Academe, for any realistic court would
have had a Kent or a Polonius to quash such silly plans; or it may
arise from the difficulty that a young dramatist might experience
in integrating a series of episodes with all their cross-currents and
influences on character; or it may arise from Shakespeare's desire
to reduce the plot to airy nothingness so that he might develop the
whimseys of the dialogue. In short, the antecedent action of *Love's
Labour's*, though it contains the entire complication and in part
the resolution of the plot, is hurriedly presented in the first two

scenes with no great effort at verisimilitude of motivation and no great vividness of dramatic effect: Shakespeare has outdone his master Lyly and attempted a comedy that concentrates on a single episode like Classical tragedy; and, as a consequence, the action shown on the stage is so slight in situation and event that the play depends almost entirely for its effect on the extraneous heightening of lyricism and badinage.

The tradition of Classical tragedy and epic perhaps influenced Plautus to begin his *Menæchmi in medias res,* and to explain the antecedent action, not in the first but in the second act. Shakespeare's *Comedy of Errors,* founded on the *Menæchmi,* has an even more complex pre-play, but sets it forth, as does *Love's Labour's* in Act I. In the very first lines, the Duke explains the law against Syracusans, and condemns Ægeon to death at sundown; and Ægeon in reply narrates the story of his marriage, of the birth of his twin sons, of his adoption of lowborn twins to serve them, of his shipwreck and the loss of one of each set of twins, and of his travels to find the missing boys. The whole is an arid stretch of merely rhetorical monologue occasionally broken by comment from the Duke; and the entire first scene is thus sacrificed to a long and somewhat unconvincing explanation of the existence of two pairs of identical twins in the same town and yet unknown to each other. Thus those who arrive in time heard a tedious brief introduction; and those who were late would not understand the fundamental fact of two sets of twins and so would lose the point of the comedy. If the theme of the piece be the separation and reunion of a family, then the complication of the plot, as in *Love's Labour's,* is entirely relegated to the antecedent action; but here the resolution runs a much longer course of episode and ludicrous situation; and so the comedy depends more on event and less on the incidentals of poetry and style. In short, the pre-play is as long as in *Love's Labour's;* it is no more effectively presented; it is not even interpolated, like that of Plautus in the midst of the action; and it shows an advance only in Shakespeare's effort—too coincidental to be quite convincing—to give the initial situation on which the curtain rises some motivation and verisimilitude. Shakespeare had not yet mastered the management of antecedent action, and this effort comes off somewhat tardy.

Perhaps because the plays that follow were not modeled on

Lyly or on Plautus, or perhaps because Shakespeare was not satisfied with his earlier use of the device, their antecedent action was
reduced to lowest terms; and, at the same time, he experiments with
its more vivid presentation. In *Two Gentlemen of Verona* the story
is told *ab ovo;* and apparently nothing of import happened before
the general situation depicted in the first and second scenes: Valentine is going to the Emperor's court to complete his education;
Proteus is in love and stays at home; and Julia seems to prefer
Proteus to her other admirers, though of course she conceals this
feeling. The story of Shakespeare's source did not seem to require
antecedent action, and he got along without it; but still he explains
the initial situation somewhat baldly in the beginning of the play.
Likewise, in *The Taming of the Shrew* there is no pre-play; and
the long Induction bears no relation to the plot. The stories of
the wooing of Katherine and of Bianca are told, it would seem,
from the beginning. There was no pre-play in the old comedy that
Shakespeare used as his source; and the early dialogue sketches
the general situation on which his piece is founded. In these two
plays Shakespeare would seem for the nonce to have foregone the
concentrated totality of Classical technique.

The plot-structure of the chronicle history play differs from
Elizabethan tragedy and comedy in that the episodes are loose-knit
and digressive, as they were in Holinshed. This laxity of integration does not require the preparation of a carefully depicted pre-
play; and, indeed, if one attempted to sketch the tangle of events
that led up to the diverse actions of the plot, a whole play would
be necessary; and, in such series as *Henry VI* and *Henry IV*, Shakespeare solves the problem in just this fashion. *King John* is perhaps
the first of the chronicle plays to come entirely from Shakespeare's
hand; and it shows little or no advance over *Love's Labour's* and
A Comedy of Errors. After some forty lines on the claim of Lewis
to the English crown, the whole first act is given over to the Falcon-
bridge trial, which bears but slight relation to the main course of
the plot. The only antecedent action is the usurpation of John in
the place of his nephew Arthur; and this is flatly declared in the
initial lines of the first scene. *Richard III* shows a distinct advance.
It gives the opening lines to the character of the discontented Duke
and to his plots to crush his rivals to the throne. Clarence, already
ruined, comes in guarded on the way to execution; he does not

suspect Richard's hand in his overthrow; and so we see dramatically portrayed both the character of Richard and his intrigues and their success, even in the exposition of the pre-play. The scene is vivid and shows the economy of a master.

In all the plays so far, Shakespeare has put the antecedent action at the very start: this arrangement has the double disadvantage of spoiling the first effect and making it impossible for late arrivals to understand the pre-play. In *Richard II* he attempts with some success to lead off the plot with action; and he opens with the quarrel of Bolingbroke and Mowbray. The antecedent political situation that will develop into Richard's overthrow and death first appears in the second scene. The third scene continues the story of the first, and shows the King's impolitic vacillation at the duel and his banishment of Bolingbroke. Thus Shakespeare strikes the keynote of Richard's weak and calamitous reign and prepares the way for Bolingbroke's later return in triumph. This introduction successfully dramatizes the initial situation, the characters, and the setting of truculent feudalism; but Shakespeare meets the problem of the antecedent action, not so much by making it vivid and effective as by placing it in the second scene, where it will not spoil the first impression. *Henry IV, Part I,* as a sort of sequel to *Richard II,* needed but little pre-play; and, indeed, every patriotic Elizabethan was likely to know the early life of the hero of Agincourt. The rebellions that dominate the plot grow out of the usurpation of Bolingbroke depicted in *Richard II;* and even Henry's plan for a crusade, which opens the play, is apparently partly to expiate the crimes by which he achieved the crown and partly to take up the attention of the nobles and unite the distracted realm. Thus *Henry IV* develops the characters and resolves the situations created in *Richard II;* and, since the relation of the two plays is that of prologue and sequel, the later piece largely takes for granted the spectator's knowledge of the antecedent action. The same situation obtains in *Henry IV, Part II;* and even the Induction spoken by Rumor does not concern itself with early events. The Prologue of *Henry V* likewise looks forward into the play rather than back into the pre-play. The first scene opens, like *Henry IV, Part I,* with plans for a crusade which has to be postponed because of a war nearer home, and then proceeds to the heroic tale of Agincourt and the less heroic tale of Falstaff's rag-tag followers. In short, this group of historic dramas on the founding of the House of Lancaster is so closely bound together and deals with events so generally known even to the groundlings that Shakespeare hardly needed to explain the antecedent action. In general, moreover, the chronicle histories are too episodic in structure to require much exposition of the pre-play; and, to effect a start, the dramatist merely slits the thin-spun narrative of Holinshed, gives the briefest indication of the initial situation and perhaps a vivid incident to point the local color of the age, and then hurries to the battles, sieges, and disasterous chances that constitute the argument. In short, aside from *Richard III,* in which Shakespeare depicts the pre-play with both vividness and economy of art, and *Richard II,* in which he wisely interpolates it after the first scene, the chronicle histories show little advance in this aspect of Shakespeare's technique.

The more unified construction of tragedy should require of *Romeo and Juliet* and *Julius Caesar* a more significant and more artistically presented pre-play. The former tells the story almost from the start. Its Prologue sets fort the initial situation of the rival houses, and points forward to the consequently tragic love-affair; and the street-brawl in the first scene dramatizes the feud and the anger of the Prince. The only real antecedent action—though it is but distantly connected to the actual plot—is Romeo's love for Rosaline, which is also vividly depicted not only in the dialogue but also in the young man's woebegone appearance. This material Shakespeare interpolates after the initial brawl. Thus in his introduction, he combines, even better than in *Richard III,* the clarity of explanatory dialogue with the vividness of action to express the initial situation, and, furthermore, arranges the early scenes, as in *Richard II,* so that, after the Prologue, a hurly-burly of derring-do will take the eye of the spectators, and the less engaging matter of Romeo's love-sickness will come later when the attention of the audience has been gained. Shakespeare, moreover, even shows the influence of the antecedent action on Romeo's character: the merry comrade of Mercutio and Benvolio suffers from the melancholy of unrequited love. This is Shakespeare's first truly artistic treatment of the pre-play; but the action itself is slight; its inclusion was probably dictated chiefly by its presence in the source, and thus its significance is incidental. In *Julius Caesar,* a looser dramaturgy suggests chronicle history rather than tragedy; and the use of antecedent action, therefore, is not highly significant. Caesar's recent victory over Pompey is told in the first scene, in which the tribunes try to disperse the holiday crowds. And, here and there throughout the play, the earlier events of Caesar's life, his affection for Brutus, his conquest of the Nervii, his fever, and the swimming match with Cassius, are woven into the dialogue. Undoubtedly, the full biography that Plutarch had supplied made these allusions possible, and encouraged Shakespeare to attempt what he so often accomplished in his later dramas, to supply by hints and touches here and there the entire life of a major character, so that we know his ancestry, education, and previous career. These early efforts at tragedy, though they show only a partial command of integrated tragic dramaturgy, required of the playwright a nicer and more telling use of antecedent action—not one mere undigested scene or monologue at the beginning of the play, but rather an interweaving in the course of the plot of previous events, as Ibsen does in *Ghosts*, so that the action seems to grow out of a constantly remembered past, and we have the illusion of a continuity like that of life itself.

The comedies that Shakespeare was writing at this time seem somewhat to reflect this growing artistry in the use of antecedent action. In the *Midsummer Night's Dream*, the complication of each of the several plots, as in *Love's Labour's* and the *Comedy of Errors*, is relegated to the pre-play, and the comedy itself is merely their resolution: Hippolita has accepted the hand in marriage of her conqueror; Lysander has already won the love of Hermia from Demetrius whose suit has the parental blessing; Helena already loves Demetrius, who abhores her; and Oberon and Titania have already quarreled over the Indian boy. All of these elements but the last appear in the opening scene. The conflicting love affairs of Lysander and Demetrius are dramatized in the irate father's suit before the Duke; otherwise the artistry improves but little on that of the earlier comedies.

In the *Merchant of Venice*, likewise, each part of the plot stretches back into the past: the dialogue of the first scene shows that Antonio has many ships abroad and seems worried about his ventures, and further that Bassanio has spent his patrimony, borrowed from Antonio, seen and loved Portia, and hopes by marrying her to recoup his fallen fourtunes. The second scene shows us that Portia's father before his death arranged for her choice of a hus-

and, that various suitors have taken the trial of the caskets, and in the train of one of them was young Bassanio of Venice. The third scene depicts the business rivalry of Antonio and Shylock and Shylock's bitterness, which is already changing his nature from its natural melancholy to a fiery choler. The middle of the second act opens the minor plot, the love of Lorenzo and Jessica. Thus the introductory exposition occupies most of the first act and runs on into the second; but Shakespeare has learned to save it from aridity by combining it with action—Antonio's bargaining with Shylock and Portia's rejection of the Prince of Morocco. In *Love's Labour's* Shakespeare saved the expository opening scene by the wit of the style; in *A Midsummer Night's Dream,* by wit and poetry; in *The Merchant of Venice* he adds to both of these, as he did in *Romeo and Juliet,* the spice of pertinent action and of clash of character. In *The Merchant of Venice,* moreover, Shakespeare has learned where in the course of events to raise the curtain: in the earlier comedies he put much or all of the complication in the pre-play, and so reduced severely the action in the piece; in *Romeo and Juliet,* he perhaps began too early, for the Rosaline episode has little relation to the main argument; but, in *The Merchant of Venice,* the antecedent action is just sufficient to introduce each plot, and neither contains extraneous events nor impinges seriously on the complication. Although he could still refine upon his art, Shakespeare has mastered the two chief problems of the pre-play: how much material to include in it, and how to combine dialogue and action to express it both clearly and vividly.

Merry Wives of Windsor shows a certain retrogression; and, as in *Romeo and Juliet,* the initial episode, Falstaff's defiance of Shallow and of Slender, bears slight relation to the plot of the comedy; and the antecedent actions that this episode tells, Falstaff's poaching of Shallow's deer and Nym's theft of Slender's money, are significant only in their portrayal of the characters concerned and as a link with *Henry IV, Part II.* Tradition says that the play was written to order and in haste; and perhaps this accounts for such laxity of structure. One of the two plots, Falstaff's wooing of the merry wives, has no antecedent action, and is portrayed complete from the initial love letter to the final buckbasket episode. But the secondary plot, the wooing of Anne Page, has progressed apace before the curtain rises: Shallow is pressing Slender's suit;

and the Doctor is pressing his own with the help of Mistress Page
and the pretended help of Mistress Quickly; and the aristocrati
Fenton has actually captured the girl's heart. Anne's cold reception
of Slender's suit is evident in the opening scene; and the res
appears as the play goes on: Shakespeare has quite outgrown the
naïveté of placing the antecedent action in a long, dull speech o
in improbable dialogue at the beginning of the play.

Shakespeare's comic genius flowered about 1600 in three drama
of wit and poetry and vivid characterization, *As You Like It* mor
romantic, *Much Ado* and *Twelfth Night* more of the earth earthy
of Elizabethan life. In *Much Ado* the major motive of the plot
the unsuccessful rebellion of Don John, is introduced at once; and
in this same war Claudio and Benedick have distinguished them
selves. Claudio gets Hero's hand as his reward; Benedick get
Beatrice' taunting wit; and this wit gives verve to the first scenes
Thus Shakespeare integrates the antecedent action with his plo
and at the same time provides amusement. The lines suggest tha
Beatrice's raillery arises in part from a real liking for Benedick
and, if so, the pre-play has a subtle element of character chang
such as Shakespeare was later to use in the great tragedies. The
first act of the piece has, indeed, but little action, and Shakespear
would seem to revert to the device of wit, as in *Love's Labour's,* to
enliven his exposition; but here the wit is so much sharper and so
much more expressive of character and situation that it is almos
as absorbing as the street-brawl in *Romeo and Juliet.*

As You Like It has the most complex antecedent action of any
play so far—so complex that it seems not quite consistent in some
details. The comedy begins with an exposition of Orlando's statu
in his elder brother's household—an exposition in such bold, swif
strokes that it seems hardly convincing to us moderns who are no
acquainted with the unhappy plight of younger brothers under the
old system of primogeniture. The fisticuffs of Orlando and Olive
dramatize this conflict almost at once. Thus we learn of Sir Roland
the terms of his will, and the characters and activities of his three
sons. Then follows the less telling scene which sets forth the
affection of Celia and Rosalind, the hate of their respective fathers
the usurpation of Duke Frederick, and the exile of the true Duke
to the Forest of Arden. The usurper expresses his growing appre
hension at the popularity of Rosalind at court, and foreshadows he

exile. Then follows the wrestling match in which Orlando again demonstrates his prowess and Duke Frederick, his injustice as a usurper. In short, the events that drive Orlando to Arden are portrayed, not only in the dialogue, but in two fights upon the stage, the first demonstrating that he can hope nothing from his family, the second, that he can hope nothing from his liege lord; both in his home and at the court, and thus the antecedent situation, is strikingly manifest; and the evils of the court, as thus displayed, also explain the exile of Rosalind and the flight of Celia. The later acts of *As You Like It* have but little stirring action; but either the accident of his source or Shakespeare's own sense of dramatic contrast gave the introduction two rough-and-tumble scenes to point the difference between the actual world, where old servants like Adam are cast off and younger brothers reduced to mere peasants, and the idyll of Arden, where true lovers meet by sheer coincidence and wicked usurpers repent for no particular reason and seek a holy life. Certainly it is rare for the antecedent action of a play to be depicted with more sound and fury than the actual episode of the plot. The Introduction of *As You Like It* requires the exposition of both a political situation and a social, with their several consequences on the lives of the major characters, the narration of events in the family and in the State before the play began, and the delineation of at least five important characters. And yet Shakespeare dispatches all this business with dialogue and action that is at once graphic and luminous.

The pre-play of *Twelfth Night* is almost as complex and quite as well portrayed; and, like *As You Like It,* it is founded on conditions of the age that any theatre-goer would have understood from a mere hint. None of the important characters in this play is static; each is striving to accomplish, if not exactly an ambition, at least the security of his present place. The Duke, heavy with love-sickness, strives for Olivia's hand; social ambition urges Malvolio in the same pursuit. Sir Toby urges Sir Andrew, and is in turn urged forward by his longing for a permanent easy birth in the establishment. Maria, whose only fortune is her wit, lays siege to the heart and hand of the valorous Sir Toby. Feste, who foresees a match between the Countess and the Duke, runs off to gain his future master's favor. And the Countess Olivia herself, entrenched behind a barrier of grief, also seeks permanent security in an uncertain world, shrewdly selects her future mate and leads him to the altar almost by main force. She will none of the fool Sir Andrew, and before the curtain rose rejected him without a hearing; she nonsuits even the mediators of the eligible Duke; she does not seem to guess the flames that make Malvolio's heart palpitate beneath his steward's chain, or she would certainly have extinguished them. Meanwhile, Viola, fatherless and almost friendless, has just been shipwrecked on a foreign coast; she also longs for safety and a husband. Thus the pre-play concerns no less than eight characters, places each in his special situation, and suggests the means by which he is trying to extricate himself. Truly, this is the complexity of very life; and Shakespeare expresses it, with poetry and music in the case of the Duke, then in contrast, with the violence of a storm in the case of Viola's shipwreck, then with yet further contrast, in the witty dialogue of Sir Toby and Maria, then with more poetry at the ducal court, and with more wit—the incomparable quiddities of Feste—in the hall of the Countess—and so the play is ready to begin. Shakespeare has employed all the devices of witty and poetic dialogue, of action and even of incidental music to make this complex exposition palatable. The antecedent action, moreover, concerns not only the plot but also the characterization of the piece. Several of the principals are not, when they first appear, their normal selves: the personable Duke is burdened with love-melancholy; Olivia is sad at the recent death of her father and her brother; Sir Andrew is trying to assume the virtues of the alluring lover, though he has them not; and Sir Toby is his impressario and stage-manager for the nonce. Maria, Feste, and Viola show a half-hidden strain of uncertainty. In short, the play does not start from a static point of departure, but plunges into the whirl of very life, with character and event portrayed as acting and reacting on each other even before the curtain has risen.

In the great tragedies that follow Shakespeare avails himself of this subtle technique of antecedent action that he had already developed in the comedies, and even stretches it backward to include, as he did in Olivia and in Orlando, something of the parentage, birth, and education of the main characters; and thus the dramatist creates whole biographies for many of his figures. These masses of detail he weaves into the warp and woof of the five acts just as in life the past is ever reappearing in the living texture of the present. Thus, piecemeal, in shreds and patches, we see the full lives of Polonius and of Hamlet, of Claudius and of Gertrude, and, by inference, of Rosencrantz, Guildenstern, Horatio, Ophelia, and Laertes. In *Othello*, Iago's twenty-eight years appear in retrospect; we see Othello, as if he were the hero of a novel, his royal birth, his military life from the age of seven years, to his wooing, marriage, and death; and Cassio, the mathematical Florentine, implies his former life in words and actions to those who can read the social idiom of the age. Their consistent and vivid pasts, so much at one with their very living presents, make these men and women all-too-human. Like ourselves, they are part of the continuum of life, no dead deposit on a static matrix, but a reality; and this reality gives to *Hamlet* and *Othello* and the other great tragedies their significance and inevitability of theme. Antecedent action is perforce the seed from which great drama grows; and the seed must be rightly sown if the stages of growth are to be explained. Thus *Romeo and Juliet* and *Julius Caesar,* for all their excellencies, are hardly tragedies: this consummate and exacting type of dramatic art was possible only after Shakespeare had mastered in comic pieces the devices and techniques by which drama is linked to life.

The management of antecedent action raises four major problems: where to cut into the vital stream of event; how to arrange this earlier material and interweave it in the course of the drama; how to express it in monologue, talk, or action, and so give it vitality or at least some interest; and lastly how and how much to employ it to delineate character and even to show character-change before the curtain rose. Shakespeare's solution of these problems grows more and more interdependent and intricate.

At first he seems hardly to know where to begin his play. *Love's Labour's* starts so late in the course of action that it has but little plot. At the other extreme, *Two Gentlemen* and *The Taming of the Shrew* have almost no antecedent action. And most of the chronicle histories merely take for granted a knowledge of previous events. In *King John* the first episode hardly belongs in the play. The comedies of the later 1590's show Shakespeare's growing mastery of this problem: in *The Merchant of Venice* he raises the curtain at precisely the right moment, when Bassanio asks for a loan to fit him out for Belmont, thus starting one plot; and Antonio in consequence seeks to borrow from Shylock, thus starting the other. In most of his later plays, Shakespeare grasps the moving coil of events with dexterous surety.

The second problem, the placing of these earlier data in the play, Shakespeare solved at first on the mere principle of clarity; and an Induction or an initial dialogue declared at once plainly and somewhat flatly the situation and previous events. In the *Comedy of Errors* he does not even follow Plautus who put off this explanation so as not to deaden the first scene; in *Richard II* he hits upon the Plautine device; and in *Julius Caesar* he weaves, as he does in later plays, the antecedent action into the whole course of the piece.

The third problem, the style of the pre-play, engaged Shakespeare's serious efforts from the first: in *Love's Labour's* he tries to lighten the exposition with wit and in *A Comedy of Errors,* with pointed rhetoric; in *Romeo and Juliet,* and later in *As You Like It,* he represents the conflict of motives directly, by physical violence; in *Twelfth Night* he adds music. And so, by a growing diversity of effects, ever more closely related to his purpose, he gives to the introductory scenes increasing verve and interest until in the brilliant initial act of *Twelfth Night* he can portray a whole complex mass of previous events and motives arising from them, and yet never let interest flag.

The fourth problem, the delineation of character, hardly existed in such early plays as *Love's Labour's* and the *Comedy of Errors,* for their type-characters are too faint to integrate with the pre-play. *Richard II,* in its opening scenes, contrasts the King's weakness with Bolingbroke's strength, and so lays the foundation of the plot. But the subtler matter of change of feeling and character before the play began first appears in Romeo's melancholy, in Hippolita's willingness to wed her conqueror, in Shylock's hatred of Antonio, and in Shallow's of Falstaff. So the antecedent action is bound into the very warp and woof of the play, which thus recedes into the background of the life from which it springs. The mastery of this technique was a necessary part of Shakespeare's growing realism and of the deepening significance of his themes; and, in his later plays, actual life seems always to stand just out of sight behind the wings of the stage, and the actors are not mere actors but inhabitants of this intense reality that is barely beyond our vision.

Shakespeare spent ten years and wrote some twenty plays in mastering his technique, before he wrote *Hamlet*. He experimented, imitated, devised, and re-combined, cut into his stories at widely divergent points, placed the antecedent action at the beginning or dissolved it throughout the first act or even the whole play, lightened it with wit or heightened it with poetry or action, made it express fine shades of character, and in time became a master in the difficult task of introducing a drama to its audience and relating it to its own living and realistic past. Thus Shakespeare learned and developed his art.

IV

Mistaken Identity in Shakespeare's Comedies

During the eighteenth and nineteenth centuries the interpretation
of Shakespeare's characters and themes was almost entirely in the
hands of poet-critics or of impressionistic men of letters, who oracu-
larly read into his works the concepts, and especially the moral
platitudes, of their own generation, while more exact scholars
worked on editorial details or on such less immediate problems as
sources and theatrical presentation. More recently, however, Professors Stoll and Schücking, basing their work on the conventions
of the Elizabethan stage, have led the way in insisting upon a more
Elizabethan interpretation of the plays; but, unfortunately, their
own interpretations, though unquestionably pertinent and valuable,
are somewhat narrow in basis; for, as the present writer and his
students have endeavored to show in a number of special studies,
an influence upon Shakespeare even more important than the world
of the theatre was the world of Elizabethan life, which, even more
than dramatic tradition, supplied situations such as the cheating of
a gull [1] and the revenge of cuckoldry,[2] supplied character types such
as the rustic servant, the constable, and the emancipated Renaissance lady,[3] and supplied themes such as the Italian duello, the ruinous effect of rising capitalism, the change in military life from a
feudal to a professionalized army,[4] and the vivid contrast between

the Renaissance court and the still Mediæval country. Having thus investigated from the point of view of plot, character, and theme, this relation of inherited convention to immediate realism, the present writer proposes in this study to investigate this relationship from the point of view of stage-convention itself, in order to ascertain how far and by what means Shakespeare bent and changed convention to suit his immediate purposes, whether it dominated him, or he it, and especially whether he made it subservient to realism and Elizabethan *vraisemblance*.

Dramatic irony is one of the most telling effects of the theatre; and perhaps its most obvious form is the device of mistaken identity, in which a particular character is supposed by one or more of the rest to be some one other than himself. Sometimes this error is purely fortuitous; sometimes, the result of intentional disguise; but, in either case, the audience, being in the secret, sit like the gods on Olympus, and smile at the ignorance of the petty mortals on the stage. In actual life, the deception of intentional disguise is more usual than that of fortuitous mistake; and consequently the former is more probable and so more realistic in art; for a chance mistake in identifying anyone is almost sure to be cleared up, if not by a close look at his clothes and face, at least by a few moments of conversation. Among the Elizabethan upper classes, however, the artificiality of dress, which left almost no part of the body its natural shape, the bewildering changes of "new-fangled upstart fashion," [5] the wide use of face-painting, of grotesque wigs, of strange headgear, and masks and sometimes veils, must have hindered recognition; and, among the lower classes, the Mediæval uniformity of a leathern apron and a rule for carpenters [6] and the blue coats for the old-fashioned servant [7] must have made it hard at times to tell one Dromio from another. Even so, however, such matters as voice-intonation, build, and facial contour could not be entirely changed; and one rarely reads of Elizabethans actually mistaking one another except in cases of intentional disguise. Mistaken identity, however, in one form or another, has been a common device of all drama and especially of the Latin comedy that Shakespeare must have known so well. He himself, indeed, employs it more or less in almost every one of his comedies; and the contemporary use of boy-actors for women's parts made the masquerading as men of Portia, Viola, and Imogen a particularly common and convenient device of the Elizabethan stage. The present writer, therefore, proposes to examine mistaken identity as characteristic of Shakespeare's use of stage-convention, and, if possible, to ascertain how far he leaves it a mere comic convention as he found it in Plautus, and how far he develops and changes it, both from Plautus and from the sources of each play, not only in order to make it more significant in plot, character, and theme, but to give it for his Elizabethan audience a greater *varisemblance*.

Shakespeare's early comedies, the *Errors, Love's Labour's, Two Gentlemen,* and *A Midsummer Night's Dream,* not only all employ mistaken identity, but employ more of it than any known sources of the plays in question. In *A Comedy of Errors,* though mistaken identity is the very basis of the Plautine source, Shakespeare actually doubled the use of the device, by introducing twin servants as well as twin masters; and, since the mistake is a mere fortuitous coincidence and not intentional on the part of any of the characters, he clearly casts aside all thought of convincing realism, developing his play as a farce for its laughter rather than its truth to life, or meaning. Even granted two sets of twins, masters and servants, could they go through a whole day, constantly mistaken for one another, and no one guess the truth? Here convention is indeed given a free rein, in accordance with the theories of Professor Stoll, and character and theme are quite subservient to it. In *Love's Labour's Lost* the young ladies at the time of the Muscovite masquerade intentionally deceive their lovers as to who is who, so that each lover addresses his suit to the wrong girl. The use of mistaken identity is more convincing; but it is short and unimportant in the development of plot and in the portrayal of character and theme: apparently as in *A Comedy of Errors,* the device is used merely for its own inherent comedy. In *Two Gentlemen,* mistaken identity shows both advance and retrogress: it is serious in tone; it expresses character, Julia's fidelity to her fickle lover; and it contributes essentially to the comic conclusion of the plot. Proteus' employment of his former mistress as a page is the result of her intentional disguise rather than mere chance; but, even so, one doubts whether he could fail to recognize in "Sebastian" the voice and features on whom his ears and eyes had dwelt so long. In *Two Gentlemen,* therefore, mistaken identity, though more significantly used than in *Love's Labours',* is distinctly less convincing. In *A Midsummer Night's Dream,* the slip of Puck in anointing the wrong Athenian's eyes, although coincidence, is perhaps acceptable in a fairy play; and his mistake is important in the plot, even if not expressive of character or theme. In all these early plays, except perhaps *Two Gentlemen,* Shakespeare seems to be using mistaken identity chiefly for its own sake as a device for merriment; and its relation to plot, character, and theme, and its inherent realism, would seem to be secondary matters. The convention appears merely as a convention to be accepted by the spectator under the license of farce or romance or fairy lore, not an expression of human actuality or a vehicle for the revelation of the depths of human character.

In the comedies of the second period, though Shakespeare does not always make mistaken identity serve directly the higher purposes of plot, character, and theme, he regularly strives to give it a greater realism: the mistakes are all intentional deceptions assisted by darkness, disguise of dress, or like auxilliaries; and we are made, as far as possible, to feel that these deceptions would probably have succeeded in real life as well as they do upon the stage. As an element of dramatic technique, the device still interests Shakespeare; for in all of the earlier comedies of the second period, the *Shrew,* the *Merchant, Henry IV,* and *Merry Wives,* he either developed it beyond his sources or entirely added it to his original. In the first period he used it for farce and for romance; in the earlier plays of the second period he seems to be trying it out as a convention for high comedy. The disguise of Bianca's lovers in the *Shrew,* though developed from the merest hint in Gascoigne, is rather the conventional situation of Italian comedy, realistic in Italy, but hardly so in Elizabethan England where lovers needed no such subterfuge to see the maiden of their choice. It is of slight importance in the play, but interesting in the double uncertainty of the lovers, each doubting the identity and purpose of the other. This device is similar to Shakespeare's doubling of the mistaken identity in *A Comedy of Errors;* but, in the *Shrew,* even though the mistake appears only in a single scene, Shakespeare pictures the lovers as more than a little suspicious of deception; and one feels that he defers much more to the audience's sense of probabilty. In *The Merchant of Venice,* the ring episode brings to a merry climax the mistaken identity of the trial scene. It is more serious and poetic in tone than the wooing of Bianca; but it is more loosely bound up with the rest of the play. Portia's elaborate preparation for the trial scene, however—the letters from Bellario and the enveloping lawyer's gown—the fact that Bassiano had not the slightest hint of her coming, that he had seen her but twice or thrice before, and that his attention was centered upon the distresses of his friend, all these considerations help to make the mistake convincing; and Shakespeare seems to have omitted nothing that would make it so. Even at that, the mystery of the ring is shortly solved; and we are not allowed to think that Portia's happy stratagem was long kept a secret. The Falstaff plays show Shakespeare deliberately adding scenes of mistaken identity to English history; and the Gadshill episode, in which Falstaff recognizes Prince Hal and Poins only *ex post facto* in the tavern, and his deception by "Master Brook" in *Merry Wives,* are at once ridiculously funny and revelatory of plot, character, and theme. Both incidents, moreover, are realistic and convincing: how could he recognize the Prince disguised and in the dark? how could he know that "Brook" was Master Ford, whom he had never seen? These are perhaps the triumphs of Shakespeare's use of the convention. They display the poor gull, Falstaff, fooled, like Malvolio, to the top of his bent and taking to verbiage to cover such a retreat as he can make; they show character in convincing circumstances, and, like true comedy, make us laugh at the pretentious shams of cloaked iniquity. Here, mistaken identity has become a device for high comedy and a primary means by which Shakespeare exhibits the character of Falstaff, the greatest comic creation of his art.

During the later comedies of the second period, Shakespeare uses mistaken identity only as it appears in his sources, without augmenting it; and so one judges that his interest in it had declined. The fact that it inheres in his originals helps him to integrate it in his plots; and he is at some pains to make it also express character and to give it a verisimilitude that carries considerable, if not always complete, plausibility. In *Much Ado* the appearance of Margaret at the window in the place of Hero is carefully prepared for and motivated; and night and distance make the deception probable. Shakespeare, moreover, instead of presenting this deception directly, and so risking an unconvincing scene on the sunlit stage of the Globe, has Borachio merely relate to Conrade the circumstances of this trumped-up rendez-vous. In *As You Like It,* Orlando had hardly seen enough of Rosalind to recognize her, especially dressed in men's clothes and in the Forest of Arden, where he would not expect her to be. The comic irony of the love-making is adroitly managed, though on lines already marked out by Lodge; the plot is advanced and the characters of both lovers more clearly indicated. In *Twelfth Night* mistaken identity occupies a larger place; and partly because it is so crucial in the action, and partly because the confusion between brother and sister is largely fortuitous rather than intended by either one, the effect is perhaps less convincing. A comparison, however, with Shakespeare's use of such chance mistakes in *A Comedy of Errors* shows how far the dramatist had progressed toward realism. In the *Comedy of Errors,* the doubling of Plautus' twins certainly did not make for greater probability; and the lines place no emphasis on similarity of physique or dress; whereas, in *Twelfth Night,* he used no more of mistaken identity than his comic denouement required; and Viola carefully informs the audience that she plans to imitate her brother's dress;[8] and the Duke, moreover, testifies to the perfect likeness of the two: "One face, one voice, one habit, and two persons." Even so, Shakespeare apparently felt doubts of his success, and so makes the mistake last only for an hour or two rather than an entire day as in the *Errors,* and hurries through the scenes in which it is most prominent. Such slips occasioned by mere accident are hard to reconcile to the spectator's sense of artistic likelihood. Even in *Much Ado* and *As You Like It,* where he employed the more inherently convincing effect of intentional deception, he prepared the way carefully so as to make the mistaken identity a realistic probability rather than a mere stage convention. Indeed, the fact that Dr. Munro refers to the first period of Shakespeare's comedies as the "Mistaken Identity Group"[9] as opposed to other types that followed, shows how utterly Shakespeare had assimilated this old convention to his dramatic purposes; for every comedy of the second period has one or more episodes founded on mistaken identity, a fact that Munro had apparently quite overlooked. In *Henry IV*, in *As You Like It,* and even in *Twelfth Night,* Shakespeare had progressed far beyond the naïve Plautine technique of *A Comedy of Errors:* he had mastered the effect, turned it to his highest purposes in the revelation of character, and was already beginning to discard it.

Mistaken identity, even in its more acceptable form of intentional disguise, apparently attracted Shakespeare but slightly during his two later periods. *Troilus and Cressida* and *The Tempest* have nothing of it—unless one terms such things as Prospero's invisibility a case in point. In *All's Well* and *Measure for Measure,* it is essential to the story of the source; and, as in *Much Ado* and *As You Like It,* the dramatist was on the whole successful in giving it realism. In *All's Well* the comic outcome depends on Helena's successful deception of her husband; and Shakespeare makes its as convincing as he can. In *Measure for Measure* the Duke disguised as a Friar becomes a sort of chorus, reiterating the theme throughout the middle acts; and his absence from the government is the *sine qua non* of the plot and of the consequent revelation of character. In the romances, likewise, at the end of his career, Shakespeare does not seek occasions to use mistaken identity. In *Cymbeline,* to be sure, he added to his source Imogen's disguise as a shepherd in the mountains in order to save her life and make possible a comic end; but the fact that her identity is unsuspected by the mountaineers seems otherwise of little significance. In the *Winter's Tale,* Florizel's exchange of garments with Autolycus is likewise useful in resolving the comic complication; but the matter is of minor import in the play. The great tragedies occasionally employ chance mistakes of identity, as when Hamlet kills Polonius, believing him to be the King, and occasionally intentional disguise, such as Edgar's appearance as a half-crazed vagabond in *Lear;* but, in tragedy, characters must know who each other is if their actions are to be significant and their motives clear and consequential in effect; and mistaken identity widely used would impair the logic of a great catastrophe. Thus, in Shakespeare's developing technique, the device becomes more and more a mere accident preserved from the source or an unimportant matter incidental to greater things.

As the contrast between court and countryside gave place to weightier themes, and the depiction of rustic servants to more complex characters, so mistaken identity was superseded in Shakespeare's art by subtler forms of dramatic irony, in which, not the mere identity, but the acts and particularly the motives, feelings, or point of view of a given character were misunderstood by one or more of his companions. Thus Hamlet accuses his mother of a murder that she knows nothing of; on a still subtler plane, the Fool, in trying to console King Lear, reminds him of the very things that give him pain, and drives him further to insanity; and Desdemona, in the very self-abnegation of her repeated pleas for Cassio, confirms Othello in his jealousy. Such misunderstandings are the very stuff of life; for what man ever completely understood the thoughts and motives of another; or do we even of ourselves? These errors need no obvious properties such as night and masks and dressing in disguise to make them probable. Thus Shakespeare's art gained depth and subtlety: the fortuitous mistakes of Plautus lead to intentional disguise, which Shakespeare exploits in the high comedies of the second period; and this leads on to the highest types of dramatic irony, misapprehension of the motives and the mental habits of our fellows. Even in the second period, these delicate ironies begin to show themselves: Shylock leaves his house to the safe-keeping of Jessica on the very night that she elopes; Falstaff has the faith, or impudence, to think the young king will reward him for his vices, and that two merry but respectable married women cannot resist his charms; Benedick obtusely fails to recognize the love of Beatrice; and Malvolio has the shocking assurance to suppose that a great lady like Olivia could possibly select him for a husband. Thus in the very plays that show mistaken identity developed to its height, Shakespeare was learning the use of subtler ironies, which by degrees he made more and more important in his plays, until, in *Othello,* they govern the whole movement of the plot and the relation of almost every character with the rest: Brabantio never guesses the affection of his daughter for Othello; Iago fools all of the others; yet he himself does not understand Desdemona's purity of soul; and Othello himself understands neither Iago nor Cassio nor Desdemona. Indeed, dramatic irony is the substance of this tragedy quite as much as mistaken identity is the warp and woof of *A Comedy of Errors.* So gradually, from the stage-convention of mistakes in face and person, Shakespeare progressed to the use of intentional disguise and finally to the portrayal of those every-day misunderstandings of our fellow men, the realism of which depends not on our acceptance of some stage-convention, nor on such outward things as clothes and darkness, but on true insight into human character. He is no mere slave of convention, but its master; and he can develop or discard it at the behest of a higher artistic purpose.

V

Shakespeare and the *Conversazione*

The courtly speech of the Renaissance included, not only the common coinage of elegant etiquette, but also formalized and mannered conversations governed by plan and precedent. For story-telling, like that in the *Decameron,* and other amusements of the sort, a chief, or "queen," was generally appointed, either by right of birth or by lot or by election; and he (or more often *she*), crowned with a wreath of laurel, ruled over the festivities. Sometimes, as set forth in Castiglione, debates, like those in the Mediæval Courts of Love, took place on such subjects as marriage or Platonic Beauty, or the relative position of the courtier and the lady-in-waiting. Sometimes the talk was informal; sometimes those present spoke in a prescribed order—always with much compliment and courtliness of phrase. Sometimes, as in Romei's *Discorsi* (1586), a gentleman would deliver a set speech like Guarini's on Human Love; and the ladies would raise "doubts" and questions which he must answer. Perhaps the fullest discussion of this custom appears in Stefano Guazzo's popular work, *La Civil Conversazione* (1574) translated a few years later into English. Book IV details at length a "conversation" between six gentlemen and four ladies one winter evening at the court of the Duke of Sabbioneta. His Grace was acclaimed lord of the company; but he refused to allow his feudal rank to give

48

him precedence; and so, by using Petrarch's sonnets as a sort of *sortes Virgilianæ,* they fixed by lot on Signora Giovanna as queen, who chose judges and declared that Solitude should be the topic for he occasion. Each person had to select a place for retirement, and argue by aphorism and proverb in favor of living there alone. The contestants spoke in turn; and the two judges chose the winner. As penalty, all the others had to answer riddles before they were let go in to supper. While eating and drinking, the company discussed food and banqueting and kindred topics, quite informally. Then a musician came in, and sang a poem in honor of the Duke. Appropriate compliments were exchanged, and His Grace turned the talk to Melancholy and its effect in shortening human life. One of the guests declared that he would entertain the group next evening; and the queen proposed that, in place of the Game of Solitude played earlier, they now play the Game of Society—riddles interwoven with compliments. Then followed a debate on whether the eyes or he tongue be more provocative of love. So with pretty speeches and anecedotes, the evening drew to a close.

Many such dialogues and discourses were printed and widely read throughout Renaissance Europe. Sixteenth Century France borrowed its social customs largely from Italy; and indeed, Italian influences dominated France for over a century from the Italian expedition of Charles VIII (1494) to the marriage of Louis XIII (1615).[1] Sixteenth century England was no less affected: much of he courtesy literature of contemporary Italy was translated into English, and more or less inspired such authors as Elyot, Ascham, Whetstone, Greene, and above all Lyly, whose *Euphues* was all the rage at Elizabeth's court in the 1580's. His comedies have short dialogues on general subjects such as Flattery and Love *(Endymion, II, i, and III, iv),* and were a major influence in forming Shakespeare's style; and Shakespeare, from both his reading and his friends, must have had direct knowledge of the Italian social conventions that were so popular at court. Crane dates from about 1600 "the influence in England of Italian Games and other modes of social diversion";[2] but the number of translations of Italian courtesy books before this date[3] suggests that the influence began somewhat earlier. Sir Edward Sullivan has brought forward verbal parallels as evidence that Shakespeare knew Guazzo's volume, but did not find significant influence of Book IV, which deals so concretely with the *conversazione;* [4] and Crane's excellent *Italian Social Customs of the Sixteenth Century* merely discusses Shakespeare's use of Italian stories for plots, and suggests an influence of Bembo's *Asolani* on a very short passage in *A Midsummer-Night's Dream.* [5] Scholarship, in fact, has rather neglected the use of the *conversazione* as a set form in his plays.

Many in Shakespeare's audiences knew court life at first hand— some of them in Italy as well as in London. The dramatist's portrayal, therefore, of courtly characters and situations, especially in a play that approached the realism of comedy of manners, had to depict aristocratic conventions and amusements as they actually existed among nobles and their followers. Something of these matters he seems to have picked up early in his career—indeed, he may have known about them at Stratford. As early as *King Richard II (III, iv),* he enumerates bowling, dancing, story-telling and singing; and, in *As You Like It* when Rosalind and Celia plan to "devise sports," the former suggests "falling in love" and the latter a satiric discussion of "the good housewife Fortune," and so introduces a short *conversazione.* An allied form of entertainment was the practical joke, which Shakespeare uses in *Love's Labour's* when the Princess and her ladies change favors so that Navarre and his courtiers make love to the wrong persons in the Muscovite masquerade. The ring episode which closes *The Merchant of Venice* is a more serious practical joke. A common accompaniment of the *conversazione* was the sprightly repartee of courtly usage; and dignified statesmen such as Henry V (when he had turned away from his wild youth), the good Duke in *As You Like It,* Polonius [6] in *Hamlet,* and Gonzalo [7] in *The Tempest,* quite properly improved the occasion with apt moralizing; but most such passages are monologue. In *Love's Labour's* the characters speak whole sonnets extempore; and the elegant Don Armado caps couplets with his page (III, i, 76 *et seq.*) : such poetic devices sometimes appear in the *conversazione.* Guazzo describes the use of riddles; and the Countess Olivia propounds one to her jester.[8] Clearly Shakespeare was well aware of the techniques of amusement by which nobles and ladies passed their time while awaiting their master's pleasure or in turn supplied diversion for an hour of royal relaxation. Surely, one might expect to find something of the *conversazione* in his plays. A master of realism like Shakespeare surely would avail himself not only of stage-conventions such as mistaken identity but also of the social conventions of the age.

A complete *conversazione,* as detailed by Guazzo, would hardly be possible in drama; for it would too much delay the action, and so dampen dramatic interest; but, on a limited scale, it could be used, and would provide realistic background for courtly scenes. The Elizabethan theatre-goer, furthermore, enjoyed wit or moralizing for their own sake far more than we. The *conversazione* would appear in the plays as a sort of brief essay in dialogue, comparable to the writings of Plato that were then so popular, but on lighter subjects and more charged with persiflage and lyricism and compliment, as befitted princely hearers. It is a formal discussion by two or more persons of a set, general subject. It is not a mere exposition of the plot like Prospero's telling Miranda of their expulsion from Milan; and it is not a monologue apropos like Horatio's lecture on demons while he is waiting for the appearance of the Ghost. Portia's discussion of her lovers, though it follows a set scheme, is not general enough in subject; Lucio's obscene repartee in *Measure for Measure* (i, ii) has neither a definite topic nor a set progression; and Lear's testing of his daughters' love, though it follows a clear-cut plan, is too personal in theme. In short, the form must be trenchant dialogue in a definite progression usually marked by some rhetorical or logical device, such as question and reply; and the content must be a general subject, such as love or virtue. An investigation of the *conversazione* in Shakespeare should take into account its occurrence in the plays of different types and different periods, its composition, its subjects, its speakers, the plans it follows, and its relation to the play as a whole, plot, character, setting, style and theme, as it reflects and expresses these dramatic elements.

All Shakespeare's dramas together present fewer than a score of pertinent examples. They appear in plays of all his four periods, but as a rule only in certain types of comedy. The chronicle histories are too much concerned with politics and war and too purely forthright English to give place to such imported elegancies. Prince Hal and Falstaff, to be sure, discuss the latter's way of life—sleep, food, drink, loose women, thieving, music, and an occasional repentance—but it is all too casual and too personal for a *conversazione.* *Merry Wives* is likewise too English, and *Measure for Measure* too sombre, for the device; the Roman plays have none; and the hurried plot of a Byzantine romance, such as the *Winter's Tale,* hardly gives time for a set conversation-piece. Most of the instances appear in comedies that portray court-life in the real or the ideal: *As You Like It* has no less than seven: *Love's Labour's* and *The Merchant of Venice,* two apiece; six other comedies, one each, but the best example of all is in *Othello,* the only one in tragedy: as a courtly play of contemporary Italian setting, it might properly contain a *conversazione.*

A rapid survey of these seventeen passages would seem to be in order. *Love's Labour's,* as a court comedy, is full of merry repartee that accords with this type of play. The King and Biron in the first scene hold a *conversazione* on study, and Biron claims to win the debate. Later Don Armado and Moth converse on love (I, ii, 56-104). *Two Gentlemen* likewise opens with a formal debate, in this case on the wisdom, or folly, of love: Proteus and Valentine cite the authority of "writers" as in a university disputation; and Proteus in his soliloquy at the end of the scene returns to the subject to summarize the debate as a contest of Love vs. Honor. In the first scene of *A Midsummer-Night's Dream,* Lysander and Hermia, in similar vein, discuss the course of true love. The trial of wives that closes *The Taming of the Shrew* suggests the courtly parlor games of the day, and ends with a sort of *conversazione* on woman's subjection to her husband. *The Merchant of Venice,* using as a text Antonio's sad mood, opens with a dialogue on melancholy. The beginning of Act V, moreover, supplies the lyrical *conversazione* on night. Viola and the Duke Orsino in *Twelfth Night* join in a set discourse on woman's capacity to love (II, iv, 92-120). *As You Like It* has one or more in every act: Celia and Rosalind open the long second scene with a talk on the deliberately chosen subject of fortune; in Act II, the rightful Duke, who loves to "cope" with Jaques, debates with him the evils of satire; in Act III, Rosalind and Orlando discuss time and love; and Corin and Touchstone argue on the courtly life, as against the pastoral; in Act IV, Jaques and Rosalind talk of melancholy; in Act V, Jaques and Touchstone satirize the fashionable duello in a *conversazione* on the degrees of a lie. In the first scene of *All's Well,* Parolles and Helena discuss virginity. In *Othello,* Iago tries to entertain Desdemona, while she waits for her husband's ship to arrive, with a cynical *conversazione* on woman. Finally, the second act of *The Tempest* opens with a sort of parody of the *conversazione* in which the political wisdom of Gonzalo contrasts with the vapidities of the others in the *entourage* of the usurping Duke of Milan. All of these plays are more or less Mediterranean, and some of them definitely Italian in setting. All are courtly; and the *conversazione* is regularly carried on by courtly characters. Even Corin belongs to the pastoral tradition, which the Renaissance accepted as a courtly literary convention. The only exception is Iago; and the elegant Cassio is constrained to apologize for his ineptitude at the art (II, i, 164-165). This association with Italianate courts and courtiers suggests that such dialogues arise not so much from academic influence [9] as from the amusements of the Italian nobles: of course the catechistical method of the schools is clearly apparent in Evans' quizzing of little William Page in *Merry Wives,* and such exercises may at times combine with the influence of the *conversazione.*

The exigencies of drama hardly allowed extremely long conversations on merely general topics; and the passages just listed vary from twenty-three lines in the talk of Lysander and Hermia on love to seventy-two given to the same topic by Rosalind and Orlando: perhaps the greater importance of these latter lovers explains their greater length. The *conversazione* is usually early in the play, and near the beginning of an act, for it is too general for tense dramatic climax. Occasionally, as in *The Merchant of Venice,* it is used in the last act to impart the tone of final serenity. Love and women furnish at least half the subjects—a reflection of an eternal human interest and also perhaps of the Mediæval Courts of Love. Sometimes there is a spice of satire, as in Iago's acidulous commentary on women. In Shakespeare, the *conversazione* has usually two speakers, which is well within the maximum of nine mentioned in Guazzo.[10] Indeed, in the shortened form required in drama, many speakers would be impossible.

These speakers sometimes choose a subject deliberately; often, they follow a set plan; and occasionally one or another winds up the talk with a definite conclusion. In *Love's Labour's,* Biron announces the subject: "What is the end of study? let me know." He and the King proceed to debate the matter with couplets and a sonnet that emphasize the formal nature of the talk; and finally Biron claims to have won the case for "barbarism." Although Biron attacks "base authority," and declares that study is useless, the argument is conducted with very little of fact or logic; but at least the debate has a formal beginning and a formal end; and after all, Biron does not really take it seriously and in the end signs the oath to study: indeed, it is quite in the tone of courtly persiflage. Armado likewise introduces with a question his *conversazione* with little Moth: "Comfort me, boy: what great men have been in love?" So the talk starts to follow the plan of illustrative examples— Hercules and Samson—but then it is sidetracked to the colors that are associated with lovers and so lapses to personal topics. It has a clear beginning and a beginning of a set plan, and then by degrees fades away. The dialogue on love by Lysander and Hermia starts with a personal question—"Why is your cheeck so pale?"—and so progresses to the general matter of the sorrows and tribulations of love. There is no clear logical progression, but the exclamatory, line-length speeches capped by a conclusion from each of the speakers sets off the whole in a sort of rhetorical mold like that of the couplets and the sonnet in *Love's Labour's*. The *conversazione* on night in *The Merchant of Venice* is a lyrical contest rather than a debate; and, at the end, Jessica remarks:

> I would out-night you, did no body come;
> But, hark, I hear the footing of a man.

The speeches form irregular stanzas, each beginning with a sort of anaphora, or refrain, "In such a night. . . ." The conversation between Viola and the Duke on Woman's capacity for love, like Biron's on the value of study, is a debate, but in less formal guise.

The conversation-pieces in *As You Like It* are quite as clear-cut as those in the early plays. Celia and Rosalind discuss amusements; and Celia announces the evils of Fortune for discussion; but the talk proceeds casually and comes to no conclusion. The Senior Duke delights to "cope" with Jaques; but the latter avoids him as "too disputable" (II, v, 30-31). At last, they meet at dinner, and engage in a sort of *conversazione* on evil and satire, interrupted by Orlando, demanding food. This turns the talk to other matters, and leads up to the famous speech on the seven ages of man. Corin and Touchstone compare the courtly and the pastoral ways of life in a debate that opens with a question, and continues with "reasons" and witty examples. Touchstone claims to have won the argument just as the entrance of Rosalind brings it to an end. Later in the scene, the questions of Orlando give point and plan to his dialogue with Rosalind on time, until he becomes so fascinated with his charming interlocutor that he deserts mere impersonalities to ask: "Where dwell you, pretty youth?" This in due course leads to their *conversazione* on love, in which Rosalind undertakes to cure Orlando of his malady. After a brief introductory dialogue, she recounts the symptoms of the disease, and then, in proper scientific order gives the treatment. He agrees to try her cure, and the scene concludes. In Act IV, Rosalind and Jaques start to argue on the advantages of melancholy; Jaques analyzes its types, but Rosalind is not convinced. In Act IV in response to Jaques' questions, he and Touchstone launch upon a discussion of the seventh cause in duelling. They roughly follow the plan of popular handbooks of the period; but the conclusion is merely the non-sequitur that Touchstone is "a rare fellow"; for, after all, the talk was merely an excuse for him to exercise his wit. In short, the examples in *As You Like It* are set off rather clearly from the surrounding text, and generally follow some sort of plan.

In *All's Well*, Helena's talk with Parolles on virginity progresses by a series of questions from the former: "Man is enemy to virginity; how may we barricade it against him? . . . Is there no military policy, how virgins might blow up men? . . . How might one do, sir, to loose it to her own liking?" The *conversazione* between Desdemona and Iago also follows question and reply, and is logically arranged according to types of female excellence: "fair and wise," then dark and wise, and so forth. Desdemona in the end declares that he has come to a "most lame and impotent conclusion." The abortive *conversazione* in *The Tempest* has no clearly marked progression: it consists of Gonzalo's reiterated political wisdom in contrast to others' ill-timed and silly witticisms: Gonzalo tries to make it a set conversation, but the levity and derision of his companions forbid.—Some of these examples, just reviewed, have a clear and logical plan, perhaps based on a science like medicine, or on some other branch of popular knowledge; but more of them, especially in the early plays, use some poetic means such as refrain or couplet, or some rhetorical device such as question and answer. Most of them are clearly marked at the start, but not many reach a clearly defined conclusion: often, the *conversazione* is interrupted, or it may turn to personal matters more apposite to the plot.

Shakespeare puts this social convention to numerous dramatic uses; and it is made to contribute to plot-structure, characterization, local color, brilliance of style, and clarity of theme. For example, the *conversazione* between the King and Biron in *Love's Labour's* anticipates the solution of the main plot: Biron's skepticism about the celibate student life prepares the way for the general breaking of vows and the love affairs that form the main action of the play. In *Twelfth Night,* Viola's talk with the Duke on woman's capacity to love is the first salvo in her courtship of her noble master, and so initiates that plot. The *conversazione* on love between Rosalind and Orlando is the turning point in their love affair. The trial of wives at the end of *The Taming of the Shrew,* capped with Kate's lecture on wifely obedience, is the consummation of the whole action, both major and minor, in the comedy. Thus the *conversazione* may introduce the plot, or form its central crux, or point up its conclusion. On the other hand, as in the case of the dialogue on night in *The Merchant of Venice* and the piece on time in *As You Like It,* it may not advance the plot one whit.

Although the *conversazione* was supposed to be impersonal, it often throws light on the characters of the speakers, very much as an informal essay does, even though its subject have little direct relation to the autobiography of the author. In *Twelfth Night,* for instance, the Duke's part in the dialogue with Viola brings out his belief in the superiority of men over women—an attitude that seems to motivate Olivia's rejection of him, and this rejection makes possible his later marriage with Viola. At the same time, the dialogue reflects Viola's depth of feeling and her passion for the Duke. In *All's Well,* the conversation on virginity displays Parolles' coarse outlook on life and also Helena's outspoken desire for a husband— the latter, the basic motive in the story. In *Othello,* the *conversazione* shows Iago's cynicism toward women, which governs his whole attitude toward Emilia, Desdemona, and so toward Cassio and Othello; and it also shows Desdemona's somewhat naïve and light-hearted reaction: he believes in his cynicism so much that it motivates his whole part in the plot: and she believes in it so little that she later cannot even realize that Othello can be jealous. In *The Tempest,* characterization actually dominates and re-makes the *conversazione:* the two usurping monarchs and their courts have just been wrecked on the island; and the good old counsellor Gonzalo, who had formerly served Prospero and saved his life, takes stock of the situation seriously, shrewdly notes that there is something more than natural in the shipwreck, and proceeds *solo* with an intermittent *conversazione* on the ideal government of such an isle.[11] Meanwhile, the usurping Antonio and the wicked Sebastian, who is planning to kill his brother and also become a usurper, make vain fun of him and so display their inborn unfitness to the serious matters of rule. Character in the *conversazione* appears most clearly in the later plays, where it often serves the same purpose as the soliloquies in *Hamlet,* to show the inner personality—thoughts and motives—when the conscious mind is not roused to the alert by some immediate personal problem.

To the Elizabethans, Italy was a Land of Heart's Desire, and as such, served as a popular setting for plays, especially for courtly comedies. Court life, in fact, throughout western Europe was highly Italianized, and any play that pretended to this courtly local color might well have place for a *conversazione*. *Love's Labour's* is just such a comedy, courtly in both subject-matter and appeal; and it has two examples. *As You Like It,* with all its pastoral artifice, portrays two courts; and it has no less than six. All of these dialogues are spoken by characters connected with the good Duke or his court: apparently, as already suggested in *The Tempest,* a wicked usurper and his followers would hardly indulge in this pleasant and elevating pastime. In *The Merchant of Venice,* Antonio's melancholy, brought out in the initial *conversazione* anticipates and prepares for the serious tone of the comedy; and lyrical dialogue on night that opens Act V suggests the calm after the storm when Bassanio is happily married, and Antonio is saved. Indeed, the *conversazione* can be as rich in atmosphere as a lyric; and sometimes it is a dramatic lyric in dialogue.

It contributes also to style; for it is an excellent vehicle for either aphoristic wit or not-too-violent emotion; and it is so used in both *Love's Labour's* and *As You Like It*. It may be outright satiric, as when Celia and Rosalind determine to "mock the good housewife Fortune from her wheel, that her gifts may henceforth be bestowed equally." In fact, it is a mannered convention of Renaissance elegance that, set like a jewel in an appropriate ring, lends brilliance to everything around it.

Most important of all, the *conversazione* gives emphasis to the theme of the play. The theme of *Love's Labour's* is the predominance of love over study in youthful minds; and the opening debate argues just this proposition. Also on the inescapability of love, even for the greatest soldier, is the conversation between Moth and Don Armado; and the Don pretends to act the part of a great soldier. The dialogue between Lysander and Hermia declares that "The course of true love never did run smooth"; and the several plots of *A Midsummer-Night's Dream* clearly illustrate this proposition. As its title implies, *The Taming of the Shrew* is on the relations of man and wife; and this is the topic of the *conversazione* at the end. In fact, all the conversation-pieces in Shakespeare express the themes of their respective plays except the one on night in *The Merchant,* and Rosalind and Orlando's on time, and Jaques' three on hunting, on melancholy and on the duello. Sometimes, this relationship is direct, as in *The Shrew;* sometimes oblique and subtle, as in *The Tempest,* where the talk by inference contrasts the healthy with the evil in political life; and the theme of the play is the curing of such evil by restoring a banished Duke and his daughter to their rightful place.

Throughout Shakespeare's career, from his earliest to his latest work, he uses, in appropriate plays, the Italianate *conversazione*. This social convention, or parlor game, had spread all over Europe as a device for courtly amusement, and so in abbreviated form could hardly have escaped some use in plays of contemporary courtly setting. It was, moreover, a useful vehicle for lyricism, moralizing or wit, all three of which delighted Elizabethan theatre-goers. Its subjects are diverse, but love and woman predominate. In its shortened form two speakers usually suffice, sometimes in question-and-answer, sometimes in debate. Such dialogues have usually a clear-cut beginning and sometimes a set conclusion. Shakespeare uses it to express plot, character, setting, style, and theme, and so weaves this piece of general dialogue into the texture of the play.

Perhaps the most perfect *conversazione* in Shakespeare is the talk between Desdemona and Iago on womankind. Romei in his *Discorsi* describes a *conversazione* on just this eternal theme; and it figured largely in Mediæval satire and in the Courts of Love. Desdemona and Emilia have just arrived in Cyprus; but Othello, who should have preceded them, has not yet come; and so, naturally, she is worried. Cassio tries to pass the time with elegant compliment, and also greets Emilia, according to current custom, with a kiss, Iago directs a slighting remark to his wife; Desdemona defends her; Iago persists; Desdemona calls him "slanderer"; and thereupon, Iago extends his satire to all of womankind. Emilia declares that she would not have him compose a eulogy on her; but Desdemona offers herself as a subject. Iago, however, declares himself too "critical." Desdemona again urges him to "assay"; but the result is a dialogue on women in general, apparently quite impersonal. As Desdemona remarks, she is merely trying to pass the time politely until Othello comes. Iago labors with his "invention," and produces a couplet. So the *conversazione* proceeds by question and answer to its "most lame and impotent conclusion"; and Cassio finishes the matter by excusing Iago's most uncomplimentary attitude toward Desdemona's sex: "You may relish him more in the soldier than in the scholar"; i.e. Iago is not courtier enough to play well at this courtly game. Here, in little, appear the clashes in point of view between the well-born Desdemona and Cassio on the one hand, and the coarse Iago on the other; and this *motiv* is basic to plot and character in the tragedy. Iago reduces the *conversazione* to his own low level, just as he later tries to drag down all the principals in the play; and the theme of the *conversazione* is also the theme of *Othello,* womanhood, its flaws and its nobility.[12]

VI

Bastardy in Shakespeare's Plays

Shakespeare's plays reflect not only social conventions such as the *conversazione* but also serious social problems, and one of these is the age-old matter of the child born out of wedlock.

The differing standards of morals for men and for women and the strict class system of the sixteenth century, which allowed the nobility more or less to extend the *droit du seigneur* to all their social inferiors, tended to make illegitimacy an accepted commonplace of Elizabethan life,[1] despite the ban of Christian ethics and the disapproval of strict moralists; and Shakespeare's plays of necessity present a number of examples of real or imputed bastardy: the Bastard of Orleans in *Henry VI, Part I* introduces Joan of Arc to the Dauphin, and occasionally appears in the roles of soldier and diplomat; Richard III brands as bastards the two Princes in the Tower; in *King John,* the trial of Faulconbridge, which hinges on his illegitimacy, dominates the whole first act; in *Much Ado,* the bastard Don John creates the main complication of the comedy; Thersites, in *Troilus and Cressida,* admits his illegitimacy,[2] and "bastard Margarelon"[3] boasts himself the son of King Priam: Caliban, in the *Tempest,* is a "bastard"[4]—if one may apply the term to such a creature—Leontes, in *A Winter's Tale* declares Perdita illegitimate; the "serviceable" Oswald, in *King Lear,* is called a bastard, and most important of all is the bastard Edmund, whose machinations consummate the tragedy. The Bastard of Orleans is merely an incidental figure derived from Shakespeare's historical sources, and plays no great part in the action; Perdita and the Princes in the Tower are actually legitimate; Margarelon is unimportant; and Caliban is beyond the human pale; but several of the other characters just mentioned not only are significant in their respective plays but also seem to require study, especially as bastards: Don John's illegitimacy, indeed, is Shakespeare's own addition to the source, and furnishes the chief complicating motive of *Much Ado;* and the busy Oswald in *King Lear* is entirely Shakespeare's own. Bastardy touches the plays chiefly in two regards: the question as to who is legally a bastard, and the supposed effect of this dubious status on the character and actions of those concerned.

Elizabethan law in effect declared that, no matter what evidence might be adduced, any child born of a married woman *(feme covert)*, unless her husband was beyond the seas *(extra quattuor maria)* during the entire time of her pregnancy[5] was *ipso facto* legitimate (i.e. a *mulier*); and even the sworn statement of his parents could not make him a bastard *(quasi nullius filius)*. Thus "the strongest presumption" of the law favoured legitimacy: this presumption doubtless arose partly because the need of the state for soldiers would otherwise make such children an unwelcome public charge,[6] and partly because a nobleman, for any frivolous reason, might otherwise attempt to disinherit by this means his eldest son[7] in favour of a younger, and so defeat the law of primogeniture and bring confusion to the feudal system of inheritance. In early times, moreover, under the old principle of the *droit du seigneur (jus primæ noctis)*, which gave the right of the first bridal night to the husband's overlord, the eldest child would commonly be the offspring of the suzerain and not of his imputed father; and feudal law, drawn from old tribal custom, doubtless intended that the overlord's son should inherit, for this bound society together, and made the vassal loyal to his actual, as well as to his titular, parent. Of course, the child born out of wedlock, like Edmund in *King Lear*, had no inheritance; and a child born before the marriage of his parents *(bastard eigne)* presented a vexing problem; for Canon Law accepted him as legitimized by the later marriage;

but Common Law branded him bastard [8], and throughout the Middle Ages there was constant conflict on the point between the clergy and the nobles; [9] and the result, as in the case of the other numerous conflicts between the two legal systems of the realm,[10] was confusion worse confounded.[11] In a society governed by the principles of primogeniture, the question of bastardy was especially important: it determined in effect who should wield the *patria potestas* in a great family, and thus, in a civil war, might decide the destinies of the nation; and Shakespeare, especially in his plays on Mediaeval history, could hardly avoid at least occasional treatment of this theme.

In the rather informal trial for bastardy of Philip Faulconbridge in the first act of *King John,* Shakespeare took pains to follow the common legal knowledge of his day,[12] although his source, *The Troublesome Raigne,* paid little attention to it.[13] Robert accuses his elder brother Philip of bastardy, and so lays claim to the paternal estates. Biologically, Philip Faulconbridge is clearly a bastard, as Shakespeare's play makes even more evident than does his source; [14] and, in conformity with the old custom of the *droit du seigneur,* he is the son of his supposed father's feudal overlord, the late King Richard. Legally, however, King John is correct in declaring him strictly legitimate; for, though his own defense is very flimsy,[15] the burden of proof rested entirely on his accuser, who must prove either that no marriage existed—this would make both brothers "love begot"—or that their father was *extra quattuor maria* at the time of his birth and for the entire previous nine months. Robert attempts the latter argument; but he can only say that his father was absent from England for the first fourteen weeks of his mother's pregnancy, and the King accordingly nonsuits him:

> Your father's wife did after wedlock bear him,
> And if she did play false, the fact [deed] was hers;
> Which fault lies on the hazard of all husbands
> That marry wives.[16]

His resemblance to King Richard persuades the Queen-Mother Elinor to accept him as her grandson. She induces him, despite his unassailable claim to legal legitimacy, to "bequeath" his paternal lands to his younger brother, to admit his bastardy, to take, as a bastard should, the name of his natural father, Plantagenet, and to accept knighthood and a place among her followers: thus the matter is settled quite extra-legally, but to the satisfaction of all concerned. To look in Sir Philip's character for the traits that the Elizabethans would associate with bastardy is rather superfluous; for, according to law and custom, he was legitimate; and certainly his stedfast loyalty, pleasant wit, and soldierlike honesty, do not ally him to Don John and Edmund and Thersites.

This same problem, though with a different outcome, appears in the efforts of the wicked Gloucester in *King Richard III* to make illegitimate the Princes in the Tower. He sends Buckingham to the Guildhall to "Infer the bastardy of Edward's children" because their father

> then had wars in France;
> And, by just computation of the time,
> Found that the issue was not his begot:
> Which well appeared in his lineaments.
> Being nothing like the noble duke my father:
> But touch this sparingly, as 't were far off;
> Because you know, my lord, my mother lives.

This, of course, raises the question of absence from England as a proof of bastardy; but, as in *King John,* the lines nowhere suggest that the father was away during the entire nine months; and, moreover, Gloucester's reference to his mother implies that he and she both knew that the charge was false. Until the Princes are safely murdered, he refers to them as "bastards," [17] but later in private admits them "the sons of Edward." [18] In *A Winter's Tale,* the jealous Leontes likewise tries to bastardize his daughter Perdita, and, as a reigning prince, overrides the legal fact that, as a parent, his evidence is inadmissible. Thus the question of legitimacy is important in Shakespeare, as it was in the society of his day; but the determination of the status was hardly a simple matter.

More significant as a social study is the effect, or supposed effect, of bastardy on those to whom the term actually and legally applied. Shakespeare's amplest portraits of bastards, illegitimate both by fact of nature and by law, are Don John in *Much Ado,* Edmund and probably Oswald in *King Lear,* and apparently Thersites in *Troilus and Cressida;* but, before discussing them, the present study might well investigate the attitude of Elizabethans in general and of Shakespeare in particular toward the parents and offspring of

such unions. *Bastard* was generally a term of reproach, as Shakespeare's use of it shows [19] and Edmund in his famous soliloquy [20]
tries to nullify the evil connotation of the word and the word *base*
with which the Elizabethans etymologically connected it.[21] The
degree of opprobrium, however, attached to those concerned varied
greatly according to circumstances. The Elizabethans took for
granted a double standard of morals for men and women: un-
married men were not expected to be chaste and, if they were,
risked the imputation of effeminacy.[22] The clown Costard in *Love's
Labour's* does not hesitate to express the wish that the clever Moth
had been his "bastard"; [23] and the fashionable Lucio in *Measure
for Measure* boasts of his promiscuity,[24] and declares that the
Duke approved such means of populating the realm.[25] The virtuous
Gloucester in *Lear,* with a mere conventional apology, admits his
paternity of the bastard Edmund; [26] and one can only suppose that,
though Christian morality and some of the stricter sort [27] might
disapprove, contemporary opinion hardly frowned on the father
in the case. On the other hand and for like reason, an aggrieved
husband was furious at even the rumor of his wife's misconduct [28]
as the examples of Othello, Iago, Master Ford, and Leontes Show:
and Leontes vents his anger not only on his wife but also on her
daughter, Perdita.[29] Bastard girls, indeed, like their mothers were
likely to bear the full brunt of the stigma, and seem to have been
an important source of supply for houses of prostitution.[30] Launcelot Gobbo, to be sure, expresses the pious wish that Jessica might
have been a bastard,[31] but that is only his hyperbolic way of showing
his hatred and contempt for Shylock. Bastard sons, if recognized
and reared by their fathers, might occupy a respectable, and even an
honoured place, as in the cases of the Bastard of Orleans and
Margarelon; and the latter even boasted himself the son of King
Priam: [32] perhaps Shakespeare thought of him as begotten by
signiorial privilege. On the other hand, a legitimate son would
take the imputation of bastardy, as Warwick does in *Henry IV,*
as a burning insult,[33] for it would disinherit him of wealth and
power. Thus the problem of the illegitimate child, though very
serious for wife and daughter, was a light matter to the father, and
varied somewhat in its effects upon the son, who must in any case,
however, have felt some tinge of jealousy for his more fortunate
half-brothers.

The present study, however, is interested, not so much in the reaction of society toward bastards and their parents, as in the reaction of bastards toward the society that branded and disinherited them. To the Elizabethan mind, the idea of heredity was closely connected with politics; for the nobles justified their vast estates, descended through generations, on the theory that virtue, especially courage and loyalty, were inherited by a divine dispensation; [34] and the converse of this appears in the law attainting of treason all the issue of a traitor.[35] Nenna declared the preëminence of "bloud," and thought the "prowesses" of the nobility derived from their ancestors.[36] Peacham,[37] Stephens,[38] Heywood,[39] and Bodenham [40] defended the institution of aristocracy as derived through heredity from heaven. Bryskett, with this in mind, declared high birth essential to high office; [41] James I advised his son to prefer "men of the noblest blood" to serve him; [42] and even the Inns of Court,[43] at the suggestion of the King, closed the legal profession to all but gentlemen born.[44] Shakespeare's characters occasionally express this theory: the dissolute Prince Hal fails to run true to the "greatness" of the blood of his "ancestors"; [45] and Suffolk declares that "True nobility is exempt from fear." Noble heredity was supposed to breed not only valour but loyalty: Laertes, demanding vengeance for the murder of his father, cries out, "That drop of blood that's calm proclaims me bastard"; [46] Brutus accuses of bastardy any Roman who can tell a lie; [47] in Goneril's cruelty Lear sees a proof that she cannot be his daughter; [48] and he is horrified that "Gloucester's bastard son" should be "kinder to his father than my daughters, Got 'tween the lawful sheets." [49] The theory of Divine Right of Kings, moreover, set forth in *Macbeth* and *Measure for Measure,* amply confirms this doctrine.[50]

This Elizabethan theory of hereditary virtue associated loyalty and truth with the well born; but conversely, it associated the corresponding vices with bastards and with the lower classes; [51] and the "base born" in Shakespeare's plays usually illustrate these base effects [52] Don John in *Much Ado* is a conspicuous example. In depicting him, *Shakespeare* departs from the main source of the play, the *novella* of Bandello, to follow Spenser's version of the story in Book II, Canto iv of *The Faerie Queene,* in which he is "a groom of base degree"; and Shakespeare, taking his hint from the word *base,* has made Don John a bastard. Critics have well described him as "envious," "sulky," and a "natural villain." [53] At the beginning of the play, he has recently been in rebellion against the Prince his brother; and they have just been "reconciled." He feels, however, that he cannot stay long in favor; and he plans to strike the first blow in the quarrel that he believes must be renewed. The Prince is taking an active part in the suit of Claudio for Hero's hand; and this gives Don John the motive for his plot to make a scandal, break up the match, and ruin the innocent Hero. At the end of the comedy, when his conspiracy is discovered, the Prince declares him "compos'd and fram'd of treacherie"; and he is "tane in flight, And brought with armed men back to *Messina.*" Disloyalty in both public and private life is the keynote of his character.

In *King Lear* this theme of bastardy and the evil that it brings both to the individual and to society achieves its fullest development; and the courts of Goneril and Regan are appropriate settings in which bastards might hope to flourish. Such is the busy Oswald, unless Kent is merely venting his spleen when he calls him "whoreson" and "the son and heir of a mongrel bitch," and a knave who should not "wear a sword"; and Edgar sums up his character as panderer for Goneril and Edmund:

> a serviceable villain,
> As duteous to the vices of thy mistress
> As badness would desire.

Oswald is no coward, as his flight with Edgar shows; and he might claim some praise for loyalty to his wicked mistress; but his part in the play is nevertheless disgraceful.

A more certain, and a more fully developed, example of bastardy is the notorious Edmund, who for his own advancement plots successively against his brother, against his father, and with both Goneril and Regan. In the very beginning of the play, his father, the Earl of Gloucester, makes clear the facts of his birth and early life: he is about a year younger than Edgar, the Earl's legitimate son; and he was born of a "fair" mother for whom apparently his lordship had considerable attachment. At an early age, Edmund was sent travelling into foreign countries—presumably to Italy if one may judge from his Machiavellian arts—and now, after nine years, he has just returned; and his father introduces him to the

Earl of Kent as his recognized bastard. Edmund's bastardy is very
bitter to him, and he cries out against his lack of inheritance:

> Why bastard? wherefore base?
> When my dimensions are as well compact,
> My mind as generous [capable] and my shape as true.
> As honest madam's issue? Why brand they us
> With base? with baseness? bastardy? base, base?
> Who in the lusty stealth of nature take
> More composition and fierce quality
> Than doth within a dull, stale, tired bed
> Go to the creating of a whole tribe of fops,
> Got 'tween asleep and wake? Well then,
> Legitimate Edgar, I must have your land.
> My father's love is to the bastard Edmund
> As to the legitimate; fine word legitimate!
> Well, my legitimate, if this letter speed
> And my intention thrive, Edmund the base
> Shall top the legitimate. I grow; I prosper;
> Now, gods, stand up for bastards!

This is his initial soliloquy, and gives the keynote of his character.
Obviously, such sentiments were outrageous to Elizabethans, who
regarded the laws of legitimacy and primogeniture as sacred.

His action in the plot of the play consists in his effort to fulfill
this ambition, to come by lands "if not by birth . . . by wit." First
is the conspiracy against his half-brother Edgar, which is crude but
efficacious: on his travels, he has learned to imitate handwriting;
and now he forges a letter to prove to his father that Edgar seeks
his life. Old Gloucester accepts this and other evidence that Edmund
has concocted, demands death for his legitimate son, and declares
the illegitimate his heir. Edgar escapes, but Edmund has achieved
his immediate purpose. Even so, he is not content; and his impatience for instant wealth and power leads him to betray his father
and denounce him as a traitor; and so, too late, Gloucester comes
to realize how he has been deceived. Goneril and Regan, with characteristic ferocity, strip the old Earl of his lands, put out his eyes,
and "thrust him out"; and his bastard son grasps these ill-gotten
gains without remorse. Up to this point, Shakespeare has merely
followed the general outline of the old story as told in Sidney's
Arcadia, and Edmund conforms to his prototype; but, beyond this,

Shakespeare adds episodes that blacken his character still more. Edmund becomes the lover at once of Goneril and Regan, and later admits that he "was contracted to them both"—a scandalous state of affairs, not only because it implies actual bigamy but also because both have living husbands, and, even worse in the eyes of Elizabethans, this would put the "Half-blooded" Edmund on the throne of England. But Edmund, though infamous, is not a coward; and at the end he fights, and fights bravely, for his life. As he dies, he admits his crimes, but offers no apology or excuse:

> What you have charged me with, that have I done;
> And more, much more; the time will bring it out.

Only at the very moment of his death, he determines "some good . . . to do, Despite of mine own nature"; and he tries to save Cordelia from the death he has plotted for her; but he fails, and so his one good impulse goes for naught.

Edmund is the villain paramount in a tragedy of villains; and Shakespeare added to his sources to make these particularly shocking to the court of James I. Indeed, Edmund is the personified antithesis of all that was regarded as good in the state, in society and in religion. He is a younger son, and yet in his brother's lifetime usurps his place, and rises almost to the very throne, the seat of God's Anointed. Yet worse, he is "base" born. Being a natural son, he takes "Nature" for his goddess, and so renounces both religion and the laws of human society. With unspeakable impudence, he even calls on the gods to "stand up for bastards." He uses witchcraft and astrology, and so allies himself with the devil and all his works. James I was especially horrified at witchcraft; [54] and it was generally considered one of the worst of crimes. If the present writer is correct in believing that James himself is glanced at in the play in the person of Albany—and James was titular Duke of Albany—then Albany's horror at Edmund's duplicity is particularly significant; and Albany is especially outraged that the "Half-blooded" Edmund should become Regan's husband and so king. The tragedy is a picture of society in convulsions: the old King's unwarranted division of his realm precipitates the crisis, [55] but its darkest developments and its most ghastly scene, the putting out of Gloucester's eyes, result from the machinations of the bastard Edmund.

Thersites in *Troilus and Cressida* accomplishes less evil than does Edmund; but he is even more despicable, for he has not even personal bravery to recommend him. He is generally recognized as the most foul-mouthed character in Shakespeare; and such actions as he does perform are not of much account; for, like Jaques and the Fool in *Lear,* he is a sort of cynical chorus to the play. Still further like his prototype in *Lear* he is a professional jester, and, as such, is allowed to utter what scurrilities he will. Of this license he takes the amplest advantage: wise old Nestor brands him as "A slave whose gall coins slanders like a mint," and with his usual nice reticence Thersites declares himself "a scurvy railing knave; a very filthy rogue." He does not hesitate, furthermore, to announce his bastardy, "bastard begot, bastard instructed, bastard in mind, bastard in valour." Even his patron Ajax, within the space of forty lines, calls him a "Dog," a "bitch-wolf's son," a "Toadstool," a "Cobloaf" and a "whoreson cur," to which Thersites trippingly replies that Ajax is a "mongrel beef-witted lord" and a "scurvy-valiant ass," whom he wishes had the "itch from head to foot," whereupon Ajax beats him. Such are the amenities of this very un-Homeric household. Even after Achilles and Patroclus enter, Thersites continues to rail, and declares that his master "wears his wit in his belly and his guts in his head"; and, when he departs with a final insult flung at the whole company, Patroclus calls his going "A good riddance." His corrosive cynicism extends to the whole Trojan war: "all the argument is a cockold and a whore; a good quarrel to draw emulous factions and bleed to death upon"; he wishes that "the whole camp" had the Neopolitan bone-ache [syphilis]" he mimics and mocks both Greek and Trojan heroes:

Now they are clapper-clawing one another; I'll go look on. That dissembling abominable varlet, Diomed, has got that same scurvy doting foolish young knave's sleeve of Troy there on his helm: I would fain see them meet; that that same young Trojan ass, that loves the whore there, might send that Greekish whoremasterly villain, with the sleeve, back to the dissembling luxurious [immoral] drab, of a sleeveless errand. O' the t'other side, the policy of those crafty swearing rascals, that stale old mouse-eaten dry cheese. Nestor, and that same dog-fox, Ulysses, is not proved worth a blackberry. They set me up in policy that mongrel cur, Ajax, against that dog of a bad kind. Achilles: now is the cur Ajax prouder than the cur Achilles, and will not arm today . . .

He spares neither Agamemnon on the one hand nor Menelaus on the other. He even accuses Patroclus to his face of being "Achilles' male varlet"; and thereupon follows such a masterpiece of vituperative filth as could hardly be paralleled outside the Orient. Helen is a drab, and Cressida a slut; and the last we see of Thersites, he is calling out obscenities at Paris and Menelaus as they fight. Here indeed is a bastard, different from Don John, but, like him, without any redeeming feature.

The Elizabethans certainly did not look on illegitimate sons as attractive characters; and Shakespeare, in this as in other things reflects the opinion of his age whether he really agreed with it, or found this complaisance necessary in his rôle of popular dramatist. Of his actual bastards, Caliban may be ruled out as beyond humanity, and Orleans and Margarelon as very minor characters; but Don John, Thersites, Oswald, and above all the villainous Edmund, show a resemblance that seems to arise from their anomalous family status. Indeed, the great houses of Tudor England maintained in that society a tribal organization and a tribal point of view; and, in the strictly limited confines and closed corporations that made up English life, one must fit into a recognized place, or be an outcast. Thus probably in actual social fact, bastardy tended to produce these very traits of guile and cynicism that Shakespeare has portrayed; and in *King Lear,* Edgar, in summarizing the theme of the Gloucester plot, sets forth the social moral of bastardy:

> The gods are just, and of our pleasant vices
> Make instruments to plague us.
> The dark and vicious place where thee he got
> Lost him his eyes.

VII

The Date of *A Midsommer Night's Dreame*

Francis Meres' reference to *A Midsommer Night's Dreame* in 1598 fixes the latest possible date for the play; and its place in Shakespeare's stylistic evolution, as determined by the computations of Fleay, König, and Ingram,[1] points to 1594-95. Of the nine other items of evidence cited in the variorum edition, only two have withstood the attacks of Wright and of Furness: most scholars agree that the play was probably written to celebrate a noble marriage at which Queen Elizabeth was apparently expected to be present; but, as critics do not agree as to whose marriage was thus celebrated, the matter of date still remains open. Titania's summary of the bad weather for the preceding year seemingly alludes to the period from the spring of 1594 to that of 1595; for Churchyard, Strype, Stowe, and Forman[2] testify to the unseasonable rains and ruined crops; and Professor Rickert, though she connects the play with the Elvetham festival of 1591, seems to give weight to this evidence.[3] Professor McCloskey, moreover, taking Bottom's song, "The Woosel cocke, so black of hew" as a parody of a poem that came out in 1594, suggests for Shakespeare's play the date 1595.[4]

The present writer might add further evidence for 1595. After the night of misadventures in the woodland, Demetrius, just before dawn, refers to "yonder Venus in her glimmering sphere"; and again, later in the scene, Puck declares, "yonder shines Auroras harbinger," apparently a second reference to Venus as morning star.[5] A computation based on the transit of Venus across the sun on December 7, 1631 N. S., shows that the planet was in superior conjunction on March 1, 1595, and remained west of the sun until inferior conjunction on December 18. Its greatest western elongation—i.e., its greatest angular distance from the sun and therefore greatest prominence in the sky—was May 12 N. S., which would be May 2 according to the Julian calendar then used in England. Thus in 1595, it was a bright and very obvious morning star from the latter part of April into June; and further computation shows that this is the only year between 1592 and 1598 in which Venus was clearly visible at this season as a morning star. The movements of the heavenly bodies were commonplaces in the almanacs of the day; Venus would furnish an especially apt allusion in a nuptial comedy; and Shakespeare would hardly have introduced two needless references to it unless they fitted the occasion.

The year having thus been fixed as 1595, it remains to ascertain more closely, if possible, the month and day. Titania's speech about the weather and the reference to Venus as morning star point to late spring or early summer; and several other details in the play agree: Theseus remarks that the day of "Saint *Valentine* is past"; and Puck in the Epilogue says that the ploughman's task is done. The summer flowers that attend on Titania are hardly significant; for she remarks that summer is always with her. The title suggests mid-summer, i.e., July 6; but that is rather late for several of the foregoing allusions; and it conflicts with the suggestion of Theseus that the lovers whom he finds in the forest "rose up early, to obserue The right of May," i.e., for the customary celebrations of May Day morning.[6] Moreover, neither July 6 nor astronomical midsummer, which would take place June 11 according to the Julian calendar,[7] would fit the new moon referred to in the play.[8]

Indeed, the play is full of lunar reference, much of it perhaps merely metaphoric; but some of it clearly astronomical. The Duke's wedding is to take place when the new moon is "a silver bow"; and the courtly lovers, who plan to elope the night before, hope for at least some moonlight to help them on their way. Moreover, as Oberon remarks, there actually is some "Moone-light"; and

Quince's almanac announces that the moon "doth shine" on the evening following, but apparently so faintly that the part of Moonlight had to be personally represented by an actor. Clearly, the last two nights of Shakespeare's comedy are supposed to be graced by a new moon. Taking 708.75 hours as the average lunation, one can readily calculate from the known dates of solar eclipses and other new moons the time of an astronomical new moon in April 1595; and a new moon apparent to the popular eye would occur two or three days later. Harvey mentions an eclipse of the sun on June 20, 1582, O. S. just after five A.M.; [9] Wright notes a new moon on May Day, 1592, O. S.; [10] Von Oppolzer's monumental work records a solar eclipse on October 12, 1602 N. S., i.e. October 2 O. S.[11] All these dates agree in showing an astronomical new moon on April 29, 1595 O. S.; and the thin crescent might be dimly visible on the following evening and more clearly on May first. On the years immediately preceding and following, moreover, no new moon fell near to May Day. This date, furthermore, would show Venus as a morning star at its greatest brilliance. The present astronomical calculations, therefore, would agree with the earlier evidence that has generally been accepted and even more definitely fixed the date on May Day, 1595 O. S.

VIII

The Mercurial Richard II

The substance of this paper was given as an address before the Philadelphia Shakespere Society, November 5, 1941.

Shakespeare's King Richard II is certainly not a simply conceived heavy villain like his Richard III; and, indeed, no more complex figure appears in his early plays. Richard's seemingly disparate traits of character, in fact, have made some critics feel an unconvincing disunity in his psychology, as if his personality were not all of a piece: this might arise from Shakespeare's adherence to his source; for the play closely follows Holinshed, who, as a historian, was more interested in the *doings* of history than in the psychology of the *doers;* or perhaps it arises from the influence of Marlowe's *Edward II,* an influence that has been both asserted and denied.[1] In any case, this complexity, verging on inconsistency, seems to demand the critical application of contemporary psychology; and the fundamental questions to be asked are just what traits did Richard have, and did contemporary theories of the mind accept this combination as a recognized type of personality? As in the case of Duncan,[2] the plot that Shakespeare chose presented a difficulty, a Divine Right king, who, nevertheless, must be made to lose his crown. Shakespeare fitted Duncan into the sanguine type, a paragon of virtues but easily deceived, and thus met both conditions; but, neither on the basis of popular history nor of Marlowe's Edward, could Richard II be made a paragon of virtues; and

74

Shakespeare does not picture him as deceived but rather as ignoring repeated warnings. The problems were somewhat similar; but the dramatist's solution is clearly not the same.

Richard's most obvious trait is his protean instability. In the end, he seems to recognize this shifting ego in himself: "Thus play I in one person many people, And none contented." According to Elizabethan dramaturgy, the keynote of a major character should be struck at his first appearance. In *Richard II* most of Act I concerns the quarrel and abortive trial-by-combat between Bolingbroke and Mowbray; and Richard's part in this as royal arbiter repeatedly shows him weak and vacillating. The two antagonists are, as Richard remarks, "High-stomach'd . . . full of ire, In rage deaf as the sea, hasty as fire," in short, violently choleric. At the outset, Mowbray scorns arbitration; and the two accuse each other as traitors and liars, and add insult to injury. Despite all this, Richard repeatedly tries to persuade them to "purge this choler without letting blood." He stoops to entreat them to give up each other's gage, and finally covers his failure weakly: "We were not born to sue, but to command"—a sentiment he might have thought of earlier in the proceedings. He orders the trial to take place at Coventry. In the third scene, at Coventry, the two contestants are duly sworn; and Richard, though he had given his word to Mowbray to be "impartial," publicly embraces Bolingbroke, and wishes him well. Last words are said, and all is ready. Then suddenly Richard throws his warder down, and commands both to "lay by their helmets and their spears." He then dooms Bolingbroke to ten years' exile, and Mowbray to exile for life, and makes both swear that they will never be friends or join against him. He brusquely refuses Mowbray's plea for clemency; but, hardly has Mowbray gone, when Richard, without even being asked, commutes Bolingbroke's sentence to "six winters," because of the tears in the eyes of old Gaunt, the culprit's father. Thus Richard weakly breaks his every promise, and retreats from his every stand; he allows and then forbids the combat; despite his royal place as judge and also his plighted word, he is not impartial; and his favoring of Bolingbroke and Gaunt seems partciularly stupid; for he feared the former's popularity with the Commons and dreaded his return, and he wished only the latter's death so as to seize his lands. In vivid contrast, Bolingbroke later dispatches a similar but much more complex business at the beginning of Act IV: in two and a half lines without ado, he remands the "Lords Appellants" to trial, and no more is said.

The later acts repeatedly illustrate Richard's inconstancy. He apparently slights the Queen, but at their permanent separation becomes most affectionate; he showers favors on Bushy, Bagot and Green, but at the first ill news unreasonably takes for granted their treachery, and declares with bitter curses, "their heads shall pay for it." Scoop acidly remarks that "Sweet love" seems to turn easily to "deadly hate." Richard forever vacillates between policies of peace and war with Bolingbroke, whose illegal return from exile calls the King back from the Irish revolt; and he lands in an England that he has consistently misgoverned, expecting that his mere Divine Right to the Crown will raise him an army. His vice-regent has perforce surrendered; and his Welsh allies have just disbanded. He thinks of peace, and promises to meet all Bolingbroke's demands; then he utters a defiance, then says he'll "be contented" to lose the crown and have "an obscure grave" or even be buried ignobly as a suicide, and indulges in pretty rhetoric. Any fixed policy would have been better than none. Anent his abdication, he also vacillates. First, he sends York to say that "with willing soul" he makes Bolingbroke his heir; he is brought in; and, when Bolingbroke asks him, "Are you contented to resign the crown?" he cryptically replies: "Ay, no; no, ay." Most indiscreetly, he seems to imply that he is glad to be rid of it, but not to Bolingbroke. He confesses his faults in moments of extravagant remorse, but does not seem actually to realize them, and bawks and mammers at signing an admission of his misgovernment. In fact, he seems incapable of following any policy on anything.

This is quite different from the "sainted" Duncan, who usually knew his own mind, though often knew it wrong. Richard is not, like Duncan, the happy, sanguine man under the influence of the planet Jupiter, but rather belongs under the astral sign of Mercury, which ruled inconstancy: his "halting" undoes him; and "two opinion . . . almost pull him a-pieces. . . ." [3] Mercury, moreover, was thought to be "mutable"; [4] and men under its influence were "wayward, wauering . . . violent . . . inconsistant . . . lyars . . . proud . . . instable." [5] This is the astral influence of the witty Mercutio and the "infirme" Macbeth,[6] and Richard is their cousin german.

The mercurial type was thought to change its humor with its environment; and Richard runs the gamut of the humors. When first he is introduced with "Youth at the prow and Pleasure at the helm," he seems the handsome, fortunate, sanguine man; and even later, Bolingbroke remarks that he is by nature "A happy gentleman in blood and lineaments." But his luxurious years show him also as phlegmatic, "luxurious, given to idleness and pleasures." [7] He is "basely led by flatterers," mere "caterpillars of the commonwealth." The Queen's Gardiner calls him "the wasteful king." Richard himself admits that his extravagant court has emptied the treasury; York and Gaunt blame his follies on his love of luxury, his "rash fierce blaze of riot" and his "light vanity." The land is "declining," and "The king's grown bankrupt" like an outlaw, not because of glorious foreign wars, for he has "basely yielded upon compromise That which his noble ancestors achieved with blows."

But Richard also at times is choleric. York compares him to "young hot colts"; he starts without pause to suppress the Irish rebels; and, on his return, when Aumerle criticizes his weakness, he replies, "Thou chidest me well"; and, for the moment, he determines to fight. Just as he is both choleric and phlegmatic, he has the parallel conflicting traits of being proud and cowardly: and both of these were possible to the mercurial man.[8] Gaunt warns Richard that he will "depose" himself; and Richard admits that these prophesies "Make pale our cheek"; but, at the same time, his pride makes him angry at the old man. For a moment, he "looks like a king, his eye As bright as is the eagle's"; but he soon succumbs to bad fortune, "both in shape and mind Transform'd and weaken'd"; and the Queen is shocked that he will "pupil-like, Take . . . correction mildly, kiss the rod, And fawn on rage with base humility." He endures the indignities of Bolingbroke's coronation procession, "His face still combating with tears and smiles, The badges of his grief and patience." He cringes to Bolingbroke, and at the same time charges him with treason; but, at the last, his choler once more asserts itself; and even his murderer declares him "As full of valour as of royal blood." Indeed, in the last unseemly scuffle at his death, he defends himself rather well for one who had so often wished to die. Of its own nature, the mercurial temper was thought to be debilitating, cold and dry like melancholy; [9] and

the latter acts after the deposition show the erstwhile king luxuriating in a pitiful melancholy. Indeed, age cannot wither nor custom
stale his infinite variety of humors.

Mercurial men were supposed to be ingenious; [10] and it was
said that their inconstancy "proceeds from cloudy imaginations,
fancies, fictions, and forced dreames, which keepe the mind from a
sober and peaceful considerateness." [11] They were much given to
"fantasie" and "imagination"; and they were prone to "philosophy"
and "curiosity [affectation] in writing." [12] All this suggests the
lyric ecstasies in which Richard begins to indulge even before his
fall. On hearing each new piece of evil news, Richard takes refuge
in fanciful lyricism, and oscillates between extravagant boasting and
grovelling despair, between a false content that he can now enjoy
the simple life and a spurious longing for "death." His much-speak-
ing perhaps fooled himself, but not his followers; and the good
Bishop is led coldly to remark:

> My lord, wise men ne'er sit and wail their woes,
> But presently prevent the ways to wail.

Richard is the arch-sentimentalist, luxuriating in his woe: "Despair"
is "sweet" to him; he hates "comfort," and will "pine away"; he
cries, "A king, woe's slave, shall kingly woe obey." Even at the
very end, he still consoles himself that his downfall will make a fine
"lamentable tale." Truly, Richard was more a poet than a king—
and not a first-rate poet either, for his matter lacks high seriousness,
and his manner is too hyperbolic to be convincingly sincere.

In fact, the mercurial type suffered from "depriuation of common
sence" and "lethargie," and might even, like the melancholy man
who was also cold and dry, fall into "madnes." [13] Common sense
is certainly at the antithesis of Richard's every thought and act. His
mismanagement of the trial-by-combat has already been discussed.
His appointment of the sick and aged York as his vice-regent when
he leaves for Ireland is equally unwise: in defiance of York's advice
he has just seized Gaunt's estates; and, when Bolingbroke returns
to lead the rebellion, York is so divided in his sympathies and
"weak with age" that he knows "not what to do," and so goes to
Bolingbroke and says he will "remain as neuter." Richard believes,
or affects to believe, so utterly in his sacred vocation as a Divine
Right king—despite the obvious lack of divine solicitude for his

unhappy fate—that he repeatedly compares himself to Christ; and, though he is completely at the mercy of the rebels, he compares them in wild and whirling words to Judas, and calls them "traitors." The powerful Northumberland he particularly insults, and then calls him "insulting"! A politic Mark Antony would have sought to conciliate and divide his triumphant enemies; but Richard frantically blunders on. He admits his own "weaved-up folly," and yet is outraged at its consequences. Indeed, in the deposition scene, he has so utterly lost poise that "madnes" could not have gambled further from good sense.

Richard, in brief, if clearly mercurial: he is a very weathercock of inconsistency; he varies his humor as quickly as his judgments and opinions; and, when separated from the happy influence of his favorites, he falls into a melancholy without restraint or poise; he has the "imagination"—or at least the fancy—of a poet; and, like many poets, especially the lesser fry, he has not a shred of common sense, let alone tact or diplomacy. He has, indeed, the lyrical incompetence that the Romantic critics have falsely attributed to Hamlet; [14] and the Elizabethans would doubtless have regarded him with pitying scorn.

In *Richard II*, the King is deposed because of his misgovernment; in *Henry IV*, he is on the whole excused. This play presents three separate explanations of his fall: according to the first theory, set forth by Bolingbroke, the King fell through shallow levity and bad companions; but he himself was popular, and so could not have been altogether bad:

> The skipping king, he ambled up and down,
> With shallow jesters and rash bavin wits . . .
> Enfeoff'd himself to popularity.

According to the second theory, set forth by Northumberland and York, Richard was an "unhappy king," a "sweet lovely rose"; and he fell because of evils inherent in the age:

> . . . we are all diseased.
> And with our surfeiting and wanton hours
> Have brought ourselves into a burning fever,
> And we must bleed for it; of which disease
> Our late King Richard, being infected, died.

Thirdly, moreover, according to Bolingbroke's late admissions, his own artfulness ruined Richard; and he "did pluck allegiance from men's hearts," and so got the crown through "by-paths and indirect crook'd ways," All these three views show an increasing sympathy for Richard, and a corresponding tendency to blame Bolingbroke. Shakespeare is once more true to nature in portraying Richard's reign as happier in more and more distant retrospect.

The original questions of Richard's character and its close relation to the psychological theories of the age have now been answered: Richard was mercurial according to the current concept of that complexion; but one might further ask whence Shakespeare drew the idea that Richard was mercurial: from Holinshed, or perhaps from Marlowe? Holinshed gives little support to Shakespeare's conception of Richard. The royal favorites are not mere shallow flatterers of an unstable king, but won his favor because they served him faithfully and so were "enuied of manie." [15] Holinshed's Richard does not show vacillation in giving up the crown; [16] and, when imprisoned, he does not indulge in extravagant fantasy, but is "with sorrow almost consumed, and in manner halfe dead." [17] Holinshed, however, added a summary of Richard's character that gives the King's personality such a variety of humors that only the mercurial complexion could explain it: [18] he is handsome and goodnatured and "much giuen to the pleasure of the bodie" (and therefore sanguine); he is "prodigall" (and therefore phlegmatic, under the influence of the moon); he is "ambitious" (and therefore choleric); and at last he is "consumed" with grief (and therefore melancholy); and withal, he is easily led astray (and therefore mercurial). [19] Such a conglomeration must indicate either that perfect balance of humors that caused mental and physical perfection or the weak mercurial character; and as Richard's career prohibits the former theory, only the latter remains. Thus Shakespeare may have inferred Richard's mercurial temperament from Holinshed.

Holinshed, however, does not seem to deal consciously in terms of humors. Of course, Shakespeare had himself previously used the humors for psychology in *Love's Labour's;* but, perhaps he owed something of it also to Marlowe's *Edward II.* Marlowe's nobles, like Shakespeare's, are clearly actuated by sharp martial choler in contrast to the king; but Edward is licentious and dissolute rather than mercurial: indeed, he is so "brainsick" and "bewitched" with Gaveston that nothing but overt force can separate the two; he is a determined sabyrite; and this "wanton humor" [20] is clearly phlegm under the astral influence of Venus, which was "giuen to idlenes and pleasures ... and lusts." [21] Edward, moreover, is so sunk in luxurious indolence that he makes no effort to suppress rebellion, as Richard did in Ireland. The two, therefore, are clearly not of the same complexion, though neither was fit to cope with robustious feudalism; and so they both fell before their choleric nobles. After his fall, however, King Edward declares, "grief makes me lunatic," and he seems to grow melancholy—a humor that like the mercurial complexion, was cold and dry and suggested debility: he vacillates like Richard, and cannot decide whether to abdicate or no; and this Edward of the later scenes may have given Shakespeare the hint for his mercurial and unstable Richard.

Richard II, moreover, seems to be significant in its influence on Shakespeare's later tragedy, especially political plays such as *Macbeth* and *Lear,* in which a monarch must fall through his own inherent weakness: in *Macbeth;* the great usurper is clearly mercurial; [22] in *Lear,* the old king lapses into a senile melancholy, which like the mercurial complexion was cold and dry.[23] A mercurial hero is a very human figure in his wavering uncertainty, and also makes a perfect protagonist for Greek tragedy, a man potentially good but too unstable to play the part for which life cast him. Thus in *Richard II,* Shakespeare is reaching from the loose chronicle plays toward close-knit and significant political tragedy; and the emphasis on Divine Right in all three plays increases the parallel.[24] The excellence of *Richard II* as a piece of artistry is a matter *de gustibus,* and so not to be argued; but its importance in Shakespeare's evolution from Marlowe's influence toward the great tragedies of his prime is not to be minimized, especially in its application of the humors to great tragic personality.

IX

The Date of *Romeo and Juliet*

The date of *Romeo and Juliet* is still an open question. The first quarto appeared in 1597; but some critics place the tragedy, or at least an early version of it, as far back as 1591. The Nurse's reference to an earthquake eleven years before [1] would point to this date, for in 1580 an earthquake was actually felt in England. On the other hand, the allusion to the "first and second cause" of a quarrel [2] would suggest a later year; for Saviolo's *Practise,* which discusses the "causes" of a duel, was published in 1595. The style of the play, moreover, very similar to that of *A Midsummer Night's Dream* (1595), supports this date; and, furthermore, Weever's reference to the popularity of Romeo as a character seems to have been written at about this time. The first quarto describes the play as having been performed by "the L. of *Hunsdon* his Seruants"; and the use of that title shows that the tragedy must have been on the stage between 22 July 1596 and the following April.[3] Of course, it may have been written as early as 1591 and extensively revised in 1595 or 1596; but the evidence is inconclusive.

Romeo and Juliet is full of astrological references; and these references are linked to the days of the week and month and to the phases of the moon: indeed, Shakespeare marks the passing of time with unusual clarity and precision. The play begins on Sunday with a brawl followed by the Capulet entertainment where the lovers meet, and, about midnight, the famous "balcony" scene. On Monday the lovers are married, Tybalt killed, and Romeo's banishment decreed. On Tuesday Romeo's exile begins, and Juliet promises to marry Paris, and takes the potion. On Wednesday she is found apparently dead; Romeo returns to Verona; and, that night, both lovers commit suicide in the Capulet tomb.[4] On Monday Lady Capulet and the Nurse in a long, and otherwise rather pointless, dialogue emphasize the fact that Juliet was born "On Lammas-eve," *i.e.* 31 July O. S., and that her birthday is "A fortnight and odd days" from the time of speaking. A fortnight would bring the date back to 17 July; and the 'odd days'[5] would bring it either three days farther back to 14 July or five days back to 12 July. If it were seven days before, Lady Capulet would surely have said three weeks. Thus the play would seem to have been set in a year when Monday fell on either 12 July or 14 July. The former was Monday in 1591 and in 1596; and the latter was Monday in 1595. According to the Julian calendar then used in England, moreover, these are the only three dates in the decade of the 1590's that would fit these circumstances.

The phases of the moon, implied or stated here and there in the text, supply further evidence that should determine which of these dates is preferable. On Sunday, in the "balcony" scene, Juliet is "bescreen'd in night"; and a "mask of night" covers her face; and it is "dark night." Nevertheless Romeo can recognize her from below, and he swears "by yonder blessed moon." These passages are consistent only with a thin old or new moon; and, as the scene takes place near morning, the moon must be in its final quarter. This inference is supported by the allusion to "the pale reflex of Cynthia's brow"—or "bow," as some critics prefer—early on Tuesday morning;[6] and apparently on Thursday morning in the graveyard just before dawn there is no moon at all. In short, all this consistently implies the last stages of a waning moon, with a new moon invisible on Thursday or Friday. If Monday was 12 July, then there should be a new moon 15 or 16 July; if Monday were 14 July, then there should be a new moon 17 or 18 July; and this necessary relation of lunar phases to the days of the week and of the month should serve as a significant check on the three possible dates already found.

Taking 708.75 hours as the synodic period of the moon, one

can compute the lunations for July 1591, 1595, and 1596 from the solar eclipses of 12 April 1582 O.S.[7] and 2 October 1605 N.S.[8] In 1591 the new moon occurred on 11 July, *i.e.* on Sunday night; and, consequently, it is impossible that Romeo could swear by 'yonder' moon just before dawn; for on that night no moon at all would have been visible. In 1595 the new moon occurred on 24 July; and this would mean that on 13 July, eleven days before, the 'balcony' scene would have been flooded with a moon almost full, and the graveyard scene would have had almost a quarter moon. There remains only July 1596; and this fits perfectly; for there was a new moon, and therefore no light before dawn on Thursday, 15 July, 15 July O.S., during the graveyard scene; and on the Sunday night preceding, *i.e.* 11 July, there was a thin crescent of the old moon until late after midnight for the 'balcony' scene. Thus the play is astronomically dated 11-15 July 1596, very much as Dante's *Divine Comedy* is placed in Holy Week 1300. Significantly enough, moreover, this would bring the unlucky thirteenth of the month in the ill-starred Tuesday when Romeo's banishment begins and when Juliet is forced to consent to marry Paris.

All this can hardly be coincidence; for, given the day of the week, the mathematical probability that it would by accident fit both the changes of the moon and also the two possible days of the month can be calculated as one chance out of 155. As none of this material appears in Shakespeare's sources, one can hardly escape the conclusion that he deliberately gave the play this definite date; and the reason for his doing so is not difficult to find. *Romeo and Juliet* is full of astrological reference that depends more or less on the calendar; almanacs were common reading-matter; and, when Shakespeare consulted his almanac, he naturally made the dates and the astronomy conform. This definite fixing of the plot by year and day suggests that the tragedy was written, or at least extensively revised, in 1596; for Shakespeare would naturally consult a current almanac: he would hardly trouble to compute—even if he knew how —the week-days and lunations of a year ahead; and the quarto of 1597 precludes a later date. Possibly a version of the play existed in 1591;[9] but the evidence scattered up and down the text points to 1595-6; and the astronomy clearly implies the latter year—about the time when we learn from the title-page of the first quarto that it was actually on the stage.

X

Shakespeare's "Star-Crossed Lovers"

Romeo and Juliet seems a tissue of improbable coincidence: Capulet's illiterate servant happens by mere chance to ask Romeo to read the list of those invited to his master's entertainment; Romeo, by a most unusual chance, decides to attend his arch-enemies' festivities, and so chances to fall in love with Juliet; at just this time, the Prince chances to make a stringent edict against brawling, and Romeo chances to kill Tybalt and so is banished; and, also at just this time, Old Capulet chances to betroth Juliet to the Count Paris. Any one of these chances might singly be accepted; but why should they all occur within two days and just in the right order to set the plot in motion? Even more a matter of fortuity is the catastrophe: by chance, the Friar's letter to Romeo miscarries; by chance, Romeo meets and kills Paris at the tomb; by chance, the Friar is too late to intercept Romeo; and, by chance, Juliet awakens just too late to save her lover's life and just too soon for her father to save her from suicide. Indeed, never was love-affair more perfectly ill-timed; and yet, as if to emphasize this very fault, the master-dramatist, more than in any other play, marks, scene by scene, the days of the week and sometimes the very hours of the day. Truly as Rümelin declares, "mere accident" [1] seems to guide the order of events; and, if this be so, the play has no integration of plot, does not illustrate the inevitable working of any general truth, and so can have no theme; without a theme, it has no ethos or significance; and, for all the gorgeous trappings of Shakespeare's lyric style, it is not tragedy but mere melodrama.

Indeed, the critics have had difficulty in assigning to *Romeo and Juliet* any universal meaning. Ulrici, Rotscher, Vehse,[2] and more recently Erskine[3] seem to feel that it expresses the evils of civil feuds; but, in sharp contrast to Shakespeare's later, political tragedies,[4] neither the action nor the dialogue emphasize the general injury to the state that feuds were supposed to effect; and, furthermore, the Prince himself declares that his objection to brawling arises chiefly not from such dangers but from the killing of his kinsman Mercutio.[5] Tieck and Maginn seem to consider that the tragic outcome derives from Romeo's impetuosity and too great haste; but is it Romeo's haste that brings him to the Capulet feast or that so crucially keeps the Friar's letter from arriving? Dowden says that "the moral theme of the play is the deliverance of a man from dream into reality":[6] but surely such a change would improve the hero's chances for meeting the problems of life, and so result rather in comedy. Horn, more vaguely, suggests that the play expresses "the grand irony of life"; and Bodenstedt and Erskine feel that "tragic fate" directs it; but the ironies are as nothing compared with those of *Hamlet, Othello,* or *Lear;* and there is no fatal antecedent action, as in the *Œdipus,* that decrees an inescapable tragic consequence. Thus most critics, despite the obvious predominance of coincidence, seem to feel that the play has some sort of system or governing purpose; and they accordingly assign it various vague and rather divergent themes, none of which closely fits the plot or explains its sudden leaps without causality from one episode to another. Shakespeare generally gave the stories that he used a timely realism and *vraisemblance;* and his utter failure to link the events of *Romeo and Juliet* in any certain, or even probable, connection is a strange departure from his usual artistry.

In the main trend of the story Shakespeare follows rather closely Brooke's poem, which is generally recognized as the chief source for the play. Brooke tells the tale as a "wofull chance," with little effort to explain the chances that occur; and he and Paynter, Shakespeare's other possible source, agree in repeatedly ascribing the course of events to "Fortune" or "false Fortune"[7] Shakespeare, however, makes little reference to Fortune as governing the action; and these references appear too late to explain the motivation of the plot.[8] A few passages somewhat casually ascribe the direction of events to "God" or "heaven"[9]; but the play has no clear-cut Christian moral, unless it be the evils of brawling, as indeed Paynter suggests, or the wickedness of a secret marriage, as Brooke implies; and the catastrophe is not the inevitable consequence of either of these things. Nevertheless, over the play hangs a certain tragic fate. Juliet cryptically answers Paris, "What must shall be"; and reiterated premonitions suggest an evil end: the Prologue refers to the "death-mark'd love" of the two protagonists; Lady Capulet, the Nurse, and Friar Lawrence give voice to ominous predictions; Romeo twice dreams—the second time that his lady found him dead; both lovers are "pale" and melancholy at parting; Romeo, even while arranging his marriage, casts his defiiance at "love-devouring death"; he says that the killing of Mercutio "but begins the woe"; and he declares that he and Paris are "writ in sour misfortune's book." Juliet compares her love to the dangerous speed of lightning; her "all-divining soul" sees Romeo "As one dead in the bottom of a tomb"; she describes her case as "past hope, past cure, past help"; and, as she takes the potion, "a faint cold fear" as to the outcome "thrills" her veins. Is all this only the convention of dramatic prolepsis—a mere pious pretence of inevitable catastrophe where no inevitability exists? Is Shakespeare no more than a theatrical charlatan, or did he really see in this tissue of circumstance a *rationelle* and motivation that is not clear to us?

Not only is the play replete with ominous predictions, but many of these predictions are associated with the hours and days and with the heavenly bodies that mark time. The Prologue refers to Romeo and Juliet as "star-crossed lovers." At the very beginning of the action, when Romeo starts for the Capulet feast, he says:

> . . . my mind misgives
> Some consequence, yet hanging in the stars,
> Shall bitterly begin his [its] fearful date
> With this night's revels, and expire the term
> Of a despised life closed in my breast,
> By some vile forfeit of untimely death . . .

In Act II, Friar Lawrence invokes the good will of "the heavens,"
but he fears that "after-hours will chide" all those concerned in
the marriage. When Capulet forces Juliet to the unwelcome match
with Paris, she cries out: "Is there no pity sitting in the clouds . . ."
and later, "Alack, alack, that heaven should practise stratagems"
against her. At Juliet's seeming death, Lady Capulet and the Nurse
blame the day and hour as "Accurst" and "black" and "lamentable,"
as if the very calendar were responsible; and the Friar, even more
clearly, imputes the misfortunes of Capulet to astral influence:

> The heavens do lour upon you for some ill;
> Move them no more by crossing their high will.

In Act V, when Romeo learns of Juliet's supposed death, he
cries aloud, "then I defy you, stars!" And when he is resolved to
kill himself, he says that death will "shake the yoke of inauspicious
stars From this world-wearied flesh." Friar Lawrence imputes the
killing of Paris to "an unkind hour," as if the blame lay on the
heavenly bodies that mark the passing time. Thus, if Shakespeare
meant what his characters seem to say, astral influence actually
governs the lives of these "star-cross'd lovers"; and, like so many
of Chaucer's figures,[10] they are the puppets of the stars and planets
and of the days and times of day.[11]

Although the stricter theologians looked askance and a few
astronomers such as Copernicus must have had doubts, nevertheless the sixteenth century generally accepted astrology as a science:[12]
Queen Elizabeth regularly employed the learned Dr. Dee to compute for her the lucky days and hours for undertaking her affairs;
and, though only specialists mastered the more esoteric mysteries
of casting a horoscope, yet all classes devoured books of popular
astrology, edition on edition,[13] so that Ben Jonson could make it
the basis of his masque, *Mercury Vindicated*. Everyone knew that
the moon governed the rise and fall of tides; and what was man
that he should escape such power?[14] Indeed, the farmer had to
know the changes of the moon for the planting of his crops; and almanacs, which supplied this astrological information, were so plenti-
fully produced that the Lambeth Palace Library, for the year of
1595 alone, has no less than six by as many different publishers.
Shakespeare himself makes constant reference to astrology; and
Schmidt's *Lexicon* lists thirty-six examples of his use of *star* as

"influencing human fortune," and four uses of *astronomer* as "astrologer."

To the Elizabethans, astrology had come down with some accreations from its Babylonian origins. They knew Greek astrology, partly from pseudo-Aristotle, Galen, and Ptolemy, and partly through Arabic and Mediæval authors; and a bevy of translators such as Warde,[15] Dariot,[16] and Lemnius,[17] and popularizers such as Moulton,[18] Harvey,[19] and above all assiduous compiler Thomas Hill,[20] supplied them with the traditional lore of astrology and its associated pseudo-sciences. Indeed, the Greeks, by a curious schematism, had linked astrology with their other learning; and the result, as transmitted by the Middle Ages, was an integrated and complex theory that embraced and co-related physical and biological knowledge. Human beings were divided into four types, depending on which "humour," or bodily fluid dominated their physique; and each of these humours was associated with a certain day, with certain planets and constellations, with a chemical "element," a season of the year, a period of a man's life, a colour, a metal, and a bodily condition of heat or dryness. This astro-biological lore, being largely a matter of tradition, shows less variety and disagreement that one might expect in different Elizabethan authors; and, without attempting to plumb the mysteries of "judicial" astrology, *i.e.* the casting of horoscopes, one can, at least approximately, set forth the more obvious phases of the subject.

Perfect health of mind and body arose from a perfect balance of the four "humours"; but, in most men, one humour or another predominated, either by nature from birth or by the circumstances of the occasion. Blood, supposed to be generated in the stomach, gave to those whom it controlled a sanguine temper; it was considered hot and moist and was associated with youth and springtime. Sanguine persons were thought to be under the influence of the constellations Gemini, Libra, and Acquarius, and of the planet Jupiter, and so were of a jovial disposition. This disposition especially prevailed from midnight to six in the morning, and its day was Thursday. Its colour was white, its metal electrum, and its chemical element the air. The sanguine man was handsome and lucky, and Jupiter was called "the greater fortune." A superfluity of phlegm, supposed to be genera'ed in the liver or perhaps the stomach, made a man easy-going, slow-witted and "phlegmatic"; this humour was cold and moist and moderately fortunate, and was associated with the element water, with women and children, and with autumn; such persons were under the influence of the constellations Cancer, Scorpio, and Pisces, and under either the planet Venus, which was grouped with Friday, copper, and yellow, or the moon, which was grouped with Monday and silver. The phlegmatic humour achieved its greatest power from six in the evening until midnight, and especially on Mondays. A superfluity of bile, called "choler," generated in the heart and found chiefly in the gall bladder, made a man wrathful or "choleric"; this humour was hot and dry, and was associated with fire, youth, and summer; such persons were presumed to be under the influence of Aries, Sagittarius, and especially Leo, and of the ill-omened planet Mars, whose day was Tuesday, or, more luckily, of the sun, whose day was Sunday; their hours were from six in the morning until noon, their metal was gold, and their colour red. A superfluity of black bile, generated chiefly in the brain and found chiefly in the spleen, made a man melancholy; this humour was cold and dry, and was associated with winter and old age; such persons were under the influence of Taurus, Virgo, and Capricorn, and of that ill-omened planet Saturn, and were therefore of saturnine disposition; their metal was lead, their colour grey, and their chemical element the earth. The present study proposes to examine the chief characters of the play to ascertain how well they fit into these four types, and how well their actions and the outcome of these actions accord with their days and times of day.

Gervinus [21] and Law [22] note the sharp contrast between Tybalt, Benvolio, and Mercutio; and this contrast, upon close examination, seems to spring from the fact that each represents a distinct type in the medical and astro-biological theory of the day. Tybalt is clearly of the choleric or wrathful type: he is always ready to fight, a quality that brings about the tragic catastrophe; he is "fiery" and "furious" and admits his "wilful choler"; [23] and Benvolio refers to "the unruly spleen of Tybalt deaf to peace." [24] Although the spleen was often associated with melancholy, yet it was also considered the seat of anger; [25] and, as the choleric man, of disposition hot and dry, [26] was supposed to be much given to anger in its entire gamut from mere "chyding" to "fighting, murther, robbery, sedition," [27] Benvolio's reference to Tybalt's "unruly spleen" is quite appropriate to the latter's choleric nature. Choler, moreover, might properly predominate in early maturity [28]—about the right age for Old Capulet's nephew—and in the hot, dry months of summer when the play takes place. Of Tybalt's personal appearance, Shakespeare gives no direct clue; [29] but certainly the timing and the outcome of the events in which he participates agree with the dominant hours of the choleric man: Capulet manages to quiet him at the festivities when Romeo appears; for it is between 6 P.M. and midnight in the phlegmatic period of the day; and Tybalt's fight and death on Monday afternoon are quite correctly timed: the day itself was phlegmatic and the time of day melancholy, and consequently his martial powers would have ebbed at noon, when the choleric part of the day was over. A complete accord of each character and his every act with the appropriate times would hardly be dramatically possible; and yet the part of Tybalt, minor and fragmentary though it is, agrees with the scheme of the Elizabethan pseudo-sciences, as to his bodily humour and his psychological bent, as to his age and the season of the year, as to the timing of events by the day and time of day. Nothing of this appears in Shakespeare's sources: the season is winter, with the days and hours only vaguely marked. Could Shakespeare, by mere accident, have introduced so many consistent details; and would an Elizabethan audience, steeped in such lore, have failed to realize their significance?

Also choleric, perhaps by nature, perhaps because of the season of the year, is Old Capulet. His wife, quite properly, thinks this humour inappropriate to his age; and, when in the first street-brawl he demands his sword, she suggests that a crutch would be more fitting. He is "too hot," *i.e.* too angry, toward Juliet; and his impetuous, headstrong nature, like that of Tybalt, directly contributes toward the tragic catastrophe. His blood is still young; and, even at night, he complains of heat rather than of chill; and, though he is "old," he seems to long for his "dancing days" and the masquerades of thirty years before. Such another testy old gentleman is Montague, who itches to fight the "villain Capulet." Among the Elizabethans, decrepitude set in at about the age of forty; for they lived hard and were primitive in their hygiene and sanitation. [30] Thus Capulet, whose reference to his "dancing days" would place his years about fifty or beyond, is certainly enjoying a very green old age. [31]

In sharp contrast to these choleric types is the phlegmatic Benvolio; and Shakespeare points and repoints this contrast.[32] As Benvolio's name suggests, he is easy-going and friendly. "Fleame" was thought to be cold and moist and "wearyish"; and Benvolio is "weary." [33] Such men were supposed to be affable, slow, dull, forgetful, soft of flesh, of small appetite, fat, short, posesssed of little hair, of pale complexion, and given to dreams of rain and swimming.[34] Mercutio, to be sure, compliments Benvolio by calling him "as hot a Jack . . . as any in Italy"; [35] but the latter's obvious preference for peace gives the lie to such a description: at the very beginning of the play he tries to avoid a brawl; and he opens the crucial third act with a speech of similar import to Mercutio:

> I pray thee, good Mercutio, let's retire:
> The day is hot, the Capulets abroad,
> And, if we meet, we shall not 'scape a brawl;
> For now these hot days is the mad blood stirring.

He urges the swashbucklers to drop their swords and "reason coldly"; [36] and, after the fray is over, he refers to "The unlucky manage of this fatal brawl." [37] In the first act, moreover, he pursues his phlegmatic humour by not pursuing Romeo.[38] Heat was supposed to make persons of this temperament more sanguine; [39] and perhaps this influence makes Benvolio hopeful of avoiding brawls and, at the beginning of the play, of curing Romeo's love-sickness; but the heavens prevent his purposes; and, as the momentum of the tragedy develops, he drops out of sight, like the Fool in *Lear,* as if his phlegmatic temper and sanguine hopes and lucky influence were inappropriate to the catastrophe.

The name Mercutio, which Shakespeare derived from his source, doubtless suggested that the character be depicted as of the mercurial cast; and, indeed, this may have supplied the hint from which Shakespeare conceived his whole astrological tragedy.[40] The mercurial temper is most difficult to define; for persons under that planet's influence might by attraction partake of any one of the four humours, and so were chameleon-like in their variety:

Mercurie in all things is common and mutable, he is good with the good, and euill with the euill, with the Masculine, masculine, with the Feminines, feminine, hote with the hote and moyst with the moyst, infortunate with the infortunes, and fortunate with the fortunes, especially when he is ioyned or corporally applying vnto them, or beholdeth them with some good aspect.[41]

Just so, Mercutio changes to the wrathful type at the entrance of the angry Tybalt; and this same quick adaptability he urges vainly upon Romeo.[42] The Mercurial man was supposed to be a "nimble person" and a go-between in love-affairs;[43] and Mercutio by nature has "dancing shoes with nimble soles"[44] and he joins with Benvolio in trying to distract Romeo and cure him of the unhappy love for Rosaline. This type, moreover, was supposed to be "volatile, sprightly, and ready-witted."[45] Both Brooke and Paynter agree in calling Mercutio "pleasant and courteous" and popular with ladies; and they add that he had a fiery mind but cold hands—a suggestion of the inconsistent mercurial temperament. Shakespeare's Mercutio is certainly garrulous: he "talks of nothing";[46] he "loves to hear himself talk";[47] and he "will speak more in a minute than he will stand to in a month";[48] and, on occasion, he takes the stage for forty-two lines on the "inconstant" topic of dreams.[49] He calls himself "the very pink of courtesy,"[50] and readily adapts his talk to the occasion, witty, consolatory, or obscene;[51] and he is so susceptible to environment that he seems to feel the chill of night more even than Old Capulet.[52] He is quite fitly killed on Monday afternoon—a phlegmatic day and a melancholy time of day that would depress the mercurial temperament and subject him the more easily to Tybalt's onslaught.

Juliet's old Nurse should also, perhaps, be accounted of the mercurial type.[53] Juliet, to be sure, impatiently accused her of having the phlegmatic and melancholy symptoms of old age, "unwieldy, slow, heavy and pale as lead"; but, at the time, she is doubtless under the phlegmatic influence of Monday, and certainly her interminable garrulity and her willingness to shift from Paris to Romeo and back suggest that by nature she shares Mercutio's cast of mind. These minor characters, especially Tybalt and Mercutio, conform rather closely to their astrological prototypes; and an examination from this point of view of the two principals in the play would seem to be worth making.

Juliet is clearly of a hot, passionate temperament. She falls in love with Romeo at first sight, and she even dares to gainsay her father's orders to his face. The Nurse calls her "hot" and tells an anecdote of her babyhood that the credulous might interpret as a sign of passion. At the beginning of the play, she is not quite yet fourteen, and so has hardly had an opportunity to show her nature;

but the stars had given her this nature even from her birth, and Shakespeare carefully impresses on the audience the horoscope of her nativity; and twice we are told that she was born on "Lammas-eve at night," that is when the sun was in the house of the constellation Leo.[54] Those born under Leo were supposed to be choleric and passionate if not incontinent, inclined to be stout and often barren; and the type was associated with youth and summer.[55] If then Juliet is of this hot complexion, her planet should be Mars or the sun; and with the latter the text constantly associates her: she shines so brightly that she shames the torches; she is called the "sun"; Romeo refers to her "light"; Friar Lawrence compares her to "the sun" clearing away Romeo's sighs; Juliet herself compares her love-thoughts to "the sun's beams"; she is a "lantern" and "her beauty makes This vault a feasting presence full of light"; and, at her death, the Prince declares that "The sun for sorrow will not show his head." The Nurse cannot find Romeo for her until the sun is in the ascendant at high noon; and the poison, counteracting her natural impulse, makes her "cold and drowsy." Some of these references may be mere metaphor, but they are too numerous and too apt to Juliet's choleric nature to be entirely accident; and, moreover, metaphor was so commonly a part of the method of scientific thought that a metaphoric use does not preclude a strictly technical one. Juliet, therefore, like Tybalt and Old Capulet, is hot and dry, but only moderately so, for she is under the influence of the sun rather than of Mars.[56] Choler was supposed to be most active in summer;[57] and the characteristics of this type were amply chronicled in contemporary pseudo-science: such as one was slender, of moderate stature, "lyuely, daper, quycke"[58] and "prouoketh to ye works of Venus";[59] and "neyther can they so well rule theyr own affections because in their reasonings and discourses they be so very earnest and hastye."[60] Thus the heat of summer clearly brings out in the maturing Juliet the traits of character fixed by her birth when her planet[61] the sun was in the sign of the zodiac Leo.

The most complex of all these figures is Romeo. He first appears as an example of the melancholy type, and so suffers under the influence of Saturn,[62] which was styled "the greatest infortune." Even before he enters, his father describes his tears and sighs, and declares that his "humour" is "black and portentous." He has been avoiding the sun, and "locks fair daylight out"; and, when he enters, he declares that the love for Rosaline that afflicts him is a "choking gall." [63] Clearly, Romeo, whatever his natural humour, is suffering from love-melancholy. Heaviness and the metal lead were particularly associated with this bodily condition; [64] and Romeo is "heavy"; [65] he "cannot bound a pitch above dull woe"; he has "a soul of lead"; and he compares his love to a "heavy lightness" and a "feather of lead." Melancholy often brought on madness; [66] and Mercutio fears for his sanity; and Benvolio proposes the proper cures of diversion and counter-attraction. [67] Romeo's condition is like that of Orsino at the beginning of *Twelfth Night;* but his case is more violent, perhaps because, as the learned Friar says, his disposition is not well "temper'd." [68] At all events, he is obviously given to "extremities."

On falling in love with Juliet, however, Romeo rebounds to his natural self. Melancholy is cold and dry, unhappy, and saturnine; but Romeo, in the bloom of youth and lofty station, could partake of such a humour only because of some immediate, overpowering impulse, for "Trouble and affection" can change one's disposition. [69] Romeo, by nature sanguine, [70] quickly returns to his innate merry self. Indeed, at the very moment that he climbs Juliet's garden wall, he would seem to renounce his former bitter mood: earth, as a chemical element, was associated with melancholy; [71] and Romeo cries out: "Turn back, dull earth, and find thy centre out." This tendency to variable extremes was in itself a sign of a hot disposition; for such a humour was described as "variable and changeable." [72]

In the last four acts, Romeo clearly shows the effects of his sanguine humour. His whole love affair betrays a cast of mind that is hopeful against obstacles, and impatient of cold reason; and this very quality helps to induce the tragic ending. Even as he leaves Juliet, condemned to exile from Verona, he is still hopeful, and protests against "Dry sorrow" because it "drinks our blood"; and he prosecutes his wooing and insists upon the marriage, with an untimely haste. His association with the moon, to be sure, rather suggests the phlegmatic; but this may be mere contrast to Juliet as the sun; and folklore, moreover, takes the moon as the source of moisture that causes decay and growth; [73] and so perhaps Romeo, of a hot and moist complexion, might be associated with it. Romeo's sanguine humour, moreover, fits with his good looks:

the Nurse catalogues his physical attractions *seriatim* in the best sonnet style; [74] and the sanguine man was supposed to be "mery, pleasant [witty], fayre, and of a ruddy colour," [75] to have "comely" stature and a handsome appearance "consonāte to manly dignity." [76] Indeed, blood was the "best of all the humours" and was associated with youth and spring.[77] Romeo is by nature "mery" and "pleasant" and can overcome even the volatile Mercutio at persiflage: [78] truly, he seems to show all the good qualities of the sanguine man. He has also the weakness of the humour: blood could produce "riot and wilfulness"; [79] and those who had a superfluity, when "too much chafed," are prone to act "like mad-men"; [80] quite of this sort is Romeo's rage against Tybalt, and his rage against himself when he has killed Tybalt, "The unreasoning fury of a beast." In short, Romeo, in his rapid changes from saturnine love-melancholy to his natural joyous disposition, and then on occasion to unreasoning rage, is a rather clear portrayal of the sanguine man: he woos Juliet in one night and marries her next day in defiance of all obstacles; he has the sanguine man's good looks and wit and dignity of bearing, and also his wilful fury under provocation. The choleric Tybalt, Capulet, and Montague, all under the influence of Mars, the choleric Juliet under the influence of Venus, the phlegmatic Benvolio, the mercurial Mercutio and the Nurse, and the sanguine Romeo, now under the power of love-melancholy and now of fury: all of these surely make of *Romeo and Juliet* an astrological tragedy of humours.

The Elizabethan pseudo-sciences, however, were associated not only with human character but also with the calendar; and, as the month and the days of the week are rather clearly marked throughout the play, a review of the action day by day should indicate how far the periods of predominance of certain humours govern the outcome of the episodes. The reference to "Lammastide," *i.e.* August 1, as "A fortnight and odd days" to come clearly places the action in the "hot days" of the middle of July, when "the mad blood [is] stirring"; and summer was associated with the hot, dry, choleric temperament. In the very first scene, moreover, the word-play on "choler" strikes at once the keynote of the season as well as of the action. This setting in the heat of summer is Shakespeare's own deliberate change from his two reputed sources, in both of which the story begins in winter and drags on into spring. Shakespeare, in fact, even has Juliet declare that "summer's ripening breath" has matured their "bud of love"; and thus one may impute both the love and the hate that motivated the tragedy to the season of the year and the sign of the zodiac.

The old Mediæval system of "elections" according to which each hour after dawn brought one luck or misfortune under a changing astral influence, varying according to the time of dawn and according to the day of the week—all this system was far too complex for an audience to follow, and would have required too much rapid calculation on their part to be effective: Shakespeare, therefore, was obliged to use some simpler method wherever he proposed to govern his plot by the luck or ill-luck of days and hours. In his sources the action of the play consumes several months; he begins it on Sunday and ends it early Thursday morning.[81] The first act and the first two scenes of the second occupy Sunday, that is Juliet's day. The opening street brawl apparently takes place in the morning, a part of the day when the choleric humour was predominant; and the second scene, in which Romeo reads the list of guests to be invited to Capulet's supper, seems to occur that afternoon; and, at about the same time, the third scene in which Lady Capulet and the Nurse discuss Juliet's age. Scene four is in the evening; and the maskers are hurrying to the Capulet residence. Benvolio declares: "Supper is done, and we shall come too late"; and Romeo answers him:

> I fear, too early: for my mind misgives
> Some consequence yet hanging in the stars,
> Shall bitterly begin his [its] date
> With this night's revels . . .

This speech, spoken by the hero and coming at the final climax of the scene, seems particularly significant: Romeo quite properly fears bad influence at that time of the day; for the evening would not usually be favourable either to his naturally sanguine disposition or to the melancholy humour that for the time afflicts him. Indeed, how else can one explain his fear of being "too early" coupled with his misgivings of bad astral consequences? In the fifth scene, the maskers arrive as the hall is cleared for dancing; and, at first sight, Romeo and Juliet fall in love, converse in a perfect sonnet, and then kiss and part. The time of day is phlegmatic, and Tybalt's anger is restrained by Capulet; but, even so, it is no lucky hour for the two lovers. In the first scene of Act II, Romeo gives the slip to his merry companions; and, in the second, he is under Juliet's window. This famous dialogue in which the two plight their troth clearly takes place in the sanguine period after midnight; for, near the end, Juliet remarks that it is "almost morning."

While "gray-eyed morn smiles on the frowning night," Friar Lawrence is out gathering herbs; he meets Romeo and advises prudence. The next scene is in the late morning. The Nurse, having searched since nine o'clock, at last comes upon Romeo in the company of his merry friends. Her slowness in finding him is stressed both here and in a later scene; but the situation and the dialogue that explain it seem alike without dramatic reason; and perhaps one should suppose that the Nurse, though perhaps by nature mercurial, has, with advancing age, grown phlegmatic or even melancholy. If melancholy, her lucky hours did not begin till noon; and, just after Mercutio says that it is noon [82], the Nurse finds Romeo, and so can make the appointment for him to marry Juliet that afternoon. Thus the marriage takes place in the time of day dominated by the unlucky melancholy humour, for melancholy was associated with Saturn and his malefic influence. That same fatal afternoon, Mercutio and Tybalt are both killed, and Romeo, "fortune's fool," is banished by the Duke. These are the critical hours of the play; and Juliet may well wish the sun's "fiery-footed steeds" to hurry by, for evening will bring less dangerous auspices. So Juliet is wed; and that night the marriage is consummated; but the unfriendly streaks of morning bring in Tuesday, the choleric day of Mars and of dead Tybalt's vengeance, for on that day Romeo's exile starts.

Old Capulet, meanwhile, intent on marrying Juliet to Paris, sets Thursday for the happy event, and then moves it forward to Wednesday, and on this same unlucky Tuesday forces the already wedded Juliet to consent. This Tuesday, which comprises most of the fourth act, is a welter of ill-omened preparations; Romeo hastens to depart; the Capulet household is preparing for the wedding; and Juliet is preparing, by the use of the Friar's drug, to frustrate their preparations. She takes the potion with deep misgivings, as well she may. The working of this drug has caused great trouble to commentators. The Friar declares that it is supposed to

last "two and forty hours"; and his calculations must be true, for
he reaches the tomb about the time that Juliet actually awakes.
Forty-two hours, however, from Tuesday night when she takes
the potion would bring her waking to the following Thursday afternoon or early evening; and, in fact, she wakes very late at night
and apparently on Wednesday. The present writer hazards the suggestion that "two and forty" is a textual slip for "four and twenty,"
which would agree with both the metre and the circumstances.[83] On
this same Tuesday occurs one of the most fatal chances of the
tragedy: the Friar's letter fails to reach Romeo, and so Romeo
fails to do his part in the plan that was to unite him with his bride.

Wednesday, the day of changeable Mercury, begins with the
discovery of Juliet's seeming death; and, indeed, Wednesday is full
of change and violent reversal; the wedding is quickly turned into
a funeral; Juliet seems to die, then lives, then dies; the hopes of
the good Friar change to bitter failure; and Romeo, fresh from
happy dreams, hears of his wife's death and believes the news, returns, kills Paris, and takes poison. When Juliet is first discovered
in seeming death, the Nurse and Lady Capulet lament the "Ac-
cursed, unhappy, wretched, hateful day" no less than fourteen
times: surely they thought that the day had something to do with
their misfortunes Mercury was supposed to be good or evil depending on its relation to other influences: [84] Juliet's cold body is found
in the morning; the funeral apparently takes place in the afternoon,
when melancholy was the predominant humour; and the death of
the lovers, before midnight. The final reconciliation of the rival
houses seems to occur in the early hours of Thursday,[85] a sanguine
day and time of day: perhaps by this Shakespeare meant that the
reconciliation was well-founded and permanent.

Elizabethan scientific theory, in short, does much to explain
the plot of *Romeo and Juliet,* and reduces considerably the amount
of apparent coincidence. Shakespeare changes the time of the
tragedy to mid-July, when "summer's ripening breath" matures
both the love of the protagonists and the hate of the rival houses.
The sub-major figures, in their characters and actions and sometimes even in their physiques, fit into the scheme of humors. The
passionate character of Juliet, necessary to her part in the tragedy,
agrees with her association with the sun and her birth under the
sign of Leo; and the impetuous fervour of Romeo, careless of re-

sults, is consonant with his sanguine disposition. Some of the actual coincidences, moreover, can be traced to the day or time of day: the choleric morning hours would seem to give rise to the initial brawl; and this brawl in turn causes the Prince's edict, which in turn causes Romeo's fatal banishment. Romeo's going to the Capulet festivities "too early" makes possible his meeting with Juliet and his falling in love with her; the phlegmatic hours of evening explain Capulet's success in restraining Tybalt at the moment; and the thoughtless abandon of the balcony scene is quite proper to the sanguine hours after midnight. The crucial deaths of Tybalt and of Mercutio, furthermore, take place in the afternoon, when ill-omened melancholy was supposed to rage; and Romeo's banishment and Juliet's wedding fall on Tuesday, the unlucky day of Mars. Indeed, again and again, not only the forebodings of the characters but also the auspices of the humors and the calendar point to a tragic catastrophe: the "death-mark'd love" of "star-cross'd lovers" cannot end happily. Thus the theme of the play is not the evils of civil factions, as in Paynter, or the wickedness of "stolne contractes," as in Brooke, but rather, as in Greek tragedy, the hopelessness of defying the heavens' will. Both the Elizabethan theory of tragedy that derived from Seneca and Horace [86] and the general taste of the age [87] demanded an obvious moral theme; and Shakespeare, snatching a grace beyond the reach of Chapman or Kyd or Marlowe, seems to have turned popular science to his purpose to give the plot of his drama something of the inevitable sequence of Hellenic tragedy.

XI

Patterns of Style in *Romeo and Juliet*

In ordinary conversation figures of speech come naturally to our lips
—in fact, words change in meaning largely through the metaphors
developed in slang. In poetry, also, the strong emotion of the lines
produces a wealth of figures of many sorts; and, when we are
witty, we play on words in ways that have been noted and named
by rhetoricans.

The dramas of Shakespeare, therefore, as realistic dialogue and
also as poetry and as wit, should be, and are, rich in stylistic heightening. The major figures of speech—or colors of rhetoric, as they
used to be called—fall into four somewhat overlapping types: type
I, the figures of sound, such as alliteration, cacophony, onomatopoeia, and perhaps one ought also to include meter and rhyme; type
II, the figures of sentence-structure and arrangement, such as the
rhetorical question, sentence-climax or anticlimax, parallelism, antithesis, ellipsis, and epigram; type III, the figures of comparison
or association, such as simile, metaphor, personification, metonymy,
and allusion; type IV, the figures of wit, including pun, double meaning, sarcasm, irony and dramatic irony, hyperbole, meiosis, oxymoron, paradox, and the like. The actual examples are at times
difficult to identify, especially in Elizabethan speech, in which so
many meanings and pronunciations of words differ from those of

the present day; and sometimes two or three figures are subtly combined and so are hard to distinguish; but analysis reveals them in Shakespeare just as it did centuries ago in Homer and Vergil. The changes in the plays between verse and prose, and the ebb and the flow of the tempo,[1] obviously relate to plot and character: surely, the figures of speech that heighten the style should likewise reflect the personalities of the speakers and the passing situations of the plot; and these figures, like Shakespeare's changes of tempo, might fall into certain patterns in a scene or a whole play and have consistency and a *rationale* at once of their own and in accord with plot and character.

Romeo and Juliet is usually considered one of Shakespeare's most poetic plays, and it is full of Elizabethan wit and of the lyricism of the contemporary sonnet craze, and so seems an appropriate subject for stylistic study. Shakespeare's plays, unlike Classical and French drama, are written in a variety of styles, wide as the social gamut of their characters; and, indeed, constant variety was necessary, or the groundlings in the theatre would become bored and noisy. The 236 lines of the first scene of *Romeo and Juliet* run through five distinct stylistic phases separated by change of speakers: first, the low-life wit of the servants down to line 60; second, the brawl in broken sentences down to line 78; third, the Prince's declaration demanding peace to line 102; fourth, the talk of Benvolio and Montague about Romeo down to line 154; and fifth, the lyrical dialogue between Romeo and Benvolio about the former's love affair. These five styles—low comedy, rapid action, high oratory, serious conversation, and somewhat stilted lyricism—are common to most of Shakespeare's plays; and the verbal technique by which Shakespeare expresses each of them is surely worth the study.

Doubtful cases being generally omitted, Shakespeare seems to use well over a hundred figures in these 236 lines; and, of these figures, only ten are in the sixty lines of prose, and some hundred in the 176 lines of verse. In short, as one might expect, the prose averages only one figure every six lines; and the verse one every two lines or oftener. If one redivides the scene into seven arbitrary sections approximately equal, one finds these figures distributed unevenly, section by section: nine in the first, which is chiefly vulgar wit; eleven in the second, in which the brawl takes place; fourteen in the third, in which the Prince enters and speaks; sixteen and eighteen in the next two sections, in which Montague and Benvolio talk; some thirty in the sixth section, in which Romeo describes his pangs of love; and sixteen in the last section, in which Benvolio suggests a remedy. These last two sections, moreover, are not only entirely in verse but also very largely in rhymed couplets. The number of figures consistently increases up to the last section, so that the sixth has three times the heightening of the first; and this quite accords with the lyrical climax of the scene, the portrayal of Romeo in love.

The types of figures also show changes that clearly relate to the varying speakers and to the passing situations. In the initial talk of the servants, seven of the figures of speech are witty word-play as previously noted under type IV; and the other three are parallel structure at times combined with anaphora and antithesis, all of type II. In the brawl, as one might expect, most of the figures are ellipses of unfinished sentences (type II). Thus the first 78 lines of the scene are dominated first by Type IV and then by Type II. The Prince's speech that follows uses almost entirely figures of music and comparison (type I and III), in sharp contrast to the types of heightening that precede.

In much the same style, though less oratorical, the dialogue between Montagu and Benvolio continues down to Romeo's entrance at line 153. Alliteration is the predominant figure, with some metaphor, personification, allusion, and rhyme. With Romeo's entrance comes a great increase in all four types of figure; for, like the free fantasy of a symphony, it combines the two stylistic themes that came before. There is a wealth of metaphor with some personification and allusion (type III); no less than ten examples of oxymoron (type IV) in lines 174-180 and a sprinkling thereafter of witty word-play; there is much alliteration and rhyme (type I); and Romeo's repeated examples of oxymoron balance the servants' wit with which the scene began. In short, the early part of this scene stylistically depends on figures of types II and IV; it proceeds to the more poetic figures of types I and III; and its climax depends on a rich combining of all four types; and so it builds to an artistic culmination not merely by increasing the number of figures but also by adding to their variety. Certainly, this scene has a consistent pattern of style that leads to a climax of contrasting poetic effects.

Individuals have characteristic habits of speech, just as *prosateurs* have certain favorite figures and turns of expression that characterize their styles. Shylock uses Biblical phraseology,[2] and surely other persons in Shakespeare's plays reflect some universal trait. As already noted, the servants naturally express themselves in vulgar word-play, conventional, obscene puns in parallel phrasing; and the Prince's lines owe their smooth oratorical flow largely to his reiterated alliterations: "peace, Prophaners . . . pernicious . . . purple . . . pain" and so forth. One might expect that Montague and Benvolio in their fifty lines of dialogue would use contrasting rhetorical effects; but apparently they are not important enough to be contrasted, for both are given to alliteration, like the Prince, with occasional metaphors and other figures for variety. When Romeo enters, however, a distinction at once is evident between him and Benvolio, which continues through the eighty verses of their dialogue: though Benvolio speaks some twenty lines and part-lines, he has but half a dozen figures, chiefly metaphor; whereas Romeo, though he speaks but three times as much, has almost ten times as many figures as Benvolio. Obviously, his lines are much richer in poetry; and his figures show the widest variety, with alliteration and rhyme, parallel structure with some asyndeton, antithesis, and ellipsis, much metaphor sometimes combined with allusion and personification, some punning word-play (so dear to the Elizabethans) and paradox and above all oxymoron, which give to his speech a witty artficiality that suggests that his pangs of love are not too deep. In short, Romeo, with less than one-fourth of the lines in the scene, has over half the figures and a greater variety than any other character; and so his description of his love supplies the climax of the scene not only dramatically but also stylistically.

The scene that follows has a similar lyric climax, with Romeo and Benvolio supplying the dialogue. Aside from the couplet rhymes, the figures are various, scattered and not very numerous, perhaps because the dialogue is ordinary talk. Even here, however, their number is notably greater toward the end: the first twenty-five lines, in which Paris and Capulet converse, have only seven figures; whereas the last twenty-five, with Romeo and Benvolio, have twice that number, chiefly alliteration. The third scene, being also work-a-day talk, is also rather poor in heightening. Scene four is somewhat more fanciful, especially in Mercutio's conceits; but it has hardly enough figures to show a clear-cut pattern. In fact, the shorter and less emotional scenes generally show rhetorical pattern somewhat vaguely if at all, and so may be omitted from this study.

The last scene of this initial act is taken up with the Capulet ball and the first meeting of Romeo and Juliet; its 142 lines show stylistic changes rather similar to those of the first scene of the act. The text falls into six parts. (1) The rapid dialogue of 13 lines spoken by the servants who prepare the feast has only four figures, chiefly ellipsis. (2) Capulet's welcome to the guests down to line 38 has 9 figures, chiefly alliteration. (3) The next 12 lines, spoken almost entirely by Romeo, contain, beside many couplet rhymes, 17 figures, including some of all four types: five alliterations (type I), parallelism, ellipsis, and chiasmus (II), simile, metaphor, and allusion (III) and at least three cases of hyperbole (IV). (4) The dialogue down to line 90 between Tybalt and Capulet has occasional couplet rhymes, together with 9 alliterations, and one example each of hyperbole, metonymy, refrain, and metaphor—only 13 figures in 39 lines as compared with 17 in Romeo's 12 lines. (5) The dialogue between Juliet and Romeo that follows in the form of a sonnet and a quatrain has four alliterations, three metaphors, a hyperbole, and a pun: once more the lines that express Romeo's love are greatly enriched with heightening as contrasted with the other dialogue. (6) The scene ends with rapid talk between the Nurse and Juliet, contrasting with the lovers' impassioned lines, and marked by only two ellipses appropriate to Juliet's haste. Indeed, in this scene, as in the first, Romeo has an overwhelming number and variety of figures in proportion to his part in the text; and Shakespeare is clearly using lyrical heightening to emphasize the hero's love, which is the dramatic crux of the tragedy. In several regards, in fact, this scene is parallel to the first one in the act: it begins with servants' rapid talk, proceeds to polite conversation and thence to lyricism in the then-popular sonnet style to express Romeo's feelings; and, at the end, both scenes revert to the commonplace once more with very little heightening. As in Scene One, alliteration and rhyme seem to be the commonest figures; but they disappear in the low-life prose; and, in the most elaborate passages, they are overshadowed by metaphor and other figures of comparison.

The short first scene of the second act, in which Benvolio and Mercutio seek Romeo after the ball, is written in the light tone of casual conversation, doubtless to contrast it with the Balcony Scene which follows. Mercutio's speech, as usual, is fanciful and allusive, but the number of figures in the scene as a whole is not extraordinary. Then comes the Balcony Scene with 190 lines heavily loaded with figures, a rich lyricism without relief that ran the risk of wearying the groundlings. The scene has at least 142 figures, some of the alliterations and metaphors going through several verses. It may be cut at entrances, exits, or other critical points into six sections at lines 32, 60, 106, 138, and 157; and the appended table summarizes the major facts of style-analysis:

Lines	Number of figures	Type I (sound)	Type II (sentence-structure)	Type III (compari-son)	Type IV (wit)	Juliet's lines & figures	Romeo's lines & figures
1-32 32 lines	33	14 (chiefly allit.)	4	11	4	0 0	32 33
32-60 28 lines	22	6	6	5	5	20 16	8 6
60-106 46 lines	30	19	3	4	4	29 15	19 15
106-38 32 lines	21	12	4	3	2	26 16	5 5
138-57 19 lines	12	7	2	2	1	12 5	7 7
157-190 33 lines	24	10	2	8	4	21 12	12 12
190 lines	142 figures	68 figures	21 figures	35 figures	20 figures	107 lines 64 figures	83 lines 78 figures

The first section of 32 lines is Romeo's long soliloquy; it has more figures than it has lines. It is very rich in vowel-alliteration; and, if the pronunciation of Elizabethan vowels were certain enough to allow the counting of assonance (e.g. "gaze . . . lazy-pacing . . . sails . . ."), this would considerably increase the number of the figures of sound, which are generally the most numerous throughout the scene. In the five sections that follow, the number of figures is slightly less, so that, oddly enough, the passage richest in lyricism seems to be the first; but mere number is not always a safe criterion in aesthetics. After the first section, the scene is a dialogue between the two lovers, with a few brief interruptions from the Nurse. Juliet has 107 lines with 64 figures, and Romeo 83 with 78 figures, so that his lines would seem to be more richly lyrical than Juliet's. Her verses, moreover, are much more given over to mere alliteration; and so Romeo's heightening has greater variety. On the whole, the scene has so much stylistic unity that it shows but little pattern; and this is not surprising, for the same two characters speak throughout, and the whole is written in the very apogee of lyric style from which one could hardly vary without the danger of anticlimax. This is probably the longest scene of pure passion in all Shakespeare, and it cannot be matched even in *Antony and Cleopatra*. The following scene, with the Friar's advice to Romeo in studied metaphor and moralistic epigram, gives contrast to this ardent passion of the lovers: thus the Balcony Scene, though it has no great variety in its hundred and ninety lines, is quite different from the scenes that precede and follow.

Act III, Scene i has about the same speakers, the same rapid changes of style, the same varied sorts of material, as the first and last scenes of Act I. It falls into four parts, as the appended table shows. (1) The first thirty-six lines are witty dialogue between Mercutio and Benvolio, with the figures of type IV predominant. (2) Lines 36 to 80 are the quarrel between Tybalt and Mercutio, the latter having three-fourths of the figures, though he has less than half the lines. His taunting of Tybalt expresses itself in comparisons and wit; but, oddly enough, figures of sound are most numerous, perhaps because the dialogue is in verse. The number of figures per line, moreover, is smaller than in the other three sections. (3) Lines 80 to 138 show the killing of Mercutio and of Tybalt with figures of type III predominant, but also many of types I and II. In this section, almost all the heightening is in Romeo's lines, and indeed, he averages a figure for every verse. (4) Lines 138 to 194 comprize the dialogue between Benvolio and the Prince, with a great preponderance of alliteration as in their speech in Act I. Altogether, this scene has 109 figures in 194 lines—richer in heightening than Act I, but not as lyrical as the Balcony Scene. As usual, the musical figures are the most numerous. These four sections, doubtless because of their changes in speakers and in variety of

Act III, Scene i.

	Figures of Type I (sound)	Type II (sentence-structure)	Type III (association)	Type IV (wit)	Mercutio's no. of lines & figures	Benvolio's	Romeo's	Tybalt's and the Prince's
Wit Lines 1-36 — 25 figs.	3	6	6	10	25 / 21	10 / 8[1]	— / —	— / —
Quarrel 36-80 — 19 figs.	9	1	5	6	20 / 14	4 / —	9 / 4	Tybalt 7 / 1
Fight 80-138 — 34 figs.	10	9	13	2	17 / 9	9 / 3	26 / 26	— / 2
Ben. and Prince 138-194 — 31 figs.	20	6	5	0	— / —	28 / 16	— / —	Prince 16 / 11
194 lines 109 figs.	42 figs.	22 figs.	29 figs.	18 figs.	62 lines 44 figs.	51 lines 27 figs.	35 lines 30 figs.	

[1] Benvolio and Romeo share some figures.

content, show much more contrast than the sections of the Balcony Scene, but not as much as the two scenes analyzed in Act I. Curiously enough, the figures are most thickly scattered in the first section, perhaps because, in the two sections that follow, the characters' clash of wills and violence of action supports the dramatic effect without the heightening of style.

Again, as in Acts I and II, Romeo's lines have the greatest number and the greatest variety of poetic effects. Mercutio depends on little more than wit; Benvolio and the Prince, as they did earlier, on alliteration; and Tybalt's nine lines are so blunt and straight-forward, to accord with his choleric nature, that they have only one figure of speech. Thus the pattern of the style seems to be clearly associated with character and also situation. As in Act I, Scene i, the fight evokes ellipses; and the Prince's formal discourse, not-too-obvious alliterations. The style, moreover, shows not only correlations with plot and character but also a consistent pattern of its own: the figures of wit regularly decrease section by section (10-6-2-0), as Mercutio's part declines. The musical figures, on the contrary, increase (3-9-10-20). The figures of sentence-structure and of association follow a course parallel to each other, first down, then up, then down; and they are commonest in the section where Mercutio and Tybalt are slain. In short, the scene shows a consistent stylistic pattern that is largely integrated with plot and character, and, like Act I, Scene i, rises in the next to the last section to a climax of swift and effective action, supported and reflected by a wealth and variety of figures of types I, II, and III.

Act III, Scene v naturally falls into four parts divided at lines 58, 126, and 196. The first of these is the passionate farewell of Romeo and Juliet with interruptions, as in the Balcony Scene, by the Nurse. Indeed, this dialogue is a brief but intense echo of the Balcony Scene, with a greater depth of tragic tone. Its 58 lines contain over eighty figures of speech: whereas the Balcony Scene averages about one figure in 1⅔ lines, this dialogue averages one figure in less than three-fourths of a line, so much more heightened is the verse; and some figures, such as alliteration and parallel structure extend over several lines. The variety of figures also is very great. Type I has 32 examples, 29 of them alliteration and also cases of repetend, cacophony, and onomatopoeia, and a couplet rhyme. Type II has twenty examples, nine of them parallelism, and also antithesis,

ellipsis, anaphora, and rhetorical question. Type III has 17 examples, eleven of them metaphor and personification, and also
prolepsis, metonymy, and apostrophe. Type IV, which one would
hardly expect to find at all, has twelve examples, five of them
irony or dramatic irony, and also hyperbole, oxymoron, and word-
play including puns. Indeed, these 58 lines contain some twenty
different sorts of figures; and one doubts whether Shelley himself,
that virtuoso in lyrical effects, anywhere shows a greater concentration or a greater variety. Some of the commoner figures, like alliteration and metaphor, form a sort of groundswell of the heightening,
maintaining the emotional level and giving unity of tone; and some,
like cacophony and prolepsis, lend piquant variety appropriate to
the sense or the emotion of the line: thus the style is unified but not
monotonous, and adjusts itself to the changing content without
losing emotional continuity. As in the Balcony Scene, Romeo's lines
are richer in figures than Juliet's, and somewhat more varied: she
has 42 figures in 32 lines, and he has 39 in 24; and almost half of
her figures are alliteration. Thus the first section of this scene adapts
its lyric style not only to the passion of the lovers but also to their
individual habits of speech as already distinguished in the Balcony
Scene.

The three following sections of this scene, beginning respectively
at lines 60, 126, and 197, contrast sharply with the first section in
both content and style and less sharply with one another. The 66
verses between Juliet and Lady Capulet have only 45 figures, 23 of
them being type I, chiefly alliteration, 13 of them, type IV, and a
sprinkling of types II and III. This is a complete contrast both
in number and variety with the section between Romeo and Juliet
that precedes. Juliet's lines are hardly richer in figures than Lady
Capulet's, but the former has somewhat more variety, for most
of Lady Capulet's are mere alliteration. The following section in
which Capulet urges the match with Paris on his unwilling daughter,
is somewhat richer in heightening, with 59 figures in 70 lines. The
types, moreover, are almost evenly distributed, with 17 of type I and
13 of each of the other three. Capulet speaks all the lines but ten
and he has all but five of the figures—a much greater concentration
of heightening than he shows in Act I, Scene v, perhaps because
of his anger at Juliet. The last section, in which Juliet and the Nurse
discuss the former's plight, has 36 figures in its 56 lines, with a

considerable preponderance of types I and III. Juliet's 28 lines with 29 figures are, as one might expect, more lyrical than the Nurse's 15 lines, with six. The four sections of this scene show considerable contrast: the first has a great number and variety of figures; the second has much fewer with a preponderance of types I and IV; the third is richer again, and also like the first has a fairly even distribution among the four types; the fourth has slightly less heightening, with a preponderance of types I and III. This scene is a sort of reversal of the pattern in Act I, Scene i, with the first and the last sections cut off; but there the lyrical outburst came as a climax, whereas here it starts the scene. The pattern is clearly symmetrical: the first and third sections have a great number and variety of figures; and the second and fourth have fewer and more largely of type I.

Act IV, Scene v falls into three sections: to line 33 is the Nurse's reaction to Juliet's death, to line 95 are the laments of the family and the Friar's consolation, from there to the end of the scene is the dialogue between Peter and the Musicians, a sort of comic relief, like the Scene of the Drunken Porter in *Macbeth*. The first two of these sections are very similar except that the former is hardly more than a monologue, and the latter has two major speakers— Capulet and the Friar—and three minor speakers; but none of them is markedly differentiated as to style. Both sections, being very emotional, have more than one figure per line. There is the usual preponderance of figures of type I; and, in both, the rhetorical figures of type II are almost as numerous. The second section, however, has a surprising number of figures of type IV; but the number of ellipses is not surprising in such rapid dialogue. The third section of the scene is quite different in both content and style, and reminds one of the jesting Servants who opened the first act. Both have comparatively few figures; and these 47 lines have only 25, about equally divided between the four types. Indeed, this witty dialogue has hardly half the number of figures of type IV that the preceding section has—a commentary on the Elizabethans' fondness for wit, even in serious talk. Over half the lines and about three-fourths of the figures are Peter's; and he dominates the dialogue. On the whole, the scene seems to run down to a deliberate anti-climax. It is not really tragic; for Juliet's death, discovered in the first section is only apparent; the mourning for her is too exclamatory to be impressive; and the scene ends with a flourish of low-life wit. The real catastrophe is in the act that follows.

Act V, Scene i has only 86 lines; but they fall into a symmetrical pattern in four sections, ending respectively with lines 11, 34, 57, and 86. In the first and third, Romeo speaks alone. The former of these soliloquies has more figures than verses and a considerable variety, with alliteration predominant and a scattering of dramatic irony, metonymy, metaphor, and epigram. This is Romeo's characteristically rich and varied style. The other soliloquy, which comprises the third section, has fewer and less varied figures: indeed, Romeo's reaction to the news of Juliet's death is a striking contrast to the exclamations and hyperboles of the Capulet family in the preceding scene. They pour out their hearts with words; but Romeo quietly resolves on suicide, and proceeds to make the necessary preparations. The second section of the scene, when Romeo first hears the tragic news, has but 15 figures in 23 lines; and, although Romeo's style is somewhat more heightened than Balthasar's, it is certainly plainer than usual. Events are now beyond the expression of rhetoric or even poetry; and nothing but bare action and plain statement can show Romeo's deep resolve: he can only die. In the fourth section, in which he buys the poison from the Apothecary, his phraseology is somewhat more elaborate again, as it was in the first section when he was alone; but that was hopeful and this is deep despair. Thus, of the two soliloquies in the first and the third sections of the scene, one is elaborate and one simple; and, of the two dialogues, the first is simpler and the second, more elaborate; and the tones and styles of the whole scene contrast with the artificial rhetoric of the Capulets and with the rude comedy of Peter and the Musicians that ends the preceding scene. Shakespeare weaves a complex web of stylistic contrast between scenes and within longer and even shorter scenes to give his audience the variety that they craved.

Act V, Scene iii, which closes the tragedy, falls into six parts, divided at lines 21, 73, 120, 186, and 227. In the first, Paris comes to put flowers on Juliet's tomb, and almost three-fourths of the figures are alliteration—a type of heightening that Shakespeare seems to prefer for minor characters like the Prince, whose emotions he does not care to emphasize. In the second section, Romeo kills Paris, and, as usual in violent action, the number of figures decreases. The third section is Romeo's passionate soliloquy ending with his suicide, and the number of his figures rises to one in three-fourths of a line, as rich in heightening as his former impassioned outbursts. In the fourth section, divided between the Friar, Juliet, and the Watchman, the proportion falls to one figure in two lines. In the fifth, when the Prince and the two fathers find the bodies, it rises somewhat, but not to Romeo's lyric height; and the last section, in which all is explained and the rival families make peace, averages only one figure in two lines. The heightening of this scene generally reflects the content of the lines, and is consistent with the speech-habits previously apparent in different characters: the Prince is still alliterative, and Romeo still richly lyrical. As elsewhere, alliteration is by far the commonest figure; and, as the number of other figures declines, alliteration seems proportionately to increase, as if Shakespeare substituted it for subtler devices of style in the less important parts; and Romeo seems to have a smaller proportion of alliteration than any other character. Alliteration is the musical base of all this heightening, at least in the verse; but generally the alliterating sounds are too far apart for it to be too obvious; and sometimes other figures overshadow it not only in their prominence but also even in numbers; and, in Romeo's soliloquy, as elsewhere in his speech, the metaphors are more striking. The following table summarizes the style-analysis of the scene.

After a full examination of the evidence, the late Professor Adams [3] concludes that the youthful Shakespeare taught for a time in a country grammar school, where, of course, Classical rhetoric would be an important subject. In any case, Shakespeare, if we may assume even that he attended Stratford Grammar School, could not have been ignorant of the flowers of rhetoric; [4] and Sister Meriam Joseph has recently shown the influence of the Classical figures of speech on the dialogue of the plays.[5] For that matter, even if Shakespeare had never heard the Greek names of these figures, his characters would still use them, just as the most ignorant people do today, unconsciously when haste or wit or emotion prompts. Surely, therefore, it is not surprising that in a lyrical play like *Romeo and Juliet,* these figures should be so abundant: indeed, Shakespeare seems to be quite conscious of their use; and he must have realized that they fall into patterns, not only consistent but sometimes even symmetrical, and often synchronized with plot and character. Thus

No. of lines and figures	Figures of Type I	Type II	Type III	Type IV	Main characters	No. of lines	No. of figures	Comment
Lines 1-21 22 figures 1 in 1 line	15	3	2	2	Paris	19	19	Chiefly alliteration
21-73 39 1 in 1⅞ 11.	18	4	12	5	Paris Romeo	13 35	8 28	Alliteration and Type III
73-120 64 1 in ¾ line	24	12	24	4	Romeo	47	64	Types I and II at first; later Type III also
120-186 33 1 in 2 11.	17	8	5	3	Frair L. Juliet 1st Watch	23 13 12	14 9 5	Type I at first with increasing variety
186-227 34 1 in 1¼ 11.	20	5	7	2	Prince Capulet Montagu Frair L.	15 5 5 5	14 6 2 4	Prince especially alliterative
227-309 42 1 in 2 11.	25	10	5	2	Prince Friar L.	21 41	14 18	
	119	42	55	16				

Romeo, the impassioned lover, has a greater concentration of figures than any other character, even the nimble-witted Mercutio; Juliet has somewhat fewer than Romeo; and this is true in scene after scene. The boorish servants and the fiery, blunt-spoken Tybalt have least of all; for the former have no important emotions, and the latter expresses himself in action. Situation also is reflected in the style: the violence of a street brawl produces few figures, except perhaps ellipsis; the Prince discourses with formal dignity and smooth alliteration; and Romeo runs the whole gamut of stylistic heightening.

The present study has analyzed the eight longest and most important scenes; and perhaps on this basis, one might venture some further tentative conclusions. In a series of recent studies the present writer has been investigating the tempo of Shakespeare's plays; and one might ask whether any correlation appears between tempo and the quantity and type of stylistic heightening. As tempo can be counted only in verse dialogue, the following table uses only the poetry from the eight scenes considered. This table suggests that the

Scene	Tempo (slow : fast)	Heightening
I, i, 60-235 (Street brawl)	1 : 1½	1 fig. in 1¾ lines
I, v, 13-142 (Ball)	1 : 2—	1 fig. in 2¼ lines
II, ii (Balcony Scene)	1 : 1—	1 fig. in 1¼ lines
III, i, 48-91, 100-194 (Tybalt dies)	1 : 2+	1 fig. in 2— lines
III, v, 1-60 (Lovers' farewell)	1 : 1—	1 fig. in ¾ line
III, v, 60-243 (Betrothal)	1 : 2—	1 fig. in 1¼ lines
IV, v, 1-95 (Juliet seems dead)	1 : 1½	1 fig. in 1 line
V, i (Apothecary shop)	1 : 1	1 fig. in 1+ line
V, iii (Graveyard)	1 : 1+	1 fig. in 1⅓ lines

amount of heightening is in inverse ratio to the speed: at all events, the two scenes or part-scenes with the fewest figures (I, v and III, i) are two of the three fastest; and the one with the most figures is one of the two slowest (III, v, 1-60); and, in Act IV, Scene v, ellipsis accounts for the greater number of figures than one would expect, for ellipsis is one of the few figures that tends to speed the verse. In short, the style of the poetry seems to be somewhat integrated with the delivery of the lines.

One might further enquire how far the heightening of the style correlates not only with the timing but also with the humors of individual characters. During most of the play, Romeo is obviously a sanguine lover, and he speaks with the even, moderate tempo that characterized that humor; but how far is his great number and variety of figures also characteristic of his humor? This is an hypothesis that can be tested only by the examination of many other sanguine characters. Perhaps the Prince is sanguine; but he uses fewer and less diverse figures than does Romeo: and his speeds show so great a variety that one hesitates to say that they reflect any one humor; but, in his play, Shakespeare often sacrifices consistency of timing to theatrical effect. Tybalt is strikingly choleric, under the violent astral influence of Mars; and, though his lines are few, they show evidence of great speed, as one would expect of the choleric type; and, in contrast to Romeo, he uses very few figures. The choleric type is regularly swift in speech; but dare one add that it is also very plain-spoken, with little stylistic heightening, perhaps because it expresses itself in action rather than words? Romeo and Tybalt are certainly a contrast in humor, speed, and style. Capulet in his first scene is like Tybalt in all three respects; but later his delivery slows and his style grows more elaborate; but Shakespeare's patterns of humor and of tempo do not always agree in the earlier plays. Juliet is choleric under the benign influence of the sun, a humor that approximated the sanguine: she has about the same average speed as Romeo but fewer figures. Mercutio, who represents the mercurial complexion, speaks rather fast, and, perhaps for that reason, has comparatively few figures. Benvolio's speed does not agree at all with his phlegmatic humor; but his few figures, as in the case of Mercutio, agree with this rapidity. In short, some correlation seems to exist between humor and style, though not always between them and tempo; and these correlations might be the subject for some further study.

The results of this paper are rather tentative; but at least they show the existence of style-patterns in the play, and suggest that these patterns are integrated with situation and character and probably with tempo and humor also.

XII

The Objective Genitive and "Run-awayes Eyes"

Nothing is more idiomatic and more difficult for a foreigner than English usage of prepositions; and in Elizabethan times these uses were quite as complicated and not always the same as they are today. Idioms relating to *of* and to the genitive case are certainly no exception; but Abbott's *Shakespearean Grammar* ignores the matter entirely; and even Franz's more recent work is incomplete. Fundamentally, the genitive should express either birth-origin or possession; but other common uses developed such as the partitive genitive, the genitive of time as in *a journey of two hours,* a genitive of material as in *a house of stone,* and other uses in which *of* seems to stand for some other preposition such as *from,* as in *a man of Rome.* Schmidt's *Lexicon* more or less clearly distinguishes several such uses in Elizabethan English; but occasionally his examples do not seem to fit too well under their respective headings; and this suggests that Elizabethan English has more types of the genitive than he provided for.

In the loose syntax and semantics of Elizabethan, adjectives were used both subjectively and objectively, and in this respect could be distinguished only by guesswork or by the context: *mortal,* for instance, might be used subjectively and applied to a person to mean *subject to death* as in *mortal man;* or it might be used objectively to mean *causing death* as in *mortal injury* or *mortal taste* (the latter in *Paradise Lost*). Today, most adjectives have been normalized in their subjective use; but a few, like *awful,* as in *awful accident*—i.e. an accident causing awe in the beholder—retain their old objective sense and indeed are regularly used in it. The genitive case, in a way, turns a noun or a pronoun into an adjective by making it modify another noun or pronoun; and in the common Elizabethan idiom of "thieves of mercy" (meaning *merciful thieves*), a phrase introduced by *of* is actually substituted for an adjective. Therefore, it is not surprising that this double adjectival usage—subjective and objective—should become an idiom also of the genitive case; and the objective use still occasionally appears today in such an expression as *the love of God,* meaning *love for God,* i.e., not God's love for man, but man's for God. In this use, *of* regularly stands in place of *for;* and, in modern English, the substitution of *for* usually brings out the meaning more clearly.

Today this ambiguous twin-sense has largely been discarded, like other linguistic ambiguities that were dropped in the eighteenth century; but Shakespeare's text shows many examples both of the objective adjective and the objective genitive. The latter is especially common after verbal nouns; and, in most cases, the substitution of *for* would improve the sense for the modern reader: "Your lives shall pay the profit *of* the peace" (*R. and J.,* I, i, 89) ; "I humbly do desire your grace *of* pardon" (*M. of V.,* IV, i, 402) ; "To appeal each other *of* high treason" (*Richard II,* I, 27) ; "Pity *of* him" (*M. of V.,* II, iii, 42) ; "hate *of* you" and Love *of* you" (*T. G. V.,* I, i, 96; II, iv, 5 and III, i, 46) ; "The fear *of* your adventure" (*A. Y. L. I.,* I, ii, 187) ; "whom *of* succours we entreated" (*Henry V,* III, iii, 45) ; "I have an eye *of* you" (*Ham.,* II, ii, 30) ; "I humbly do entreat you *of* your pardon" (*Othello,* III, iii, 212) ; "in change *of* him" (*T. and C.,* III, iii, 27) ; " 'Tis pity *of* him" (*A. and C.,* I, iv, 71) ; "since *of* your lives you set so slight valuation" (*Cymb.,* IV, iv, 48) ; "for fear *of* the storm" (*Temp.,* II, ii, 116). Sometimes the objective genitive is used without a preceding verbal: "I have no mind *of* feasting forth" (*M. of V.,* II, v, 37) ; "*of* this my privacy, I have strong reasons" (*T. and C.,* III, iii, 190) ; and "The date is out *of* such prolixity" (*R. and J.,* I, iv, 3) ; "Let us take the law *of* our sides" (*ibid.,* I, i, 31; cf. 39) ; "No sudden mean *of* death" (*ibid.,* III, iii, 45) ; "Now you do know the reason *of* this haste" (*ibid.*, IV, i, 15) ; and "Poor sacrifices *of* our enmity" (*ibid.*, V, iii, 304). Sometimes even pronouns in the genitive have an objective sense, as in "*my* love" (e.g. *All's Well*, III, iii, 79, and *Henry VI, Pt. III*, II, vi, 5) meaning the love of someone else *for* me, and in "Ne'er saw her match" (*R. and J.*, I, ii, 92), meaning a match *for* her; and "*your* attendance" (*Twelfth Night*, I, iv, 10) clearly means attendance upon you, and Kittredge notes it as a case of the "objective genitive." [1] In the noun, this idiom often appears without the *of*, and simply in the genitive with an apostrophe: "my *sceptre's* awe" (*Richard II*, I, i, 118) refers to the awe of subjects *for* my sceptre, for of course an inanimate object like a sceptre could not in itself experience *awe;* "for the *fault's* love is the offender friended" (*M..for M.*, IV, ii, 116) refers to someone's love *for* the fault; "a *brother's* dead *love*" (*T. N.*, I, i, 31) alludes to Olivia's love *for* her brother; "let there be weighed Your *lady's* love against some other maid" (*R. and J.*, I, ii, 95-96) refers to Romeo's love *for* his lady; and again "*confusion's* cure lives not in these confusions." (*ibid.*, IV, v, 61). Perhaps another example is Romeo's bitter exclamation, "O, I am *fortune's* fool" (*ibid.*, III, i, 133), which seems to mean a fool *for* fortune to treat as she pleases. These cases of the objective use of the genitive have been gleaned somewhat at random; but one might note that eight of them come from *Romeo and Juliet*, at least one in every category; and, therefore, the idiom does not seem to be a rarity in that play or indeed in Shakespeare generally.

Probably the most famous *locus desperatus* in all the text of Shakespeare is the "run-awayes eyes" (*R. and J.*, III, ii, 6). Juliet is waiting with utmost impatience for her secret tryst, and longs for the sun to set and darkness to

> Spread thy close curtain, love-preparing night,
> That runaway's eyes may wink, and Romeo
> Leap to these arms, untalked of and unseen . . .

The earliest commentary on this passage seems to be that of Warburton in 1747; and, for more than two centuries since then, critics have produced such a library of comment that the Furness variorum edition requires twenty-eight pages merely to summarize the mate-

---

[1] *Twelfth Night,* ed. Kittredge, p. 96. See also examples in II, i, 34 and 35; and "*thy* excuse" (I, v, 3) clearly means an excuse *for* thee.

rial down to 1870. The difficulty is obvious: Romeo is the legal run-away after killing Tybalt; and yet, why should *his* eyes be blind so that he will not be seen to visit Juliet? The *pursuers'* eyes or the *constables'* eyes would make sense; but surely the fugitive would need all his eyesight to reach Juliet and then escape. The earliest critics read sense into the passage by arbitrarily making "run-awayes" refer to the sun or stars or night or Cupid or love or to Rumor, as personified in the play's Prologue. This is very like the psuedo-allegorical interpretation of the Bible and of the Koran that has plagued criticism of those works for centuries: it is mere unsupported guesswork. The Victorian age, despite the fact that "run-awayes," spelled with slight variations, appears in all the quarto and folio texts, attempted a bewildering variety of emendations, with scant regard for the manner in which their suggested readings came to be mistaken for "run-awayes." The error can hardly stem from a printer's "foul case"; for the chance is incredible that all the printers of the early quartos and the first folio, scattered over a full quarter century had exactly the same letters misplaced in the boxes that held their fonts of type, and that each independently picked out just these wrong letters or made precisely the same sophistication in printing this very word. If the error, moreover, was in the manuscript, or arose from misread handwriting, then the handwriting must have been equally misleading, and misleading in just the same way in at least two separate manuscripts; for the first quarto and the first folio texts, being different to the extent of over seven hundred lines, could not have been printed from the same copy. The suggested emendations, furthermore, when written in Elizabethan "secretary" script, rarely show the slightest resemblance to "run-awayes" likewise written in the common Gothic handwriting of the age. In short, though Clarke and Collier insist that "It is generally admitted that *run-awayes* must be wrong," yet the evidence of the several early editions is unanimous in its favor; and no explanation seems available as to just how such mistakes as have been suggested could have arisen, and arisen in the same way in otherwise divergent texts. Furthermore, of the score or more of emendations that have been proposed, not one has satisfied more than two or three editors: this is a sharp contrast to the general acceptance for the last two centuries of Theobald's famous emendation of "a Table of greene fields" (*Henry V*, II, iii, 16), in which "a Table" is a paleographic mis-reading for "a' babbled." More recently, editors have tended to revert to the original text, often adopting the explanation first set forth by Hunter that "run-awayes" refers to *runagates* or *prowlers* in the streets who might see Romeo on his way to keep his tryst and report him to the authorities. Unfortunately, however, no such runagates are mentioned here or elsewhere in the play, except that Romeo himself is later called a "runagate" (III, v, 88) ; and, as Romeo has just been banished and so must flee the city, he is the obvious candidate for the application of the word *runaway,* especially if one interprets it as *runagate.*

The present writer would suggest that "run-awayes" in the passage under discussion does refer to Romeo, and that it is a clear case of the objective use of the genitive, and means, not the eyes *of* runaways, but eyes spying *for* runaways; and the text might then be freely paraphrased thus: Juliet urges night, which helps lovers, to lend darkness so that eyes on the lookout *for* runaways may be closed, and so Romeo will be able to come to her arms unobserved. This explanation has two advantages: it does not require the emending of a text that is almost certainly correct, and it gives the obvious sense of the passage in conformity with Elizabethan grammar and idiom.

XIII

Contrast of Tempo in the "Balcony Scene"

Not only the meaning but the textual detail of Shakespeare's dialogue reflects the tempo at which he expected a given passage to be
delivered: vowel and consonant combinations lead the voice to *lento*
or *andante* or *allegro* or *presto;* ellipses and over-long lines suggest
haste; the use of the emphatic *do* suggests deliberate speech; and,
most important of all, the presence or the absence—evident in the
meter—of slurrings between words as in *don't* or *for't,* and within
certain words, such as *ever* and *heaven,* show the tempo of the
verse.[1] Such evidence may show the speech-characteristics of a role,
slow or fast, smooth or jerky; and this in turn seems to show how
Shakespeare at times adjusted his lines to the speech-peculiarities of
the actor for whom he wrote the part: in this way, one may even
guess some characteristics of Shakespeare's own speech, from the
parts he played. In an important role, moreover, changes in tempo
should synchronize with the situation, the emotion[2] and even a
fundamental evolution in a given character; and such would seem
to be the case in the tempo of Desdemona. The present study is
concerned with the more superficial relation of tempo to literary
and dramatic style.

Contrast is one of the most striking of devices; and, indeed, without it, poetry and prose would both sink to drab monotony. In

Romeo and Juliet, a play of wit and lyricism, style is the dominant dramatic element; the two protagonists might well show some contrast in their style of speech; and this contrast might well appear in the tempo of their respective roles. In Acts I and II, both characters speak somewhat slower than the rapid norm of the Elizabethan stage, in which the evidence for rapidity preponderates by almost three to one. In Act I the role of Romeo, strangely enough, shows slightly more evidence for slow than for fast speech; and, in Act II (omitting the Balcony Scene) it is slightly shaded in the opposite direction. Juliet in Act I—though the evidence of her part is hardly enough to furnish proof—seems to be even slower than Romeo; and, in Act II (again omitting the Balcony Scene) she is, like Romeo, slightly more rapid. In short, the tempo of the two lovers in most of the first two acts displays no striking contrast, and is notable only for being rather slower than the average speech of the Shakespearean stage.

The Balcony Scene is an utter contrast in tempo to the scenes before and around it, and shows a striking contrast of speed between the two lovers: Romeo's lines supply almost four evidences for slow speech to one for fast, a complete reversal of the norm; and Juliet's, on the other hand, are nearer the usual ratio, and are more fast than slow by about two to three. In Shakespeare's text Romeo has about eighty lines, and Juliet almost one hundred and ten, that is an approximate ratio of three to four; but Romeo may actually have had more speaking-time. Elizabethan actors, as Hamlet suggests, spoke "trippingly"; but, in this play that according to its prologue took only two hours on the stage, the two chief characters in their most famous scene pronounce their lines much slower than the norm, and in the case of Romeo, with an extreme deliberation that reminds one of the dazed and halting speech of Desdemona in the last act of *Othello.* When the lovers meet again in Act III, the speech of both of them is somewhat slower than the norm; but, as in Act I, the contrast is but slight: in Romeo, the evidence somewhat favors rapidity; in Juliet, the opposite—just contrary to the very striking contrast in the Balcony Scene. In Act III, as a whole, the evidence for Romeo somewhat favors the fast; in the third scene, Juliet is fast by a count of more than two to one; and, in the fifth scene, she is slow by a count of about three to four. In Act IV, Romeo doesn't appear; and Juliet's lines are slow by two to three.

In Act V, Juliet's few lines show an even balance of evidence; and Romeo's show almost twice as much evidence for rapid tempo. In short, Romeo's part, outside the Balcony Scene, does not stray far from a ratio of one to one. This is slow for the Shakespearean stage; but, in the Balcony Scene it is retarded even more to the astonishing ratio of four slow to one fast, a ratio that appears nowhere else in his part. Juliet's role for the entire play averages about the same as Romeo's, but with greater variation; and her proportion in the Balcony Scene of two slow to three fast re-appears in Act IV, and is nearer the Elizabethan norm than Romeo's. Shakespeare seems to have intended the Balcony Scene to move slowly, with an *andante* lyricism; and he further accentuated it with great contrast in the speeds of the two speakers. For all his fiery protestations, Romeo speaks almost *largo* and generally *legato,* as a contrast to his lady's greater variety and speed.

Some actors say that Romeo's part is one of the most ungrateful major roles in Shakespeare, because he is a mere foil to Juliet; and his more monotonous, heavier tempo would seem to agree with this: he acts as a sort of bass accompaniment while Juliet carries the air: at all events, the length and importance of his speeches dwindle as the scene progresses, and he has few of the purple passages. In short, Shakespeare, in dramatically building up the scene, seems to have been sacrificing Romeo for a brilliant lyric climax in the part of Juliet, and the contrast in tempo doubtless contributed to this effect. No other reason for it is apparent; and one finds it in no other scene. It does not seem to inhere either in the characters of the speakers or in the momentary situation: if lovers should prolong their accents, why does not Juliet do so? Indeed, it seems to be a mere trick of style, without deep dramatic meaning, devised purely for theatrical effect, like the artificial lighting of a Rembrandt. Shakespeare's comparative failure in *Romeo and Juliet* to integrate tempo with plot or character (as he later did in the part of Desdemona) is not surprising; for he had not yet mastered the complexities of tragedy. In short, Shakespeare uses contrast in tempo to heighten the effect of a lyric scene, even though there is no clear reason for this contrast; the device, though somewhat specious, was doubtless effective.

One might ask further how far modern actors instinctively adjust their rendition of the lines to the tempos that Shakespeare appar-

ently expected, how far their "feel" of interpretation leads them to
conform to the expression-marks inherent in his texts. Of course, the
modern stage with its proscenium arch will not allow—especially not
in a large, echoing theatre—the speed of the Elizabethan actor's
speech; but, in the Balcony Scene, the contrast is so great that modern Shakespearean actors, though scaling down the average tempo,
might retain the difference between the slow-speaking Romeo and
the faster Juliet. Sothern and Marlowe were for many years a
standard of Shakespearean production; and a comparison of the
tempos indicated in the original text with a recording of the Balcony
Scene as they presented it should indicate how nearly at least two
modern actors reflect the contrast that the dramatist seems to have
intended.

As recorded for the victrola, this scene is reather heavily cut,
especially the earlier speeches of Romeo. In fact, the 190 lines of
the original are reduced to about 120; and, of these lines, Romeo
has about thirty-four; the Nurse, a few interjections; and Juliet the
lion's share. The evidences of speed apparent in this abbreviated
version accentuate the contrast apparent in the uncut text. Romeo's
part supplies three evidences for fast as against eighteen for slow
tempo, a proportion of six to one in favor of retardation; and
Juliet's ratio shows forty evidences of speed to fifteen for slow
tempo, a ratio of one to almost three in favor of speed. In short,
these calculations show the same deliberate Romeo as the uncut text,
contrasting with the same impetuous Juliet, whose lines show more
speed and so a greater variation than her lover's slow and more
even pace.

How do Sothern and Marlowe deliver these 120 lines? Some
speeches are too short to give clear evidences of tempo; and the
tempo sometimes changes within a line; but a rough estimate,
gleaned from repeated playing of the record, may well serve: as
Mr. Sothern interprets Romeo's role, twenty-nine lines are clearly
slower than the average, and five lines faster, exactly the same ratio
of six to one that the uncut text affords; and, as Miss Marlowe
interprets Juliet, forty-four lines are fast, and thirty-five lines are
slow—a ratio of about four to three-plus, somewhat slower than the
evidence that Shakespeare's text suggests, a change perhaps dictated
by the size and construction of modern theatres. In short, the actors
have maintained the contrast that Shakespeare seems to have in-

tended, although they doubtless keyed the whole passage down to a slower tempo to make it audible beyond the proscenium arch. The following diagram is set forth in approximate ratios:

	Romeo		Juliet	
	Fast	Slow	Fast	Slow
Evidences for tempo in Shakespeare's uncut text (190 lines)	1	4	3	2
Evidences for tempo in text cut for Sothern and Marlowe (120 lines)	1	6	3—	1
Tempo of lines as given by actors	1	6	4	3+

The instinct of the actors, therefore, would seem to have guided them aright in their timing of this scene; but, unfortunately, the matter is not quite as simple as mere ratios would imply; for Sothern and Marlowe do not always pronounce specific passages as Shakespeare's indications seem to require. Mr. Sothern's part, being almost entirely slow, both in Shakespeare's text and in his own rendition, only rarely errs; but even he gives *andante* time to the line, "The exchange of thy love's faithful vows for mine," in which the meter clearly requires the slurring of the first two words into one, and this implies rapid delivery. Miss Marlowe's part, having much more variation, has many more opportunities for mistakes in tempo. For example, she pronounces very slowly:

> O Romeo, Romeo! wherefore art thou Romeo?
> Deny thy father and refuse thy name;
> Or, if thou wilt not, be but sworn my love,
> And I'll no longer be a Capulet.

Yet "Romeo" is slurred into two syllables three times in the first line (Cf. line 51 where the meter shows it slowed to three syllables); and the contraction "I'll" in the last line also implies speed. Miss Marlowe doubtless felt—and properly—that the speech required emphasis; but retarded tempo was apparently not the type of emphasis that Shakespeare intended: perhaps change in voice-inflection or in volume would be more effective. Later, Miss Marlowe renders rapidly, "And I will take thee at thy word," and also "I am too quickly won," though the lack of slurring in both cases suggests a slower delivery. Miss Marlowe on the whole rightly realizes the *rubato* delivery appropriate to her role in this scene; but, again and again, she renders slow passages fast and *vice versa*. Shakespeare's contrast between the two speakers is apparent; and yet the interpretation of the tempo is often in opposition to the expression-marks that his text supplies.

These studies of Shakespeare's tempo seem to have various scholarly uses in throwing light on the dramatist's characterization and his style, and on the Elizabethan presentation of the plays; but perhaps their most significant value might be as a guide to actors' interpretation of the lines; for timing is all-important on the stage. The human voice allows three chief means of emphasis: change in volume, change in tempo including pauses, and change in intonation. If an actor feels sure that a passage requires emphasis, such a study as this can often show him whether Shakespeare intended emphasis by change in tempo or by some other means; and it can certainly indicate the sort of speed required for his part as a whole and often for individual speeches. Perhaps acting editions should be prepared in which tempo is marked on the margins; and then, if the actor insists on flying in the face of the evidence, he at least knows that he is doing so. Musicians rarely take great liberties with the expression-marks of Beethoven; and one might ask how far an oral interpreter has the right to vary those of Shakespeare.

XIV

The Theme of *The Merchant of Venice*

Shakespeare's earliest plays, such as *Love's Labour's, Henry VI,* and the *Errors,* are too loose-knit and lacking in verisimilitude to have a very convincing or a very significant theme; but, in time, he seems more and more to feel the social contrast of Mediæval rural England as opposed to the Renaissance life of the court; and, in *Richard II,* he seems conscious of some of the political principles that govern monarchy. In like fashion, *The Merchant of Venice* begins to reflect the economic trends of the Renaissance: the increase of wealth and the growing power of money and of the bankers and the merchants who controlled it, the risks they ran, and the whole system of loans-at-interest on which modern capitalism is built. Shylock lends; Antonio borrows, and lends again to Bassanio, who in turn must make good the original loan from Portia's riches. Indeed, this is a chain of dependent credits not unlike modern high finance.

Although Shakespeare generally shows toward his characters a wide human interest, yet he clearly detested Shylock, whom he portrays as unprincipled in business and unfeeling in his home. Shylock finally pays a dreadful penalty—worse even than his prototypes [1] in *Il Pecorone* and in Shakespeare's other sources—and not even the magnanimous Antonio has any sympathy for him. The playwright seems to have expected his audience to hate him even more than they hated the notorious Richard III, whose overthrow had brought to the throne the glorious House of Tudor. This unwonted "sæva indignatio" of Shakespeare is usually attributed to an anti-Semitism inherited from the Middle Ages and kept alive by the illegal presence of Jews in London, and especially aroused at the time by the alleged attempt in 1594 of Lopez, the court physician, to poison the Queen. As a matter of fact, however, the prejudice of the Middle Ages must have been dying out, even in clerical circles,[2] for under Cromwell the Jews were permitted to return; moreover, such few Spaniards of Jewish descent as lived in London [3] had for the most part been long since converted to at least outward Catholic conformity, and so were indistinguishable from other Spaniards—those who were not could hardly have constituted a pressing problem; and the *cause célèbre* of Lopez, though perhaps the occasion for one or two anti-Jewish plays, is too far removed both from Shakespeare's character and from his plot to have furnished the chief motive for either.[4] Shylock, the Machiavellian Jew, would seem, indeed, to have been a study not in Elizabethan realism but in Italian local color; [5] for Italy (especially Venice where the Jews were go-betweens in the Turkish trade)[6] had become, since their expulsion from Spain, their chief refuge in Western Europe. Merely as a Jew, therefore, Shylock could hardly call forth the contemptuous abhorrence manifest in the play, for that side of his character was the stuff of exotic romance; and, furthermore, Shakespeare's one appeal to the sympathy of the audience for Shylock is the latter's defense of his race and religion: "Hath not a *Jew* eyes? hath not a *Jew* hands, organs, dementions. . . . ?" [7]

Between Shylock and Antonio the conflict is not a matter of religion, but of mercantile ideals, as Shylock declares in an aside at the entrance of Antonio:

> I hate him for he is a Christian:
> *But more,* for that in low simplicitie
> He lends out money gratis, and brings downe
> The rate of usance here with us in *Venice.*[8]

The audience is amply informed that Shylock hates Antonio because the latter has called him "Usurer," and spat upon him, and "thwarted" his "bargains"; [9] and Antonio openly glories in having cast such slurs. Upon the Rialto he has railed at Shylock, not for religion, but for usury—as Shylock puts it, "all for use of that which is mine owne." [10] In the crucial third act, Shylock twice reiterates this theme; [11] and Antonio himself assures the audience:

> He seekes my life, his reason well I know;
> I oft deliuered from his forfeitures
> Many that haue at times made mone to me,
> Therefore he hates me.[12]

Race and religion, then, are not the main theme of the play; [13] it is rather conflicting economic ideals.[14] In Elizabethan parlance, "usurer" meant anyone who took even the lowest interest on money.[15] Antonio follows the Mediæval ideal, and, like Chaucer's Merchant, is supposed "neither to lend nor borrow" [16] at interest; and Shylock, like the modern capitalist, makes interest the very basis of his business.

Again and again, in Shakespeare, this allusion to usury recurs, and commonly with a fling at its un-Christian ethics and its bitter consequences. It is "forbidden"; [17] and the usurer is a simile of shame; [18] the citizens in *Coriolanus* are outraged that the senators pass "edicts for usury to support usurers"; [19] and *Timon* is full of attacks upon the system as undermining the Christian virtues and the state.[20] In other Elizabethan dramatists also [21] the usurer is a common object of hatred shading into contemptuous ridicule. Partly Classical, partly Mediæval [22] in origin, he is often, like Vice in the old Morality plays,[23] both wicked and comic: Shylock is clearly in this tradition,[24] and follows directly upon Marlowe's Barabas, who also combines moneylender and Italianate Jew. The widespread currency of this theme and the intensity of emotion that it aroused suggest that it could not have been purely a dramatic convention,[25] and that it struck closer home to the Elizabethans than a mere Mediæval tradition or a bit of Venetian local color. Like the *miles gloriosus,* the Elizabethan usurer owes something to Latin comedy; but, like Falstaff, Shylock is more than a Classical survival: if not a characteristic London type, he at least exemplified an immediate and crying problem, the iniquity of English usurers and the interest that they charged; and this theme in *The Merchant of Venice* can hardly be the accidental petrified remains of Shakespeare's "clerical predecessor," the author of the lost play *The Jew;* [26] for it is too prominent both in this and in other plays by Shakespeare.

Indeed, the question of the moral and the legal justification of interest came close home to every Elizabethan, and was crucial in the transition from feudal society to modern capitalism. The hardships of this transition appear in the "misery and squalor" of the age.[27] Gold was pouring into Europe from America; [28] prices were rising, and merchants grew rich,[29] but classes with fixed incomes suffered intensely. The rural aristocracy, whom political life was drawing to London, could no longer live directly off the produce of their estates, but required ample supplies of ready money,[30] which they had to borrow at an interest inflated by competition with the merchants who could afford to pay exorbitant rates; and the economic depression of the 1590's accentuated their distress.[31] Even miners, weavers, and other classes of artisans worked on small loans often at ruinous interest.[32] The increasing need for large capital, both in industry and in commerce, required similar large-scale organization of finance; [33] and the devolution of the Mediæval guilds, begun by the exactions of Henry VII and continued during the sixteenth century, put much of this business into the hands of almost unregulated individuals or of new organizations. The players themselves sometimes had reason to be bitter at the demands of Henslowe and others who supplied them with buildings and furnishings; [34] and thus both audience and actors had personal motives for hating the usurer.

The policy of the government was fluctuating: of necessity, it was a constant borrower itself; [35] and yet the church,[36] the Bible,[37] and the classics [38] stood utterly opposed to interest; and the outrageous exactions of many usurers had inflamed public opinion.[39] In 1543 all former legislation against usury was repealed; 10 per cent was legalized; and severe penalties were placed on the common chicaneries by which this rate might be actually increased.[40] Shortly after, in the reign of Edward VI, this law was repealed; but in time an outcry arose against the "lack of penal statutes against usurers"; [41] and, in 1570, the government again attempted regulation. Under the name of an act against usury, Elizabeth legalized 10 per cent,[42] a very moderate rate, but still declared the taking of any interest to be a sin.[43] Even the government apparently dared not too openly defy popular opinion.

This general bitterness against usury appears both in scattered literary allusion and in formally reasoned polemics. Stonex has found it in Stubbes, Lodge, Greene, Nashe, Chapman, Rowlands, Jonson, Middleton, Dekker, Shirley, and others.[44] In 1599, Marston attributed the wealth of Mecho to "damn'd Vsury." [45] Barnfield was caustic;[46] Overbury called usurers "Devillish";[47] Rowley termed them "living carrion";[48] Adams and Nashe associate them with Satan.[49] Such a popular tract as the *Kind Hartes Dreame* (lic. 1592) glanced at the subject. Learned polemics, written chiefly by divines,[50] draw arguments both from authority and from contemporary conditions. Philip Caesar quotes at length from the Bible, Aristotle, Cato, and Roman law,[51] adds the early Church Fathers [52] and Luther and Melanchthon,[53] and declares that usury enriches men without work,[54] and that since there is no wear in lending, no price should be paid.[55] Warton declared usury against the Bible and oppressive to the poor.[56] Lodge exposed the whole system by which a "Solicitour" would frequent taverns, allure "Novices" to borrow at ruinous rates, help them riot the money away, demand the indorsement of friends and relatives at each extension of the loan, and so in the final forfeiture empoverish whole families.[57] Henry Smith, the popular preacher of the day, delivered and printed in London a *Sermon* branding usury as against the law of nations, against the law of nature, and against the law of God.[58] He noted the customary evasions of the Elizabethan statute, and ended with a rebuttal of opposing arguments. Similar in rationale are the six sermons on the topic by Mosse: usury ruins the individual and the state, and all authority condemns it.[59] Such is the reasoning in Sanders,[60] in The *Death of Usury*,[61] in Pie,[62] and in Fenton.[63] As late as 1615 Digges contrasted "well-minded Merchants," such as Antonio, with usurers who, like "greedy Caterpillars," prey upon society.[64]

Until after 1600 there were no published polemics on the other side; but one can gather the verbal excuses of usurers from the clerical rebuttals. Some permissive authority was found in the Bible [65] and in Calvin's *Epistle*.[66] The custom was defended as necessary for the support of widows and orphans who could not otherwise derive profit from their funds; [67] it was widespread [68] and so became an economic necessity for all; [69] often it was mutually helpful; [70] surely money should not be kept from legitimate business;[71] and, finally, the law of the realm permitted 10 per cent.[72] The first fully reasoned defense of interest would seem to be Bacon's "Of Usury," [73] in which, with remarkable clarity of vision, he sees the struggle not as a matter of religious authority but as a class conflict between the mercantile and the agrarian interests.[74]

Shakespeare, however, took the regular attitude of the 1590's. Indeed, most revelatory of the dramatist's point of view are the excuses that Shylock gives for his trade: they are not the arguments just summarized, but the very reasons urged most bitterly against it. Like the devil, he quotes Scripture to his purpose,[75] though the audience doubtless had by memory more than one text that forbade it. He parodies Aristotle's attack on usury as if it were an argument in favor.[76] He declares that he is unjustly hated "all for use of that which is mine owne"; [77] and anyone would have told him that since a usurer's goods were got by a sort of theft, they were not his own.[78] Of course, it was this feeling on the part of the audience that justified the treatment of Shylock at the denouement. He calls Antonio a "prodigal," [79] though the term is clearly misapplied; for usurers preyed on the youthful heirs of noble families, and so, to the horror of the age, brought ruin on ancient houses. He hates Antonio for reducing the rate of interest "here with us in *Venice*," [80] and so upholds the extortionate charges of the day. With a callous presumption, he publicly demands "justice" for his compounded iniquities; he calls upon his oath in a "heaven" [81] whose law he flouts; and he claims the support of the Venetian commonwealth, whose well-being his practices were supposed to undermine.[82] To the Elizabethans all this was mordant casuistry; and, by making Shylock himself call up almost every argument against his own way of life, Shakespeare, with keen dramatic irony, implies that not one honest word can be said in his favor. For Shylock the Jew, there is no such rationale of bitterness; and so utter and thorough a philippic must surely have been intentional.[83]

Not only does *The Merchant of Venice* reflect the Elizabethan attitude toward interest, but the details of the play constantly refer to current business customs. Such a "merry bond," signed under pretense of friendliness,[84] was not without precedent in actual fact.[85] Bassanio, to seal the bargain, follows the usual etiquette of asking the lender to dine; [86] and later Shylock actually goes to a feast, like a true usurer, to help use up the borrowed sum and so insure a forfeiture.[87] The accounts of Sir Thomas Gresham show that in Antwerp alone the feasting of Queen Elizabeth's creditors cost him £25 a year.[88] Shylock, moreover, carefully avoids the term "usury," is insulted at being called a "usurer,"[89] and, with an exquisite delicacy, objects even to having his "well won thrift" described as "interest"—though this euphemism was commonly allowed by contemporary moneylenders.[90] London usurers—perhaps because they had risen from poverty by extreme penuriousness—were supposed to run their households in a stingy, not to say starvling, expenditure;[91] and Shylock and Gobbo mutually complain of each other in this regard.[92] Usurers regularly wished the forfeiture rather than the repayment of the loan; and in Lodge's *Looking-glasse,* the young gentleman, like Bassanio, offers much more than the nominated sum; but the moneylender, like Shylock, refuses and demands the forfeiture. Contemporary London, therefore, would seem to have supplied both the commercial decorum and the business trickery of Shakespeare's Venice; and this suggests that the dramatist intended to bring before his audience with immediate realism his economic theme.

Even the idealized Antonio reflects Elizabethan London. He "was wont to lend out money for a Christian curtsie,"[93] according to the highest ethics of the age; and he was not without living prototypes. In 1571 the House of Commons considered a bill to establish banks to loan money at a mere 6 per cent;[94] a few years later one Stephen Parrott projected a bank that would make loans for pure Christian brotherhood, "a good, godly and charrytable work";[95] and, as late as 1598, Berwick-on-Tweed made pawnbroking a town monopoly in order to reduce the exactions of creditors.[96] The comparison of Antonio to a "royal Merchant"[97] suggests England as well as Venice;[98] for the London merchants had grown rich, and in their "comely entertainment" were not to be "matched by any foreign opposition."[99] Hunter, on Shylock's word, declared that Antonio condemned interest "through simplicity," and that, as Shylock says, he was a "prodigal" wasting an ample patrimony;[100] but the dramatist clearly expects us to admire his probity rather than condemn his ignorance and waste. Even Cardozo[101] thinks him an "angelic simpleton" for signing the bond. As a matter of fact, Antonio knew well the exactions of usurers, and realized that if he would accommodate his friend, he must accept hard terms. Elsewhere he appears as a skilful merchant who does not risk his "whole estate Upon the fortune of this present yeere";[102] and, like a shrewd man of affairs, he does not seem overanxious early in the play to divulge his business secrets. He is, indeed, the ideal merchant, very much as Othello[103] and Henry V are the ideal of army life; and, just as Shakespeare heightened his effect by contrasting Hotspur and Prince Hal with the poltroonery of Falstaff, so, in *The Merchant of Venice,* he put Shylock and Antonio side by side as comparative studies in business ethics.

Shylock the Jew was merely Venetian local color; Shylock the usurer was a commentary on London life.[104] The moneylender had been hated for centuries; and, in Shakespeare's day, the difficult transition from the Mediæval economic system to modern capitalism especially subjected both rich and poor to his exactions. Efforts to find realism in Shylock have generally looked to Venice or to the Orient[105]—regions of which Shakespeare knew none too much and the groundlings even less: the crux of the play is nearer home; and it reflects the current uses of commercial life and the current attitude toward them. Nevertheless, *The Merchant of Venice* is not strictly a problem play like *All's Well,*[106] or even mainly one, as is *Othello,*[107] for it is written *ex parte;* to Shakespeare there is but one answer, and so there is no problem; and, moreover, the old stories upon which it is founded dictated a happy ending that forbade the logical conclusion of the theme and kept the play a romantic comedy; but, to the Elizabethans, it had a verve and realism that is lost upon the present reader. Just as the stories of the romances were changed and reinterpreted century by century, so Shakespeare gave timely significance and telling vividness to his borrowed origins; and this intensified reality is perhaps his chief contribution to Elizabethan drama. Usually the matrix from which his play developed was a plot, as in *King Lear;* sometimes both plot and character, as in *Henry V;* and, on this matrix, he built a drama that, almost certainly in details of setting and style and often in motivation and theme, shows the immediate impress of his age. *Julius Caesar* is full of English setting;[108] the background and motives of Desdemona are thoroughly Elizabethan;[109] in *Twelfth Night* he transplanted an English household and staff of servants to the confines of Illyria;[110] the character of Falstaff is a realistic foil to the romantic wars of chivalry; and, in *Merry Wives,* even the plot would seem to have been borrowed from common contemporary situations. *The Merchant of Venice* is a romantic comedy built of old folk material, to which has been added a realistic theme and motivation; and this theme, although Shakespeare has not yet learned to make it entirely implicit in his plot, obviously portrays the downfall of hated usury and the triumph of Christian charity in the person of a princely merchant.

XV

The Psychology of Shylock

Claude Dariot's *Iudgement of the Starres* appeared in Wither's English translation in 1583 and again in 1598. It was a recognized standard work on the interlocking pseudo-sciences of astrology, alchemy, medicine, and so incidentally psychology; and it generally followed the Greek tradition, derived through Arabic and Mediæval transmission, that associated these studies, part for part, with one another. Men under the astral influence of Saturn, for example, who were thought therefore to be cold and dry and to suffer from the manic-depressive tendencies of "melancholy," it briefly describes as follows:

> He signifieth ould men, fathers, grandfathers, and such like, husbandmen, beggers, Iewes, Moores, digers for metals or stones, potters Curriers, sink-clensers, & all such base trades, obstinate in opinion, laborious, of deepe cogitation couetous, enuious, solitarie, mournfull, few woords, rauenous, deceiuers, superstitious, treasorers, deepe memorie, experience, and knowledge of many things, possessions, buildings, tillage, inheritances, it causeth imprisonments, and secret enemies.[1]

This description covers Shylock's every major trait of character and every major activity in the play: a father, a Jew, a follower of the base trade of usury, rich in "possessions," "couetous, enuious," a deceiver of Antonio and "obstinate" in hating him; and thus his devious and intractable humor "causeth imprisonments and secret enemies." Despite all this, the present writer holds no brief for the particular influence of Dariot's popular treatise on Shakespeare's comedy; for these were the traits that contemporary writers regularly attributed to the atrabilious type, and Shakespeare was following popular science and not a single author. Leminus, for example, though he does not specifically mention Jews, gives a very similar list for those afflicted from "natural melancholy":

> . . . churlish, shyning, wayward and ill to please, stubborne, intractable, obstinate, greedy of worldly goods, & couetous of money, pinching and sparing, whē they haue got it, & and not daringe to spēd or bestow upon thēselues such thinges, as the necessity of mãs life for use requyreth.[2]

He adds that they have "slow pace," downcast eyes, "grim" looks and few words. Obviously, an enquiry into the psychology of Shylock must start with a survey of his actions and character in relation to the recognized melancholic type.

Shylock is melancholy in his social aspects as a father, a usurer, and a Jew; but he is even more melancholy in his anti-social aspects as an alien and an outcast of society. Melancholy people were thought to be reserved and unattractive, if not actually disliked. Lemnius and Dariot both call them taciturn; Walkington imputes to them great extremes, and says that they are either devils or angels, and that this humor is the "greatest enemy to life." [3] Lemnius calls them "churlish . . . and ill to please"; and no wonder that such were found to be "solitarie." [4] Certainly, Shylock with his "sober" house and his dislike of masques was a social pariah in the festive society of sixteenth century Venice; and no one in the play has a good word for him. He is "The villain Jew" and "The dog Jew," even before he has committed any overt act against Antonio; and later the Doge himself though bound by law to protect him, calls him "a stony adversary, an inhuman wretch Uncapable of pity." His very daughter declares that his house is "hell" and that she is "ashamed" to be his child; and his servant Gobbo loathes him, calls him "the very devil incarnal," and wants him given "a halter." Gobbo claims that Shylock has done him "wrong"; and this wrong, if not imaginary, apparently pertains to food and clothing; for Shylock complains that Gobbo is too "huge" an eater to keep, and

Gobbo leaves his service to enjoy the fine new liveries of Bassanio: all this accords with Lemnius' description of the melancholy type as, even when rich, "pinching and sparing" in their habits.

Perhaps Shylock's most fundamental melancholy trait, however, is his rapacity as a usurer; and, if his bitter ravings truly reflect his inmost soul, he cares more for his ducats and his jewels than he does even for his daughter. Antonio for years has been foiling Shylock's covetous extortions by loaning money without interest; and, when the comedy opens, Shylock has long nursed a bitter enmity against him. Melancholy was thought to be an acrid humor; and melancholy men were especially susceptible to resentment: indeed, Elyot imputes to them "Anger long and frettying" [5] such as Shylock's. Laurentius thought that melancholy might make a man act like one possessed; [6] and Lemnius declared melancholy men prone to "enuy, emulation, bitternesse, hatred, spight, sorcery, fraude, subtlety, deceipte, treason, sorrow, heauinesse, desperation, distrust and last of all to a lamētable and shamefull end." [7] Thus from melancholy covetousness arose a bitter melancholy hatred, and this combined with the further melancholy characteristic of deceit, made this type of melancholic man "a brocher of dangerous Matchiavellisme, an inventor of stratagems." [8] Thus Shylock dissembles and fawns on Antonio while he plots against him; he lies and pretends to be calculating his wealth while he is really gloating at getting him in his power; he even whines, "I would be friends with you, and have your love." Antonio is still suspicious, but he has to sign the bond. Indeed, this early crucial scene between the two is built on Shylock's hatred and deceit, sprung from his usurous rapacity, and sharply contrasting with the open probity of Antonio. Shylock's hatred, once fixed, would be tenacious; for the melancholic temper was "stubborne, intractable, obstinate"; [9] and neither the Doge nor Portia's famous plea can move him to compassion.

The Elizabethans, in the scheme of the pseudo-sciences that they had inherited, linked certain temperaments and facial and physical types of men, with certain animals. [10] Shylock is called a dog and a "cur"; and probably this is a mere term of general opprobrium; [11] but the repeated references to him as a wolf and "wolfish" would seem to refer to the widespread contemporary belief that made the wolf a symbol of deceit. [12] Thus Shakespeare, both by realistic depiction of his words and deeds and by a traditional symbol accepted in the science of the age, represents Shylock as evil and dangerous, a very pitfall to the upright and unwary.

The cold, dry temperament of Shylock's melancholy, through years of smoldering hate, has become the hot, dry temperament of hidden choler. Lemnius describes this inner burning as the most dangerous of the numerous varieties of melancholy. It is "unnatural," i.e. not innate; it "is compact and made of yealowe or yolkie Choler aduste. . . . If it be immoderatelye and too much enflamed, it bringeth the mynde into furious fitts, phrenticke rages, and brainsicke madnesse." [13] Doubtless, Shylock's unhappy status in the community and also Antonio's contempt, expressed so clearly when they first appear together, had greatly aggravated this dangerous humor; [14] for choler was thought to be especially "inflamed by the contempt and bad opinion of others." [15] His memory treasures every insult that Antonio has given him. [16] His combined humors express themselves even in his dream of "money-bags." He took this as a fearful premonition; and "dreadful dreames" were believed to be a sign of melancholy [17] and even more of choler.[18] Shylock's melancholy, in short, which belonged to him as an elderly father, as a usurer, and as a Jew, by degrees was passing into a venemous choler like Iago's; [19] he hardened his heart in evil; and only a power that could break his heart could change him. Such is the Shylock that the scenes unfolded to Shakespeare's audience.

Shylock realized his condition; and, in time, it was borne in on those about him. He tells the Doge that it is his "humor" to take Antonio's flesh; and the Elizabethans did not use such well-known scientific terms unmeaningly. He declares in evidence before the court that he has no reason to demand his bond except "a lodged hate"; and, indeed, his melancholy, because of the loss of Jessica and his other misfortunes, has so completely turned to choler that the very avarice from which this hate originally sprang is quite submerged, and he refuses twelve times the original loan. This refusal, so important in proving his "malice" against a Venetian citizen and thus in establishing Portia's case against him, seems at first glance an inconsistency in the covetous nature of a confirmed usurer; but the change in his humor from melancholy to choler explains it; and choler is doubtless the "humor" that he mentions to the Doge as actuating his revenge. Indeed, his entire purpose has become to "plague" and "torture" Antonio; and "plague" was no mild word

to the Elizabethans. His victim early comes to realize this meta-
morphosis in his nature, and calls him "cruel" and a "bloody
creditor," and refers to his "envy" and his "fury," as if he were
quite beside himself; and indeed Shylock has almost lost his reason.
The Doge, likewise, and Gratiano comment on his untoward bitterness.

Even as early as the second act, his suspicious nature expresses
such a change: he suspects his daughter's talk with Gobbo; he even
suspects Bassanio of flattering him; [20] and suspicion was a sign not
only of melancholy but of choler. Bright notes among the characteristics of the former, "feare, distrust, doubt," and he describes such
men as "suspicious." [21] Coeffeteau, likewise, found them mistrustful,
and compared them to jealous husbands and lovers.[22] Thus not only
Shylock's bitterness against Antonio that is evident when first they
meet but also his suspicious attitude toward others show that even
early in the play the process of "adustion," i. e. burning, was changing his cold, dry melancholy into a hot, dry choler quite in accordance
with the pseudo-science of the age.

Such a hatred, maturing over years, could not but culminate in
revenge; Huarte describes a dangerous melancholy as appropriate
to "blasphemers [Jews?], wily, double, friends of ill-doing; and
desirous of revenge"; [23] and Coeffeteau dwells repeatedly upon the
vindictive nature of choler.[24] Even before the middle of the play,
Shylock, with bitter rage, has vowed to have "revenge." For him,
"Every offense" is at once transformed to hate; and hate means
death to the offender. At the very outset of the play, he cries,
"Cursed be my tribe if I forgive him!" Later Jessica declares that
she has heard Shylock "swear"

> To Tubal and to Chus his countrymen,
> That he would rather have Antonio's flesh
> Than twenty times the value of the sum
> That he did owe him.

He has an oath in heaven to take the full penalty of his bond, and
has sworn it "by our holy Sabbath." He himself tells Portia in the
trial scene: "by my soul I swear There is no power in the tongue
of man To alter me." He is so carried away that he can see no wrong
in his hate, and exclaims, "My deeds upon my head!" He cannot
recant or change; and, when he fails, he is broken.

Shylock was probably born melancholy as a result of his race and religion; or, if not, he would have acquired the humor from his time of life and his profession. His years as a social outcast in Venice and especially his bitter rivalry with Antonio had heated this cold, dry humor to the hot, dry temperament of choler, which was aggravated by his daughter's elopement and her theft of his gold and jewels. This choler made him vindictive and led him to revenge; and his vindictive refusal of Bassanio's proferred gold and his refusal of Portia's plea for mercy before all the court gave evidence that his chief object was not merely recovering his loan but killing a Venetian citizen; and, on this charge, Portia defeats him. Thus Portia's procedure in the trial becomes significant; and thus the very comic outcome of the play depends, at least in part, on Shylock's psychological evolution from melancholy and choler to revenge and so to ruin. According to the psychology of the age, each step in this change arose from the preceding; and the whole evolution, as in great tragedy, was not only natural but inevitable. Evolutions of somewhat similar pattern, and likewise based on the science of the time, appear in Iago, whose choleric jealousy led to his fearful vengeance and then to retribution,[25] and also in Coriolanus, who fell from pride to choler and so to revenge and ruin;[26] and perhaps Shylock should be considered a psychological study in preparation for these later protagonists of tragedy. In any case, he ranks with Romeo and Kate the Shrew as a study, early in Shakespeare's career, of psychological change that results from the impress of situation and event on a human soul. With Romeo, the reaction from the melancholy of unrequited love to his natural sanguine temper is necessary before the plot can start;[27] with Kate, her cure from the violence of choler constitutes the plot itself; with Shylock, the change from melancholy to vindictive choler, expressed in his refusal of Bassanio's money, finally resolves the comic complication. Such a Shylock cannot be the sympathetic figure that some critics and actors would portray; for this type of choler was recognized, as in Iago, as a social menace, just as the usurer was recognized in Elizabethan life. Shakespeare hated Shylock for his trade, and so conceived the background of his motives as utterly deceitful and vindictive.

XVI

The Speech-Tempo of Shylock and of Thomas Pope

Just as in music the composer by expression-marks, such as *presto* and *accel.*, indicates tempo to the performer, so Shakespeare has left indications, though more indirect, of the varying speeds at which he meant his lines to be delivered. Some of these indications are quite certain, some more doubtful; some show great change from the normal, some but slight; some passages have many, and some few. These expression-marks fall into half a dozen types, some of which are common and some rare. For example, the ellipsis of grammatically essential parts, such as subject, verb, or relative pronoun, would show rapidity; whereas cacophonous consonantal combinations and many heavy vowels would force slow speech. Lines metrically over-long establish some presumption of rapidity; but a commoner and better evidence of haste is the slurring—apparent in the meter and perhaps also in some spellings of early texts—of such words as *spirit* (pronounced as *sprite*), *never, heaven, being* and also such contractions, apparent in the meter if not in the spelling, as *'tis, there'd* and *for't*. Since meter gives the best and the fullest evidence, speech-tempo is far clearer to discern in the verse than in the prose. To illustrate such an investigation, a single passage taken at random will, perhaps, suffice, Antonio's speech at the end of the first scene of *The Merchant of Venice:*

> Thou know'st that all my fortunes are at sea;
> Neither have I money, nor commodity
> To raise a present sum: therefore go forth;
> Try what my credit can in Venice do:
> That shall be rack'd, even to the uttermost,
> To furnish thee to Belmont, to fair Portia.
> Go, presently inquire, and so will I,
> Where money is; and I no question make,
> To have it of my trust, or for my sake.[1]

In "know'st," both the meter and the spelling show a slurring that implies speed; and likewise the meter demands that "Neither have" be slurred into two syllables—a indication of great rapidity; rack'd" is a case parallel to "know'st"; and the meter furthermore shows that "even" is pronounced, as it often was in Elizabethan English, as if it were *e'en.* "Portia," again according to the meter, has two syllables, not three as in line 166 above. Words like "question" ending in *-tion* or *-sion* might have their suffixes in one syllable or in two, the latter being strong proof of slower tempo. Here the meter requires a slurred ending, and consequently implies some speed. In short, no less than six separate pieces of evidence scattered throughout these nine lines show that they must have been spoken fast. The second and fourth items, being less common forms are stronger evidence than the other four. It is possible that some slowing of speech occurred between the items, especially in the third and fourth lines that contain no evidence either way; but it seems a fair presumption that the passage as a whole was given fast. Without question, Shakespeare's plays were generally rendered in a swift and tripping tempo: this accords with Hamlet's advice to the actors; the Prologue of *Romeo and Juliet,* moreover, refers to that tragedy as taking "two hours" in performance; and the size and the construction of the Elizabethan theatre, in which the actor, speaking in the midst of the audience, could easily be heard, support this same conclusion. Speed, therefore, was Shakespeare's norm; and the present writer's study of tempo in various of the plays, amply confirms this view.[1]

In general, *The Merchant of Venice* certainly follows this rule. Omitting prose passages, in which the proofs of tempo are but scanty, Act II of the play yields some 165 evidences of speed against some 65 of slower delivery: presumably about three quarters of the lines are to be given fast; and no single scene offers more evidence for slow, than for fast, speech. The last act of the play, likewise, has more than twice as many proofs of rapidity than of slowness. The two characters in the play that might be thought especially deliberate in their speech are Antonio and the Duke; but neither varies much from the general average, about three or four to one. In fact, the tempo of this play is in the normal stage-tradition of Shakespeare and the Elizabethan theatre.

Shylock appears in five scenes distributed throughout the first four acts; and he speaks almost four hundred and fifty lines, for the most part verse. An analysis of his tempo shows it to be astonishingly slow, a general average of about seven slow to eight fast, and this average is approximately maintained in all his five scenes, except for his mere sixteen lines in Act II, Scene iii, when it falls to an average of four to seven. Indeed, the Trial Scene, in which he speaks over a hundred lines, gives more proofs of slow tempo than of speed. Shylock is easily the slowest speaker in the play. The evidences for slow and fast, moreover, are commonly so intermingled in his lines that they suggest, not so much dramatic emphasis, or deliberation on his part, as a jerky habit of utterance, a speaking in short breath-groups by fits and starts. Much of his dialogue is in snatches; but, even when he gives a long set discourse, more or less prepared beforehand, such as his defense in the Trial Scene, the evidence is in sharp contrast to that of Antonio's speech already analyzed:

> What judgement shall I dread do | ing no wrong?
> You | have among you many a purchased slave,
> Which, like your asses and your dogs and mules,
> You use in abject and in slavish parts, [cacophony?]
> Because you bought them: shall I say to you
> Let them be free, marry | them to your heirs?
> Why sweat they under burthens? let their beds
> Be made as soft as yours, and let their palates
> Be season'd with such vi | ands? You | will answer
> 'The slaves are ours': so do | I answer you:
> The pound of flesh, which I demand of him,
> Is dearly bought; 'tis mine and I | will have it.
> If you deny me, fie upon your law!
> There | is no force in the decrees of Venice,
> I stand for judgement: answer; shall I have it?

These fifteen lines contain some thirteen items of evidence, nine for slow speech interlarded with four for rapid. If F be taken for the fast, and S as a symbol for the slow, and a vertical mark indicate a line or more between items, then the tempo might be diagrammed as follows: S S F F | S | S | F S S S | F F | S. Not only are the fast items mingled with the slow, but also all the units separated by vertical marks that have more than one item, contain both slow and fast. In the first two lines, for example, which contain four items of evidence, the first line and a quarter are clearly slow; and then, before the clause is ended, comes a sudden burst of speed for no clear dramatic reason. A line that has no evidence follows, and then a line with such cacophonous consonantal combinations that it cannot be spoken rapidly. Or take the ninth line that starts fast with "season'd," slows up within three words at "viands," and continues slow in the next sentence with "You will." If the speed stopped at the question mark, contrast between question and reply might explain the change in tempo; but why should it suddenly slow down at the words "with such"? Jerky delivery seems to be the only possible answer. Shylock's speech, though full of indications of slow tempo, is not really slow: it is rather uneven and *rubato,* as if he were constantly trying to catch his breath. This is truly a sharp contrast to the *legato* speed of Antonio.

Shylock's first speech in verse, just as Antonio enters (I, iii, 36-47) ; yields eleven items of evidence, six of them slow: the exclamatory first line is probably fast; then follow "Christian" in three syllables, a needless "that" put in after "for" and the consonant-combination "and brings down," which cannot be hurried. After two lines that show no evidence, but may well go fast, "I will" suggests the slow speech of determination; and it is immediately followed by the slurred, and therefore rapid, form of "ancient" and "nation," each in two syllables, and "Even" slurred to one. There follow a needless "do" for emphasis, a slurred "interest," and "Curséd" to give stress to the exclamation that follows. In short, the ten lines might be diagrammed: F S S S | S F F F S | F S; and they seem to show the same mutability as the example cited earlier, though here at least some of the changes have more reason. Shylock's next speech—eight lines that begin, "I am debating . . . "—starts slowly, becomes faster but jerky with exclamation and ellipsis and the slurring of "signior," and then slows down at the end with "last man." His fifteen lines beginning "No, not take interest . . ." show great variety, and may be diagrammed: F F F S | F F F S F | F S | F | F—an unusually rapid speech for Shylock. This shows six changes of tempo in fifteen lines; and, if only one had evidence for the passages represented by the vertical strokes, one might discover more evidence of retardation. Even more is this true of the twenty-four lines that start, "Signior Antonio . . . ," for clues are missing from eight full lines in the middle: F F F S | F F | | S | S | F F F S F. The evidence of Shylock's speeches in Act II Scene v points the same way. For example, the one beginning, "I am bid forth to supper . . ." runs: S F | S F F F S F S. His part in Act III is entirely prose. In short, whatever the situation, emotional or matter-of-fact, the evidence points to a *rubato* style of delivery, with many variations, sometimes hard to explain on ordinary dramatic grounds.

Surely all this was not an accident, nor does it reflect Shakespeare's inability to write smooth lines if he chose. Both as an actor and a playwright, Shakespeare must have understood thoroughly the fundamentals of dramatic style and delivery. Why did he give Shylock this curiously jerky, at times breathless, speech? Several explanations suggest themselves. Perhaps Shakespeare thought of Shylock, since he was a Jew and an "alien," as a foreigner who could not command the language fluently. But Shylock does not use foreign phrases like some of the French characters in the Henry plays; nor do the intricacies of English idiom seem to confuse him. As Jespersen has pointed out, his Hebrew background influences his diction and his allusions; [2] but what he speaks is plain, clear English. Moreover, all Europe knew that Jews, as go-betweens in the Oriental trade, were, though not citizens, permanent residents in Venice, which, like the Papacy, protected them for sound financial reasons. So Shylock's being a Jew and a foreigner hardly explains the peculiar tempo of his speech.

A somewhat similar jerkiness appears in the rôle of Roderigo in *Othello*. Here it seems to arise from the nervousness of a weak and wavering character: Roderigo is never sure of himself or of Iago, or indeed of anything; but Shylock is certainly not weak, and his exasperation and his bitterness—if one can call them nervous—are of quite a different cast. The parallel of Roderigo seems to offer no solution.—Possibly these strange contrasts of Shylock's tempo were a part of the comic effect of the character as interpreted on the Elizabethan stage. Doubtless, a clever actor could often make them so; but they sometimes appear in speeches that have no other comic elements; and therefore this explanation seems hardly adequate.

According to Professor Baldwin,[3] the rôle of Shylock first belonged to Thomas Pope, one of the original members of Shakespeare's company of actors who specialized in satiric comedy and the *miles gloriosus*. His other rôles included Don Armado in *Love's Labour's*, Aaron in *Titus*, Mercutio, Speed, Buckingham in *Richard III*, Philip in *King John*, Mowbray in *Richard II*, Falstaff, Benedick, Casca, Jacques, and Sir Toby. He seems to have had poor health. Though one of the most important members of the Company, he retired at forty-four; and he died at forty-eight. Ben Jonson describes him as "fat"; [4] and the evidence suggests that, like his own rôle in Falstaff, he was a "swollen parcel of dropsies." [5] Dropsy—which today is regarded as a symptom rather than a definite disease—commonly arises from affections of the heart or the kidneys; and the fluids secreted give a puffy corpulence to the body. Because of pressure on the chest, the sufferer is likely to be very short of breath and therefore to speak jerkily or with an irregular, gasping utterance. Could Shakespeare have calculated the jerky tempo of Shylock's part to the speech-habits of the actor who he knew would take it?

Most of the rôles probably played by Pope are in prose, and so have meagre evidence of tempo; but several of them, notably Sir Toby, seem to show a tendency to short, jerky breath-groups, suggestive of a dropsical speaker. The measurements, moreover, used in the present study apply to five of the more poetic rôles assigned to Pope by Professor Baldwin; and these might well be examined to see whether they show the same characteristics as Shylock's lines. If so, the double advantage will arise of confirming Professor Baldwin's assignments and of showing a new way that Shakespeare adapted his writing to his actors.

The part of Buckingham in *Richard III* (1593) is important in all five acts. About one third of the items of evidence indicate slow tempo—not very different from the norm in any Shakespearean

play; and the tempo does not seem particularly jerky. The part of
King Philip, written about the same time, is hardly more to the
purpose. Mercutio in *Romeo and Juliet* (1596) generally speaks
much faster than does Shylock, as his mercurial garrulousness would
require; many of his lines are in prose, and even many of those in
verse offer slight evidence; but several of the shorter speeches
show sudden and repeated change of tempo: his lines in the fourth
scene that begin "Tut, dun's the mouse . . ." seem to follow the
pattern, F F S F S; and lines 96 to 103 later in the scene run F. S S.
F S. He speaks similarly in II, i, 23-29, and of course in his gasping
ejaculations after he is wounded. On the other hand, most characters
speak jerkily at times; and perhaps this evidence is not sufficient to be
significant. The part of Mowbray in *Richard II,* which seems to date
from 1595, shows increase in slow passages, many of them interlarded with the fast, as in the part of Shylock. His first speech for
example runs: S F | F S F F F F | F S | S F S F S S. *The Merchant
of Venice* was probably composed within the twelvemonth following.
This jerkiness seems even more apparent in the part of Casca written a few years later just before Pope retired from the company in
1599, presumably because of failing health. Perhaps because Casca
is "dull," or perhaps because of Pope's growing malady, or perhaps
for both and still other reasons, Casca's lines, like those of Shylock
in the Trial Scene, actually show more evidence for slow, than for
fast, tempo; he speaks often in short snatches; and slow and fast
are curiously commingled in the few passages of verse he utters.
Perhaps the best example is from the beginning of the third scene:
F S S F S F F F S S | S | S. Even short speeches may show this varia-
tion: " 'Tis Caesar that you mean; is it not Cassius?" Here he
seems to change tempo twice within a line.

   In short, as far as this type of evidence can show, the verse
passages of the parts taken by Pope seem to grow more and more
spasmodic in their style—if only Falstaff and Sir Toby spoke at
length in verse, the matter might be settled once for all! Does this
apparently increasing jerkiness of style in Pope's later rôles reflect
the progress of his disease? Or is it Shakespeare's more and more
skilful adaptation of the lines to the actor's trick of speech? Or is it
a comic technique that he started in Mercutio and Shylock and continued in Roderigo even after Pope had died? Perhaps it is all three.

Or perhaps the evidence for Shylock's distinctive style is too insecure a basis for such theories, for style is an evanescent thing at best, and hard to reduce to simple diagrams; but the conclusions of the present study seem to fit too nicely for mere coincidence with those of Professor Baldwin in his study of the Shakespearean Company.

XVII

Shakespeare's Speech as an Actor

If Shakespeare adapted his verse to fit the jerky, almost breathless speech of Thomas Pope, might he not also adapt the parts that he wrote for himself to his own habits of speech? The usual tempo of Shakespeare's plays—and apparently of all Elizabethan drama—was distinctly fast: Hamlet advises the players to speak "trippingly on the tongue"; *Romeo and Juliet* is called "two hours' traffic of our stage"; stenographers, intent on stealing the text for pirated editions, made countless blunders in their transcripts; and the small size of the theatres, with stages that placed the actors out in the midst of the audience, made possible great rapidity of speech. The studies of the present writer in several plays bear out this supposition: *The Merchant of Venice,* and *Othello* for example, seem to yield two or three items of evidence for fast delivery for every one of slow. Of course, some types of evidence are stronger than others; but a rough diagram can be made of any given passage: if F stands for an item that shows rapidity, and S for slowness, and if one vertical stroke stands for a line that shows no evidence and two for two or more such lines, than the Ghost's speech of nine verses in *Hamlet* that begins, "I find thee apt . . ." would diagram as F | F F | S F | |. Evidence of speed appears in "shouldst," "wouldst," " 'Tis" and "Abused," which the meter requires one to say in two syllables and not in three, as the Elizabethans sometimes pronounced it. The one evidence of slow tempo is "forgèd," in which the meter requires that the -ed be spoken separately. Apparently, therefore, the whole speech is fast except for the "forged process of my death"; and, since the correction of this false report is the whole point of the Ghost's appearance, one might properly ascribe this slower tempo to the need for emphasis. The human voice can stress a word or a phrase by any one of three types of variations; mere volume of sound—the shout or the whisper—a somewhat crude effect that Shakespeare deprecates in *Hamlet;* change of intonation, especially the circumflex of surprise or irony; and change in tempo, used most extremely in the abrupt pause of aposiopesis. The first method is usually too obvious to be artistic; the second is somewhat limited in application; the third, therefore, should be the commonest means of vocal emphasis; and a study of it should not only assist in the appreciation of the lines but also show something of Shakespeare's own habits of speech.

Tradition has long ascribed the parts of Adam in *As You Like It* and the Ghost in *Hamlet* to Shakespeare as an actor. The sixty-six lines spoken by Adam seem to have been written for rendition in a tempo far slower than the average of Shakespearean drama. His three short speeches in the first scene are all prose; but what evidence there is suggests deliberation: the first speech has "yonder" rather than the shorter *yond;* the second has combinations of consonants that would be hard to enunciate rapidly; and the third has the full forms, "I have" and "I would." Adam's two short speeches in II, vi and vii, when he is dying of hunger, certainly show no proof of tripping tempo. Most of the positive evidence is in the four speeches in II, iii, in which he warns Orlando against Oliver. The following fourteen lines contain eight evidences of slow speech against four for faster, and, despite its exclamatory inflections, must go slow:

> What, my young master? O my gentle master!
> O my sweet master! O you mem | ory
> Of old Sir Roland! why, what make you here?
> Why | are you virtuous? why do people love you?
> And | wherefore are you gentle, strong and viliant?
> Why | would you be so fond to ov | ercome
> The bonny priser of the humorous Duke?

Your praise is come too swiftly home before you.
Know you not, master, to some kind of men
Their graces serve them but as en | mies?
No more do | yours: your virtues, gentle master,
Are sanctified and holy traitors to you.
O, what a world | is this, when what | is comely
Envenoms him that bears it.

Adam's part in the verse-dialogue of this scene presents thirty-two pieces of evidence, over two-thirds of them for slow speech—an utter reversal of the norm. The meter does not allow for many common slurrings such as *memory* and *Why would,* and *what is;* and most such slurrings as appear are too usual to suggest great speed.

The lines of the Ghost in *Hamlet,* being more numerous and all in verse, offer even better evidence. Eighty-two of these verses are in I, v, and six in III, iv. The former scene is predominantly slow except for one bitter passage that begins, "Ay, that incestuous . . ." and ends, "To those of mine." These eleven lines contain seven evidences of speed and none of slowness; but, even including this outburst, the count for the scene is only thirty-one for fast to twenty-five for slow, far slower than average. The six lines of the Ghost in III, iv, contain no evidence for fast and six for slow tempo. Thus the items for the Ghost's whole part stand thirty-one to thirty-one; and this is far slower than the 1 : 2 or 1 : 3 ratio that is Shakespeare's average. The slow tempo of Adam and of the Ghost are quite in character; for both parts must express great dignity, the one of age, the other of the spirit world.

Professor Baldwin,[1] basing his investigation on the known casting of several plays and on the practice in "stock" of casting a given actor again and again in similar roles, has assigned to Shakespeare fifteen other parts, beginning with the Duke of Ephesus in the *Comedy of Errors* as played in 1589 and ending with the Duke of Florence in the 1607 performance of *All's Well.* All these parts are minor and contain less than a hundred lines, but they have a certain importance and dignity, for they are generally the fathers of the heroines or the rulers of the state. Most of them are written in poetry; and all except that of Vincentio in *The Taming of the Shrew* contain enough lines of verse to allow of some conclusion as to tempo. Of these fifteen parts, eleven, like Adam and the Ghost, are distinctively slower than normal. Antonio in *Two Gentlemen of*

Verona, shows twelve evidences of fast against twelve for slow speech; and this makes him two or three times slower than the norm. Charles VI in *King Henry V* has six slow to ten fast. Prince Escalus in *Romeo and Juliet* has sixteen to twenty. The Duke in *The Merchant of Venice* has twenty to twenty-seven; and Friar Francis in *Much Ado* has thirteen to nine. Professor Baldwin is uncertain whether in *Julius Caesar,* Shakespeare took the part of Cinna or of Cicero; but as far as the present study is concerned, the question is not material: both parts, though very short, show more evidence for slow tempo than for fast—indeed, in Cicero, it is eight to one. The Sea Captain, who, according to Baldwin, Shakespeare played in *Twelfth Night* is neither aged, nor a father nor a ruler—nor even a gentleman—and yet the evidence is six slow to ten fast. Indeed, the lack of dramatic reason for his deliberate speech suggests that his speech reflects Shakespeare's own habit of utterance. Friar Peter in *Measure for Measure* and Duncan in *Macbeth* show an approximately even balance of evidence; and, in *All's Well,* the extremely short part of the Duke of Florence shows a ratio one to two. This investigation definitely supports eleven of Baldwin's ascriptions of Shakespearean roles.

The other three ascriptions present some difficulties. The first of these roles is that of the Duke in the *Comedy of Errors* as performed in 1589. The part has almost ninety lines, and yields about four items of slow evidence to forty-two for fast. In other words, it exceeds the norm in speed, and does not show the grave deliberation that one might expect either of Shakespeare as an actor or of an exalted noble; and one might infer that the novice playwright knew neither ducal decorum nor his own *forte* as an actor. Perhaps he did not write this early role with himself in mind; or perhaps he did not think to adapt it to his habit of speech; or perhaps he was not yet skillful enough to do so. In short, this part, for all its speed, may have been played by Shakespeare.

The sixty odd lines of the Duke in the third scene of *Othello* offer a more preplexing problem; for Shakespeare by then was in his full stride as poet and dramatist, and must have realized his own capabilities as an actor. The part is small, but it dominates most of a crucial scene. The Doge and the magnificoes are represented as hearing a rapid succession of contradictory messengers report on the Turkish naval maneuvers that threaten Cyprus. Then Brabantio's charges against Othello interrupt them; and they must settle these before the Moor can go to defend the island. Military exegencies give the scene a breathless haste; and this appears in the Duke's speech, which is about one to six, about twice as fast as the usual speed of Shakespeare's plays. Even the sententious lines in which he tries to console Brabantio for the elopement show more evidence for fast than slow delivery. Of course, the Doge is depicted as a great ruler in the council chamber rather than in public, and the Cyprus affair cried haste; and these reasons may explain his rapid, decisive speech; but they suggest that Shakespeare did not take this part. The roles of Gratiano, Lodovico and Montano are likewise too fast. The role of Brabantio, though rather longer than Shakespeare usually takes, is possible; for, though the father's bitterness and inner turmoil give it speed, Brabantio seems by nature a slow speaker: he often starts gravely and then, under stress of his feelings, his speech gains momentum. Baldwin, very plausibly assigns the part to John Heminges, who also played Polonius and Kent, and a change in this ascription would involve considerable recasting; and this is improbable. A more attractive theory is that Shakespeare took no part at all in *Othello;* for the play was written well on in his third period when he seems already to have been retiring from the stage. In fact, Professor Baldwin assigns him no acting part in *Lear,* which was written about that time. In short, the present writer doubts that Shakespeare played the part of the Duke, or any other part, in the first performance of *Othello.*

The part of Lepidus in *Antony and Cleopatra* is also questionable, though it is too short to show positive evidence. Lepidus appears in six scenes scattered through the first half of the play; and he speaks almost thirty speeches but only one long one. The evidence for tempo is thirty for fast as against eight for slow—not far from the norm of Shakespeare's plays. The part does not seem to fit the Shakespearean pattern set forth by Baldwin as well as most of the others that he lists; and it is the latest part that he assigns to Shakespeare. In short, the present writer would question it for the same reason that he questions the Duke in *Othello.*

Of the seventeen roles that Baldwin assigns to Shakespeare, the present study clearly supports fourteen, and seriously questions only two. One might ask whether this method might suggest other parts that Shakespeare played. Boyet in *Love's Labour's* is just the sort of dignified elderly gentleman that Shakespeare might have taken; but his tempo averages one slow to three fast; and this is much too rapid unless one wishes to rely on the same explanations that give Shakespeare the role of the Duke in *A Comedy of Errors*. The part of the Duke of Athens in the *Dream* seems too long and too important for Shakespeare; but the speeches in verse show about an even balance of slow and fast, and so approximate Shakespearean tempo. Professor Baldwin gives Shakespeare no rôle in this early play; but, if the playwright had one, it may well have been the Duke. In *Lear*, the part of Burgundy is too brief for valid evidence, and that of France if too fast to be assigned to Shakespeare. The part of Gonzalo in *The Tempest* is just the sort that Shakespeare might have taken—or John Heminges also. It shows but few more evidences for fast than for slow time, and so is within the Shakespearean range of speed; but it is probably too important and certainly too late to be assigned to Shakespeare with great certainty. In short, the present writer is not inclined to add to Professor Baldwin's list, except perhaps the rôle of the Duke of Athens.

The data set forth in the present paper support Professor Baldwin's ascriptions, and furthermore imply that Shakespeare as an actor spoke with dignified deliberation. Was this merely part of his histrionic technique, or was it also his habit in daily life? The slow speech of the Sea Captain in *Twelfth Night* suggests that it was habitual; and this in turn (if one care to climb the dangerous heights of hypothesis) suggests that Shakespeare, like most modern actors, merely played himself in all his rôles, and was, in short, not truly an actor at all, but a mere "stage personality". At all events, the parts he took do not suggest that he was a "star". Be these hypotheses as they may, the fact remains that, as in an earlier study, this evidence on the whole supports the conclusions of Professor Baldwin; and, if Shakespeare took the parts that Baldwin and the present writer agree upon, Shakespeare, on the stage at least, could hardly have followed Hamlet's advice to the players to speak their lines "trippingly."

XVIII

Kate Minola, a Medical Case-History

Katherina Minola should have been a charming and courtly young lady: she is depicted as the product of a culture—the culture of Renaissance Italy—that gave high praise and high reward to court-liness. Moreover, she is "fair"; she is "young and beauteous"; and, as her furture husband somewhat plainly puts it, she is "a lusty wench." Her father's wealth and position, furthermore, have as-sured her of some cultural opportunities, at least in music; and, indeed, she has been "Brought up as best becomes a gentlewoman." She should be capable also in domestic matters; for her father as a widower would presumably depend on her to superintend his household;[1] at least, she certainly knows enough to object to her husband's ill-treatment of his servants. All these accomplishments, Shakespeare develops far beyond his source, which merely groups her with her sisters as "fair dames";[2] but they are all to no purpose, for Katherine is a confirmed and violent shrew. She is "Renoun'd in Padua for her scolding tongue", and "Kate the curst"; even her father calls her a "shrew" and a "hilding of a devilish spirit." Her actions bear out this description: she drives her music-teacher from her with "vile terms"; and she ties her sister's hands and strikes her. In short, Kate's temper ruins all her good qualities.

In Shakespeare's source, Kate seems clearly to be acting a part:

she intends either to "match" her future husband, or at least to test his "manhood" before she submits to his control. In Shakespeare's play, though Petruchio tries to excuse her as "curst" only "for policy," her violence is really part and parcel of her actual disposition; and indeed Shakespeare suggests the causes that produced it: the taunts of Hortensio, her natural jealousy of her sister who has suitors when she has none, and her father's peremptory manner of addressing her. She reproaches him with making her a "stale" or public laughingstock; and she bitterly resents the groom's late arrival at her wedding and his outrageous dress and ill-mannered speech and action even in the midst of the ceremony. Kate is proud and high-spirited; and, as she says, she has "never needed" that she "should entreat"; and apparently either by nature or through years of habit, she has come to get what she wants by making life miserable for those around her. Her violent humor is no mere pretense like that of Corporal Nym, but an actual condition that is part of her very self.

According to medical tradition, which came down to the Renaissance from Galen, the body contained four "humors," or fluids: blood, a predominance of which made one sanguine; phlegm, which made one slow or phelgmatic; bile (choler), which made one wrathful or choleric; and black bile (melancholy), which in extreme cases might produce a sort of manic-depressive phychosis. Bile, commonly called by its Greek name "choler," was supposed to be hot and dry. Elyot says that this heat is "kendlyd in the harte," and so courses throughout the body;[3] and, according to Coeffeteau, it "enflames the blood and spirits, which are about the heart, by means of the gall, which in this heat exhales it selfe, and ascends vnto the braine, where it troubles our imagination".[4] Walkington considers choler rather a disease of "the mouth of the stomach".[5] A predominance of choler in the system, moreover, was supposed to produce a lean and muscular physique[6] and numerous other bodily traits on which not all authorities agreed.[7]

On its psychological effects, however, there was little disagreement. Choleric people were supposed to be "obstinate"[8] and yet "inconsistant,"[9] "propt of wit,"[10] but given to "furie,"[11] and this last was their outstanding trait, and led to "chiding," or even to "murther, robbery, sedition."[12] This humor, therefore, was appropriate to "All warriers, brawlers . . . theeues."[13] Astrologers asso-

ciated the type with the warlike planet Mars, which was considered
an unlucky influence; [14] and choleric people were generally feared
and disliked.[15] The Huguenot La Primaudaye, writing in a more
moralistic vein, treats choler as a sin; [16] and Coeffeteau considered
it the most violent and dangerous of all the humors: [17] the heat of
choler is "full of bitterness," and "tends to the destruction of the
object which it pursues"; [18] and those afflicted with the malady
should be treated like "monsters and serpents" whom one should
"strive to smother as soon as they are disclosed." [19] Kate's violence
of disposition clearly puts her in the choleric category; and Grumio,
in trying to cure her, says that she must not have "choleric" food.
Coeffeteau attributes to Aristotle a distinction between three types
of choler: [20] the first "sudden," a burst of anger such as anyone
might have, rather than a bodily disease; the second, a smoldering
hatred from a wrong; the third a protracted violence. Kate's symptoms point to the last of these three types; and, if this diagnosis
be correct, truly her case was parlous.

In the Middle Ages, a young woman of position might select
either of two careers: she might become the betrothed of God by
entering a convent, or she might take unto herself a human husband
—or rather her father might select one for her. In the Renaissance,
at least in England, but one career remained after the suppression
of the monasteries, the career of marriage; and failure to get a
husband brought on a girl the shame of spinsterhood.[21] No wonder
that "Katherine the curst" is mentioned in the play as the "worst"
possible "title" for a maid; and that Kate bitterly resents Hortensio's fling, "No mates for you!" She may object to her father's
choice of a husband for her, and, with a fine irony, call her future
lord "a mad-brain rudesby full of spleen [violent anger]"; but, for
all that, she knows that she is lucky to get any husband, and not
"lead apes in hell." Grumio declares that she might best be mated
to the devil, for her husband will "be married to hell"; but Petruchio
more auspiciously compares his humor and hers to "two raging
fires" that will the more quickly burn each other out. Indeed, marriage was considered the severest test for persons of the choleric
type: Walkington thought that such were too "variable" [22] to make
a happy match; Coeffeteau warned them to avoid the company of
other "quarrelsome persons"; [23] and Ferrand considers the choleric
the most unhappy in married life, especially if linked to another of

its own complexion: "But if two Cholerick Persons meet together, this is rather a slavery then true Love, it is so subject to Outrages and Anger, notwithstanding the neerenesse of their coplexions." [24] Indeed Katherine might deem herself lucky to get any husband at all; and Petruchio was taking a great chance.

In both Shakespeare and his source, Petruchio's violence is merely a role assumed for the occasion: his marrying of Kate in fact suggests that his actual temper must have been sanguine! He has a tough fibre; and, as Grumio predicts, "scolding" does "little good upon him." He seems to come from an impoverished country family; and having had his fling of travel and town life,[25] he is ready to settle down and marry for money as a prudent gentleman should. He has decided that he will "tame" the girl and make her "Comformable to other household Kates." His cure, while its lasts, is as violent as the disease, but he knows no "better" way; and, if anyone else does, let him tell it, for " 'Tis charity to show." As it is, however, he goes round to work; and, having wooed the lady with persistent good humor, no matter what she said or did, he now weds her with an equally persistent lunatic humor, and lets her do and say what she will in the way of threat and entreaty. For all its apparent lunacy, however, his treatment has basis in medical and scientific theory. The disease had a "deepe root," [26] and so would require drastic treatment; and, to prepare himself for this most strenuous role, Petruchio might well quaff off the customary sweet "muscadel" at his wedding,[27] for sweet wines were especially supposed to augment choler in the system,[28] and he is planning to out-Herod Herod.

So Petruchio takes his wife in hand, determines to "curb her mad and headstrong humor"; he rails and rants at wedding-guests and servants; as Peter says, "He kills her in her own humor"; [29] and, as if he were taming a hawk, he sees to it that she shall have little food or sleep: they leave the wedding before the banquet; she has no dinner, and no sleep that night. This is quite in the best tradition of Galen; for "much eating is also dangerful to this [choleric] humor".[30] Choler, moreover, was very hot and dry; [31] and, on the way home, Petruchio took care to expose his wife to mud and mire and cold, so that she arrived "almost frozen to death" at a cheerless house in which apparently the servants have not yet made the fire. Next day, she again complains of the "cold cheer." The weather suggests winter; and choler was supposed to have most of its power in the late spring and summer: [32] just as Shakespeare changed the date of *Romeo and Juliet* to August so that "summer's ripening breath" might enhance the love of the two protagonists, so in *The Taming of the Shrew,* he adds to his source a description of the journey after the wedding with its detail of the cold, inclement season, for this was doubtless intended to play its part in the curing of Kate's choler. In Shakespeare's source, Kate is denied mustard as "too choleric" a condiment: [33] perhaps this passage gave Shakespeare his hint for the medical treatment of her case. At all events, he likewise has Grumio declare that mustard is "too hot" for her, and that she must avoid "choleric food." Shakespeare's Petruchio, furthermore, orders "burnt" meat off the table, and closely follows good medical tradition [34] in declaring:

> 'Tis burnt; and so is all the meat.
> What dogs are these! Where is the rascal cook?
> How durst you, villains, bring it from the dresser . . .
> I tell thee, Kate, 'twas burnt and dried away,
> And I expressly am forbid to touch it,
> For it engenders choler, planteth anger;
> And better 'twere that *both of us did fast,*
> *Since, of ourselves, ourselves are choleric,*[35]
> Than feed it with such over-roasted flesh.

The ultimate insult is on the bridal night when she sits up while he improves the occasion by "making a sermon of continency to her." This is a wrong almost comparable to that of the forsaken Mariana in *Measure for Measure;* and yet it also is a part of the therapeutic process; [36] for choleric persons were supposed to be over-passionate. The last stage of the treatment was especially tantalizing: Walkington, following Galen, declares that much motion is bad for choleric people; [37] and, when Petruchio and Katherine set out for her father's house, he threatens, at her every sign of choler or even at the slightest contradiction, to quit the journey and go back home; and the ability to stand rough travel without a return of her disorder was good proof of her cure. In short, Petruchio is not merely ill-treating his wife to break her spirit, but rather applying contemporary medical knowledge to combat her disease.

The cure certainly justified this strenuous therapy; and Shake-

speare traces the steps in her recovery by showing her change in
psychological attitude. Kate's first reaction to her mad wooer is
self-pity; and indeed even her father feels that Petruchio's treatment of her "would vex a saint." At the wedding, the bridegroom
seems even "curster than she . . . a devil, a devil, a very fiend";
and she rebels when he hurries off before the nuptial feast, and
says that she will remain at her father's, and threatens to "be
angry"; but her wedded lord and master carries her off almost by
main force; and, for the first time in her life, she learns in that
mad journey to beg for "patience." Petruchio's wooing and his
violence at the wedding are portrayed as making little or no change
in Katherine's humor; but the cold and mud of the journey counter-
act her hot, dry choler, and start the cure. In the country, moreover,
she has broken with all the old associations of the luxurious town;
and the severe regimen of cold and hunger and watching tempers
her choleric spirit until she learns to "entreat." But even so, she
is not yet fully cured; for, shamed by the presence of Hortensio,
she declares: "My tongue will tell the anger of my heart"; but,
on the return journey to her father's, the threats of Petruchio to
give up the trip finally reduce her choler; and, to please her husband,
she will even call the sun the moon, and address old Vincentio as a
young girl—indeed, she even kisses her husband in the public street
at his command. This "new-built virtue" not only wins the wager
at the end of the comedy but even induces her grateful father to
augment her dowry by twenty thousand crowns. She lectures the
assembled company on the duties of a wife,[38] and even forces the
other wives to obey their husbands' orders. Despite Lucentio's fling
in the last lines of the play, the cure seems to be complete; and,
if Kate ever does come to dominate her husband and his household,
it will be in the fashion of the Countess Olivia, by craft and not by
violence.[39]

   The foregoing interpretation of Shakespeare's *Shrew* resolves
several of the difficulties that have troubled critics in the play. It
explains the unseemly behavior of a well brought-up young lady,
and her father's reaction to that behavior. It presents Petruchio,
not as a mere brute breaking his wife's will because she dares to
cross him, but sympathetically, as Shakespeare clearly intended to
present him: he is the worldly-wise physician-husband who has
learned in his travels how to meet all occasions. His methods are

severe, but at that they are more kindly than those of Coeffeteau, who would treat choleric persons quite in the fashion that violent lunatics were treated in that age. This interpretation of the play, moreover, suggests the function of the long "Induction," which some critics have considered quite extraneous. The comedy of the "Induction" centers on the cure of Sly's supposed fifteen years of "melancholy," a dangerous humor which like choler might lead to madness: thus these two humors have reduced both Kate and Sly to social uselessness; and both characters are shown as happily restored, to the joy of Sly's wife and of Kate's husband. Thus even the most boisterous scenes of the play are redeemed from mere crude farce; they have a meaning and a human interest with which one can sympathize. This psycho-medical background, moreover, is almost entirely Shakespeare's own addition to the stark old comedy from which he took his plot. The final cure justified the means; and, in the end, Petruchio has made Kate over into what she should have been, and she is no longer "Kate the Curst."

XIX

The Date of *Henry IV*

Richard II introduces the trilogy of *Henry IV, Parts I and II,* and *Henry V;* and scholars have generally believed that the plays were written in that order. At any rate, *Richard II* seems to be the earliest in style and structure; and it can hardly have been composed later than December 9, 1595 when Hoby invited Cecil to a performance of "King Richard." *Henry V,* the last of the trilogy, is generally dated 1599 because of the allusion to Essex' expedition to Ireland during that spring and summer. This leaves four years during which the two parts of *Henry IV* might have been composed. This gap, however, can be further closed; for, in 1598, Meres lists *Henry IV* among Shakespeare's works, and under date of February 25, 1597/8 the quarto of *Part I* was entered in the Stationers Register, and was published later that year.[1] Since, moreover, the *Famous Victories* seems clearly to be an influence on Shakespeare's play, and since the earliest extant copy of it is dated 1598, some scholars have taken 1598 as the date for both parts of *Henry IV,* and "few" have put it as early as 1596.[2] The *Famous Victories,* however, was presented on the stage before 1588, and was entered for publication in 1594, and so at that time may well have been printed,[3] and, indeed, might have been available to Shakespeare even in manuscript. Consequently, this earlier terminus for the date of *Henry IV* is open to question. Indeed, one might ask why Shakespeare, having begun the series with *Richard II,* waited several years before continuing it; and one might also wonder how and why a play as popular as *Henry IV, Part I* got into print so soon after it was written.

Several other pieces of evidence, more or less cogent, have been adduced to date these plays. George Chalmers favored 1596 for *Part I* because the scarcity of oats in that year would give point to the remarks of the First Carrier;[4] and Morris favored the same date for *Part II* because the current scandals relating to empressment would lend significance to the empressment scene in Act III.[5] According to scholars who prefer a later date, these allusions could have been made two or three years afterwards, but they would have lost their timeliness. Hotson, who considers Shallow a satire of Gardiner, would date the play sometime before November 26, 1597 when the latter died.[6] Chambers and others prefer the latest possible date because of the "Maturity" of the style; but stylistic evidence is doubtful in determining a year or two. Hudson, likewise, prefers 1597 in order to give time for the change of names from Oldcastle to Falstaff. Such a change, however, under pressure from the Court, could have been done in short order; and the evidences of "Oldcastle" that linger in *Part II* suggest just such a hasty revision. Since Cobham, moreover, who was Lord Chamberlain and is generally held responsible for the excision of "Oldcastle," died March 6, 1595/6, the change doubtless took place before his death; and, therefore, *Part II,* and *a fortiori Part I,* must have been written and submitted to censorship before March 1596. In short, Hudson's own evidence tends to disprove his date of 1597, and suggests one a year or two earlier. Indeed, all of these items of evidence—the high price of oats, the scandals of empressment, the change of Oldcastle's name to Falstaff, and, one should perhaps add, the death of Gardiner—suggest an earlier rather than a later date for both parts of *Henry IV,* 1595—96 rather than 1597—98.

One piece of evidence remains. When Henry V, at the end of *Part II,* becomes King, he re-assures the Chief Justice and other lords:

> Brothers, you mix your sadness with some fear:
> This is the English, not the Turkish court;

> Not Amurath an Amurath succeeds,
> But Harry Harry.[7]

Most critics ignore this reference to the death of the Sultan Murad (Amurath) III in 1596 (N.S.) on January 18; and Malone, who did the first serious work on the date of *Henry IV* took it merely as evidence that *Part II* was written at some time after that date. The passage, however, seems to be somewhat more definitive; for, as a matter of fact, "Amurath" did not succeed "Amurath," and so history falsifies the statement in the play. Mohommed III as eldest son succeeded Murad III though popular demand gave support to a younger son Amurath. Shakespeare then is not, as Malone implies, reviewing an event that had taken place, but rather previewing an expected event that did not actually take place. A brief review of Ottoman dynastic history in 1595—96, therefore, is perhaps revelant.

From the great days under Suleiman the Lawgiver (*reg.* 1520—66), called by the West "Magnificent," the Ottoman Empire fell into rapid decline; and, in the reign of Murad (Amurath) III (*reg.* 1574—96 N.S.), the army and the women of the harem competed for power at court. The Sultan's chief wife, Safie, born of the noble Venetian family of Baffo but captured in childhood and sold to the harem, dominated the state, and made a traffic of the great offices. For a time, she had been the Sultan's only wife; and his eldest son, Mahommed, who was unpopular because of his harsh yet dissolute character, was her child. By other wives and concubines, Murad had no less than 103 children, twenty of whom were boys; and a younger son, named Murad after his father, was the popular choice for the succession. After twenty-two years of dissolute misrule, Murad III died on January 18, 1595/6. The eldest son Mohommed was away in Magnesia; and Safie, who was doubtless aware of the popular movement to substitute the younger Murad for her son and knew that such a change would end her power in court, conspired with the Pashas to keep the Sultan's death a secret until Mahommed could return to Constantinople. This secret was well kept for ten days, during which he arrived, was clandestinely proclaimed, had all his brothers strangled at a feast to which they had been invited, had all his father's pregnant wives drowned, and then announced his father's death and his own acces-

sion. Popular sentiment was aroused and also the anger of the
Janissaries, who had expected to make profit out of the selection of
the new Sultan; and, to divert attention, Safie, though a Venetian
by birth, proposed a general massacre of Christians. She was dissuaded from this course; but one infers that the Christians, doubtless foreign as well as Greek, had expected Amurath to succeed and
doubtless given him some support. By concessions to the Janissaries
and to the religious authorities, Mahommed III, whose reign was
even weaker than his father's, was confirmed on the throne; and
Safie continued her rule of favoritism and corruption.[8]

Since 1580, Elizabeth had had diplomatic relations with the
Sublime Porte; and the Turkey Company was carrying on a brisk
trade in the Levant, and commanded enough influence in London
to quash the rival designs of the Shirley brothers in Persia.[9] From
these and other sources, news of affairs in Turkey must have
reached London rather promptly; and, in the winter of 1595—96—
at least until the news of Mohommed's succession had time to
arrive, presumably during February—those who took an interest
in matters Oriental might well expect an Amurath to succeed an
Amurath. Shakespeare certainly took such an interest: he followed
the Persian exploits of the Shirleys,[10] and seems to have noted the
death of the Tsar Boris[11] and to have known something of the
Moghul Akbar's new religion.[12] Therefore, writing before the news
of Safie's palace *coup* reached London in February, 1596, he might
well make the reference to the Ottoman succession that appears in
the last act of *Part II;* but, a few weeks later, such a reference would
be merely erroneous and therefore stupid, for King Henry V would
certainly not compare himself to a Prince who had failed to succeed
to the crown; and, a few months or years later, the reference would
be quite pointless, for young Amurath by then would be forgotten.
The change, moreover, of "Oldcastle" to "Falstaff" in *Part II*
surely took place before Cobham's death on March 6, 1596 while
he was still sufficiently active to direct his affairs as Lord Chamberlain. In short, two independent items of evidence, "Amurath" and
"Oldcastle," require a date for *Part II* before March, 1596.
Henry IV, furthermore, can hardly have been written before 1595:
Richard II, the first of the series, is usually dated in that year; the
empressment abuses, though of long standing,[13] became an open
scandal early in 1596; and the Amurath reference would not be

probable until the reign of the dissolute Murad III seemed to be drawing to a close. These pieces of evidence taken together suggest the winter of 1595—96 for the composition of *Part II*, and for *Part I*, a few months earlier in 1595,[14] immediately after the writing of *Richard II*.

XX

Falstaff, an Elizabethan Soldier

Whether or not Falstaff is a "scoundrell" (as Anstis called him in 1721) and a coward has been discussed for two hundred years;[1] his namesake, Sir John Fastolfe in *Henry VI, Part I* is depicted as a "craven"; but the Romantic nineteenth century[2] was generally so blinded by his wit as to overlook or try to explain away his apparent delinquencies, and even holds him up as a sort of philosopher of humour, a serio-comic critic of the militarism of his age. To Bradley, for instance, he is "the humorist of genius," a typification of "god-like freedom."[3] In 1914, however, Stoll attacked this interpretation as too fine-spun for acceptance by an Elizabethan audience; and, by drawing parallels from similar situations in other plays, he maintained that the character and actions of Falstaff were the very stuff of dramatic convention, and, as contemporary dramas showed, were regularly stigmatised by the Elizabethans as cowardly and dishonest. He placed Falstaff in the tradition of the *miles gloriosus,* the type of rascally braggart soldier borrowed from Roman comedy, and pointed out that Shakespeare, by giving Falstaff the characteristics and actions of this type, must have intended the audience so to interpret him.[4] Publishing in the same year, Forsythe likewise took Falstaff as the rough, blunt soldier of the Elizabethan stage, who supplied comic relief and linked the more aristocratic characters to the humbler figures of the secondary plot.[5] In spite of striking parallels in support of this view, some critics are unwilling to call one of Shakespeare's most brilliant creations a mere borrowing from dramatic convention;[6] and surely it is possible to see in Falstaff an essentially realistic creation[7] and yet to admit such moral lapses as may appear.[8] But, beyond some cursory remarks of Fortescue's,[9] no one seems to have brought such a hypothesis to the test, although most scholars agree that Shakespeare generally filled in the outline of his sources from contemporary English life.

Since the sources of Henry IV give only the slightest suggestion of Falstaff's character, I propose to seek his prototype in contemporary society; and, to this end, present two hypotheses: that actual Elizabethan conditions furnish ample analogies for the actions, and so for the character, of Falstaff; and that the audience, knowing such actions and such types of character in daily life, would see them, not as dramatic conventions, but as a holding of the mirror up to nature and so judge them not with nice ethical reasonings, as Bradley supposes, but in a rough-and-ready fashion, very much as they judged such people and such actions in the world around them.

Shakespeare clearly intended Sir John Falstaff to appear as an army officer. He is shown on a peace footing, with his soldier-comrades and his lady-loves, his food and lodging, his brawling and drinking, his chronic insolvency and his means of evading its consequences. He appears likewise at war, in preparation and recruiting, in military peculation, in actual battle, and in the dubious rewards of victory. Practically all the common elements of a soldier's life are involved; and, in a sense, they comprise practically all that Falstaff does in the three plays in which he appears. Logically then, one should study his character as an army officer, rather than in any other group of Elizabethan society;[10] and the following paragraphs propose to show how closely his behaviour squares with the actual doings of officers as depicted in the military books and other literature descriptive of the times.

Army life was on a very low plane,[11] partly because the organization and the method of recruiting were changing from the feudal to the modern professionalised system, and partly because Renaissance society, without the organized capital of modern industrialism, could hardly finance this new system which political necessity imposed. Soldiers, in consequence, were very little and very irregularly paid; [12] and, as no provision was made for them in peace time or in old age, they often had to live by their wits and turn professional bully or downright highwayman. As Harman says ". . . the hardiest soldiers . . . if they escape all hazards, and return home again, if they be without relief of their friends they will surely desperately rob and steal." [13] This situation created a vicious circle; officers got their positions by favouritism [14]—very much as Hal procured for Falstaff a "charge of foot"—and sometimes even by actual sale, and mis-used their commissions to enrich themselves.[15] Therefore, men of probity avoided military service; [16] and, therefore, the profession, "dispised of every man," [17] sank lower and lower in the general esteem. Doll Tearsheet was voicing a general sentiment when she declared that captains such as Bardolph made "the word captain odious." [18] Under such conditions, the few chivalrous exceptions, such as Sidney, were all the more conspicuous; and this decadence of army life explains why the worldly-wise Bacon advised Essex to seek civil rather than military preferment.

During war-time the two main types of peculation practised by captains had to do with recruiting and with the padding of musterrolls; and Falstaff seems to have been guilty of both. Riche [19] and Digges,[20] who had ample reason to know the facts, agree in blaming the system of recruiting for the low type of soldier. Men of substance evaded the draft by bribing the constable or the captain; and levies were consequently made up of "Rogues, Runagates, Drunkards, and all sorts of Vagabonds and disordered persons" [21]—such men as Falstaff's crew. If the local officials, a Dogberry or a Justice Shallow,[22] were proof against corruption, the recruiting officer, such a one as Bardolph or Falstaff himself,[23] would surely accept the proffered bribe. Thus the army was drawn from the very jails [24] and roadsides, and constables prided themselves on "a verie wise peece of service, when they heve rid the countrie of this scumme of idle loiterers" [25] Riche goes on to describe the whole system in a passage that closely parallels the exploits of Falstaff and Bardolph, and that leaves little doubt either of Shakespeare's realism or of Riche's indignation:

It was my fortune not namie yeares sithence to passe along the streets, where I sawe a companie of townes men, that were weaponed with olde rustie bills, who were haling and pulling of a fellow by the head and shoulders (I had thought to some place of execution) and demanding of one of the companie what offence the fellow had comitted: I was answered that it was an idle Rogue that had bene a rennagate about the countrey, & they had pressed him for a Souldier.

But I pray (said I) doth your Commission warrant you to presse Rogues, to serve for Souldiers?

With this demaund, the Constable of the Warde began to grow very hote and angry, and he told me flatly, he was not ignorant how farre his Commission did extend: and as for these Rogues, Vagabonds and other like excrements of the Common-wealth, he thought it a happie riddance to purge the Countrey of that infection, and by sending them to the warrs, to keepe honester men at home in their places.

I durst not render any rough reply to the Constable, least he should complaine that I went about to disturbe him in the execution of his Office: but in a curteous maner I asked of him, that if the place where he dwelt were so distressed, that an enemie were ready to approch, to made spoyle and hauocke of their liues and goods, and to make a pray of the Citie or Towne wherein he dwelt, whether would he and the rest of the inhabitants his neighbours, retaine such men as they had pressed for the seruice of their Prince, to fight in their defence and to repose themselves in the trust of their seruice?

In faith sir no (quoth Maister Constable) for we would sooner commit them all to prisson, then to put weapons into their hands, that would be more readie to take the spoyle of vs, then to hurt our enemies.

Then I perceiue Maister Constable (said I) you can quickly conceiue of the good or ill that conerneth your selues, but you cannot so easily discerne of the generall good, that doth as nearely concerne your Prince and Countrey: but God blesse the place you dwell in from any such distresse as we haue spoken of, and God defend, that either the soueraigne dignitie of our gracious Prince, or the honour of our Countrey, should euer depend in the fidelitie or seruice of that rascall rabble, thus raked vp and sent to the warres.

The Constable presently chops me vp this answere: Sir, I perceiue by the sound of your words, you are a fauorite to the Captaines, and I thinke you could be contented, that to serue the expedition of these times, we should take up honest house-holders, men that are of wealth and abilitie to liue at home, such as your Captaines might chop and chaunge, and make marchandise of, sometimes by retaile, sometimes by the great, (as men use to buy Oxen in Smithfield) a whole company bought and solde together, not to him that was of best experience, but to him that would give most money? But sir, God defend that any man of honest reputation

should come in place to be extorted, where beside the exactions of Victual-
lers, they shal be infected with vnwholesome and vnseasonable prouisions,
oppressed by the *Prouant Maister,* cheated and purloyned by so many
scraping Officers as it would but breede anger to be spoken of. . . .

For this argument Riche had no answer, and was "put to a *Non
plus*."

As the foregoing quotation suggests, officers stole from their
soldiers; and, even at that, their extravagant and disordered lives
sometimes obliged them to pawn their own arms and come into
battle, as Falstaff did, without full equipment.[26] They stole the
soldiers' pay,[27] and even the money for their food;[28] but the most
lucrative form of peculation was the padding of muster-rolls,[29]
accomplished by enrolling one soldier in two different "bands" so
that the Captain might draw pay for two,[30] or by neglecting to
report the dead and missing and so pocketing their wages. This
drawing of "dead pay," as it was called, made it profitable for a
commander to lose in battle as many of his men as possible; and
Digges declares that some would actually lead soldiers into "some
desperate unfeasible Service . . . to have their throats cut, and then,
having choice horses to save himself by flight, and his confederate
Favorites, with the pay of the dead they may banquet and riot their
fill."[31] Thus Falstaff, in spite of his cowardice, led his men to a place
of danger so that "not three" of his "hundred and fifty" were left
alive,[32] for, indeed, as he says, he feared the "shot" (tavern-
reckonings) of London even more than he did the "shot" of
battle;[33] and, knowing this abuse, surely an Elizabethan audience
would infer that he had led his men to slaughter so that he might
steal their "dead pay."[34] Such were the means by which Bradley's
"humorist of genius" attained his "godlike freedom."

If the officer on active service had his financial problems and his
dubious ways of meeting them, the officer in peace time was no better off. The rigid system of nobility, clergy, and guilds grouped the
upper classes into sharply defined, closed corporations; and the
widespread vagabondage of the day shows how little was the opportunity of the casual intruder. Society was too tightly organised
to assimilate the numbers of soldiers or even of officers who returned from the wars; county families were "in debt," and knights
were "poor";[35] and the government assumed no responsibility.[36]
These outcast soldiers repaired to London and lived a riotous life,[37]

very like that of Falstaff and his crew, sometimes begging from their friends,[38] sometimes robbing [39] as petty thieves, like the well-named Nym, or as highwaymen like Falstaff, and sometimes turning a doubtful penny by acting as "companion" [40] to some wild young nobleman or as bully for some harlot such as Doll.[41] Many a timorous soul who had never smelt powder, for mere self-protection, assumed this calling though he had it not; and so

> to preuent quarrels, because he loves not every day to fight; he heares downe strangers with the story of his own actions, & wil attribute the honor of a victory to his owne valour [cf. Falstaff in battle!]; now he that is but weake of *faith,* & wil not beleve these woders, must be terrified with the *stab.*
>
> It is a good warrant as for him that would swager, sweare, and be every day drunke, to be called *Captaine.* . . .[42]

Thus the actual soldiers were amply supplemented by the fictitious. Brathwait sets forth the whole system, and might almost be describing Falstaff and his "roarers"; the "Roisters," he says, were ruled by "Censors" or "Moderators," who adjusted differences among them:

> And these [censors] have beene *Men* in their time, (at least accounted so) but now their fortunes falling to an ebbe, having drawne out their time in expence above their meanes, they are enforced (and well it were if Misery forced them not to worse) to erect a *Sconce,* whereto the *Roarers* make recourse, as to their *Rendevou:* And hereto also resorts the raw and unseasoned *Youth,* whose late-fallen patrimonie make him purchase acquaintance at what rate soever; glorying much to be esteemed one of the *fraternity.* And he must now keep his *Quarter,* maintaine his prodigall rout with what his Parcimonious father long carked for; prepare his *Rere-suppers,* and all this, to get him a little knowledge in the Art of roaring. And by this time, you may suppose him to have attained to some degree, so as he can looke bigge, erect his *Mouchatoes,* stampe and stare, and call the *Drawer* Rogue, drinke to his *Venus* in a *Venice-glasse,* and to moralize her *Sex,* throwes it over his head and breakes it. But for all this, he hath not fully learned his postures: for upon discourse of valour, he hath discovered his Cowardize; and this gives occasion to one of his *Cumrades* to triumph ore his weaknesse. [43]

The analogy to contemporary criminal types seems undeniable; and Bronson points out that Gadshill is clearly the "setter," i.e. informer, of the band of highwaymen.[44] Wine, women and brawls—

not an edifying trilogy—made up the lives of these "foot-land-rakers." [45] The dramatists of the day must have seen this life to the full in the liberties south of the Thames; and their plays constantly reflect it.[46] *Henry IV* shows plenty of contemporary brawling and rowdism; [47] wine was the very staple of Falstaff's diet, and by his own admission the basis of his "courage"; and the relation of Falstaff and his band to the Quickly establishment is all too obvious: brawls, wine and women. Even something of his wit, for which Stoll seems to find no adequate analogy in the *miles gloriosus,* must have belonged to his living prototypes; for those who must "live by their wits" will surely acquire some verbal dexterity to save themselves in tight places. And, indeed, tight places were numerous, for, with all his rascalities, the "Swaggerer" lived in fear of arrest for debt,[48] and, like a true "gentleman of the shade," slept in seclusion all day as did Falstaff, and gave public vent to his bravery only under cover of night. Indeed, Falstaff on a peace footing runs as true to his living prototype as Falstaff at war.

Of Shakespeare's realism little doubt can remain; and it is highly probable, if not certain, that Falstaff's friendship with Shallow,[49] his love-making with Dame Quickly, with Mistress Page, and with Mistress Ford, and the Gadshill robbery, with its sequal of unpaid tavern bills, were all more or less motivated by the need of money, indeed, the economic realism of Balzac and of Dumas *fils* had its precursor in Falstaff. Most of Shakespeare's soldiers in the tragedies were supposed to be real historic personages, or at least figures of an earlier, supposedly heroic time, and so are idealised: Macbeth, Banquo, Macduff, Antony, Brutus, Othello, and Henry V. In the comedies and problem-plays, however,[50] realistic characters and situations are more usual, and especially the common Elizabethan situation of the Elizabethan youth and his hired protector. In the case of Iago and Roderigo, the soldier-mentor merely uses the youth and fools him to the top of his bent; in the case of Sir Toby and Sir Andrew, the latter at least is a fool; and, in the Falstaff plays, a young prince, the idol of the English people, and of Shakespeare, makes a fool of his bully, and when he has used him, casts him off—as princes were supposed to do according to the best canons of Machiavelli. Bradley need not be so concerned over the "rejection" of Falstaff; it was the only realistic conclusion possible in an age when soldiers went unrewarded and when politics looked

only to the convenience of the prince. Beyond the parallels cited by
Stoll and the materials assembled in the present study, refutation
of Bradley seems unnecessary; but perhaps one should point out
that the respect of Westmoreland, Colevile, and other officers toward Falstaff was, as Lancaster remarks, more of their "courtesy"
than of his "deserving"—in an age when courtesy was the basic
virtue. And lastly, if the Elizabethans considered Falstaff to be as
elevated a character as Bradley would have us believe, why should
Lord Cobham object to the dramatist's honouring his ancestor with
all these admirable qualities?

Recognising Falstaff as a common type in the London of the
day, the Elizabethans surely could not quite suspend the feelings
and judgments that they associated with his living prototypes. What
they thought of lying and deceit, of brawling, drunkenness, and sexual license, would doubtless vary with individuals. Even the serious-
minded were tolerant of deception in an age when absolutism in
Church, State, and army required constant compromises of personal
sincerity. Brawling was such a commonplace of Elizabethan life that
though some might protest one could hardly take it very seriously.
The sober citizen might frown upon drunkenness and sexual vice;
and military writers inveigh against them as incompatible with
war-time discipline; but the most approved courtesy books regularly
took for granted "Batcheler-sensuality," [51] and no serious social
stigma was attached to such irregularities. At these things, an
Elizabethan might laugh, and even at Falstaff's recouping his
fortunes by the slaughter of his men; for human life was cheap. His
peculation might arouse disgust in such as Riche and Digges; but
most people would doubtless have shrugged their shoulders at these
time-honoured abuses. All these things, furthermore, because they
are less dangerous, appear less offensive in art than they do in life;
the Middle Ages delighted in Reynard the Fox, and we to-day enjoy
the biography of a rascal like Villon because we know that he cannot
play his tricks upon ourselves. Over all Falstaff's misdoings, moreover, plays the flame of Shakespeare's wit, illuminating the comedy
of character and situation. Granting all this, however, one thing the
Elizabethan could not pass over or condone: Falstaff was an arrant
coward; he ran away at Gadshill, and at Shrewsbury tried to filch
the reward of another's valour. In a brawling age, when one's daily
safety on the street depended on being ready with one's weapons,

cowardice was universally despised and its outward signs well recognised. Poins threatens to stab Falstaff for the mere jesting imputation of such a weakness; [52] and Falstaff, true to his nature, hastily retracts. "For surely," says Digges, "cowardize in Man (especially professing Armes) hath ever been accounted the foulest vice." [53] Overbury describes the "Vaine-Glorious Coward in Command" as having gotten his commission through influence, as noisy and railing, and declares that he "loves a life dead payes." [54] Indeed, cowardice is the very crux of Falstaff's character, as an army officer, to which his other traits but appertain; and his cowardice above all must have made the runaway hero of Gadshill and the supposititious slayer of Hotspur a rather despicable figure of fun. Quite contrary, therefore, to the views of Tolman and Bradley, Falstaff's character to an Elizabethan would seem somewhat to improve in *Part II* and in *Merry Wives;* for the license of the latter plays might be more easily condoned than the poltroonery of *Part I.*

Surely Shakespeare wrote the Falstaff comedies neither to make his hero the expression of some fine philosophy nor to concoct a clever compound of dramatic convention, although some of his characteristics may come from such traditions as the *miles gloriosus*.[55] He seems rather to have aimed at contemporary realism with a lambent play of laughter. Not only Falstaff but his confederates are soldier-types of the period: Nym, whose very name suggests his "taking" ways; Bardolph, who carried his lantern in his nose; Pistol, whose fantastic elegancies of speech bespoke a bowing acquaintance with the court; and Falstaff himself, who seems to represent the old military aristocracy run to seed,[56] the foil of Henry V, in whom the Elizabethan saw epitomised the Golden Age of valour.[57] Perhaps in Falstaff and his crew Shakespeare wished to satirise, by contrast with this Golden Age, the decadence of his own times, much lamented by Riche and other military writers of the day; but his touch is too light for satire, and his attitude too genial; and so the present writer would rather think that he aimed merely to depict men and things as they are, "to show virtue her own feature, scorn her own image, and the very age and body of the time his form and pressure."

XXI

Falstaff and the Plautine Parasite

The wide and rapid conquests of republican Rome, by crowding the slave-markets, produced a plethora of cheap labor; and, in consequence, the free citizens of the metropolis fell by degrees into two classes, the idle rich, who did not need to work, and the idle poor, whose work was now done by slaves.[1] The former lived only for amusement; and many of the latter lived on the former by supplying this amusement. These latter, in return for a fine dinner, though only seated on a stool at the lowest place at table, pandered to the taste of their more fortunate fellow-citizens in flattery, wit, and women. They frequented public places, hoping to be asked to dine, and accepted on the slightest provocation. Hunger was their ruling passion; and thus their brains, in devising sedulous adulation or Attic salt to tickle their patrons' jaded palates, or in maneuvering the stratagems of an amorous intrigue, were always at the service of whoever filled their bellies. They even dared at times to spice their chit-chat with a dash of impudence, which they might have to retract with undignified expedition. So lived the Roman parasite. Naturally even the patron, or *rex,* of such a one held him in casual contempt, and, to supply a trick of novelty, would sometimes play practical jokes on the unhappy creature, who, for his dinner's sake, must extricate himself as best he could and take all in a merry humor.[2] Latin comedy, despite its debt to Menander and his school, from whom it largely borrowed plots, was intensely realistic; and the parasite was one of its commonest stock characters; for the parasite, as semi-professional funny-man of Roman life, at once the source and butt of daily humor, was the natural vehicle for the comic Muse; and, indeed, several of those in Plautus have little part in the main action of the plays, and seem to be introduced as "character" rôles, developed merely for their witty speeches and their clowning.

In the Renaissance Plautus and Terence were widely read and sometimes even performed by students in the schools. Udall's *Ralph Roister Doister*, the first English comedy, is clearly in the Plautine tradition; and, in the person of Matthew Merygreeke, it depicts the Plautine parasite, who opens the play by frankly stating that he will serve any man for "meat and drink." At times, he uses flattery, but for the most part he bases his pretension to his keep on the solid foundation of helping to provide his patron Ralph with the mistress of his momentary choice. Merygreeke has been Anglicised in detail of speech and action, and probably he had his living prototypes among the rag-tag roarers whom any man of substance might pick up at "Humphrey's tomb" in Paul's and take to dinner for Christian charity; but in general outline he is rather clearly founded on the Artotrogos and the Palaestrio of Plautus.[3] Gascoigne's *Glasse of Government* (1575) and the Acolastus of Gnaphæus also have their parasites; in the *Misogonus,* Orgalus and Oenophilus, who introduce the hero to the courtesan, seem to owe something to the type; and Edwards' *Damon and Pithias* contains the parasite Eubulus. Thus parasites had become stock figures of the sixteenth century English stage.

The presence, moreover, in the Renaissance of a somewhat similar type—often returned soldiers who had no means of peaceful livelihood—reinforced the Classical tradition. Miss Welsford puts Falstaff and Ben Jonson's Carlo Buffone into this group.[4] Riche says that such a one is a "jest-monger," a "temporiser" or a "formalist" —swaggerers and quarrellers.[5] Breton classes parasites with panders, jesters, and jugglers, and condemns them in extenso:

A Parasite is the image of Iniquity; who the gaine of drosse is devoted to all villanie. He is a kinde of thiefe . . . he breakes into houses with his tongue and pikes pockets with his flatterie. His face is brazed that he cannot blush and his hands are limed to catch holde what hee can light on. . . . He is sometime a pander to carry messages of ill meetings and perhaps hath some eloquence to persuade sweetnesse in sinne. He is the hate of Honesty and abuse of Beauty, the spoyle of Youth and the misery of age.[6]

Shakespeare presumably knew the England and the English drama of the age and he certainly knew Latin comedy: he based the plot of *A Comedy of Errors* on the *Menæchmi,* and borrowed incidentally from other Plautine plays. Terence he had doubtless read in school.[7] He seems, moreover, to have been particularly conscious of the parasite as that character appears in Classical comedy; for all his four uses of the word associate the type with frivolous amusement, with degenerate luxury, with flattery; and his "Most smiling, smooth, detested parasites"[8] suggests the worst side of such a character. Shakespeare's conception of Falstaff is usually said to be founded, more or less, on the *miles gloriosus,* though he is a bit too jolly for the type,[9] and Glendower and Hotspur are more purely boastful soldiers; but Falstaff is so complex a character that he may well be, in effect, a combination of interlocking types; and the present writer contends that one of those types that went into the making of Sir John's vasty girth and flippant wit and scandalous rascality is the Plautine parasite; for, indeed, what else is he to Shallow and to the "merry wives" and especially to Prince Hal, but parasite extraordinary plenipotentiary?

The parasite of Plautus was omniverous of good food: it was the be-all and end-all of his life. Gelasimus delighted in "drinking bouts" and "draughts of honied wine," and declared that never since he was born had his hunger been fully satisfied.[10] Peniculus, whose name refers to the sponges used to wipe off the Roman dining tables, opens the first scene by announcing, "Youths call me Peniculus because, when I eat, I wipe the tables clean";[11] and food is the *Leitmotiv* of his entire talk. Saturio boasts that all his ancestors have "filled their bellies" by the parasite's trade; he jocosely renames himself "Essurio," the hungerer; and his aim in life is to gobble all day long.[12] The parasite of Diabolus in the *Asinaria* bargains for a meal in payment for his intrigues;[13] and likewise Artotrogus, the "Bread-devourer," as *quid pro quo* for his egregious flattery, receives from Pyrgopolynices a promise of provender for life.[14] Ergasilus is "a bottomless pit"; he puts himself up for sale for a dinner; [15] no one ever lived "more full of hunger"; and, to satisfy this inner urge, he will play either buffoon or pander.[16]

Perhaps it is no mere accident that Falstaff is more, and more continuously, interested in food than any other character in Shakespeare. He turns to the culinary even in metaphor.[17] He calls for breakfast. He calls for "sack"; and likewise in sack he drowns the unhappy memory of the buck-basket *contretemps*.[18] His post-prandial delectations are chiefly bibulous,[19] and, one suspects, his pre-prandial also. Food and drink, he declares, are the basis of all true manhood—especially drink.[20] Like a true parasite, he protests that he cannot grace Shallow's board, and then permits himself to be induced.[21] His diseases arise apparently from surfeit and repletion; [22] and his figure, "in waist two yards about," [23] reveals the aptness of his contemptuous nickname, "Sir John Paunch." [24] This mountain belly—as Ben Jonson would have called it—he supports at the Prince's cost; [25] and when he boards himself the outlay is so ruinous that he has to dismiss most of his followers.[26] We are told the items of his bill for food and drink, chiefly for drink; [27] and no wonder that the Hostess of the tavern bitterly complains that he "hath eaten me out of house and home; he hath put all my substance into that fat belly of his," so that indeed she must pawn her plate if she would keep him.[28] He sponges on her and tricks her with promises to pay, which are not kept.[29] Indeed, he has good reason to fear the "shot" of tavern bills more even than the shot of battle; [30] and when he returns from the wars, the hostess has him arrested for his debts; and he evades prison only by a miracle of lies.[31] He lives off anyone he can: in London, off the Prince or Mistress Quickly; [32] in the country, off Page and Ford, when they permit, and especially off Mr. Justice Shallow.[33] Indeed, the Prince's description of his life and character, delivered shortly after his first appearance in the first Falstaff play, certainly suggests the valiant trencherman:

. . . there is a devil haunts thee in the likeness of an old fat man; a tun of man is thy companion. Why dost though converse with that trunk of humours, that bolting-hutch of beastliness, that swollen parcel of dropsies, that huge bombard of sack, that stuffed cloak-bag of guts, that roasted

Manningtree ox with the pudding in his belly, that reverend vice, that grey iniquity, that father ruffian, that vanity in years? Wherein is he good, but to taste sack and drink it? wherein neat and cleanly, but to carve a capon and eat it? wherein cunning but in craft? wherein crafty but in villany? wherein villanous but in all things? wherein worthy but in nothing? [34]

But Falstaff pays for his solid pudding by a wealth of empty praise. Just so Gelasimus promises to flatter his *rex* with *perieratiunculas parasiticas;* [35] so Peniculus, after some prompting, plays toady to Menæchmus [36] so Saturio calls his patron, "my Jupiter on earth"; [37] so Gnatho in the *Eunuchus* of Terence flatters Thraso; [38] but, most of all, achieving a very adulation in *excelsis,* Artotrogus overwhelms his braggart captain by ascribing to him deeds that no human being could perform; and in return receives his "mess of olive pottage." [39] Indeed, Plautus runs the whole gamut of flattery, from the fawning pleasantries of Ergasilus [40] to this flood-like Homeric gusto of Artotrogus, who out-Herods the braggart in his very trade of braggadocio. Falstaff also can flatter, even a Chief Justice in a pinch; [41] he can fawn and whine, and make a quick *volte face* when his impudence has overstepped the bounds. [42] The parasite was, after all, though not a servant, only a mean dependent, and he must curry favor with the source whence came his dinner.

To curry this all-necessary favor the Classical parasite played, even more than flatterer, the rôle of *derisor,* or buffoon. Gelasimus has "witticisms to sell," and declares, "If anyone wants a droll fellow, I am to be bought." [43] Ergasilus depends on his clowning for his keep and describes parasites as "needy drolls." [44] Saturio even studies books of jokes to supplement his extemporaneous wit. [45] Indeed, all of the parasites of Plautus display great verbal cleverness. On Falstaff's ubiquitous wit it is hardly necessary to descant. It is his most attractive trait of character and has so charmed critics that they are prone to overlook his many frailities. Indeed, it gives an overtone of comedy to every scene in which he plays; and, like a true parasite, he depends more upon it than on flattery to hold the interest of his patron. As with Saturio, not all his jokes are purely extemporaneous, and he welcomes his experiences with Shallow, not only for their own sake, but also because he can turn them to account in regaling the Prince with their relation. [46]

Sometimes both the Classical parasite and his Elizabethan counterpart provided humor quite unintentionally. The patron and his friends did not hesitate to play practical jokes on such a guest, who could not take offense; and such situations appear in the *Captivi* [47] and the Stichus. [48] Quite in this tradition, Prince Hal and Poins turn the tables on Falstaff and his fellows when they rob the citizens on Gadshill; and Falstaff's subsequent boasting of his prowess in the tavern scene that follows finds a close parallel in the *Miles Gloriosus*. Critics may well remember that it is not the boastful soldier but his obsequious parasite who declares that he killed a hundred and fifty men at once in Cilicia, a hundred in Scytholatronia, thirty at Sardis, sixty of Macedon, and then adds up this "sum total," as seven thousand—quite as Falstaff counted up his antagonists at Gadshill in an ascending scale that dizzies the arithmetic of memory. Some critics have been disturbed that Falstaff is both a wit and the butt of wit in others; but this double rôle is easily explained if one thinks of him as a development from the Classical parasite.

On such occasions, when his patron seemed to turn against him, or at other times, when his discourse seemed to need an added spice, the parasite would provide this spice by turning to sheer impudence, and would cry out and bluster against the world in general and even against his *rex*. Peniculus, who rails more than he flatters, sometimes calls his patron names and indeed plots against him. [49] Ergasilus bitterly complains at the decline of the parasite's trade; [50] and, like Merygreeke in *Ralph Roister Doister*, threatens to break down Hegio's door when it isn't opened to him at once. [51] Gelasimus is most impudent to a prospective patroness; [52] and when he feels defrauded of the expected dinner, he curses roundly at Pamphilus. [53]

Quite of this sort is Falstaff on occasion: [54] with a rapidity that shows his friendship insincere, he sometimes addresses the Prince as "lad" or with the intimate *thee* and *thou*, and then lies and boasts and rails against him. He plays crony and hail-fellow for a price. He dares half-humorously to call the royalty of England the "rascalliest sweet young prince" in an age of etiquette and strict propriety. He declares that the son of God's Anointed has a "damnable iteration," and is "indeed able to corrupt a saint"; and when his horse is stolen by his confederates on Gadshill, he turns on the Prince, and cries:

Go hang thyself in thine own heir-apparent garters! If I be ta'en I'll peach for this. An I have not ballads made on you all sung to filthy tunes, let a cup of sack be my poison: when a jest is so forward, and afoot too! I hate it.[55]

He even calls him to his face "a bastard son of the king's" [56] and "thou whoreson." He terms his darling Mistress Quickly a "quean"; and when she has him arrested for debt, he threatens to throw her into the open sewer that ran down the middle of Elizabethan streets; and then, a few minutes later, when she drops her suit, he immediately declares, "there's not a better wench in England." Justice Shallow he flatters to the top of his bent but ridicules behind his back as a notorious liar (save the mark!), as "a forked radish, with a head fantastically carved upon it with a knife," as "the very genius of famine, yet lecherous as a monkey," as a "justice-like serving-man"; and, after he has abused their friendship beyond hope of making up, he browbeats him to his face and scorns even to answer his and Slender's accusations of mayhem and poaching.[57] Falstaff, indeed, is no respecter of his social inferiors, his equals, or his betters: he seems to respect only those who may provide his dinner and only when they do it. He is like the Roman parasite not only in being at once a wit and the butt of wit, but also in combining flattery and fawning with impudence and brag.

One of the chief rôles of a parasite was the part of Pandarus. Peniculus ran errands for Menæchmus to his mistress; [58] Artotrogus apparently acts as procurer for his valiant Pyrgopolynices; [59] the parasite of Diabolus is a master of such intrigue; [60] and Saturio would even sell his daughter to gratify his gluttony.[61] The free and easy morals of Roman—or Greek—life differed but little from the practice of the Renaissance.

Elizabethan bachelors were hardly expected to be chaste; and consequently someone must arrange for the gratification of their desires. Even as a youth, Falstaff was an habitué of bawdy houses.[62] Gluttony, moreover, and the drinking of heavy wines encouraged such vices. To be sure, he does "entirely deny" that he is a "whore-master"; [63] but what else is his position in the notorious House of Quickly? Elsewhere, moreover, he admits that he "went to a bawdy-house not above once in a quarter—of an hour." [64] Apparently, he caught diseases from the unspeakable Doll Common; [65]

reiterated rumor credits him with having introduced the Prince to these pleasures of the town; [66] and the Chief Justice, who should have been well informed, declares it as a fact.[67] No wonder that Hal calls him "thou globe of sinful continents." [68] He apparently procures for Hal through the kind offices of the Quickly establishment; [69] and, in *Merry Wives,* he intrigues for Ford and panders for himself. Indeed, there is very little of Falstaff, either in speech or action, that would not be appropriate to the parasite of Plautus. He leads this merry life quite in the fashion described by the *Phormio* of Terence,[70] living at the cost of others and paying his way by word of mouth and other services of comparable value; and, final compliment of all to the good life he follows, he brings up his well-born page, the gift of his darling Prince, to play the sedulous ape and copy this *modus vivendi;* and little Robin so admirably learns his part that he schemes and intrigues and lies, even to the confounding of his proficient master.

Nowhere else in his plays does Shakespeare so adequately depict a parasite. Don Armado [71] in *Love's Labour's Lost* is probably, as many critics say, an early study for Falstaff; for, like Falstaff, he seems to belong in the tradition of the *miles gloriosus;* but he has little of the parasite: he does not show an all-absorbing interest in his dinner, and does not fawn on the King of Navarre. Sir Toby Belch in *Twelfth Night* has also been declared a relative of Falstaff's; but Sir Toby, according to Elizabethan custom, had a perfect right, as uncle of the Countess, to board and lodge himself under her roof; [72] and, though he bleeds Sir Andrew and occasionally flatters him, yet he is hardly a Plautine parasite, for all his interest in "cakes and ale." Iago's relation to Roderigo is even more remote from Classical models; [73] and the flatterers of Timon of Athens dine at his table in the guise of honored friends and not as ignoble parasites.[74] Shakespeare has but one true Plautine parasite, richly anglicized, to be sure, but unmistakable both in his psychology and in his way of life.

Falstaff, like his Classical precursors, gets along without visible means of support and satisfies his gustatory cravings and his delight in deep potations by living, when he can, off a patron whom he amuses by alternate flattery and impudence, by enduring practical jokes and personal insults, and then cursing out his patron and the world, by falling even to the part of lecher and of pander. By just these arts did the Roman parasite creep or intrude or climb to his patron's feast. This conception of the fat knight as a clever parasite, whose company was fit only for idle times of relaxation, is hardly complimentary to so popular a character, of whom we would rather not think evil; but, if this be Shakespeare's conception, it cannot be gainsaid. It not only fits his speech and action in the play, but furthermore explains why the Prince should so lightly cast him off when the mantle of royalty fell on his shoulders: Prince Hal had always intended to "throw off" the "loose behaviour" of his days and nights with Falstaff; [75] and, when his former parasite, with characteristic effrontery, thrusts himself forward even into the coronation procession, calling upon his *rex* like a true parasite, "My King, my Jove! I speak to thee, my heart!" the newly crowned monarch turns on him, and says:

> I know thee not, old man: fall to thy prayers;
> How ill white hairs become a fool and jester!
> I have long dream'd of such a kind of man,
> So surfeit-swell'd so old and so prophane:
> But, being waked, I do despise my dream.
> Make less thy body hence, and more thy grace;
> Leave gormandizing; know the grave doth gape
> For thee thrice wider than for other men.
> Reply not to me with a fool-born jest:
> Presume not that I am the thing I was;
> For God doth know, so shall the world perceive,
> That I have turned away my former self;
> So will I those that kept me company.
> When thou dost hear I am as I have been,
> Approach me, and thou shalt be as thou wast,
> The tutor and the feeder of my riots . . . [76]

Thereupon the new king grants him a pension and banishes him beyond the "verge," i. e. ten miles from his royal person. This "rejection" of Falstaff [77] has caused some outcry among Romantic critics, who think, we must presume, that he was quite the proper associate for a King whom the Elizabethans looked upon as the ideal of royal virtue and warlike prowess.[78] Luckily, Shakespeare's plays—and especially the Falstaff comedies—do not take place in such a land of impossible make-believe, but in the significant human reality of Elizabethan England.

Shakespearean criticism has traveled far since the days when Falstaff was considered "entirely the creation of his [Shakespeare's] own mind"; [79] and perhaps it has now sufficiently progressed so that one might attempt to disengage the several elements in this complex creation; for Falstaff, like the melancholy of Jaques, is "compounded of many simples." In part, he comes from English history and the tradition of the golden times of Henry V; in part, from the conventions of Classical and English drama; in part, from novelle of contemporary Italy; and, in large part, from the actual pageant of Elizabethan life, as Shakespeare saw it in the Stratford lanes and the London streets. From Holinshed and the old anonymous play, The Famous Victories, Shakespeare took the figure of Oldcastle and the conception of the Prince's riotous youth. As a Lollard, Oldcastle had become a sort of Protestant saint; and possibly Falstaff's occasional lapses into the sanctimonious may derive from this origin. At any rate, Oldcastle's Elizabethan descendant, the powerful Lord Cobham, seems to have obliged Shakespeare to change the name so that his illustrious ancestor would not be held up to public ridicule; and, on a hint from Fastolf, a minor character in Henry VI, the dramatist seems to have made up the present name. From the talk of Derrick in The Famous Victories Shakespeare apparently borrowed a few verbal odds and ends; [80] and some of the jokes, of course, are from the common stock of Elizabethan comedy. These sources supply the name of the fat knight, his general situation in the play as roisterer-in-ordinary to gay young royalty, and a few clever phrases; but this is only the meagerest beginning of the Shakespearean Falstaff. From Classical drama and from the pseudo-classical drama of the Renaissance Shakespeare took the stock character of the miles gloriosus, the vain and boastful captain whose bravery is more evident in an amorous intrigue than on the field of battle, and whose vanity is his ruin; and the miles gloriosus seems to be the source for Falstaff's personal appearance, for his cowardice in war, and perhaps for his gulling at the hands of the Prince and of the merry wives.[81] From the stock figure of the parasite comes the detail of his relations with Prince Hal and Mistress Quickly and Shallow and Page and Ford, which forms the essence of the comedy of intrigue; and many of the situations in the affaire at Windsor have their analogues also in contemporary Italian stories. All these literary sources are significant; but the real flesh and blood of Falstaff, the relish and the gusto of his talk, the madcap comedy of his disreputable escapades, the *verve* of his irrepressible wit and flattery and impudence, the recruiting scene, his management of Nym and Bardolph and Pistol and Page Robin—all this is pure Elizabethan realism, the very elixir of contemporary life condensed to its quintessence: boastful soldiers and parasites rather like Falstaff, thinking such thoughts and doing such deeds and living in such a fashion, actually walked the streets of London; and when they spoke they would have talked as he did, had they had but Shakespeare's revelatory genius to prompt their lines. Dramatic situations and general concepts of character can be borrowed from a foreign literature; but humor is so national a thing, and age so easily withers it and custom stales, that each country, and indeed each period of history must create its comedy anew—quite as Shakespeare created Falstaff. It is not what he borrowed that makes his plays supreme, whether it be from Holinshed or Udall or *The Famous Victories,* or even from Plautus or the *novelle* and the comedies of Italy; it is the intense reality of Elizabethan life as his eyes could see it, his wisdom interpret it, his incisive pen record its color and light and shade and ceaseless flux. This predominance of realism in the character of Falstaff over sources and literary tradition and the convention of the stage is especially demonstrated by Shakespeare's mingling in his character the *miles gloriosus* and the parasite, two types that Classical tragedy did not combine. In Elizabethan times, however, the decay of feudalism and the military changes that gunnery imposed threw out of employment the older sort of soldier [82] and reduced him to thief or parasite; and therefore Falstaff, in combining these two major elements of his character, is not Classical or Mediæval, or Italian, but above all contemporary Elizabethan English.

XXII

Falstaff, a "Knave-Fool"

Falstaff's character, like Jaques' melancholy, is "composed of many simples": it is extracted but little from the play's known sources, a very little from the "craven" Sir John Falstolfe in *Henry VI*, and very much from the actual soldiers, and self-styled soldiers, who bullied and roared and lived by their wits in the London taverns; and it also derives in part from such old standbys of the stage as the Latin *miles gloriosus* [1] and the glutton parasite,[2] the boastful fighter in the Mediæval ritual play,[3] and the soldiers of popular and of learned Italian comedy.[4] The actual London roarer, with some help from literary sources, seems to be the background of Falstaff the soldier and the bully. The parasite, who included gluttony in his bill-of-fare of virtues, supplies the background of Falstaff's sponging on Prince Hal and of his predatory visits to Shallow and to Page; but Falstaff's merry meetings with the Prince, which give most of the merriment to *Henry IV*, reflect, in their wit and practical jokes, the Elizabethan fool and butt of others' foolery, who appears both in the life and in the theatre of the age. Indeed, Ben Jonson in *The Poetaster* seems to refer to Falstaff as a "fat fool"; and, shortly after the writing of *Henry IV*, Shakespeare's company engaged Robert Armin, the Queen's jester, to take comic parts, and Shakespeare at once wrote for him the role of Feste,[5] in

Twelfth Night, carefully adapting it to his professional style of wit and persiflage.[6] The court jester and the court players, it would seem, were not unwilling to snatch a grace from one another's art.

In actual life, servingmen of good birth but narrow means were still expected to amuse their noble masters, and sometimes proved to be veritable lords of misrule,[7] as they do in *Twelfth Night.* In Tudor comedy the fool was rarely a professional court jester, but rather a natural born fool like Launcelot Gobbo and Sir Andrew Aguecheek; and he is portrayed with growing realism.[8] But Falstaff is a sort of unofficial court jester to young Prince Hal; he is the dean of the Joyous Society to which royal heir loaned countenance, "Fol ça, fol là, fol tout par tout." [9] He is the recognized subject for any practical joke; he is called "fat fool" and "a Great Fool" and "a fool and jester." From the very outset of *Henry IV, Part I,* he is the constant subject of his Prince's amused contempt and foil to his Prince's wit. According to Elizabethan dramaturgy, a character's chief trait should appear at his initial entrance; and, in the first lines of the first scene in which Falstaff comes on the stage in *Henry IV, Part II,* he calls himself the common butt of humor, and declares, "Men of all sorts take a pride to gird at me." When he mentions his "dagger of lath," he seems to compare himself to the Vice, or Fool, of early comedy; and, like the Vice, he is much more a moving force in the plot than most of the stupidly funny clowns and country jakes of previous Elizabethan drama; [10] and, also like Vice, he prompts the hero (Prince Hal) to evil courses. Rabelaisian laughter is his livelihood, and rascally foolery, his stock-in-trade: he implies that only wine saves him from being an utter fool and coward,[11] and that he depends entirely on others' willingness to laugh; [12] like Tarleton, the Queen's former jester, he again and again saves himself by witty repartee,[13] as Poins fears that he may do after the *contretemps* in Mistress Quickly's house; [14] and he looks forward to keeping his princely patron "in continual laughter" for weeks over the worthy Justice Shallow.[15] Falstaff, therefore, seems *primâ facie* to belong in the fool tradition; and, though Ward, in treating the type, omits him,[16] Miss Welford notes the parallel between him and Ben Jonson's Garlo Buffone,[17] and even declares him "the typical buffon, seen, understood and interpreted by Shakespeare." [18] This view of Falstaff, moreover, as both the source and the butt of foolery has support in the original casting of the rôle: Thomas Pope, who seems to have created the part, had for years been playing the type of sometimes stupid, often knavish, funny man; he seems to have done Don Armado, Dromio, Speed, and Peter Quince, and was soon to do Sir Toby Belch.[19] By 1596, Pope had apparently taken on portly middle age; and the part of Falstaff may well have been created to capitalize his comic talents together with his girth. Miss Busby in a well documented study has collected some twenty traits of character and actions and turns of speech that belong to the Elizabethan stage fool; and, in the face of the Romantic critical tradition, which would make Falstaff a serious philosopher and even a pathetic figure, at least in the *Henry* plays,[20] the present study proposes to interpret him, in all three plays, as the type of knavish fool, in tastes and character and action and very turn of phrase.

The Elizabethan fool, like the Classical parasite, delighted in the fruits—not to mention the wines and other pleasures—of good living;[21] and Falstaff's concept of high life comprized a plentitude of capons and sugared sack. In *Henry IV, Part I,* he is introduced as not only fat-bellied but "fat-witted with drinking"; and the Prince says that Sir John cares only for "cups of sack . . . capons . . . bawds, and leaping houses." Poins, when he enters, reiterates the Prince's quips at Falstaff's notorious guste for "a cup of Madeira and a cold capon's leg." Surely the chivalrous and philosophical Falstaff of Professor Bradley's interpretation is not the Falstaff that a competent Elizabethan dramatist would introduce thus to his audience. Shortly, it appears that Falstaff is not only fat but too lazy to move without a horse. His preoccupation with meat and drink appears repeatedly; he is "ye fat guts" and "wool-sack"; and his unpaid tavern reckoning consists mainly of two gallons of sack. These traits are evident also in *Part II:* Falstaff enjoys to the full the pleasures that Mistress Quickly and Doll Tearsheet provide; he genially expands at the solid satisfactions of Shallow's festive board, and even helps himself, uninvited, to his host's venison.[22] In *Merry Wives* he seeks creature comforts by pursuing Mistress Page and Mistress Ford, and delights in Master Brook's gratuities. These same predilections make his journey in the foul buckbasket and sousing in the Thames especially obnoxious to him. Indeed, Falstaff, if not a *gourmet,* at least can gormandize.

He follows the Elizabethan fool [23] also in his fondness for fine clothes and the exalted social rank they were supposed to signalize. In *Part I* the Prince twits him with his delight in a "fair hot wench in flame-coloured taffeta"; and, in *Part II,* he promises his Doll luxurious apparel. For himself, he must have twenty-two yards of satin; he patronizes "Master Smooth's the silkman" to provide the necessities of war; and Mistress Quickly must pawn even her hangings and silver to pay for these indispensables. At the coronation, he laments the lack of "new liveries" for his following; and in *Merry Wives* he has fallen so low that his Page Robin is reduced to chicanery to get himself "a new doublet and hose." For all his shabbiness, however, Falstaff, like other stage fools,[24] proclaims his gentility: he says that he started service as a page in the exalted House of Norfolk; and, at the end of *Part I,* he promises to reform and live as a nobleman should; but his subsequent career belies this resolution; for, in *Part II,* though he declares himself a "gentleman" and counts himself among "men of merit," he is no better than before. In *Merry Wives* he plays up his knighthood to Mistress Page and to Mistress Ford, as he had earlier done to Mistress Quickly, and swears that he longs to make Mistress Ford his "lady." With blatant conceit, he fancies that they yearn for his attentions; and he refers to his "honour," and blandly asseverates "as I am a gentleman." Indeed, his preeminence of birth and knightly prowess do not stick fiery off, and are revealed only in vain repetitions. He aspires to the food and clothes and social status that his barren knighthood had not supplied—for knighthood was no longer practical—; and such aspirations are quite consonant with the servingman-companion of Elizabethan life and the fool of the Elizabethan stage.

Falstaff's fine food and fine clothes—when he can get them—and his affected airs and graces, all show forth in comic disparity with his cowardly braggadocio; and this ironic contrast also appears in the stage fool:[25] quite Falstaffian in this regard is Swash in the *Blind Beggar;* and the fool in *Solimon and Persida* rifles his enemy's body, as Falstaff does at the Battle of Shrewsbury; and Strembo in *Locrine,* like Falstaff, saves himself in the midst of the fight by pretending to be dead.[26] Indeed, Falstaff's cowardice is so rank and gross in nature that only the hardiest critic could gainsay it. Again and again, in *Henry IV, Part I,* he eats his words: he calls Poins a thief and a rascal for stealing his horse, and yet dares not "strike him," even though the Prince dubs him "coward." He is afraid even of the harmless travellers that he plans to rob, but when they surrender, calls them vile names. When Poins and Hal attack him in disguise, he manages to run; and Poins gives climax to the scene by exclaiming, "How the rogue roared!" Later he has the impudence to brag of his bravery in the rôle of highwayman; and Hal confounds him with the truth, and calls him a "natural coward"; but he dares take no offense. Elsewhere, he calls Poins a coward; but even Poins can make him eat his words. When he thinks Hal cannot hear, he boasts that he can cudgel him—and then hastens to retract when he learns that Hal has heard him. He pretends to the Prince that he has killed Percy in battle; but, unfortunately, the Prince had done it himself, and so unmasks the lie. In *Part II,* he allows even the servant of the Chief Justice—a signal insult from an underling— to tell him that he lies in his throat; and any such remark should have meant a duel with an equal or a thrashing for an inferior.[27] He boasts, and boasts again; and well may the Chief Justice refer to his "impudent sauciness." He abuses Hal and Poins even to the notorious Doll, and then whines to the Prince that he meant "no abuse"; and the Prince declares him moved by "pure fear and entire cowardice." In *Merry Wives,* after bragging what he will do to Ford, he "quaked with fear" in the basket of foul linen, and suffered an "intolerable fright." Again he is in terror of Ford, and yet in the end has the assurance to brag of his bravery. Indeed, the only thing that saves him at all is his "admirable dexterity of wit"; and often that wears thin. In short, he is an impudent paltroon, whose cowardice is equalled only by his clever effrontery.

Not only Falstaff's character but also the situations and actions in which he is engaged show his relationship to the fool. His huge girth and awkward motion make his attempts to run and fight at Gadshill and at Shrewsbury utterly ridiculous; and, when he pretends to die in battle, his getting down and getting up again must almost equal the acrobatic tricks that formed part of a fool's repertory.[28] He doubtless left to his subordinates the actual stealing of Shallow's deer. The Vice had started as a clever intriguer personifying Satan, but had long since become the butt of others' wit. In the Gadshill episode, Falstaff is in the stage situation of the duper duped; again he is the dupe of the Prince and Poins at Mistress Quickly's; he does, to be sure, make a dupe of Shallow; but, in most of *Merry Wives* he is gulled to the top of his bent until he cannot take refuge even in hilarity. Here he appears as the ridiculous lover, a common role of the stage fool, and, like Trotter in Greene's *Fair Em,* conducts his presumptuous wooing in a grandiloquent style. He tries to catch the merry wives with the same bait that was successful with the notorious Dame Quickly, and is repulsed with indignity. The stage fool was fond of song and dancing; and Bunch, for instance, in *The Weakest Goeth to the Wall* brightens his speech with gems borrowed from contemporary broadside balladry. Probably Pope was no singer; but Falstaff shows this trait by calling for a "bawdy song"; he thrice praises the singing of Master Silence; he himself, when tipsy, attempts a rendering of "When Arthur first in court"; and he goes to the expense of music for his dinner of reconciliation with Mistress Quickly. Falstaff, in short, like the conventional Elizabethan fool, amuses by comic acrobatics and by songs, by practical jokes of which he himself is often the victim, and by the rôle of comic lover; and, in all these situations, he is the Elizabethan fool.

The upper classes, however, depended for their amusement chiefly on verbal legerdemain. Falstaff's recipe for humor was "a lie with a slight oath and a jest with a sad brow"; and his "jest" was like to be some whimsey of style or verbiage. On the stage the fool rarely used blank verse or elevated discourse, and generally spoke in either prose or doggrel rhyme. Falstaff, likewise, uses prose, even when the Prince addresses him in verse; he uses prose to the Lord Chief Justice and to Prince John and to Coleville, though they are using meter. Once he speaks two lines of blank verse—when he is ridiculing Pistol's extravagant style of speech; and once he breaks into rhyme, "Your brooches, pearls and ouches," but continues in prose. Later he lapses into a few lines of blank verse in joyous anticipation of his success with the merry wives; and his love-letters close with a quintet in Skeltonic rhyme. Indeed, of the hundreds of lines that Falstaff speaks in these three plays, less than a dozen are blank verse. This use of prose makes all the more incongruous the passages of extravagant emotion that the fool drives to the point of parody. He indulges in crocodile laments, like Falstaff's elegy on his vanished virtue. The fat knight promises a mock-passionate speech "in King Cambyses' vein," and travesties the King speaking "in passion." In *Merry Wives* he talks to Mistress Ford in high astounding terms that cannot be sincere, and even at the end still addresses her as his "doe." The incongruity of these ecstasies is aggravated both in the fool and in Falstaff by swift transitions to slangy vernacular; and, one feels that his flights into the grandiose exist largely for such anticlimaxes. Pistol was a master of this technique; but Falstaff, as in the other devices of foolery, was a competent practitioner. Mistress Quickly calls him a good actor; and truly he had virtuosity of style.

Indeed, age cannot wither nor custom stale his infinite variety, which ranges from crass absurdity to witty repartee, from word-play to mock-moralizing proverbs. Sir John is fertile in the invention of ridiculous explanations and anecdotes, such as characterized the fool: for gross and circumstantial falsehood is his only escape from the chronic difficulties of his way of life. He swears and declares that he fought with dozens of opponents at Gadshill; he insists that his pocket was picked of (purely imaginary) valuables at the tavern; and he invents out of whole cloth an anecdote against Poins, whom he seems to regard as his rival in Hal's esteem. The mock "bill" was another convention of Elizabethan foolery; and Falstaff's letter to Hal is a sort of comic proclamation. The ludicrous monologue and the apostrophe to an inanimate object were standard conventions of the type; and Falstaff uses them three times in *Part I,* twice in *Part II,* and again three times in *Merry Wives:* he soliloquizes, for example, on the abuse of the King's press, on his page, on Shallow, on wine, on the buckbasket episode and on love. Both in life and on the stage, telling repartee was the regular refuge of the fool; and, in all three plays, Falstaff furnishes a flood of instances. The use of ridiculous nicknames, a common device of the fool, appears especially in *Part I:* Falstaff calls the Prince, "you starveling, you elf-skin, you dried neat's tongue, you bull's pizzle, you stock-fish . . . you taylor's yard, you sheath, you bow-case, you vile standing tuck . . ." He calls Bardolph "Knight of the Burning Lamp," alluding to his rubious nose, and has pat soubriquets also for the Hostess, Robin, and Pistol. Indeed, Falstaff is the pure Elizabethan fool in his use of fictitious anecdote and parody, in his ludicrous apostrophes and monologues, in his keen repartee, and in the scurrilous names that he foists on those about him.

Of all types of wit, the Elizabethans most relished word-play and such stylistic trickery as comic alliteration and mock-Euphuistic balance. Strumbo in *Locrine* parodies Euphuism; [29] and alliteration was a common device of fools. Again and again, Falstaff plays on a letter; and his discussion of camomile in *Part I*, and his balanced aphorisms and outlandish allusions in the *Merry Wives*, are redolent of Lyly's masterpiece. Like a true fool, he preverts, repeats, and puns on words, plays on the names of the recruits in *Part II*, and persists in misunderstanding the Chief Justice; and, in *Merry Wives*, he achieves a neat double meaning with the word *angels*. The slip-of-the-tongue, often intentional, he generally leaves to Mistress Quickly; but, in *Part I*, he seems to make one on "grace." Paradox and oxymoron were commonplaces of the fool's repertoire; and Falstaff repeatedly indulges in ironic contradictions: Hal is the "rascalliest sweet young prince," and, the knight attributes all his own vices to him. Falstaff's description of himself as "kind" and "true" and "valiant," and "old in judgment and understanding," forms a very climax of paradox; and his characterization of Mistress Quickly as "a poor mad soul" who thinks that he will marry her, his pretense that he has "checked" Hal for boxing the ear of the Chief Justice, and his declaration of deep love to Mistress Ford, all these are good, not to say extravagant, examples. Moreover, like the generality of fools, Falstaff chops logic and parodies the syllogism. Repeatedly, in all three plays, he amply displays the verbal quips and cranks that the Elizabethan audience associated with the stage fool and the dissolute companion of youthful noblemen.

At times, Falstaff lapses into a mock-seriousness that has been deceptive to some moderns; and his serio-comic proverbs and bits of moralizing and of satire are also characteristic of his type. The conventional fool was much given to proverbs, often misapplied; and Falstaff turns to his purpose such ancient sayings as "watch and pray" [30]—wrested from its original Benedictine meaning. Sometimes, he coins an aphorism *ad hoc:* " 'Tis no sin for a man to labour in his vocation"; "The better part of valour is discretion"; ". . . skill in the weapon is nothing without sack"; and "To wake a wolf is as bad as to smell a fox." He uses tags of Latin, often comically, "ecce signum," "memento mori," and "ignis fatuus," the last applied to Bardolph's face. Just as the fool often insisted on his own wisdom, [31] so Falstaff paraded the moralistic shreds and patches that he had perhaps inherited from his Lollard forebear Oldcastle. At times, his language has an unctuous smack of Holy Writ: "trouble me no more with vanity"; he comments on "villanous man" and the "bad world"; and he is as ready to repent as Robert Greene, especially when he finds it convenient to turn informer on the Prince's escapades. He takes a high moral tone against giving his tailor security for the clothes he has ordered, and says that he has lost his voice with "singing of anthems." Thus he is a sort of satire on himself, and provides satiric slurs at other characters, at bourgeois virtue, and at the social *status quo*. This is all quite in the vein of the Elizabethan fool. He satirizes Hal as Crown Prince; he weeps crocodile tears that "virtue" is disregarded "in these costermonger times"; and, all the while, he is himself a living diatribe on the degeneration of feudalism and army life.

In short, not only Falstaff's way of life and livelihood, his comparisons of himself to a Vice, his love of good living, and his parade of gentility and of affected airs and graces, his flagrant cowardice, his huge girth and awkwardness of motion, his situations as comic soldier and comic lover, but also his whole technique of speech, his prose occasionally mixed with doggrel rhyme and his mock-poetic flights, his absurd stories and grandiose and petty lies, his word-play and fine sayings in pseudo-moralistic vein, all these stamp him as the Elizabethan fool *par excellence*, to be so recognized by any theatre-goer of the age. Nearly all of these characteristics appear in all of his three plays; and he has hardly an action or a speech—and he speaks nearly two thousand lines—that does not have its parallel in the stage fool of the day; and, *vice versâ*, there is not a single trait of the stage-fool that Falstaff does not illustrate. He is *miles gloriosus* and parasite and glutton, and furthermore, he is, as Shakespeare's words repeatedly declare him, a "great fool" and "a fool and jester."

The Elizabethan fool shows several variations and something of an evolution. *Wit Without Money* notes three sorts of fools: "An innocent, a knave-fool, a fool politic." [32] Such stupid bumpkins as Launce and Gobbo belong in the first class; the court fools, Feste and the Fool in *Lear*, belong in the third; and Falstaff is the "knave-fool," like the *picaro* of Spanish fiction, fittingly introduced as at odds with "old father antic the law." Falstaff the knave derives from his backgrounds as *miles gloriosus* and especially as actual London roarer and Elizabethan soldier; Falstaff the fool derives from the Classical parasite and from the Renaissance fool in fiction and in life. Indeed, so broadly is his part conceived that he fits most of the items in *The XXV Orders of Fools* described in a contemporary broadside ballad: [33] he is aged; he causes ill reports; he disdains wisdom, yet preaches to others; he fails to provide in youth for his old age; he flatters and cogs and boasts. He is all three types of fool emphasized in Armin's *Nest of Ninnies*. He is sinner, social critic, and merrymaker. The stage portrayal of the fool was in transition from the stupid rustic who was a "mere booby" to "the more pretentious clown"; [34] and Falstaff seems to show the consummation of this change. The fat knight is no country clown, but rather one of Lyly's (or Shakespeare's) jesting pages come to man's estate, and reduced by the decline of feudalism to shifts and chicaneries for a livelihood. And his page Robin may well be a depiction of his own early life and bringing up. Such a theory seems to find support in the original casting of the part; for Thomas Pope had played the comic roles of Dromio and Speed and Quince and Fluellen; and apparently Shakespeare created Falstaff for this seasoned actor of broad comedy who had grown too old and portly for more lightsome parts.

The Romantic concept of Falstaff ignored, or tried to explain away, his obvious vices and poltroonery, and interpreted him, in the words of Professor Bradley, as a "philosopher of humor." In 1914, Professor Stoll attacked this theory, and showed that the Elizabethans would have recognized him as the *miles gloriosus*, and therefore as knave and coward. Since then, a series of studies have supplied yet other types of background, all tending to a derogatory view of his character: he is not only the boastful soldier of the stage but also the parasite and the glutton; he is not only a stage-convention but also a realistic figure drawn from London life, an old man trying to maintain his youthful *verve* and follies by the drinking of sweet wines, [35] a disreputable officer in the corrupt transition from feudal to modern military life. [36] The present paper presents another phase of this effort to recover Falstaff's background in contemporary life and on the stage; and, like the others, it reveals him as far removed from the good and great "philosopher" that Professor Bradley pictures. That the Elizabethans could have admired his code of honor, public or private, has already been sufficiently exploded: in the present study, he appears not only as a knave but as a "fool"; and his foolery coincides in word and action with the stage fools of the age, and, as far as one may judge, with the actual lords of misrule who catered to the great, such as

Somerset and the three knights who were "Master Fools" to James I.[37] Just such was his relation with Prince Hal; and it seems unthinkable that even the densest dullard of the Elizabethan audience would mistake Strumbo or Somerset for Plato or Aquinas, or even for Shakespeare's Prospero or Gonzalo.

XXIII

Old Age in Falstaff, Shallow, and the Rest

Shakespeare's greatness especially inheres in his true and vivid portrayal of human character—that most complex and subtle thing in all creation!—and, therefore the two most vital backgrounds for Shakespearean research are the social and the psychological; for the former expresses man in his outward relations with other men, and the latter in his thoughts and feelings and the workings of his inner life. The present writer and his students have long labored in these two fertile fields, and have tried to fill in these backgrounds for most of Shakespeare's more complex characters, not on the basis of mere modern guesswork but according to the social conditions and the psychological theories of Shakespeare's own generation. Not only individual characters, however, should be treated in this way, but also the evolution of Shakespeare's portrayal of a given type: the constable, the statesman, the choleric soldier, and the melancholy unrequited lover. Somewhat in this latter class the present study belongs; for it proposes to survey Shakespeare's treatment of old age, to define the concept both in contemporary fact and in contemporary theory, to show his portrayal of its physical and its mental aspects, and to trace through the chronology of his plays his deepening insight into a state of life that he himself hardly lived to experience.

In the tumultuous days of Queen Elizabeth, drama generally
concerned young, handsome, active persons, the lover, the soldier,
the courtier, and the prince; and, even when, as in *Romeo and Juliet,*
parents have a part of some importance, they are not necessarily
very old; for, since men married in their twenties and girls in their
'teens, parents of grown children might well be less than forty:
Capulet, though his wife twits him with his years, calls for his
sword; and Montague is no less bellicose. Bad sanitation, however,
and neglected personal hygiene shortened life-expectancy, even
among the better classes;[1] generations were short; well-born
Elizabethans laid aside dancing and tourneys at thirty-five; and, in
"the decline of his age" at forty, a gentleman was supposed to hide
his bodily decay by retiring from court.[2] Such persons would show
some symptoms, at least physical symptoms, of old age, and so
might be termed "old" by the Elizabethans, for "old" is a somewhat
comparative epithet. Many of the characters, moreover, that are
described as "old" or "aged" in the plays are too minor to show
either the physique or the psychology of their years. Even so, however, a brief survey is in order of figures described as "old." In
A Comedy of Errors, Adriana calls her husband "old"; but she is
speaking in anger, and neither he nor his twin brother show evidence
of age. More fittingly, his father, Ægeon, is called an "old man";
and Ægeon describes his bodily infirmities:

> O time's extremity,
> Hast thou so crack'd and splitted my poor tongue
> In seven short years that here my only son
> Knows not my feeble key of untuned cares?
> Though now this grained face of mine be hid
> In sap-consuming winter's drizzled snow,
> And all the conduits of my blood froze up,
> Yet hath my night of life some memory,
> My wasting lamps some fading glimmer left,
> My dull deaf ears a little use to hear. . . .

This, Shakespeare's earliest depiction of old age, stresses merely its
obvious physical symptoms. Old women, since they are hardly appropriate as lovers, are rare in Shakespearean drama; but Juliet's
"ancient" nurse would seem to be an example; and she shows some
of the characteristics of her years. Mistress Ford in *Merry Wives,*

though described by her husband as "not young," is certainly not as "old" as Pistol would imply; and she gives no evidence of senility! The hurly-burly of the history plays allows little room for the portrayal of old age; but a few vignettes appear: *Richard II* supplies "Old John of Gaunt, time-honour'd Lancaster," always resigned and philosophical, and also the "aged" Duke of York; Henry IV and Henry VIII are depicted with some appropriate details at the ends of their long and active reigns; Falstaff refers to Pistol's "old body"; and Falstaff himself is portrayed in the fullness of time and of three plays, as he unwillingly "grows old." Justice Shallow in *Henry IV* and *Merry Wives* is probably Shakespeare's most satiric treatment of old age. Much more sympathetically drawn are Adam in *As You Like It* and Nestor in *Troilus and Cressida*. In the Dramatis Personæ of *All's Well*, Rowe describes Lafeu as an "old Lord." Polonius is "old." Kent in *King Lear* at least borders on "old" age; and Lear himself is repeatedly called "old." The folio text of *Measure for Measure* lists Escalus as "an ancient Lord"; and the Duke mentions him as "old Escalus"; but the folio text of *Timon* lists "An old Athenian," who turns out to have a daughter who is barely of age to marry! In the *Winter's Tale* Perdita's reputed father is an "Old Shepherd," who hardly figures in the play. In *The Tempest* "The good old lord, Gonzalo" presents perhaps the happiest picture of old age; but Prospero, though he speaks of his "old brain," seems hardly older than any other father of a marriageable child. Of this odd score of characters, some are very minor and some of dubious age, but several might bear a further looking into.

From the Classics came two opposing conceptions of old age: from Lucian's *De Luctu*, a tradition that stresses its infirmities and defects; and from Cicero's *De Senectute*, its happier and more pleasing aspects. The swift advent of physical decay would naturally predispose the Elizabethans toward the former; and Shakespeare, especially in his earlier plays, gives repeated emphasis to these unhappy qualities. Ægeon in the passage already quoted details the most obvious matters of physique: a broken voice, pale, cold flesh, weakness of hearing and of eyesight, and one mental trait, the loss of memory. Also in *A Comedy of Errors* Adriana complains that "homely age" has marred her beatuy. Juliet's Nurse, who lacks "warm, youthful blood," has also lost whatever physical charm she ever had.[3] In *Richard II,* York is "weak with age," and old Gaunt tells the King that, though the royal mandate can hasten age through sorrow, yet nothing the monarch can do will banish wrinkles. Antonio, likewise, in *The Merchant* refers to the "hollow eye and wrinkled brow" of age. The shrivelled and piping Shallow suggests the last two periods of life as detailed by Jaques in his speech on the seven ages of man:

> The sixth age shifts
> Into the lean and slipper'd pantaloon,
> With spectacles on nose and pouch on side,
> His youthful hose, well saved, a world too wide
> For his shruck shank; and his big manly voice,
> Turning again toward childish treble, pipes
> And whistles in his sound. Last scene of all,
> That ends this strange eventful history,
> Is second childishness and mere oblivion,
> Sans teeth, sans eyes, sans taste, sans everything.

In *Much Ado,* Constable Dogberry patronizingly (and quite unfairly) describes his colleague Verges: "a good old man, sir; he will be talking: as they say, when the age is in, the wit is out." Hamlet also imputes to old age, along with "grey beards" and bleary eyes, "a plentiful lack of wit." The suggestion of mental weakness points forward to *King Lear;* and so also, in another way, does the Duke's somewhat cynical comment in *Measure for Measure:*

> Friend hast thou none;
> For these own bowels, which do call thee sire,
> The mere effusion of thy proper loins,
> Do curse the gout, serpigo and the rheum,
> For ending thee no sooner. Thou hast nor youth nor age,
> But, as it were, an after-dinner's sleep,
> Dreaming on both; for all thy blessed youth
> Becomes as aged, and doth beg the alms
> Of palsied eld; and when thou are old and rich,
> Thou hast neither heat, affection, limb or beauty,
> To make thy riches pleasant. What's yet in this
> That bears the name of life?

Even down to his last years, Shakespeare was still concerned with the physical infirmities of age: Cassandra in the *Trolius* refers to "wrinkled eld"; and, in *The Tempest,* age is associated with "cramps," and the old witch Sycorax "with age and envy was grown into a hoop."

To Shakespeare, the psychological aspects of old age were generally its more pleasing side; and he increasingly presents them. As early as *Two Gentlemen,* he associates age with experience and with "eloquence"; and, in *Merry Wives,* Mistress Quickly sagely notes that "old folk . . . have discretion"; but, not until the middle of his career, in the person of Adam in *As You Like It,* does Shakespeare give a full and sympathetic picture of old age, a picture that stresses its maturity and sweetness of character as struggling to overcome its physical infirmities. Adam is the picture of selfless loyalty: he warns Orlando against Oliver's plots, offers his young lord the savings of his lifetime, and asks only to serve him in his exile:

> Here is the gold;
> All this I give you. Let me be your servant:
> Though I look old, yet I am strong and lusty;
> For in my youth I never did apply
> Hot and rebellious liquors in my blood,
> Nor did not with unbashful forehead woo
> The means of weakness and debility;
> Therefore my age is as a lusty winter,
> Frosty but kindly: let me go with you;
> I'll do the service of a younger man
> In all your business and necessities.

Orlando is not too hopeful for the "poor old man"; and, later in the Forest of Arden, Adam nearly dies of hunger and exhaustion. The "honor" due to age appears in Helena's appeal to the Countess in *All's Well* and by inference in *Twelfth Night* when Sir Andrew says that he will not compare himself to an "old man." The "good father," who discusses with Ross the omens at the murder of Duncan, has a memory that goes back, he says, for seventy years; and such a store of experience appears in statesmen such as Polonius, Nestor, Escalus and Gonzalo. Lear is "a gracious aged man." In short, Shakespeare portrays both the physique and the mentality of age: among its less attractive qualities, a broken voice, ugliness of face and crookedness of stature, talkitiveness, lack of friends, and, above all illustrated in King Lear, its failing mental powers. The psychology of age, he generally shows more favorably: it has eloquence and discretion, and, in the person of Adam unselfish loyalty; long memory makes for wisdom and commands reverence; and it can be gracious and at times deeply pathetic.

Shakespeare's earlier pictures of old age, being more concerned with its physical aspects, are generally less sympathetic. The Elizabethans, living in a society without police, when a man's good right arm was his protection against insult or mayhem, had a certain contempt for physical infirmity and for the shifts it was often put to in order to survive. This unsympathetic attitude of the earlier plays is most clearly expressed in the persons of Falstaff [4] and of Shallow. As Falstaff had been a page in the Norfolk household fifty-five years before, he must be at least sixty-two, for one usually commenced page at seven; but he admits only to "some fifty" years, and declares himself in the "vaward of youth." His associates repeatedly call him "old," and finally he himself is constrained to admit that he "grows old." With wine, he tries to heat his blood to youthful fervor: he must be hale fellow with his patron-prince; and, when an Elizabethan soldier showed signs of age, his occupation was gone, and he had no recourse but beggery and starvation. Today we should feel the pathos of such a rôle; but not so the Elizabethans, who were too much concerned with the calamities of society at large —as portrayed in such a tragedy as *Macbeth* [5]—to waste many tears on mere individuals. Some critics to the contrary notwithstanding, the present writer agrees with Professor Stoll [6] in finding little sympathy for Falstaff in the plays: the fat knight is not only an outrageous boaster, a debauchee, an officer who takes bribes and deliberately sends his men to death so that he can steal their pay; but, worst of all to the Elizabethans, he is an arrant coward, with only his wit as a redeeming trait. Even older, and without even wit to redeem him, is Justice Shallow, who had been—or at least claims to have been—a gay blade about London some "fifty years ago." He has "lived fourscore years and upward," and long since retired to his estates in the country. He is pompous and boastful and so generally ridiculous that even Falstaff, who is progressing toward his age, makes fun of him. He is wizened with years and yet lecherous; he is avid of honorific titles and yet connives at petty corruption: in fact, he is one of the most satirically depicted figures in all Shakespeare. Indeed, the dramatist in the fullness of his second period plays, used age in Faistaff and complete senility in Shallow, as the very stuff of comic ridicule.

Here and there in the early plays, a more attractive picture is evident, in John of Gaunt, for instance, and in the Duke of York in *Richard II;* but Adam is the first full portrait of a "good old man." He is almost Shallow's age, but hale and hearty for his years, having avoided license in his youth. To Shakespeare, Adam represents "The constant service of the antique world, when service sweat for duty, not for meed." Again and again, Shakespeare idealizes the feudal classes, the nobles and their "servingmen," and seems to regret the transition to modern capitalistic society. Economic pressure was making life arduous both for nobles like Orlando and for servingmen like Adam; and both were perforce abandoning the chivalric ideals and the liberality and also the hospitality that was supposed to have characterized them in Mediæval times. Shakespeare's idealization of this "antique world" seems somewhat to have cast its glow on the declining years of Adam.

Such a sympathetic picture of old age appears, perhaps in Polonius, and clearly in Nestor and Gonzalo. Many critics and most actors portray Polonius as a senile fool; [7] but he is not so very old, nor is he by any means a fool: his daughter is of barely marriageable age, and his voice is young enough for Hamlet to mistake it for the King's; and, furthermore, with the knowledge he has, the part he plays in political affairs is shrewd, and accords with all that an Elizabethan would expect of a counsellor of state.[8] He is, in short, clearly Falstaff's junior, a man in his forties or fifties; but, if one call him a depiction of old age, he presents (despite Hamlet's slurring comments that have misled so many critics) a rather sympathetic picture. Of Nestor's great age, however, there cannot be a doubt: he is "old" and "venerable," and "was a man when Hector's grandsire suck'd"; in short, he must be eighty, an age that the Elizabethans no doubt associated with heroic early times. Achilles calls him "winter"; the dialogue refers to his "white beard," his "silver beard" and his "wither'd brawn"; and he speaks of himself as "old," and mentions his "old eyes." Shakespeare's attitude toward him follows the Homeric tradition: he is shrewd in council and rightly considered "reverend" for his "stretch'd-out life." Gonzalo, likewise, in *The Tempest* is indisputably "old"; like Nestor, he is at times perhaps too talkative; but his terse wisdom

and political foresight are not to be despised; even the flippant
Ariel calls him "the good old lord"; and the wise Prospero addresses him as "Holy Gonzalo, honourable man." Great age was
certainly unusual among the Elizabethans. When it occurred, its
weaknesses were much in evidence: and, when Shakespeare presents it in a pleasing guise, he is dealing either with pastoral un-
reality as in the case of Adam, or with a long-past heroic period of
history as in the case of Nestor, or in a pure romance as with
Gonzalo.

Late in his work, in the person of King Lear, Shakespeare finally
drew a fullscale portrait of extreme old age, showing its subtle
evolution and the psychological processes involved; and a proper
understanding of this character requires some grasp of the popular
and scientific theories of the time.

The Elizabethans, following the tradition of Aristotle, usually
divided man's life into three major parts, and each of these into
two or more subdivisions. Of these major parts, old age was, of
course, the last. The Mediæval encyclopedia of Bartholomæus
Anglicus, still popular in the Elizabethan translation of Batman,
began *Senecta* at forty-five or fifty, and divided it into old age and
dotage.[9] Lemnius, also popular in translation, divided his third
period of life into "full ripenesse" and "Old Age," the latter beginning at sixty-three or sixty-five and turning into "dotage." [10]
The famous French physician of the Renaissance, Andreas Laurentius, begins old age at fifty, and divides it into three parts, "greene"
old age, a period of wisdom and prudence like that of Polonius,
lasting to seventy; a period of transition; and finally a decrepitude
that precedes death.[11] "Dr. Arcandam" approximates Laurentius
in his three divisions, but suggests that age may set in as early as
thirty-five.[12] Cuffe has an entire monograph on the evolution of
man's life, with much citation of Classical authority and extended
reference to astrology and to the humoral theories of Galen. His
scheme is generally similar to those of Bartholomæus and Lemnius:
a period from fifty to sixty-five under the sanguine and fortunate
influence of the planet Jupiter, followed by "decrepit old age" under
the melancholy and unlucky influence of Saturn.[13] Only "Dr. Arcandam" seems to have enough sense of actual contemporary conditions to begin old age as early as thirty-five; the others are clearly
following Classical tradition. Medical writers regularly agree with

Cuffe that the latter years of life are astrologically unfortunate, and that the body is dominated by black bile, the melancholy humor. This was the humor of physical decrepitude and mental instability, and it easily gave way to the childishness of dotage: this is the evolution so aptly pictured in King Lear.

Lear is repeatedly called "old"; and, as early as the second act, admits as much to Regan. Indeed he is "Fourscore and upward," and shows both the physical and the mental effects of his years. He has "white hair," and is "infirm" and "weak" with age, even before the middle of the play. Physical exposure and "Passions and Perturbations of the Mind" [14] burn out the last remnants of his kingly choler and his vital fluids, and leave him cold and dry and weak in body. Lear's mind also soon shows the effect of this decay; and most of his symptoms follow the theories of Lemnius, Cuffe, and other contemporary authorities: even in Act I, his "discernings Are lethargied"; soon his memory begins to fail; [15] he grows "talkative"; [16] and shows a "waiward pettichnesse:" [17] As early as the fifth scene, he foresees and fears approaching madness, and in Act II senses the beginning of *hysterica passio*. In Act III his "wits begin to turn," and he complains of melancholy "cold"; and the Fool prophetically declares: "This cold night will turn us all to fools and madmen." By the end of the act, his wits are "gone." In the next act, he is "mad," and has illusions of sight,[18] and raves and imagines Kent and Edgar as judges in a court condemning his two older daughters. Toward the end of Act IV, his cure begins by the medically accepted means of music [19] and complete rest.[20] But the defeat of Cordelia brings on the final tragedy of his death. Thus Lear is a case-history of physical and mental decay brought on, partly by misfortune, but largely by advancing years, very much as Kate the Shrew is a case-history of choler in an earlier period of life.

Nearly all of these details that give such realism to Lear's time of life are Shakespeare's own; for the sources from which he took the story do little more than mention the King's age. Holinshed's *Chronicle* says merely that he "was come to great yeeres, and began to waxe vnweldie through age"; he does not go insane, but is restored to his throne and rules happily for two more years, until his death. The *Mirour for Magistrates* goes a step further, and calls him a "doting foole"; but, after Cordelia restores him, he rules

"Three yeares in peace." The story in Spenser's *Faerie Queene* refers to his "feeble age" and his "drouping day"; and, after he is
restored to his crown, he finally dies "made ripe for death by eld."
The old comedy of *King Leir* does little more: "One foot already
hangeth in the grave"; and, early in the play, Lear admits that his
"pale grim death" approaches. He "weepes" at Goneril's ill-treatment, and appears exhausted at Regan's court; but he does not go
mad as in Shakespeare. At last, Cordelia restores him to the throne,
and the play leaves him ruling happily. In short, the depiction of
Lear's senility is Shakespeare's own; and this greatest portrait of
old age in all world literature was done by a dramatist but little over
forty: so much for those critics who insist that Shakespeare's greatest characters are but aspects of his own biography! Probably,
Shakespeare first chose the old story because it aptly illustrated the
dangers of abdication and of division of a realm—two themes especially dear to James I, for he ruled as a God-appointed Divine Right
monarch, who therefore could not forego the holy mandate, and,
moreover, just at this time the King was trying to persuade parlia-
ment to accept complete union with Scotland.[21] The story, therefore,
was a perfect combination of these timely themes in the hands of
the court playwright. As Shakespeare worked over this material
to make it express more strikingly the dangers of abdication and
division, he found that they demanded a tragic conclusion; and,
furthermore, Lear must be extremely old to have a motive to re-
linquish his government; and, if he is so old, his mind and body
must break under the strain of accumulated catastrophe: he could
not suffer as intensely as the situation required and still return to a
happy rule as in the old comedy of *Leir*. Thus the political theme
of the play and also the psychological verisimilitude of this title role
turned the piece into stark tragedy: such political errors could not
but bring ruin on all concerned, and especially old age could not
endure the stress and strain, and so must find an escape in madness
and in death.

Shakespeare portrays several stages of man's latter years:
Polonius in his forties or early fifties is still a competent prime min-
ister; Falstaff in his sixties still tries to cling to green old age, and
uses stimulants and bragging and above all his wit to pass for a
younger man; Shallow and Nestor and King Lear are in their
eighties. Polonius falls hardly within the range of the present study,

although Elizabethans often showed signs of old age in their forties. Shallow is treated satirically and with emphasis on the physical traits of age. Nestor is idealized, as befitted a Homeric figure, and sketched but briefly in. Lear is a full-length portrait in both physical and psychological detail, with nothing of the satire of Falstaff or of Shallow. An understanding and a sympathy for old age apparently grew on Shakespeare; we see Lear as a deeply pathetic figure; and, in Nestor and Gonzalo, wisdom and integrity of character make up for loss of physical strength; and the dramatist ends by idealizing age as much as he had ridiculed it some fifteen years before. Not only his sympathy but also his depth of psychological insight grows, perhaps first in Falstaff who shows the fear of advancing years and in Shallow who ludicrously glorifies his youth, and most of all in Lear who bows and breaks before the storms of life.

XXIV

Robert Shallow Esq., J.P.

Robert Shallow is certainly the most be-titled commoner in Shakespeare: he is "Master," "Esquire" or "Armiger," a "gentleman
born" [1] (a more or less legal status),[2] "your worship," [3] and "justice
of the peace" [4] placed "in commission" with Master Silence; [5] and
Falstaff, boastful of his influence at court, promises to make him
Lord Chief Justice upon the removal of Sir William Gascoigne,[6]
and in anticipation calls him "my Lord Shallow." [7] This worthy
justice of the peace took his local greatness very seriously; and,
when irked by Pistol, he drew himself to his whole diminutive and
wizened height, and told those present: "I am, sir, under the king,
in some authority." [8] At the beginning of *Merry Wives*, moreover,
he and Slender set forth in antiphonal responses his judicial honors,
albeit with some mangling of the King's Latin. To the title "justice
of the peace," Slender adds *coram;* for he had apparently seen
jurat coram me in attestations above the justice's signature and had
supposed it part of the title. Shallow does not correct him or decline
this adventitious honor, but proceeds to call himself *custolorum,* a
corruption of *custos rotulorum,* i.e. keeper of the records and
usually *ex officio* head of the Commission. Shakespeare's modicum
of law,[9] like the rest of his social concepts, belongs to his own age; [10]
and so he does not stick at the anachronism of placing in the reign

of Henry IV, when Shallow was supposed to have flourished, an
office that seems to have been created by an act of Henry VIII: [11]
"There shall be one . . . custos rotulorum in euery of the said twelue
shires"; [12] and presumably the muster-roles of Gloucestershire, [13]
which Shallow had in charge, were among these records that he kept.
Thus he announces himself as *"Custalorum";* and Slender, who mistakes this law-Latin, adds to the duet, as if it were another title,
"Aye, and *Ratolorum* too; and a gentleman born—who writes
himself *Armigero* [*armiger*] [14] in any bill, warrant, quittance, or
obligation, *Armigero.*" Thereupon, the good justice, whose sense of
eminence is not yet quite satisfied declares that his forebears have
enjoyed this title of *armiger* for over three hundred years; and this,
if taken literally, would mean that his ancestors had borne an
heraldic coat of arms almost since the days of William the Conqueror. In short, Shallow came of a "county family," and was justice
of the peace, and was that justice in particular to whom the records
were entrusted; and, out of all this, he and Slender make a fine showing of epithets and titles, correct and spurious. The benchers of the
Inns of Court seem to have had a *penchant* for the drama; and,
only a few years later, *Twelfth Night* was performed in their hall
of the Middle Temple. Certainly, those of Shakespeare's audience
who understood law-Latin had cause to smile at this pomposity;
and those young blades, moreover, who nursed a grudge against
the law, might have their laugh at the admiring Slender and the
very worshipful *"Custalorum."*

This grandiloquent display of "additions," as the Elizabethans
termed honorific titles, arose from the intense irritation of Shallow
and his young friend Slender. Sir John Falstaff and his rag-tag followers, presuming upon an old acquaintance with the justice during
his salad days in London, had recently visited him in Gloucestershire; and, as Shallow declares, they had "beaten my men, killed
my deer, and broke open my lodge"—apparently his private hunting lodge. The miscreants had, thereupon, fled the county to evade
the jurisdiction of their irate host, [15] and carried some of his venison
to Windsor, where, even at the moment, they were about to enjoy
it at the table of Master Page. Even while Shallow spoke, he could
doubtless sniff the feast in preparation; and this certainly did not
improve his temper. Deer-stealing was still a serious offense; [16] and
the justice, whose interest in dogs [17] suggests that he preferred to

do his hunting for himself, was not one to take it lightly. Falstaff's men, furthermore, had recently got Slender drunk and picked his pocket—so drunk, indeed, that he cannot for certain testify just which of the band was the thief. No wonder that the exasperated Shallow, who had no power outside his shire, declared that he would appeal to the national authorities and "make a Star-Chamber matter" of his grievance. "The Council," he declares, "shall hear of it; it is a riot." Since justices of the peace were appointed by the Council of State at Westminster,[18] Shallow must have been *persona grata* with that body, which exercised not only political but also exalted judiciary functions when sitting in the notorious Star Chamber; and "a riot" came particularly under its jurisdiction. Thus Shallow's boast was not quite an empty one, especially as even small affairs were appealed so constantly to London that in the following reign the custom was condemned.[19] Nevertheless, despite both law and influence, the very worshipful justice quickly turns craven at the military brag and swagger of the portly knight: apparently, he was not only pompous but also something of a coward; and his influence at court was doubtless less than the influence that he thought Falstaff had.

Shallow's office on the Commission of the Peace was ancient and honorable. In early Norman times the sheriffs had controlled law-enforcement and tax-collecting in the shires, and so had risen to great power. As an offset to this power, the Crown had developed first the office of "crowner," or coroner, especially as a financial check, and, somewhat later, about 1200 had organized the office of justice of the peace from the knights who were supposed to preserve order. In time, the J.P. also rose to be a check on the sheriff, especially on his law-enforcing power.[20] Since these petty justices were the king's personal appointees, their commissions expired at the end of a reign; and thus, when Pistol brings the happy news of the accession of Prince Hal as Henry V, he is *ipso facto* stating that Shallow no longer holds his office; and it therefore behooves the erstwhile justice to use his friend Falstaff to curry favor at court or risk permanent loss of place. Pistol might well exclaim, "A foutre for thine office!"[21] A statute of 13 Edward I, 2, sets forth the J.P.'s powers and duties and, during the fourteenth century, they so increased that by 1388 the number of the Commission was raised to six in every shire;[22] and, two years later, to eight. A salary of four shillings for each day of the session was allowed—about $30. in modern purchasing power. The incumbent had to hold the status at least of gentleman, esquire, or knight; [23] and, in 1414, a justice was required to be a resident of the shire and to own land to the value of twenty pounds.[24] During the Tudor period, J.P.'s were regularly appointed by the Council on the advice of the judges of the assize. The Crown apparently considered the office so important that it must be kept independent both of the sheriff and of the local gentry; as early as the reign of Richard II, Parliament passed a law that no steward of a lord might hold it; [25] and again, in the reign of Queen Mary, it enacted a statute that no sheriff might serve as justice of the peace.[26] Finally, Sir Christopher Wray, Chief Justice of the King's Bench, revised the Commission of the Peace in 1590,[27] and fixed it in the form that underlies Shakespeare's conception of Justice Shallow; and this conception must indicate, if not the actual condition of the office and of those who held it, at least the attitude of a London audience toward them; and, indeed, Shakespeare's satirical attitude is also reflected in *Mulde Sacke* (1620). If jurisprudence be a social science, its relation to social history, and the social standing of its practitioners, should not be quite ignored; and the worshipful Robert Shallow, though a mere character of fiction, is worth a hasty glance, as a justice of the peace, as a personality produced by his ancestry and education, as the host and client and gull of Sir John Falstaff; and his *disiecta membra,* scattered through two plays are worth collecting and fitting together—for they do fit perfectly—into the portrait of an Elizabethan country squire and *custos rotulorum,* a distinctive portrait in the long gallery that stretches from Chaucer's Franklin through Addison's Sir Roger, Fielding's squires in *Tom Jones,* and Jane Austen's country gentlemen on down to recent times.

Coke gives the highest praise to contemporary Commissions of the Peace; [28] but Shakespeare's depiction of Shallow seems to imply that Coke spoke *de jure* rather than *de facto*. Shallow, indeed, was not a model public servant: he was pompous and cowardly; he connived at gross infractions of justice and even committed them. The abuse of the King's press was especially notorious; [29] and, when Falstaff visits Shallow to raise his allotted four recruits for the war, and the Justice parades the candidates before him, Sir John picks first the wealthiest, and then, upon their offering bribes *sub rosa,*

he selects the four least competent.[30] Whether Shallow knows of
the actual bribery is not quite evident; but he expresses surprise
at Falstaff's ill-selection, and is not deceived by the Knight's trans-
parent sophistry that he prefers Shadow because "he presents no
mark to the enemy" and Wart who is lean and therefore supposedly
choleric and warlike: Wart cannot even execute a forward march;
and Shallow knows "he doth not do it right." Mouldy and Bullcalf
had bought their exemption at three pounds, a good round sum for
an Elizabethan countryman; and, if Shallow did not actually know,
he must have suspected it, and so connived at extortion and bribery.
In his own official capacity, moreover, he does not cavil at gross mis-
carriage of justice; and, even before Falstaff, his servant Davy does
not hesitate to make the following suggestion:

> *Davy.* I beseech you, sir, to countenance William Visor of Woncot
> against Clement Perkes o' the hill.
> *Shal.* There is many complaints, Davy, against that Visor: that Visor
> is an arrant knave, on my knowledge.
> *Davy.* I grant your worship that he is a knave, sir; but yet God forbid,
> sir, but a knave should have some countenance at his friend's request. An
> honest man, sir, is able to speak for himself, when a knave is not. I have
> served your worship truly, sir, this eight years; and if I cannot once or
> twice a quarter bear out a knave against an honest man, I have but very
> little credit with your worship. The knave is mine honest friend, sir;
> therefore I beseech your worship, let him be countenanced.
> *Shal.* Go to; I say he shall have no wrong.

Apparently in Shallow's jurisdiction, if one were Davy's "honest
friend," one might be the most notorious "arrant knave" and still
get off scotfree; and the casual tone of this transaction suggests that
none of those concerned considered it a serious malfeasance of
office. It implies, at least on Davy's part, a regular traffic in justice;
and one wonders what *quid pro quo* he got from his "friends" for
getting them his master's "countenance." Apparently, Shallow's
appreciation of the law had not in all these years progressed even
as far as the *suum cuique* of Justinian.

As Shakespeare's use of realism in the plays of his middle periods
grew in elaboration of detail, he increasingly showed his characters,
not merely in cross-section, but with entire biographies implied in
the dialogue: thus he does Falstaff, and even Falstaff's page, little

Robin, thus Launcelot Gobbo and Malvolio, and even some of the minor characters in *Hamlet*. He was interested enough also in Shallow to sketch that worthy's *belle jeunesse,* and to indicate what sort of youth had led to such an age. Shallow came of an old county family; and, as a young man, he had quite properly been sent to Clement's Inn,[31] one of "the lesser Inns of Chancery," usually patronized by those who were unable to enter the four Inns of Court. Perhaps this is why the justice's law-Latin was no better.[32] He boasts, moreover, that he gave these years to high living rather than high thinking; and he descants on his gay youth to "Cousin Silence"; and Slender relishes his stories and "good jests." Indeed, like Chaucer's Wife of Bath, he luxuriates in his own fascinating past; and, like Polonius, he had a taste for amateur theatricals, and had taken the role of Sir Dragonet in a play about King Arthur; he boasts of the "swinge-bucklers" with whom he "would have done anything," the worthy fruiterer named Stockfish with whom he fought behind Gray's Inn, not in a real duel, one supposes, for Shallow disliked the newfangled Italianate laws of arms, but boasts his prowess with an old-fashioned "long sword." He declares he would fight even with Sir John Falstaff—if he were "young again." He helps direct the not-too-sanguinary meeting between the parson and the schoolmaster in *Merry Wives;* and even the sensible but bourgeois Master Page believes that he has "been a great fighter" ; but Falstaff, who had actually trailed a pike (albeit ignominiously), has only contempt for Shallow's boasted exploits with drabs and fruiterers: from the supreme expanse of his own Gargantuan proportions, he ridicules the cavaliero's spare and wizened frame, and declares it shows lack of manhood; the gay and youthful Shallow, he declares, was no familiar of the great Duke John of Gaunt to whom he so readily refers, but a mere hanger-on in the train of elegance and fashion, which he imitated only from afar. Truly, Falstaff was the very man to recognize sham and conceit in others!—Shallow himself inadvertently confesses his own rusticity; for he interlards these romantic memoirs with allusions to the current prices of ewes and bullocks, very much as the impassioned vows of Madame Bovary's lover are interlarded with cries from outside about the price of cattle and pigs: the effect is not romantic. Thus Shallow had taken his fling of life in London; and these edifying years had made him the sort of justice that he was. Such often were the young

bloods of the law; and thus having mastered jurisprudence and discretion, they later retired to their respective native heaths and enjoyed just such a Shallow age.

The justice is now "old," and has long since inherited the family
estates, and is ripe with honors: the days when Falstaff was a page
and Shallow a would-be gay Lothario, are "fifty years ago"; and
elsewhere he declares that he has "lived fourscore years and upward." Most of his "old acquaintance" are now dead; and his
fondness for wise saws and platitudes further attests his age. He
had left the purlieus of the court peradventure at thirty-five. Since
then, he has enjoyed "a goodly dwelling and a rich" that doubtless
descended to him from his ancestors; he hunts in his park, keeps a
sharp eye on the working of his land and on the prices of ewes and
bullocks at Stamford Fair, exercises the exalted local functions of
custos rotulorum, and lives, in short, the life of a country squire and
a pillar of rural society.[33]

Into this life came Falstaff, now a knight; and his advent revived Shallow's memories of the gay old times in London. Shallow
has not seen him for years, and treats him with true country hospitality of bed and board, and when he leaves presses him to return.
London has still its fascination; and Shallow, even at his age, hopefully intimates, "peradventure I will with ye to court"; and his
servant Davy also longs for the gauds and vanities of city life.
Falstaff plays up to these ambitions, and makes great promises, to
be fulfilled upon Prince Hal's succession, and even offers the country
justice "what office thou wilt in the land." They drink together, and
grow very drunk from "sack at supper"—so drunk that Master
Silence is impelled to song, and Falstaff expresses unbounded ad-
miration. Shallow, in short, was planning shrewdly to make use of
Sir John at court; but Sir John, more shrewdly, was planning to
make use in Gloucestershire of Shallow. The Knight has for the
Justice only supreme contempt: he is so thin and "starved" as to be
indeed "the very genius of famine"; and Falstaff has no fellow-
feeling for such men. In the sincerity of soliloquy, he compares
master and servant, Shallow and Davy—an odorous comparison to
one who boasted three centuries of gentility! He plans to "gull"
the conceited Justice out of his money; and indeed, by the end of
the play, he had managed to get "advancements" to the tune of a
cool thousand pounds, of which the Justice, now fully disabused, will

be thankful to recover the meerest moiety. So much for the Shallow of *Henry IV*.

Merry Wives seems to be added as a sort of sequel: the events it chronicles cannot come before; for, in the latter play, Falstaff and Shallow meet for the first time since their youth.[34] The deer-stealing, therefore, set forth at the beginning of *Merry Wives*, must have taken place after Falstaff, at the end of *Henry IV*, had failed to get the Justice the high office he had promised; and the Justice, deeply chagrined and a thousand pounds the poorer, had returned to Gloucestershire. Sometime thereafter, with unblushing effontery, Falstaff, it would seem, had revisited the vicinity, and poached on his former host's preserves, and then retreated to Windsor to share his ill-gotten venison with Master Page. Thither came also Shallow, partly perhaps in pursuit, and partly to make a match for his nephew Slender with the rich and beautiful Anne Page. The story of the virtuous "merry wives," which constitutes the main plot of the play, has little to do with Shallow; but, by the way, one gathers that he fails in both his purposes: his ardent revenge quails before the knight's braggadocio; and the talented House of Page, which had put Falstaff down, disposes easily of Slender and cheats him of his prize. In Gloucester, Shallow might shine as a great light; but, in London, and even in Windsor, he is hid beneath a bushel.

Robert Shallow Esq. J.P., most worshipful *"coram"* and *"Custolorum,"* not to mention *"Ratolorum"* and the rest, strutting the stage with dried-up dignity, boasting the gallantries of his misspent youth, flaunting fine casual references to the great Duke, John of Gaunt, and to the Star Chamber and the Royal Council—yet timid at the mere bombast of Sir John: this Shallow is a study in fine ironic contrasts. He raises his eyebrows (while he shuts his eyes) at the knight's method of picking out recruits; and his own perversion of the king's high justice, he does not even trouble to conceal, but treats quite casually as a thing of custom; and, whether for the nonce, he supports the right or contravenes it, he is always petty. What a foil to the high-minded austerity of my Lord Chief Justice Gascoigne, whom Shallow would supplant. Even at the age of eighty and more years, the country justice hopes to rise at court, and curries Falstaff's favor, and swallows the knight's extravagant promises; and Falstaff uses him, and gulls him out of a cool thousand, and steals his deer to boot, and brushes aside his threats, very much as in the Middle Ages the knight and noble might brush aside a local royal officer. This rough-and-tumble of feudal life was still popular in England; and officers, moreover, who have in charge the petty enforcement of the law—laws against poaching, or against speeding traffic—are seldom popular, especially with such gilded youth of the Inns of Court as patronized Shakespeare's plays and laughed at his comic constables and his ridiculous justice of the peace.

Whether Shallow is a satire on Sir Thomas Lucy of Warwickshire, as some critics have supposed, or on William Gardiner, a London J.P. and apparently an enemy of Shakespeare's,[35] the present writer would not dare assert; but what would be the object of satirizing Lucy before a London audience that never heard of him, and is one to suppose that Shakespeare nursed a grudge for a decade against a local Stratford squire? This would make the dramatist as petty as Shallow, and a stupid playwright also. And surely a London justice, like Gardiner, seems a far cry from the rustic Shallow, with his deer-park and his interest in dogs and cattle. Shallow, indeed, may well be Lucy and Gardiner and doubtless a dozen more, for the players of the time were in constant collision with the lesser officers of the law, and Shakespeare must have known these gentry well. Shallow, like Chaucer's figures, seems to be the essence of a whole social class, matured in Shakespeare's mind and depicted with the ingrained characteristics of old age. He is pompous before cronies and inferiors, but timid in the face of crime or danger; he closes one eye at the misdeeds of Falstaff, and both eyes at his own; he is an ambitious schemer browbeaten and gulled: such are the ironic contrasts of his nature. But the subtlest irony of Shallow lies, not in the play, but in the audience, young barristers and justices-in-training, who doubtless, many a one, in the course of years, himself must turn into a very Shallow—these, with an astute and mocking artistry, Shakespeare has lured to laughter at their future selves, and, as part of their London education, has persuaded them to "exclaim," as Hamlet says, "against their own succession."

XXV

Falstaff's Robin and Other Pages

The tumults of the Middle Ages had required a lord to keep great numbers of retainers; and, in Elizabethan days, the lack of modern household machinery and of telephone and postal services, still made a multiplicity of servants—as far as the increased cost of living would allow—desirable, if not essential, among the upper classes; and, just as society as a whole was divided into persons and gentlemen, so those in service were either menials or well-born "servingmen," [1] the Elizabethan counterparts of the *servientes ad arma* in the Middle Ages and of the "gentlemen's gentlemen" of the eighteenth century. Shakespeare's plays provide plenty of both the upper and the lower sort: the menials, usually country-bred, such as Launcelot Gobbo, who so longed to cover his rusticity with Bassanio's gold braid; and also the servingmen, who ranged from the "good Reynaldo" [2] of Polonius even to ambassadors and ministers of state,[3] the eyes and hands of very royalty. This complex hierarchy of service,[4] the young playwright, lately come up from Stratford, learned only by degrees to understand and picture in his plays, especially as the whole system was in a confused transition from the Mediæval scheme of things to the modern, and consequently showed in different households varying stages of change: did not the butler-steward Malvolio, who was clearly of the vulgar,

aspire to wed a very countess, and did he not cite precedent therefore?[5] Surely at Stratford even, boorish menials had been well
known to Shakespeare; and, in London, though they might assume
a Gobbo's airs and graces and exchange their plain blue coats for
a brave livery, yet they were still the same; and, even in early plays
such as *Two Gentlemen of Verona* and *A Comedy of Errors*, Shakespeare could paint them to the life as a realistic study in the *genre*.
The servingmen of gentle blood, quite otherwise, had been more
removed from the youthful Shakespeare's ken. They were the
product, not so much of the country-side, as of training in the household of some lord, a sort of prenticeship of the gently born but
little within the purview of an artisan outsider. An understanding,
therefore, of the page and of the servingman whose profession the
former would probably inherit, grew by degrees on Shakespeare:
indeed, even after he had came up to London, he had but little
chance to study their lives and characters until he rose to some association with lords and their dependents. Thus, although pages of
necessity appear in comedies of manners such as the young playwright soon essayed, he took some years to perfect their roles and
give them piquant *vraisemblance*.

The pages in Shakespeare's earliest plays are not, indeed, very
characteristic pages, or else are so lightly sketched as to constitute
mere background. Moth in *Love's Labors*, although the fullest
drawn, is hardly realistic, and appears as a wit or as the butt of
wit, rather than as a page. Perhaps Shakespeare used him merely
because in Roman comedy a *miles gloriosus* like Don Armado had
as a foil some such diminutive follower; or perhaps he descends
from the witty page of Mediæval drama.[6] Moth ridicules the heavy-
minded Don, who in return tries to patronize him as an "infant."
Although his part in the plot is small, his character is sharply limned
—a pert but lovable little rascal, a chatterbox, yet shrewd enough
to have his own private opinion of the "immaculate Jaquenetta,"
whom his master loves. He has learned of the Don's vices, and in
time will also learn to turn them to his own account; but meanwhile,
in pure merriment, he sings in his sweet childish treble and is
glib with Attic salt except when the Princess and her ladies put
him down or when he forgets his set speech in the role of the
infant Hercules and hastens to "vanish" stagestruck. On the one
side, Moth is a changeling ancestor of Puck and Ariel, and, on the

other, a forebear of Falstaff's Robin, to whom he shows a family resemblance: each sharpens his wit both *with* and *at* his master; each is termed a "juvanal"; and each acts as go-between in his master's love-affairs. Moth, as a child has character—the elfin whimsicality of certain children—but, as a page, he might have been in any walk of life for all he says and does. Hardly as yet had Shakespeare mastered the Chaucerian art of showing in word and deed and attitude of mind the stamp of a vocation.

Shakespeare's pages between Moth and Robin are rather slightly drawn; but show some growth in his understanding of a page's life and activities, if not of a page's mental bent. In *Romeo and Juliet,* Count Paris has a "boy," who is afraid to wait alone in the churchyard while his master is at Juliet's tomb. As Paris and Romeo fight, he runs off to call the watch, and at the conclusion of the play explains to the Duke the circumstances of his master's death. He is but an incident to Act V, a convenience to Shakespeare in hastening the denounment, and yet withal, truly a child in his superstitious fears and a true page in following nevertheless his master's orders. The Induction to *The Taming of the Shrew* has a more sophisticated page, who, though cast in the part of Sly's solicitous wife, yet manages to evade the fundamental wifely obligations. He is nothing of a page, but merely the occasion for guffaws among the groundlings, a comical Moth reduced to Rabelaisian farce. Sophisticated like this page, and yet like Moth a lightsome and alluring trickster, Puck plays the part of "boy" to Oberon; and his most puckish qualities seem to derive quite as much from his background as a page as from his antecedents in fairy lore. Jessica, disguised as a page, elopes from Shylock's house to act as "torchbearer" to her future husband; but, of course, she is no real page, and appears so only for the nonce. Lucius in *Julius Caesar* is page to Brutus, for in this play Shakespeare depicts Roman society in Elizabethan terms.[7] Like Moth, Lucius sings for his master, for the actor who took these parts, as Hamlet says, may well have been a chorister. Lucius also brings Brutus wine and a taper and his "gown." The affection between the two is a charming touch in this otherwise gory tragedy; but apparently Lucius is not important enough for his fate at the Battle of Philippi to be revealed, and, having suppiled a moment of lyric contrast, he disappears, as if he were a mere stage property. These pages seem to have a part in their respective plays only for

some ulterior regard, and not in and for themselves. Their portraits
are mere external effegies but briefly shown to us. For a moment,
they accompany their lords, run errands or provide music or wit. In
minor ways they may assist the plot; but Shakespeare seems to
have included their roles mainly to provide acting experience for
youthful hirelings who were not yet capable of more important
women's parts. As children, to be sure, they have some truth to
life: Moth has his impish whimseys, Paris's page his ghostly trep-
idations, and Lucius a pathetic, childlike sweetness; but, though
Shakespeare humanizes them, he does not make them pages—or at
least he makes them pages only to the extent that their small activities are such as pages might properly perform. Their pasts and
futures, their characters as molded by their walk of life, are left an
enigmatic vacuum—like those brocaded children of the Spanish
court so sedately painted by Velazquez.

The relation between parents and children that the Renaissance
inherited from the Middle Ages was too often a mere "colde friendship" rather than "naturall loue." [8] The Mosaic commandments
had dictated the theory,[9] and economic pressure the practice, by
which "children under parents are as servants." [10] The distant relations of Gloucester and his sons in *Lear* illustrate this domestic
formality; and, likewise formal, was the household of Polonius, for
all the love between Ophelia and Laertes and their father.[11] The
study of child-psychology was yet to be; and children were considered merely adults of half or quarter size. Indeed, foreigners
accused the English of "want of affection . . . toward their children"; and commonly at seven or nine, parents put them out—
supposedly to "learn better manners"—but actually to do "hard
service" in the households of their feudal suzerains.[12] The monasteries were no more; [13] knight-errantry no longer made a living;
and "Service" in the lord's household was often the only future,
especially of a younger son or daughter. Markham in his *Health to
the Gentlemanly Profession of Servingmen* (1598) describes the
whole system as it still lingered toward the end of Elizabeth's reign:

Even the Dukes sonne is preferred Page to the Prince, the Earles seconde
sonne attendant upon the Duke, the Knights seconde sonne the Earles
Seruant, the Esquires sonne to weare the Knightes lyuerie, and the Gentle-
mans sonne the Esquires Servingman. Yea, I know, at this day, Gentle-

men younger brothers that weares [*sic*] their elder brothers Blew coate
and Badge, attending him with a reuerend regard and duetiful obedience,
as if he were their Prince or Soueraigne.[14]

Too often this system not only deprived the boy of the charm and
amenities of home and childhood but also failed to train him in any
future career. A page could no longer hope to become an esquire
and then a knight-at-arms; for first the long bow and then guns
and powder had taken away the military need, and so the economic
support, of knighthood; and England had not even a standing army
that might supply the page with bread and ale. The pacifist ideal
of Machiavelli was working out in fact, at least internally, in
England; and diplomacy and politics were taking the place of war
as a means of settling disputes. Thus the old education, whatever
its former merits, ceased to be practical; and the Tudors needed,
not champions in armor, but honest and efficient civil servants
properly educated for their tasks.[15] Knighthood was become a mere
luxury;[16] and Lord Bacon wisely advised the impecunious Earl of
Essex to seek rather a career at court or in some civil capacity. As
Ascham declared even early in Elizabeth's reign, "Great mens
sonnes are the worst brought vp"; and "commonlie," for this
reason, "Meane mens sonnes come to great authoritie"[17]—so
poorly did the old feudal education of the aristocracy fit them for
the needs of the new age. More than a generation later, Peacham
was still lamenting parents' neglect of their children's training.[18]
The drama mirrors this condition of affairs; and Falstaff, who
refers to himself as a "nobleman,"[19] and who had been a page to
the very Duke of Norfolk,[20] was apparently reduced in later years
to commencing highwayman.

This breakdown of the old system produced an educational chaos:
some brought up their children, like Orlando in *As You Like It*, in
mere rusticity,[21] or sent them at sixteen or eighteen to learn manners
at court, like Valentine in *Two Gentlemen of Verona;* some, who
could afford it, hired "skilfull Tutors," or sent the youth packing
off to the university, like Jaques and Laertes, or to the Inns of Court
to get some smattering of law.[22] Indeed, the halcyon days of pages
and of servingmen were over; and such a one must either spend his
time in "seruile toyle," selling his birthright for his bread and
pottage, or else turn highwayman as Oliver sneeringly suggested

to Orlando; and, either way, he came to "meere miserie." [23] Young Basse, himself a page, describes his "place and manner" of life, and laments its departed glory; [24] and, as early as 1578, Darell remarks that servingmen were "disdained and had in small regard." [25] Truly, one begins to realize why youths of rank, if not of fortune, so lightly risked their lives upon the sea in the hardships and desperate chances of exploring: it was either that or become a very plowman.[26] Apparently in France, the old system died out less quickly: the monasteries remained; and the need of troops to guard the frontier offered the page some future as an army officer.[27]

Though their career was an economic *cul-de-sac,* pages in England continued to persist by sheer weight of custom; and a father, to get such a place for a younger son, would offer even to pay the boy's expenses in his master's service,[28] especially if there were danger of the son's being pressed as a soldier in the wars.[29] Did not Old Gobbo bring presents even to Jewish Shylock? About 1598, Markham notes the fashion, contemporary with the Falstaff plays, that a gentleman be followed on the street, not with an armored retinue as of yore, but with "onelie one Boy at his heeles" [30] to do him service. Even thus, an empty purse finally made Falstaff dismiss his boisterous crew and keep only his page Robin, who, in return for multiferious services, led a most unedifying and unrewarded life. Ben Jonson, moreover, enumerates a page amongst the "graces" affected by the fashionable Hedon, and classes the unfortunate child with a "rich wrought waistcoat" and a monkey.[31] King James, probably because he came from Scotland, which was not so far advanced, still expected the nobles to send their sons—perhaps as a kind of hostages—to his court, for such dubious educational advantages as that court provided; and, if the King's greedy and ineffectual favorite Somerset, who had been raised as a page in the royal Scottish household, is a characteristic product of this system, then even royal pages acquired from their years of service neither personal virtues nor competence in public business. James nevertheless looked forward to the continuance of this ancient institution, and in his *Basilikon Doron* urged his son to select pages from only the best families: "And your seruants and Court must be composed partly of minors, such as young Lords, to be brought vp in your company, or Pages and such like." [32] Furthermore, he advised his son to "cast" coin among these pages as occasion warranted.[33]

Despite royal approbation, however, the system was falling into decay, so that now it merely exploited the unhappy youth, and turned him out into the world wise only in its follies and with tastes and inclinations that he could not honestly satisfy. Such was the doubtful status of page in the last years of Elizabeth, a status that Shakespeare came to realize only by degrees, and that he at last depicted in the scattered yet congruous fragments that, fitted together, tell the story of Falstaff's little Robin.

This keen depiction of the career of page, because it is thus dispersed through several plays, is lost upon all but the most discerning; for the rich panorama of the Falstaff comedies have so much of the complexity of very life, and are so dominated by the Knight himself, that Robin's occasional part, like a minor voice in the intricate pattern of a fugue, merely blends into the artistry of the whole, and by contributing to that loses its separate virtue. Only those, moreover, who know the Elizabethan age can read this palimpsest that Shakespeare puts before us, and catch the implication of the casual dialogue. Indeed, Robin is one of Shakespeare's full-length portraits—more than a portrait, he is a biography-in-little. Probably this was not the dramatist's original intention; for, in *Henry IV, Part II,* where Falstaff's "Boy" first appears, he has not even a name, and, like Don Armado's Moth, is but a childish foil to the wide girth and tall talk of his master. He is too young even to follow Falstaff to the wars, but not so young that Shakespeare had nothing to tell us of his earlier career.

This earlier career is both characteristic and significant. Impelled by doubtful generosity, or perhaps by embarrassment at so diminutive a follower, the Prince had given the boy to Falstaff; and Robin's having been page to the Prince of Wales implies that he must have been the son, doubtless a younger son, of some great nobleman—perhaps even a "Dukes sonne," as Markham declared that the page of a prince should be. Somewhere, moreover—certainly not in Falstaff's company and probably not in Prince Hal's—Robin had learned fluent French: Shakespeare apparently knew that in the Middle Ages the old Norman families still preferred that language and raised their sons to speak it. Master Page likes Robin, and Mistress Page calls him her "little gallant," presumably with some reference to his speech and manner, and the small offices that he performs are not done clumsily. Robin then came of good family; and, since he did not appear in *Henry IV, Part I,* he presumably entered the service of the Prince and then of the fat knight during the interim between Parts I and II. The Prince is quite nonchalant in thus placing the boy's future in the care of this "villanous abominable misleader of youth," as he calls Falstaff, this "old whitebearded Satan"; and such a nonchalance seems to reflect the carelessness of elders toward these children whom they were supposed to educate and start out in the world: surely Sir John, who had nothing in his pockets but unpaid "tavern-reckonings" and "memorandums of bawdy-houses," who called Robin a "whoreson upright rabbit" and who threatened for no reason to dress him in "vile apparel" and probably for very poverty kept his threat—surely such a Sir John was no proper guide, philosopher, and friend for a gently nurtured youth. The situation suggests *Oliver Twist,* but it is delineated with the colder sympathies of the sixteenth century: after all, most children either died in infancy or lived to a starveling manhood; and the Elizabethans, if they thought at all of Robin's fate, would doubtless think him lucky.

In *Henry IV, Part II,* where he first appears, Robin does not achieve even the dignity of a name, and is but little more developed than Shakespeare's earlier pages. He is only a convenience for his lord and for the playwright: he comes on the stage with Falstaff's sword and buckler; for Falstaff is old-fashioned in his arms, and does not fight with dagger and rapier as do Hamlet and Laertes.[34] The two enter in a comical procession, which Falstaff elaborately describes:

> I do here walk before thee like a sow that hath overwhelmed all her litter but one. If the prince put thee in my service for any other reason than to set me off, why then I have no judgement. Thou whoreson mandrake, thou art fitter to be worn in my cap than to wait at my heels. I was never manned with an agate till now . . .

Robin runs errands to Falstaff's physician and his tailor; he is still honest enough to be entrusted with his master's purse, though its contents is certainly no serious temptation; he carries letters; and he announces the musicians. Such had been the activities of Shakespeare's former pages; but Robin has already over-gone them: he has learned to lie for his master; and, having learned the art, will soon be lying to him. In the last acts of the play, he drops, if not quite out of sight, at least out of our hearing, for he has no speaking part. Though still diminutive, he has already picked up something of Falstaff's jargon and bombast braggadocio; and what he has learned, as with so many pages of the day, is not greatly to his credit. Indeed, as the Prince declares, the boy had been "a Christian," and now "the fat villain" has "transformed him ape"—apparently only too much ape of the "fat villain" himself. Robin, indeed, is learning all the sophistications that were the daily life of rogues and roisterers. He has learned to be witty upon his master's diseases, a taint of worldly wisdom quite beyond the simple merriment of Moth. In fact, he is so witty that Poins tosses him sixpence and the Prince a whole crown, ten times the usual "tester" that one flung at a court fool for a smart jibe; and the reader might well remember that at this very time King James was admonishing his son to "cast" coin occasionally among his pages. The Prince's largesse must have been most welcome; for Robin could have had but little from his master. Thus his education was thoroughly begun in the way he should not go; and he commences novice in the devil-may-care crew who taught him, if not by precept, at least amply by example.

In *Merry Wives of Windsor* Robin first achieves not only the dignity of a name but some importance in the plot; and the progress of his education has given him a more definite character. In the first two acts, like the good child in the maxim, he is seen but not heard; in the third act, he is both heard and seen, and takes a significant part. For the consideration of "a new doublet and hose," which Falstaff's barren service must have put him in great need of, he becomes Mistress Page's "little gallant" in the plot to gull his master. He has learned to carry a love-letter—and to make the love it simulates miscarry. He has learned with some dexterity to give, as Iago says, but "shows of service" to his lord, and keep his heart attending on himself; and he can turn and turn so slyly that Master Ford describes him as "this pretty weathercock." He has seen enough, and knows enough, to grow disgusted with the fat knight's service, in which he has been made pander-in-ordinary to white-haired lechery; for, while his master is engaged in these affairs, Robin must watch the door. Let those who would sentimentalize about "kind" Jack Falstaff bear these things in mind. Is this the training for a page, a future knight or officer, an "eyas-musket," as Mistress Ford describes him? With such misuse, why should a page be loyal? No wonder, even at the risk that Falstaff cast him forth to starve, he turns upon his master and helps the merry wives. Just so in actual life, the whole system of page and lord had broken down. Falstaff is never shown as giving Robin even a "tester"; and Robin helps to get his master a wetting and a sound cudgelling and to make him a gull to the whole town—all for the mere promise of hose and doublet. The "Boy," of sheer necessity, is learning to fend for himself; and, if his scruples will allow, he will soon commence master of such trades as his master's life has taught him. Already Shallow had called him "my little tiny thief," and already he had been accessory to the fact of gross disloyalty; and without him the conspiracy of the merry wives would have come tardy off. In the latter part of the play his name does not appear. One suspects that he may be either the "great lubberly boy" that the callow Slender marries by mistake for his beloved Anne Page, or, more likely, the "garçon" that the fiery French doctor mistakes in similar fashion. At all events, like Lucius in *Julius Caesar,* he merely disappears without leave-taking or good-bye.

But Shakespeare was not really done with Robin. Early in *Henry V,* Falstaff is dead—as he should be in a play devoted to true chivalry—and Robin, having previously fallen from the sanctuary of his noble parents into the hands of the wild and wanton Prince, and from him in a sad declension, to the service of Sir John, now in an ultimate misfortune, commences page to the thrasonical-bragging Pistol, who has not even the virtue of Falstaff's wit to redeem him. Apparently, Falstaff did not carry out his threat to dismiss the boy for his pranks and peccadillos in *Merry Wives;* for Robin follows the old man to his death-bed. Falstaff is "very sick," and accordingly repentant of his past. He warns Robin—teaching by precept, if not by previous example—that women are "devil incarnate"; and Robin thereupon calls in Dame Quickly as the most fitting ministrant to Falstaff's end. Perhaps his master's death-bed scene suggests to Robin that this kind of life leads to a lame and impotent conclusion. At all events, his disillusion grows: Lieutenant Bardolph,[35] Ensign Pistol,[36] Corporal Nym—what were they, forsooth, to recommend the life of soldiering to a youth of noble lineage? Robin well knows the "lily-livered Pistol" whose special virtues are a "killing tongue and a quiet sword," and Bardolph whose beery face glows red like a lantern in the dark, and Nym whose very means *take* or *steal* and whose "few bad words are matched with as few good deeds." No man can be a hero to his servant, especially not such men as these! Their futures are no better than their pasts: Bardolph and Nym are hanged; and Pistol marries the superlative Dame Quickly, and turns to the ignominious courses of bawd and cut-purse. Could even his much-berated brother-ensign, honest Iago, have fallen to this pitch? [37] A cut-purse had no honor even among thieves; for, lacking the dexterity to pick a pocket, he ranked as mere unskilled labor in the underworld. Pickpockets were of higher class; and, for this trade, Pistol had destined Robin, a sort of compliment to his birth and his *finesse*—a compliment, but truly what a shame! In time of battle, to be sure, the boy longed for "an ale-house in London" and "safety"; and yet the life that he must follow, if he follow Pistol, he declares, "makes much against my manhood"; indeed, if he could, he would leave such company and "seek some better service." Apparently, however, there is no "better service"; and the last we see of poor Robin in Act IV, he goes back to the camp to guard the baggage with the other boys; he is spared the disgrace of seeing his master eat Fluellen's leek; and, if he continue in this sort of life, Bardolph has predicted that he must be "hanged." Despite all good intentions, the bootless career of Falstaff is the only one before him; and changing times made this career continually the worse.

Robin drops out in the midst of the play, and so drops out of Shakespeare. Perhaps he is killed with the other boys when the French deserters loot the camp; and, if he escaped, the playwright leaves him just emerging into a life in which he has no place. He has fallen to the plane of Falstaff and his crew to live by his wits in camp and tavern, where now and then he can enjoy the fruits of high living and the dash and swagger of knight-errantry-of-the-road. Did Shakespeare deliberately leave him at this point so that we might suppose that from here his life was parallel to Falstaff's? These two biographies of the fat knight and his page, either through intention or by coincidence, supplement one another, and so display the whole cycle of page and servingman and knight-at-arms—the feudal system in its Renaissance decadence. The portrait of Falstaff is the fuller and more vivid, and therefore the more famous; but

Robin's, especially in *Henry V,* is the more instructive, and illustrates Shakespeare's insight into the social changes of his age.

In the three plays in which he has a part, Robin undergoes a threefold evolution. In *Henry IV,* he is hardly more than Shakespeare's earlier pages, an incidental adjunct to his master and the plot—a mere runner of errands, without decisive character or will. In *Merry Wives* he has developed both character and will; he has weighed Falstaff and found him wanting; and he sticks at no disloyalty to put him down. In *Henry V* he has thought on his present estate and on his future, and found that he has no future: shall he live by loot in France or by picking pockets in London? Such is the choice; and perhaps death solves it for him. He stands for a whole group of well-born youths, for a whole decadent system, for the economic tragedy of a whole social class. Thus Shakespeare saw deeper and yet more deeply into his character-types and so into all society; and he could not portray them truly without analyzing their causes and effects: at first, he presents the realism merely of external, sharp detail, like that of Jonson; but later his growing insight deepened it with a depiction of *why* and *wherefore;* and so, swiftly as Dante, he sketches a biography-in-little and the social *rationale* that made it what it was. This is the realism, not merely of vividness, but of depth, the realism of great tragedy, like *Hamlet* and *Othello:* given the characters and their situation, the end could not have been different. These comedies of the latter 1590's are indeed a preparation for the tragedies that followed.

After Robin, Shakespeare's pages lapse back into purely incidental parts, much as his statesmen do after Polonius,[38] and his rustic servants after Malvolio and Adam. *As You Like It* has two "pages" of the banished Duke, who, like Lucius, seem to be introduced merely for a song. The "Boy" in *Much Ado* who goes to fetch a book for Benedick is doubtless a page; and so also seems to be Balthasar, who sings "a good song" for Don Pedro. Viola, like Jessica, turns boy as a disguise; but she is old enough to be the object of Olivia's affection and of Sir Andrew's martial jealousy: she seems to be more servingman than page. So also does Rosalind in *As You Like It.* In *All's Well,* a page summons Parolles. Macbeth has a "lily-liver'd boy," whom some editors call a "servant." *Troilus and Cressida* presents four "servants," vague as to age and status. Autolycus, the ballad-singing rogue in the *Winter's Tale,* had started life as page to Prince Florizel; and the evil courses to which he has come down [39] are further proof that Shakespeare understood the lives of page and servingman. Ariel, like Puck, is a sort of fairy-page, both a familiar spirit and a child; and, in *Henry VIII* Bishop Gardiner has a "Boy," who lights his way, as Jessica did for Lorenzo and Paris's page for him. Once and for all, in Falstaff's Robin, Shakespeare had portrayed the type in the full stream of Elizabethan life; and nothing was left to add. About 1603, his interest turned from social to more political themes; [40] and his pages become mere background to a Renaissance court whose principals set forth the actual drama.

The alpha and omega of Shakespeare's evolution is romance: *Loves Labors* at the first; and, in the end *The Tempest*. Quite so his pages begin with Moth and end with Ariel; but, between these two, is a long line of more or less realistic pages appropriate to the realism of his middle-period plays, and a natural result of his interest in children and child-life.[41] The apex of this evolution is Robin and that later-Robin, Falstaff. Like a true realist, Shakespeare pictures them with no sentimentalizing, just as they were; he holds the mirror up to nature, and the mirror is not clouded with emotions of his own. He is the true Elizabethan; and, to the Elizabethans, tragedy involved, not a mere individual, or even a social class, but monarchs and whole nations. To them, the sacrifice of Robin and his fellows was of less-than-tragic scope in the epic of national change; and when these pages had played their part and served their social turn, whether in drama or in life, they left the stage without even a final word, without pathos or praise or blame: the rest is silence.

XXVI

The Humor of Corporal Nym

"SLICE, I say! pauca, pauca; slice! that's my humor." These are the first words of Corporal Nym when he first appears in Shakespeare's *Merry Wives*. The conventions of Elizabethan drama required that the key-note of a character be struck when the audience first meets him; and Corporal Nym's initial words express the three chief facets of his personality: as a soldier, he declares that he will stab any who affront him, even as he now threatens to "slice" young Slender; in emulation of Parson Evans' "pauca verba" some ten lines earlier, he cries out "pauca, pauca," meaning to say that he is a man of great deeds rather than idle words; and further to support his nice pretentions to the gentility of arms, he indulges in the fashionable malady of a "humor"—that is in a superabundance of one of the four bodily fluids, a superabundance that was then supposed to affect both the physique and the mental life of the sufferer, sometimes even to the point of death or madness. Thus does the worthy Corporal, in the very first line he speaks, announce his dashing bravery, his ominous silence, and the elegant affliction of a "humor," though which of the four humors he does not specify.

Nym ought to be important. He is the last of Falstaff's followers to appear; and his introduction, therefore, should have some special point. Indeed, his part occurs in only the two final plays of the

Falstaff series, in *Merry Wives* and *Henry V:* in the former, he warns Page and Ford of the fat knight's machinations against their wives, and so arouses Ford's jealousy, and so prepares the way for Falstaff's *contretemps* which form the centre of the plot; in the latter, he helps to supply the background of the war, and he voices the King's reasons for the casting off of Falstaff. Despite this importance, however, in plot and setting and theme, Nym speaks in both plays together fewer than eighty lines: apparently, he lives up to his initial declaration of "pauca, pauca"; and, as if to emphasize this trait still more, when he has made his final exit, still talking of "good humors" and "bad humors," Falstaff's "Boy" Robin once more reminds the audience of his laconic disposition, and suggests the reason for it:

> For Nym, he hath heard [from Evans?] that men of few words are the best [bravest] men; and therefore he scorns to say his prayers, lest he should be thought a coward: but his few bad words are matched with as few good deeds; for he never broke any man's head but his own, and that against a post when he was drunk.

Nym's mannered silences beget, when he breaks these silences, a mannered speech. His words are few and precious—indeed, so precious that Page calls him "a drawling, affecting rogue," and declares that he "frights English out of his [its] wits." In short, the brevity of Nym's colloquial style is purposefully calculated as an adjunct to his apparent martial prowess; and the few verbal airs and graces that his clipt talk permits likewise express his hopeful aspiration to the elegant gentility of his military betters. Nym, indeed, for all his silences, would like to fancy himself a master at persiflage: when Bardolph becomes tapster at the tavern, Nym applauds his new vocation as appropriate; for truly (says Nym) Bardolph "was [be-] gotten in drink." Apparently this *mot* is beneath the laughter of the company, and Nym, seeing his witticism fall flat, calls on the others to admire his neat whimsey; but he calls in vain. The Falstaff *coterie* was used to better joking.

Perhaps Nym's terse style and feeble jocularity are only an expression of his "humor"; for a humor might reveal itself in speech as well as in action and bodily state, and Nym's humor was pervasive. In *Merry Wives* he repeats the word in almost every line he speaks; and in *Henry V* it appears in his talk nine times. His use of it, to be sure, is so loose as to be "often meaningless;" and one almost wonders whether he knew just what a humor was. He almost never states, moreover, just which of the four humors supposedly afflicts him; and the present study, therefore, will attempt a diagnosis of his case.

Nym can hardly be a sufferer from too much blood. The sanguine type of man was supposed to be handsome [1] and generally fortunate: [2] if Nym is handsome, the play does not imply it; and his ill-fortune is obvious in his squalid way of life and his miserable end, hanged by the neck for stealing. Moreover, he is certainly not "honest . . . just, true, benevolent, liberall, faithful, milde, godly, shamefast, magnanimous, religious . . ." [3] Romeo, in his love for Juliet, exemplifies the sanguine type; and Nym is no Romeo.

Pistol describes Nym—perhaps he meant it for mere compliment —as the "Mars of malecontents"; and the "malecontent" type was often associated with melancholy," [4] the disease that arose from too much black bile in the system. This type was under the malific astral influence of Saturn,[5] and this would agree with Nym's untimely end; and Nym's "few words" [6] would also be proper to it, but this sparsity of speech was assumed rather than natural; and his other symptoms hardly accord with this disease. Despite his being "troth-plight" to Dame Quickly, he is no Count Orsino suffering from love-melancholy. Nor has he the religious melancholy of the Puritans: there is nothing Puritan [7] about him! He does not appear to experience "Passions and Perturbations of the Mind." Indeed, he is neither a Jaques nor a Hamlet.[8]

Nym, as a soldier, certainly should be under the influence of Mars: did not Pistol call him "the Mars of malecontents?" And those whose nativity placed them under this sign of the zodiac were supposed to suffer from too much yellow bile and so were of a choleric disposition. This type was given to "Chyding . . . fighting, murther, robbery, sedition"; [9] they were "angry, prompt of wit, nimble, inconstant"; [10] and the humor was appropriate to "all warriers, brawlers, contumelious, . . . quarrellers, theeues . . ." [11] Such is the natural humor of Lear.[12] But Nym, though more obviously a "warrier," is neither a Tybalt nor a Lear; and he is certainly not "prompt of wit," for all his wishful thinking.

Indeed, Nym in reality is no more a soldier than he is a master of repartee. He has little of a soldier's sense of honor and nothing of a soldier's bravery; and one even wonders whether his title of Corporal was not purely an assumption. He does, to be sure, refuse to play pander for Falstaff, and declares that he "will keep the havior of reputation" and that he would rather be honest than eat, but, in carrying out these worthy sentiments, he is not quite Caesar's wife. He may flaunt a fine virtue in refusing to carry Falstaff's seductive letter; but, in his own affairs of the heart, he would seem to the Elizabethans pusillanimous. He was "troth-plight" to the middle-aged but well-to-do Dame Quickly, whose affection Falstaff had apparently bequeathed him; but Pistol, with his pseudo-courtly graces, had of a sudden wooed and won the lady, and had, moreover, cheated Nym of a gambling debt of eight shillings; and even worse, when the latter bellowed for revenge, Pistol suggested that he "espouse" instead the "lazar kite" Doll Tearsheet. Surely all this should make a soldier fight; but Nym, after drawing his sword and returning it once or twice and threatening (quite soldier-like!) to stab Pistol "in fair terms" while he slept, is utterly mollified by the promise of the eight shillings and the threats of Lieutenant Bardolph: he shakes hands, and starts off for the wars, he and Pistol now "Yoke-fellows in arms." Indeed, for all his bluster, he will on occasion "carry coals," [13] i.e., endure affronts.

Not only in his personal affairs but also in the exercise of his profession, Nym's bravery is indeed predominantly bluster; and he acts more like a roisterer of contemporary London than like a *bona fide* soldier. He first appears in *Merry Wives* roaring down Slender's accusations of thievery. Slender says that he is one of Falstaff's "cony-catching rascals"; and Falstaff later admits himself "damned in hell for swearing" to his friends that Nym and Pistol are "good soldiers and tall [brave] fellows." The Corporal himself declares that his sword is good, chiefly for toasting cheese; and his favorite weapon is a knife, when his enemy is asleep. When he goes to the French wars, he remarks that he has but a single life, and so had better cherish it; and indeed, he does no fighting. Robin declares that he "never broke any man's head but his own, and that against a post when he was drunk"; Robin, to be sure, also says that he is braver than poor Pistol; but that is no compliment; and Nym himself admits that he "dare not fight" Pistol. Indeed, the worthy

Corporal, on a close inspection, has little in common with Shakespeare's description of the proper soldier type:

> Jealous in honor, sudden and quick in quarrel,
> Seeking the bubble reputation . . .[14]

Why, then, did Nym frequent the wars? Pistol replies for both himself and his confederate:

> Let us to France; like horse-leeches, my boys,
> To suck, so suck, the very blood to suck.

Army life in that age was on the lowest plane: officers stole the soldiers' pay; and thus even actual soldiers in the midst of a campaign were obliged to loot the countryside, whether friendly or not, for the bare necessities of life, and, in peacetime, "yong Souldiers" were left to "beg in the streets"; [15] the government was done with them, and the guilds closed most honest callings. Many ruffians, moreover, pretending to have "trailed a pike in Flanders," blustered their way to a doubtful living in the dives of contemporary London; and Nym was apparently one of these. Indeed, most editors in the last two centuries have followed Rowe in describing him, along with Bardolph and Pistol, as sharpers attending on Falstaff"; and yet there is a difference between Nym and these other two: Nym was the most proficient thief, Bardolph was "too open," and on this account Falstaff had to sacrifice him to the honest trade of tapster, and Pistol, according to Robin, was too cowardly. Lieutenant Bardolph gives at least some appearance of courage in the war, and so was probably an actual, though disreputable soldier; and Pistol, with his fine braggadocio phrases, may well have had some education, and perhaps had known the outskirts of the court; [16] but Nym is a born thief: his name, which means *take* or *steal*, declares as much; and his ability to instruct Robin in the master-craft of picking pockets, a highly skilled profession, suggests an early start and long years of training in the underworld. He boasts, moreover, doubtless from experience, that he can lead any "nuthook," i.e., policeman, a merry chase; truly, he and Bardolph are "sworn brothers in filching"; and, in the end, their peccadilloes get them hanged. One suspects that the bad technique that occasioned this sad *finale* was Bardolph's and not Nym's. Nym, therefore, was really a pickpocket who used the guise of soldier to cover his real craft.

Nym was no more a soldier than he was a wit; and his introduction in *Henry V,* Shakespeare's most chauvinistic play, forms the sharpest, ironic contrast to the tone of the main plot. But if Nym's righteous wrath over the loss of Mistress Quickly was not so easily assuaged, and if his military prowess evaporated so readily in war, how authentic are these symptoms as evidence of his choleric disposition? Nym, in short, is a sort of negative malingerer; and, for the convenience of the time assumes a choler though he has it not. He is no more suffering from a superfluity of yellow bile than he is from too much blood or too much atrabilious humor. Is, then, his "humor" entirely pretense; and is he in fact enjoying the good health that came from a perfect balance of the four essential fluids? Or did Shakespeare repeat the word merely to satirize Ben Jonson and his "comedy of Humors?" [17] What is the fact beneath his military camouflage?

The cold, phlegmatic type of man was given to "slouth"; [18] he was supposed to be "nothing quicke [lively]," and had a dull wit and base courage; [19] he was fat and soft and of a bad complexion.[20] Batman describes him as slow, dull, forgetful, soft of flesh, and fearful; [21] and Dariot adds that such were young men, "luxurious [immoral], given to idleness and pleasures . . . and lusts,[22] and elsewhere terms them "thoughtful, unstable vacabounds, fearefull, faynt-harted, prodigall . . . commanding, common people . . . walking from place to place . . . laborious fooles, delighting in iournies and varietie of life . . ." [23] Nym certainly has a dull wit and base courage; his time is given to "idlenes and pleasures" such as Dame Quickly's notorious house affords; he is a "vacabound," and when his means allow, doubtless a "prodigall;" he clearly sprang from the "common" people; and his rank of Corporal reflects his desire, if not ability, to command; his foray into France shows him "delighting in iournies and varietie of life": and his very "drawling" speech, if it be not another mere affectation, suggests the slow, phlegmatic temperament; and possibly Shakespeare meant dramatic irony in Nym's reiterated "humor"; for, while the Corporal boasted his choleric truculence, the actual sordid fact was the phlegmatic dullness of the soft and dastard sloth. Indeed, Robin judges shrewdly when he says that Nym and his two associate "swashers" are indeed "three such antics [buffoons]" that altogether they "do not amount to a man." The word "antic" with its suggestion of an actor on a stage is particularly happy in describing the "choleric" Nym, whose every word and deed—or lack of words and deeds—belies his vaunted "humor": it is a part that he has basely conned to make his silence glib, and his poltroonery seemingly truculent.

Corporal Nym, within his narrow compass of less than eighty lines, is a rather complex figure in two contrasting planes: what he really was, and what he pretended, and perhaps wished to be. Indeed, he is a very Swiftean figure of a sham; and even his faults of vengefulness against Pistol and quarrelsome truculence are not authentic; and the disparity between his actual humor and that that he assumed must have been to the audience a humorous thing indeed. Such a figure, done in so little space, is a *tour de force* of dramatic mastery; and, when one remembers how few critics have penetrated the shams even of the full-length portraiture of Falstaff, one wonders that an Elizabethan audience could actually see through the *æs triplex* of Corporal Nym's disguise, and tell the actuality from the coat of brass. In fact, however, as in the case of Falstaff, the explanation is not far to seek: pickpockets and other sharpers, such as Nym, who paraded under the guise of "good soldiers and tall fellows," were common in Elizabethan London; and, as soon as such a one by the merest hint betrayed himself on the stage, the audience would recognise the type, would look for the accustomed shams, and laugh accordingly. Thus the realism of Shakespeare's characters was an essential adjunct to the clarity of his art; but we, who do not always recognize these types, are oftentimes confused; for it is an irony of historic scholarship that what is most commonplace in one age imposes in another the greatest difficulty to ascertain and prove: the commonplace is rarely written down. Thus if an Elizabethan could read the present essay on Corporal Nym and his oddly assorted professions and his oddly assorted "humors," that Elizabethan would doubtless laugh, not only at the admirable Corporal, but also at the notion that anyone needed to elucidate such an obvious human platitude as he. This is an added, un-Shakespearean humor of Corporal Nym; and, for such an undertaking as the present, an Elizabethan, in the Corporal's *ipsa verba*, would probably suggest the short, acidulous motto, "paucă, pauca; slice!"

XXVII

Shakespeare and the Lombard Cities

In Shakespeare's time Lombardy was a geographical term without political meaning. It referred, not to a kingdom, for the Lombard monarchy had been overthrown in 774, nor to the nine provinces of present day Lombardy, but in general to the rich agricultural plain of northern Italy then dominated by the Duchy of Milan and the Republic of Venice. Shakespeare rightly calls Lombardy "fruitful"; [1] and, since he includes in it the city of Padua, which had long been under the Venetian Signiory, he seems clearly to use the name in the general geographical sense. The present study will follow his example. Of all the cities of Renaissance Italy, Shakespeare seems to have known Venice the best; and the strange pattern of what he knew about it and did not know, has been discussed elsewhere. [2] He refers also to half a dozen other north Italian towns, especially to several near Venice, to Padua, Verona, and Mantua, and, somewhat farther away, to Modena, Bergamo, and Milan. [3] These allusions are scattered through nine plays, and are especially common in two early comedies: *Two Gentlemen of Verona,* which has references to Padua, Verona, and Mantua, and *The Taming of the Shrew,* which alludes to Padua, Verona, Mantua, and Bergamo. Some of these are mere passing references; some form the setting of one or more scenes, or indeed of several acts; some seem mere names used vaguely for their romantic connotation, like the lists of proper names in *Paradise Lost;* and a few are more particularized. What did Shakespeare know of each of these cities; or at least what did he think worth putting into his plays; and what may have been the sources and the reasons for such allusions?

Several plays refer, more or less casually, to Verona: in *Two Gentlemen,* the Duke is in love with a lady there; and the Third Outlaw was banished from that city; it "brags" of Romeo; it "hath not such another flower" as Paris; it is proud of its beautiful women;[4] and Petruchio in *The Shrew* is a gentleman of Veronese family, was apparently born and bred there, and is still a resident.[5] A few references vaguely characterize the town: it is "old"—a fact to which its Roman ruins testify—and in *Romeo and Juliet,* it is "fair" —Shakespeare's standard epithet for cities and for women—and it has "streets" and "walls"—as did all Renaissance cities. Local tradition declares that the story of Romeo and Juliet actually took place there back in the Middle Ages—guides still show the lovers' tomb to politely doubting tourists—and in Shakespeare's tragedy, Prince Escalus summons Montagu and Capulet "To old Free-Town, our common judgement-place." Shakespeare does not seem to have looked up this reference or learned it from travellers, but merely took it, along with the rest of the story, from Brooke's poem; and Brooke doubtless had it from Italian sources reflected in Painter's "Villa Franca." Verona is of course a river port of sorts on the Adige, but it could hardly be said to have a "road" for ships, as appears in *Two Gentlemen;* and, again in *Othello,* Shakespeare seems to imagine it a seaport with a spacious harbor like Genoa or Leghorn; for he mentions "a noble ship of Venice [the Venetian Republic of which Verona was then a part]" that claimed Verona as its home port.[6] Even in later years, he seems to have gleaned little knowledge of the town from travellers, who certainly should have known a matter so obvious; and one need not be surprised that none of his plays has reference to the Adige, though he does once mention the River Po not many miles away.[7] Of the Roman remains, the cathedral, the baptistry, the churches of St. Zeno and St. Fermo Maggiore with their Byzantine and Mediæval paintings and carvings, not a word appears: doubtless Englishmen who went to Italy in those days gave their time to things other than sightseeing; and Protestantism had closed their eyes to early

Christian art. In fact, Shakespeare seems to have thought that the mere name *Verona* lent enough local color for the imagination of his audience. When he came to depict Petruchio's house in *The Shrew*, moreover, he apparently even forgot that he had described that young man as a citizen and resident of Verona, and presented his abode was a "country house"—so Pope and later editors call it—where no self-respecting Italian gentleman would live if he could possibly help it.[8] The realism of these scenes suggests contemporary rustic England and not Verona or the Lombard plain. In *Romeo and Juliet,* Verona is ruled by a "prince," though since 1405 it had been a dependency of Venice. This prince whom Shakespeare calls Escalus is no less person, according to tradition, than Bartolomeo della Scala (or Scaliger) who died in 1304; and, in Painter's version of the story, which Shakespeare probably knew, his name appears as "Signor Escala" or as "Lord Bartholomew of Escala." In short, Shakespeare seems to have had no conception of the buildings or the location of Verona; and his only two accurate bits of local color, the "Free-town" and Prince Escalus, are mere reflections of his sources.

The university town of Padua (Padova), also within the Venetian dominions, appears in three and by error in a fourth of Shakespeare's plays, all of them comedies. In *Two Gentlemen,* according to the folio text, Speed welcomes Launce "to Padua," when he must mean Verona [9] or Milan; [10] and Wright suggests that Shakespeare, as he wrote, changed his mind as to the locations of the scenes; or perhaps one town was as good as another so long as the name suggested the glamor of Italy. Doubtless for this glamor, he changes the major setting of *The Shrew* from the "Athens" of "Plato" and "Aristotle," as it appears in his source, to Padua, where Petruchio arrives, not to attend its famous university founded in 1222—but to seek his fortune in general and a rich wife in particular. In the same play, the Pedant comes to Padua—again not to attend the university —but "To gather in some debts." But Tranio does come from Pisa to the university—"fair Padua, nursery of the arts," to follow "A course of learning and ingenious studies"; and later Vincentio declares: ". . . my son and my servant spend all [my savings] at the university," the outraged cry of fathers through the ages. A few years later, Shakespeare has Portia go for legal counsel to her cousin, the "learned doctor" Bellario of Padua. Bologna was far more famous for its legal faculty; but Padua was nearer, was within the territories of Venice, and besides Bellario was her "cousin." Apparently, as a "doctor" of that university, she presents Bellario's opinions at the trial, and claims that she must hurry back to Padua when it is over. Shakespeare, therefore, must have been cognizant of Padua as a university town; but surely that is not why, a few years later still, in *Much Ado,* he made the soldierly and un-amorous Benedick a native "of Padua." In short, Shakespeare had learned somewhere, apparently not from the major sources of the plays concerned, that Padua had a university and was situated not too far from Venice—and from Belmont.[11]

Mantua (Mantova) surrounded by the lagoons of the Mincio, the fortress-capital of the Gonzaga family from 1329 to 1708, appears in casual references in several early plays. In *Two Gentlemen,* the Second Outlaw had been banished for murder from Mantua, and Silvia wants to leave Milan to meet Valentine in Mantua. In *The Shrew* Petruchio presents Hortensio to Baptista as one "Lucio, born in Mantua." In *Romeo and Juliet,* the old Nurse remembers that when Juliet was weaned, her parents were "at Mantua," and the city is credited with the usual laws against the sale of poisons and against breaking quarantine for the plague. Of more descriptive references there are none: Shakespeare does not even refer to its streets or walls or call it *fair*—much less mention its churches, cathedral, or enormous palace. Of the river and the lagoons that made it impregnable, he has nothing; but he may have realized the approximate location of its territory; for, when Valentine is travelling from Milan to Verona, he meets outlaws on the borders of Mantua; and, though Verona is twenty-five miles north of Mantua and a hundred miles east of Milan, yet anyone travelling between them would have to cross or skirt the Mantuan frontier. Apparetnly, moreover, Shakespeare realized that Mantua was just outside the territories of Verona and Venice; for, if it had not been, Tranio could hardly have convinced the Pedant that it was death for a Mantuan to come to Padua; and Romeo flees to Mantua when he is exiled from Verona, though of course here, Shakespeare is merely following his source in Brooke. The dramatist then seems to know something of the relative location of Mantua, Verona, and Milan; and apparently he realized that Mantua was an independent city-state. Of the town itself and its encircling lagoons, he gives us nothing.

A few references to some Lombard towns more remote from Venice can quickly be surveyed. Bologna, famed for its university and its twin leaning towers, is never directly mentioned; but the reference to the Bentivoglio family in *The Taming of the Shrew* may go back to Giovanni Bentivoglio who had ruled the city a century before and did much to beautify it. Shakespeare could hardly have taken the name from Cardinal Guido Bentivoglio (1579-1644), who was only a youth at the time; and his apparent association of the family with Pisa is altogether puzzling. His reference in *Antony and Cleopatra* to Modena, ancient Mutina, south of the Po on the old Emilian Road, shows no knowledge of the place. In *The Shrew,* Tranio's father is described as "a sailmaker of Bergamo": the city, far from being a seaport, is situated in the foothills of the Alps north-east of Milan; but perhaps its present frame for the manufacture of textiles goes back to the sixteenth century, and may explain Shakespeare's reference. It was then an outpost of Venetian rule.

Shakespeare speaks of Milan repeatedly in two plays, and mentions it briefly in two others. Like Verona and Padua, it is "fair"; [12] and it has "gates"; [13] and, in *Much Ado,* it quite correctly has a "Duchess." The reference in *King John* to the Papal Legate Pandulph as "of fair Milan cardinal" is confusing. Shakespeare follows his source *The Troublesome Reign* in combining into one the Legate Pandulph and Cardinal Gualo who, according to Holinshed, for a time superseded him; but, strictly speaking, a cardinal "of Milan" is inaccurate; for all cardinals are clergy of the Pope's own archdiocese of Rome, and I find no evidence that either Pandulph or Gualo came from Milan—or of how Shakespeare could have known it if they had. *Two Gentlemen* sets several scenes in Milan, but as usual does not even mention its famous buildings. Shakespeare, moreover, had an erroneous idea of the city's location and surroundings, and he seems even to suppose that it was a seaport. He makes Valentine go by ship from Verona to Milan, a most unlikely journey, as one is on the Adige and the other on the Olona, a very small tributary of the Po; and the way by water, even if the Olona could carry a *ship,* would be long and roundabout as compared to the straight road through Brescia, the way by which Valentine apparently returns. Elsewhere, furthermore, the Duke refers to "the rising of the mountain-foot That leads toward Mantua"; whereas the country around Milan and the whole Po valley reaching southeast to Mantua is as flat as Holland and crisscrossed with irrigation canals. In *The Tempest,* he even suggests that Milan is a seaport. The usurping duke by a palace revolution has his brother taken from his "library" and with Miranda "hurried aboard a bark," which (says Prospero) "Bore us some leagues to sea." The nearest port to Milan is Genoa, some eighty miles across the Apennines and not even within Milanese territory. This slip is as unfortunate, though not as famous, as the "coast" of Bohemia in the *Winter's Tale.* In short, though Shakespeare refers to Milan some twenty times from his earliest to his latest plays, he gives almost no authentic information about it.

Certainly, Shakespeare never went to northern Italy; and to him the names of the famous cities of Lombardy were only names. In fact, he does not even mention a score of towns that were as notable as Bergamo and Modena. Most of his references are in the early comedies; but he gives, as in the case of Florence,[14] little description beyond the adjective "fair" and vague allusions to streets, walls, and gates. He mentions by name not a single building or bridge or square—in Venice at least he gave us the Rialto!—but the Lombard towns he used merely as glamorous names, and gave a harbor if convenient or a mountain near at hand. Of course, most of these plays were written before Shakespeare started to develop local color;[15] and *The Tempest* is after all pure romance, and the groundlings cared little for exact geography. "Verona" and "Milan" without details were enough to set their eyes agog and their hearts aflame.

By the way, one might ask whether Bacon or Oxford or Raleigh, all of whom had been on the Continent, would not have supplied more and more accurate local color to the famous Lombard cities.

XXVIII

Shakespeare's "Orlando Inamorato"

Critics are so concerned with Rosalind and Jaques that Orlando gets as little attention as the groom at a wedding. They briefly dismiss him as a brave and charming extrovert, gallant and sanguine and free of suspicion and of guile. Whether he is so free was called in question by a performance at Munich in 1949, which portrayed him as soon piercing Rosalind's disguise and guessing her sex if not her identity, while letting her think she fools him. But Shakespeare's text shows little support for this interpretation. Orlando would seem to be all that the critics say; and yet certain Elizabethan backgrounds suggest that his character and career had special meanings to the audiences of the day and perhaps even to Elizabeth and her advisers: he appears as a younger brother, as a successful lover, and possibly even as an actual Elizabethan gentleman known to the actors and to many of the audience. These backgrounds seem to demand exploration and appropriate comment.

The Mediæval youngster of good family was either put out as a page to do "hard service" [1] in the household of his father's overlord so that he might in time become a knight; or he was placed in some monastery [2] to grow up into a monkish worldling like Chaucer's; or occasionally he was apprenticed to a rich merchant. [3] In the Renaissance, however, arms became a career for professional mercenaries skilled in the mathematics of gunnery; [4] the monasteries in England were dissolved; and trade was more and more considered "utterly vnfit for Gentlemen." [5] Thus, unless his father provided the son with lands or income, he could hardly rise above the place of armed retainer, or "servingman" in the household of his patron; [6] and, as the tranquility of Tudor times made retainers less and less necessary, and as the rising cost of living made them more and more a burden, the servingman generally sank to a mere menial servant—perhaps of his own brother; and, even if he escaped being cast out upon the highway by the "incertaintie of service," [7] he could look forward only to a "contemptible" [8] old age. Drayton, indeed, who seems to have started his career as page to Sir Henry Goodere, probably did well for himself even by accepting the occupation of mere poet; and, from the household of the Earl of Derby, if we may believe the "Dedication" of his *Fig for Momus,* Lodge descended to the vocation of playwright.[9] The system that in feudal times had fitted and introduced a young man to his livelihood was acutely dislocated without as yet an adequate substitute; and Peacham might well complain of the neglected education of Elizabethan youth.[10] Thus the growing demand for competent civil servants could be (and was) quite as well filled by sons of artisans.[11] Family honor and future policy required that what money there was should be spent on the eldest son; for primogeniture was an established custom consecrated in the Bible [12] and in the laws of England. The stress of the times, therefore, left the younger brother unprovided for. His father, says Earle,[13] "tasks him to be a gentleman, and leaves him nothing to maintain it." He cannot "descend to the means to get wealth" in trade; and so he stands "at the mercy of the world, and, which is worse, of his elder brother." He is "better than a servingman"; and yet they are not even respectful to him.[14] He wears his brother's old clothes. If he can afford it, he goes to the university and becomes a clergyman; if not, like Falstaff, he turns highwayman to pay his tavern-reckonings. If he is caught, his brother's pride will get him a pardon; his "last refuge" is the Dutch Wars; [15] and his only hope of a respectable living in England is marriage to "some rich widow." [16] No wonder, he is commonly "discontented and desperate." Until the founding of the colonies gave a new outlet for young adventurers, such a summary of their case was all too true. Sir John Smythe wrote Lord Burghley that the English sailors and the soldiers in Flanders were chiefly recruited from "young gentlemen, yeomen and yeomen's sons, such as disdain to pilfer and steal"; [17] and indeed, a younger son must do something "notable," or marry well, or else "become a very Farmer, or Ploughman." [18]

This situation must have been notorious; and, in *As You Like It,* Shakespeare portrays Orlando as faced with the typical problems of the younger son. In the very first scene, the audience is told and re-told that he is a younger brother; and he delivers himself of a whole speech on his status in the family. The second scene introduces him to the Duke as "the youngest sonne of Sir *Roland de Boys";* and he later declares that he is "proud to be Sir *Rolands* sonne, His youngest sonne." Celia is made to overhear and remember this remark, and later refers to him as "old Sir *Roulands* yongest sonne"; and, in the third and in the fourth acts, Rosalind twits him with the fact that mere manhood ("your having in beard") was the only "reuenew" of a younger brother. His father had left Orlando a thousand crowns; but, as Oliver refuses him even this patrimony, he is no better off than the average younger son: he feeds with his brother's "Hindes"; and he bitterly complains: "I am not taught to do anything," and again: ". . . you have train'd me like a pezant, obscuring and hiding from me all gentleman-like qualities." Thus he is sinking to the rank of menial; and the dramatic value of Adam in the play is largely his vivid illustration of Orlando's future fate, unless the young man makes a break for freedom; and, indeed, Adam's "constant service" has brought him to be turned off as an "olde dogge" in his "vnregarded" old age. If Orlando leaves his brother's roof, however, he has no choice but the beggary that Oliver taunts him with, or "A theeuish liuing on the common rode," and he is saved from this dilemma only by the little money that the faithful Adam gives him. Not content with setting forth this theme in the virtuous and beloved Orlando, Shakespeare shows it also in the wicked younger brother, the usurping Duke. Like Claudius in *Hamlet* and Edmund in *Lear* and the false Duke in *The Tempest,* he has yielded to temptation; but Orlando, great as was his provocation, never dreams of supplanting his brother on the ancestral lands. He will not offend against the divine law of primogeniture; but rather, full of youth and spirits, he tries to do something "notable" [19] to win his way. His first effort is the wrestling match; and though the wicked usurping Duke gave him no reward, yet his strength the valor "tript vp the Wrastlers heeles" and the heart of Rosalind "both in an instant"; and so finally, like the impoverished Bassanio,[20] he achieves a rich heiress, to the applause of all good Elizabethans. Indeed, this close reflection of the current problem of the younger son must have given Shakespeare's audience an immediate interest in the play.

An examination of Lodge's *Rosalynde,* from which Shakespeare seems to have drawn his plot,[21] shows that he himself supplied most of the realistic details that link the old story to contemporary life. In Lodge, the father, against all Elizabethan decency and custom, gives the chief share of his land to the youngest son; in Shakespeare, the eldest inherits the actual land; and Orlando is to get "a poore thousand Crownes"—an arrangement similar to that suggested by Markham for younger sons.[22] In both versions, the elder brother refuses him his legacy. In Lodge, the younger is degraded for "two or three years" to the "seruile subjection" of a "foote boy"; in Shakespeare, he is allowed mere board and keep, and so sinks uneducated to the companionship and the life of his brother's menials —just the situation that would actually develop. In Lodge, the younger is made a prisoner and a public show before his brother's friends, actions that family pride would hardly have allowed in fact; and finally he escapes to Arden by stratagems and feats of of strength that suggest the hero of a Mediæval romance rather than a probable human being. Shakespeare suppresses these crudities. In Lodge, Orlando is kept at home by force; in Shakespeare, by economic necessity. The Elizabethan dramatists, and Shakespeare in particular, were bound rather closely by the stories that they used; for their audience would feel cheated if the play left out any favorite episode;[23] and the fact that Shakespeare courted this danger by minimizing the fisticuffs between the brothers, implies some strong reason on his part. This sacrifice of melodramatic incident, the present writer would impute to the dramatist's desire for greater realism of detail and so for more telling immediacy of theme: Shakespeare, indeed, turned the broad farce of his source into high comedy, written not only for its fun but for its meaning.[24]

These changes clearly deepen the significance, not only of the three or four Adam-Orlando scenes, but also of the entire play. The most obvious result is condensation of plot and concentration on the later scenes in Arden. The setting and style also achieve a finer unity; for these scenes of realistic prose are reduced to a mere introductory link with actual life and a touch or two of contrast in the later pastoralism. Character, likewise, is refined, and given truer motives: from a romantic swashbuckler, Orlando is transformed into an Elizabethan country gentleman, fit to espouse the charming Rosalind; and Adam typifies at once the impending fate of Orlando and the sufferings of a class for which Shakespeare elsewhere expresses the popular sympathy.[25] The addition of realism to these scenes, however, affects chiefly the theme of the play as a whole: the scion of a noble house, newly come up from the country, wins at court both fame and fortune, first by besting the wrestler of the usurping Duke, and later, as a consequence of this success, by gaining the heart and hand of the true Duke's daughter.

The plays of Shakespeare's first period, largely imitative of the so-called "University wits," are clearly studies in the technique of his art, and show only sporadic and superficial elements of contemporary realism. In the second period he more and more enlivens the English history of his chronicle plays with such vivid additions as the Falstaff scenes; and, into the folk-stories and Italian tales that were the sources of his comedies, he not only introduces Elizabethan local color, but even re-interprets one or more aspects of the plot to give the tale a timely meaning: the old story of the merchant who signs a bond for a friend, he assimilated by numerous changes in *The Merchant of Venice* to the contemporary abuses of usury; and, in *As You Like It* he reads a new significance into Orlando's youthful struggles. These plays are still "romantic" comedies in the sense that the old tale still dominates the plot; but the growing power of the theme that Shakespeare is reading into the given episode leads directly to the "bitter comedies," more happily termed problemplays. Here, in *Measure for Measure, All's Well,* [26] and *Timon,*[27] the theme gains predominence, and the plot moves largely at its behest. In some of the tragedies also, this is true—in *Othello,* for instance, on military honor,[28] in *Macbeth,* on the dreadful effects of regicide, and in *Lear,* on the evils of abdication.[29] Shakespeare's art grows more and more a commentary on current problems, social, economic, and political. The constantly deepening realism and the constantly increasing intellectual significance of the plays of his first three periods go hand in hand—a natural evolution in a dramatist

who purveyed increasingly to the tastes of the court, and who preferred the praise of the "judicious" to that of "a whole theatre of
others." Thus, at the end of this second period,[30] even amidst the
unrealities of a pastoral romance that combines Corin and Silvius
with verses cut upon palm-trees and the spirit of Robin Hood,[31]
Shakespeare has introduced a current social theme that looks forward to the problem comedies that immediately follow. Indeed, the
theatre must have been full of young gentlemen of fortune, younger
sons of county families who had come up to court to make their
careers;[32] and they would enjoy seeing a younger son marry
a rightful heiress to dukedom, and feel that a play with so pat
a theme and so pleasing a denouement might be most properly en-
titled *As You Like It*. This love affair, furthermore, is conducted
with intriguing complications and in a most romantic setting.

Indeed, Orlando is Fortune's minion: in Act I, he starts as an outcast younger brother, with no hope of support either from his family
or from the reigning Duke. He overthrows the court wrestler with
only the unsubstantial reward of Rosalind's love; he escapes with
Adam's help from his brother's plots, comes upon Rosalind in the
Forest of Arden, and after some pretty fooling marries her with her
ducal father's consent, and so wins himself a wife and the inheritance
of a duchy, with less effort and even more by chance, than Bassanio
wins Portia.[33] In fact, aside from the initial wrestling match, Orlando's own designs and labors have little to do with all this happy
outcome: Adam and Adam's life-time savings get him to the forest;
and Rosalind, under a ruse, arranges his very wooing, and likewise
obtains the all-important consent of her father. This is a strangely
inert career for one of the world's great lovers; and, furthermore,
such an Orlando leaves the plot, as it was in Lodge's story, the veri-
est tissue of romantic accident. Shakespeare usually brought out the
motivation of his characters and integrated the loose episodes of his
sources; but here, for some reason, he has left the plot incoherent
and allowed the hero to stand stationary in the action, as he describes himself at the end of the wrestling, "a quintain, a mere
lifeless block." Indeed, it is Fortune brings the happy issue to his
career, and he must be her minion.

Such succession of pure luck was possible to only one psychological
humor[34] and one astral complexion, the sanguine, which was under
Jupiter's influence. This humor was "Hot and moist, . . . the great-

est fortune, masc[uline], diurnall, temperate, good in all aspects . . ." [35] Its physical effects were strength and longevity:

> Bloude hath preeminence ouer all other humours in susteinying all lieuying
> creatures, for it hath more comformitie with the oryginall cause of liuyng,
> by reason of temperatenesse in heate and moysture, also nourisheth more
> the body, and restoreth that which is decaied, being the very treasure of
> lyfe, by losse whereof death immediately foloweth.[36]

Cuffe in the main agrees:

> . . . those of a sanguine constitution are by nature capable of the longest
> life; as having the two qualities of life best tempred and therefore is com-
> pared vnto aire, which is moderately hot and in the highest degree moist.
> Yet not with that too thinne and fluid watrish moisture, but more
> oily . . .[37]

Surely the stars must be accountable—if any motivation underlies
the plot—for Orlando's "greatest fortune"; and, since each guiding
planet was closely linked with an appropriate humor, the predominance of Jupiter over Orlando's fate implies the predominance of
blood, the sanguine humor, in his body. Already in his dramas,
Shakespeare had governed the course of action in one play by the
stars, and in another by the associated humors; and whether such
a scheme of motivation may not lie behind Orlando's unexampled
luck seems worth investigation.

Both Orlando's birth and his time of life accord with the sanguine
temper. This humor was appropriate to "Noblemen"; [38] and Orlando, as he constantly repeats, is the son of a famous knight, whose
very name is a byword in the mouth of friend and foe alike. Orlando,
moreover, is his father's image: he is the "effigies" and the "memory
of old Sir Rowland." This would alone suggest his having all the
virtues of Chaucer's knight. He is, moreover, in the vigor of
"youth"; and Jaques calls him "this cock." The sanguine humor was
attributed to various parts of life between adolescence and old age:
Vaughan puts it even after sixty; [39] Cuffe associates it with the
"Prime" of life, from twenty-five to thirty-five or forty; [40] but
Lemnius takes it as "proper to lustye flourishinge age," the spring
of our years.[41] This last would accord most nearly with Orlando's

"youth." In short, by his birth and also probably by his age, Orlando would seem to have by nature the jovial, sanguine temper.

His fine physique would also seem to confirm this supposition. Jupiter's man was handsome,[42] of "faire stature," [43] and well proportioned.[44] Vaughan explains that the sanguine humor "watereth all the body, and giveth nourishment unto it," [45] and so it should produce beauty and strength. Hill imputes to the type moderate stature, moist and soft flesh and gentle looks, round slanting shoulders, a clear voice and long palms and fingers.[46] Other physiognomists differ from him in details, but there seems no doubt that this type was generally considered strong and handsome. Orlando, therefore, should properly overcome not only his brother but also the Duke's wrestler; before the match, he "looks successfully"; and later Adam calls him "strong." That he is also good to look upon must have been at once apparent on the stage, and may be inferred in the text from the attitude of Celia and Rosalind. Apparently, moreover, his hair was reddish brown; and this color was associated with the sanguine type.[47]

This humor was as well marked in traits of character as in physique. It belonged to ". . . honest men, iust, true, benevolent, liberall, faithfull, mild, godly, shamefast, magnanimous . . ." [48] It made men "moderate, mery, pleasant, fayre." [49] Orlando, likewise, is "virtuous" and "gentle, strong and valiant"; he will not "enforce a thievish living on the common road"; in their mutual extremity, he thinks first of Adam; he risks his life to rescue even the wicked Oliver from the lioness; and without a murmur, he suffers from his wound until he faints. Sanguine people, perhaps because of their innate chivalry, were thought to be impractical;[50] and Orlando shows no great worldly wisdom either in his relations with Oliver, or in his plan to go to Arden, or in his life when he gets there. Walkington, furthermore, in opposition to Aristotle and Petrus Crinerus, imputed to this "paragon of complexions" the sharpest intellectuality;[51] and the critical Jaques himself is constrained to compliment Orlando's "nimble wit," and certainly Rosalind had reason to observe it. He is, moreover, "liberally minded" and "affable in speech." [52] He is quite equal to courtly manners as soon as he realizes the breeding of those he meets in the forest, and at once changes to the idiom of "smooth civility." Orlando seems, therefore, to conform, not only to the physical beauty and strength of the sanguine man, but also to his charming disposition, his pleasing address, and his impractical turn of mind.

The weakness of the sanguine type was love; and love, indeed, could even drive him to the opposite humor, cold, dry melancholy, and so to madness. Such pangs and miseries appear in Romeo [53] and in the Duke Orsino; [54] but Orlando, despite his desperate case, seems always to have taken for granted a happy outcome for his tender passion, and so avoided melancholy. Nevertheless, he is far gone in love; and this is quite to be expected, for the sanguine complexion, according to Cogen, "is most giuen to Venus"; [55] and Lemnius thought such men open even to "riot, watonnesse . . . and detestable loues." [56] Orlando then was particularly susceptible, and, like Romeo whose innate temper was also sanguine, he is terribly smitten at first sight. Indeed, he cannot say a word, and becomes "a mere lifeless block." He reproaches himself with this untoward lumpishness, and cries, "What passion hangs these weights upon my tongue?" He quite understands his malady, and in agreement with the best medical authority,[57] later imputes the wound to his lady's "eyes." [58] Even in exile, he must deface the trees with hyperbolic verses. In fact, his attraction seems as hopeless as that of the moth for the star, and yet he remains unwavering. Although Coeffeteau associated the sanguine humor with "inconstancy," [59] yet Dariot and Walkington declared such men "faithful" [60] and noted for their "constant loving affection." [61] Sanguine men, moreover, were given to diseases of the liver,[62] which is described as "the shop of the Bloud"; [63] and love especially attacked this organ. [64] How far Orlando is thus affected is not made clear; but Rosalind jocularly offers to cure him and wash his "liver" clean. Thus Shakespeare closely integrates Orlando's sanguine humor and his role of lover in the comedy.

The violence of this passion and the apparent hopelessness of requital might easily have turned Orlando's genial humor into a dangerous melancholy that might have ended in madness; for love melancholy was likely to attack sanguine people.[65] Rosalind seems to suffer from the complaint, but Orlando apparently escapes. He is indeed "Signior Love"; but he experiences, not atrabilious cold and dryness, but rather the heat of a "quotidian fever of love upon him." Rosalind notes that he lacks the outward marks of love-melancholy, "A lean cheek," a "sunken" eye and the rest; and, indeed, Orlando will not join with Jaques in his melancholy railing against the world. Toward the very end of the play, perhaps the "heart-heaviness" that he complains of is a precursor of melancholy; but, on the whole, he clearly has the psychology, not of a hopeless, but of a happy and requited lover: perhaps, like Malvolio, he had faith in his "starres," [66] but, if so, he does not mention it; perhaps Rosalind and lucky accident resolve his problem before melancholy can set in; possibly he recognizes Rosalind during the courtship scenes, though the text hardly bears this out; possibly the mere presence of his lady-love, though unrecognized, keeps his humor wholesome. At all events, Ferrand declares that the love of sanguine persons was like to prove "happy and full of delight"; [67] and so it was with Orlando's.

The problems that modern critics find in Shakespeare often would not have troubled an Elizabethan; and, *vice versa,* the difficulties of plot and motivation that Shakespeare took pains to guard against sometimes do not appear in the perspective from which we moderns view the plays. Orlando's psychology offers a case in point, for the Elizabethans would usually have expected a youth so utterly and so hopelessly in love to have turned melancholy, and this would have cast a pall over the sprightly scenes that form the heart of the comedy. With truly artistic economy of means, Shakespeare justified at once Orlando's love at first sight and his continued hopefulness and the fortunate outcome required of comedy, by making his hero sanguine and jovial, for such men were gifted with the "greatest fortune"; [68] and so, just as the stars crossed with ill omen the destinies of Romeo and Juliet, so Orlando's love was fated to success, no matter how slight his efforts. Our concept of love is different; we have forgotten the four humors and the seven planetary influences, and so we do not at once recognize Orlando as the sanguine type, and so miss the motivation of the plot and see the play as an unjustified succession of romantic episodes.

Shakespeare but rarely presents the sanguine man, perhaps because it was a fair-weather humor little suited to the stress and strain of dramatic crisis. It belonged to the charming and easily successful, not to those struggling under the fardels of misfortune or of high responsibility; generally even his lovers show more or less a melancholy cast; and, if Orlando had been obliged to struggle toward his goal, he doubtless would have changed to melancholy.

He is a simple humor-type, and runs true to form without a discordant note, quite in contrast to those complex personalities who, like Shylock, were born under one humor, and by force of circumstances are bent to another. He presents in the end the placid poise of a mind at peace with the world, because the world had been kind and allowed it to fulfil its inner urge without so great an effort as to warp the feelings or distort the personality: Orlando indeed is Fortune's minion.

Shakespeare's deliberate change of the names of Orlando and his father and brothers from those given Lodge's *Rosalynde* is a matter of common knowledge; and his choice of the ancient Norman surname of de Boys, which also occurs as de Bois and de Bosco, has evoked some comment: an effort has been made to identify "old Sir Rowland" with the de Bois family of Weston-in-Arden because they had for their crest "A stag's head couped argent" [69]—supposedly referred to in the song "What shall he have who killed the deer?" The Rainsford family, however, in the same locality, had a similar crest; and on that slender basis has also claimed part inspiration of *As You Like It*.[70] Such theories have very little to substantiate them. The play shows no connection between the song and Orlando; crests with deer's heads were not uncommon; and not even tradition shows any relation between Shakespeare and this family of de Bois. On the other hand, the dramatist was "on terms of familiarity with Sir Henry and Lady Rainsford":[71] this makes the probability even less, for the song, with its salacious reference to wearing a "horn," [72] could only be interpreted as an outrageous insult to any family to which it was applied. What significance, moreover, would these local Stratford people have to a London audience? And, perhaps most important of all, they have supplied no parallels either to the plot of the play or to the characters of Orlando and his brothers. When Shakespeare wrote *As You Like It*, he had been living in London for some years; he was writing popular plays for a London audience: if the name of de Boys has any significance in the play, surely one should look for this significance in London rather than in Stratford. Perhaps Professor Sisson is right in suggesting that William and Thomas Lodge are the originals of Orlando and Oliver; [73] but the play suggests prototypes more socially exalted.

In Shakespeare's time the main line of the ancient family of de

Bois had long since become extinct. During the thirteenth century a succession of the hereditary owners of the estates had been called Sir Ernald de Boys; and French suggests that Ernald supplied Shakespeare with the names Roland and Orlando.[74] In the following century, however, Alice, daughter and heir of Sir Robert de Boys, married the admiral Sir John Howard; and thus the main line of the family and its estates were merged with the great house of Howard, from whom the Dukes of Norfolk are descended. If Shakespeare had in mind any contemporary reference in the name Sir Rowland de Boys or in Orlando de Boys, surely the Elizabethans, who were genealogically minded, would apply such a reference, not to any obscure cadet branch of the family in the Midlands, but to some contemporary representative of the main line, some person well known to the London of the day, if there were any such person whom the events and the character of Orlando would approximately fit.

Lord William Howard, made famous by Sir Walter Scott as "Belted" or "Bauld" Will, was, like Orlando, the third son of a great noble, Thomas, fourth Duke of Norfolk.[75] His father betrothed him as a child to the Lady Elizabeth Dacre, one of two sisters whose lives and fortunes were as closely bound together as those of Celia and Rosalind. They were heiresses to extensive estates on the Scottish border; but, their father dying, their uncles claimed the estates by "tail-male" and prosecuted their claim at first by litigation and in 1569 by joining in the rebellion of the Northern Earls against Queen Elizabeth's government. The failure of the rebellion nullified their claim, but still did not leave the sisters in undisputed possession. About this time, both of Lord William's parents died and left him, like Orlando, under the care of his half-brother Philip Howard, who, like Shakespeare's Oliver, seems to have taken his responsibility very lightly.[76] In 1577, before Lord William had gone to college or the Lady Elizabeth Dacre was fully grown, the two were married; and Lord William started upon a career of more than twenty years' litigation to obtain his wife's inheritance. Francis Dacre, a younger brother, claimed the estates, alleging, like the uncles, that they had been entailed upon the male heirs. Legal procedure of the day was interminable; and this claim was slowly being defeated in a series of lawsuits when one Gerard Lowther, probably the tool of Leicester, who hated the Howards, claimed most of the property for the Queen. Under Lowther's influence, the court at Carlisle in 1589 declared in favour of the Crown, Lord William being meanwhile imprisoned, ostensibly because he had become a Roman Catholic in 1584, but more probably so that he could not appear in court to contest the claim. For twelve years he and his wife were dispossessed, the Crown allowing them a somewhat precarious pension in lieu of their rights. In 1595 Lord William, despairing of his cause, begged the Queen to grant him at least some small estates in return for the large ones that she had appropriated; but still negotiations dragged on, although even Coke assured her that she had no legal right to the Dacre lands. Finally, the government allowed Lord William to repurchase his wife's inheritance for the great sum of approximately £10,000; and, in 1601, he came into full possession; and the estates were at last divided between his wife and her sister.

While these final arrangements were being completed, William Shakespeare, in the summer of 1600,[77] composed a play celebrating the final success of the third son of Sir Rowland de Bois in making his fortune by marrying a rich heiress, whose estates had been sequestered but were finally returned. In Lodge, the youth regains his lands by battle; in Shakespeare, by peaceful means. In Lodge, Orlando's struggle is a matter purely of physical prowess; in Shakespeare, it is rather economic and realistic to contemporary conditions. When Shakespeare created Orlando, did he have in mind the difficulties of family and fortune, then nearing solution, of young Lord William Howard? Surely the years of litigation had made them a commonplace of courtly circles; and Sir William himself, the "Belted Will" famous for generations in song and story, was a fit prototype for such a hero as Orlando, the "gentle, strong and valiant." Lord William lived an active life almost to the day of his death at the great age of seventy-seven; and his constant struggle to suppress banditry in the north suggests a physical prowess comparable to that of Orlando. He had, moreover, "strength and resolution" of character; and "his abhorrence of all that was base and ignoble, left unquestionably an impression strong and lasting upon the country over which his influence extended." [78] Shakespeare, furthermore, not only must have known of Lord William but may have had his personal acquaintance. Down to 1603 my Lord lived chiefly in Middlesex, and was much at court prosecuting his claims.[79]

His interests were antiquarian and literary: [80] he edited Florence of Worcester's *Chronicle;* he seems to have been one of the first members of the Society of Antiquaries; and he collected manuscripts and Roman sculpture. Unquestionably, he was interested in the drama, for his private account books show that in later life again and again he gave his patronage to the strolling players that penetrated as far north as his seat at Naworth Castle; [81] and he was a man of "great liberality" and open-handed "munificence." [82] Surely in his London days he must have frequented the theatres and had some acquaintance with actors and playwrights.

Perhaps the material here collected is mere coincidence; perhaps Shakespeare changed the name of Lodge's hero to de Boys by chance; perhaps it was mere chance that Shakespeare at just this time wrote a play showing how the third son of a great noble, through much trial and misfortune, came finally to his wife's rightful inheritance. On the other hand, the Elizabethans sometimes actually used the stage to bring pressure on a pending case in court; [83] and perhaps Shakespeare, like Prince Hamlet, selected for his play an old story that would glance at a contemporary *cause célèbre* and so have special interest. But the idealized depiction of Orlando suggests even further that perhaps the engaging Sir William had inspired or persuaded him to plead his pending case before the public in a play sufficiently similar to suggest a parallel and yet close enough to an old story to safeguard both dramatist and patron.[84] In *Timon of Athens* Shakespeare clearly implies his reverence for the hereditary aristocracy,[85] and a plea for the restitution of the Dacre estates to their rightful heiress is just the sort of cause that one might expect him to champion willingly and with effect. The charming and sanguine Orlando, moreover, as a younger son who overcomes misfortune, would lend Shakespeare's plea for his hero-lover a special cogency to younger sons who had come up to London to make their fortunes and frequented the Inns of Court, the taverns, and the theatres.

XXIX

Benedick and Beatrice

In *Much Ado About Nothing* the courtship of Claudio and Hero closely follows the social conventions of the age:[1] Claudio's "rougher taske" in the recent war has given place to "delicate desires"; he sighs for Hero in proper style; he discreetly assures himself that she is her father's "onely heire"; and then he has a highborn intermediary approach the lady and her father. This is entirely *comme il faut.* Quite different is the wooing of Benedick and Beatrice, which represents the ways of the emancipated Elizabethan woman,[2] who was approached direct and was wont to choose and refuse her lovers as she would. Thus Beatrice and Benedick quarrel instead of sigh, dispense with the help of fathers and intermediaries, and yet somehow get to the altar. Just such a contrast, Shakespeare had already used in *The Taming of the Shrew,* in which the conventional betrothal of Bianca offsets Kate's downright storm of fortunes; but Kate is reduced to marital compatibility by damp and cold and starvation; whereas, in the later play, Shakespeare leads to the comic conclusion of happy marriage by subtler, psychological means. In *The Shrew,* he cures the disease of choler in a few scenes by the recognized physical therapy forced on the patient; in *Much Ado,* the pair progress to mutual happiness without violence and by fine stages of emotional evolution; and Beatrice never so utterly

260

succumbs to wifely submission that she will not cross swords with
Benedick in witty combat: indeed, Act V in both plays presents the
same episodes in which the lover sends for his lady and she
obediently comes; but Beatrice enters with a quip that shows her
still possessed of a will of her own. The agent, moreover, that recon-
ciles the lovers is not the same in the two comedies: in *The Shrew*,
it is the husband acting as lord and master and physician-paramount;
in *Much Ado*, the Prince is a benign *deus ex machina*, abetted by
Beatrice's own secret wish and by a natural mitigation in Benedick's
harsh humor.

Indeed, Benedick in the early acts of *Much Ado* is clearly something choleric, though with less violence than Kate the Shrew. He
and Claudio are both foreign mercenaries in the service of Sicily,
the one a Paduan, the other a Florentine. He is introduced to the
audience, despite the slights of Beatrice, as a "good soldier," who
has done "good service" in the recent war and is "stuffed with all
honourable virtues." Thus the demands of his livelihood and also
the testimony of his superiors and fellows show that professionally
he is at least competent: both the Prince and Leonato refer to him as
"valiant"; the Messenger defends him against Beatrice; and the
Prince declares him honest, and loves him "well." Dariot describes
choleric persons under the influence of the sun as "valiant" and
"honest." Beatrice,[3] to be sure, slanders him as a coward, and says
that every month he plays Sir Toby to "a new sworn brother" whom
he fleeces and sets on "a voyage to the devil"; but, as her own uncle
explains, this is but part of the "merry war" betwixt the two, and
so should not be taken seriously. A brave soldier was supposed to
have a strong choleric humor [4] that overcame all other tendencies,
so that even those in whom choler was not innate, experienced it in
war. In Riche's *Apolonius and Silla*, from which Shakespeare took
the plot of *Twelfth Night*, the hero is described as too choleric on
returning from a campaign to fall in love with Silla:

> But Apolonius, commyng but lately from out the feelde from chasyng
> of his enemies, and his furie not yet thoroughly desolved, nor purged
> from his stomacke, gave no regarde to those amorous entisementes of Silla,
> whiche, by reason of his youth, he had not been acquainted with all.[5]

Likewise, Claudius in *Much Ado* remarks that while he fought in
the recent war, his love for Hero was in abeyance; and Benedick,

like Apolonius, has at the moment too much of a "queasie stomacke" to fall in love with Beatrice. Choler was "decoct or boyled in the stomach," [6] and subjected the patient to diseases of that organ.[7] If the reference, moreover, to July 6 may be taken as indicating the season of the play, then the time of the year, as in *Romeo and Juliet,* was the choleric heat of summer. In short, whatever Benedick's innate humor, his recent activities and the season of the year would tend at the opening of the play to make him choleric.

Indeed, he is clearly choleric, not only because he is valiant and loyal but also because he is "honorable"; and Dariot declared the solar choleric type "sincere" and "honest." [8] He is, moreover, "proud," though he does not realize it until Claudio and the Prince accuse him. This was a most dangerous aspect of choler, and might lead to arrogance [9] and violent revenge [10] and the wide-sweeping catastrophe of high tragedy.[11] Furthermore, despite the fact that Beatrice calls him "a very dull foole," he is very "pleasant" and "merrie," as he himself and the Messenger and the Prince and his own dialogue attest. Quick wit, though sometimes attributed to the sanguine type and to certain sorts of melancholy, was thought on the authority of Aristotle to be a common effect of choler, and so appears in Elyot,[12] Huarte,[13] Bright,[14] the *Booke of Dr. Arcandam*[15] and Wright.[16] Most of all, his attitude toward love and marriage was essentially choleric. At the very beginning Beatrice declares that he has "challenged Cupid" to a trial of skill at long range archery; Don Pedro calls him "an obstinate heretique in despite of Beautie." He complacently declares himself "loued of all Ladies" excepting only Beatrice, but he loves "none." Nevertheless, according to Leonato, he is a very philanderer, and does not hestitate to ply his arts with Margaret. In a wife he expects wealth and all the virtues—and doesn't want one at that; for he believes that all husbands are cuckolds, and so he "will live a bachelor." In the very first scene he has the consummate assurance to cast a slur even on Hero's paternity. He is clearly suspicious and jealous; he ridicules Claudio's infatuation, and believes that men in love make fools of themselves. All this agrees with the current concept of the choleric type: such men, under the influence of the sun, were "louers"; [17] and "in matter of women such a one hath no bridle nor ho"; [18] their pride and "strong opinion of honour" [19] would naturally make them jealous and suspicious of their wives.[20] In short, Benedick's choler, augmented in the recent wars, made him very chary of matrimony, and gave him the ready wit to play at lover and yet evade the altar. What a challenge to a high-spirited and adventurous young lady, to tame him as Petruchio tamed Kate!

Benedick's choler, furthermore, was not of a violent and dangerous sort. Vaughan divides choler into "open" and "hidden" [21]—the former shown in Benedick, the latter in Iago.[22] Coeffeteau, following Aristotle, distinguishes three types: the first and least virulent, sudden and soon over,[23] is most like Benedick's. Dariot carefully separates choler under the astral influence of Mars, appropriate to brawlers and ending at times in madness, from the more genial choler of the sun, which made men strong, valiant, honest, and loyal.[24] The latter is more like Benedick's, and it belonged to courtiers rather than to soldiers. Walkington divided choler into natural (innate?) and unnatural;[25] and the conclusion of the play suggests that Benedick's is the latter sort, the consequence of some special occasion, such as war. Elyot allows for four types of choler, pure, and mixed with other humors;[26] and so perhaps was Benedick's.

Indeed, the more permanent of the traits just ascribed to choler might arise also from a sanguine disposition, for both humors were warm and so had much in common. The sanguine was "the paragon of complexions";[27] it belonged to spring rather than summer, to be sure, but it was particularly proper to Benedick's "lustye flourishinge age."[28] Such men were "faithful,"[29] and "moderate, mery, pleasant witty, fayre ..."[30] and Benedick is certainly witty, and describes himself as "merrie."[31] They were "most giuen to Venus"[32] —sometimes even "too prone to Venery."[33] Benedick, moreover, is clearly handsome: how else could he play philanderer? Claudio, furthermore, describes him as "a very proper handsome man." The choleric type, though "sturdy,"[34] "strong" and "fayre,"[35] is not described as especially attractive in face and figure; but sanguine men were famous for their beauty.[36] Beatrice, moreover, twice in the play implies that Benedick is sanguine by nature: the melancholy humor was cold and dry; the sanguine, its opposite, was hot and moist; and she describes Don John as "very melancholy" in contrast to Benedick, who would therefore be sanguine. She goes on to remark that Don John is very taciturn, a melancholy trait;[37] but that Benedick is too talkative, and much blood was thought to make one "pleasant" and "mery." [38] Elsewhere, moreover, she taunts him that his halting wit "strikes him into melancholy"; and the sanguine type when crossed turned easily into its opposite. Benedick, therefore, was by nature made of much less stern and martial stuff than his initial "valiant" choler would suggest: innately, he is the brilliant courtier rather than the soldier; he is probably sanguine in normal circumstances; and, like Apolonius, would naturally revert to this humor when the effects of his recent campaign wear off. Like Hamlet and like Orsino in *Twelfth Night*, he does not at first appear in his normal humor.[39] If he is naturally choleric, it is the affable and loving choler of the sun, such as appears in Juliet. In short, Benedick is more the brilliant courtier than the brawling soldier: but he has no notion of marrying—least of all marrying Beatrice.

The fine stages in plot and character that bring these two together are expressed in some detail. In the very first scene Benedick says that his tyranny of the fair sex is only a pose, behind which apparently he hopes to escape matrimony. Indeed, he admires Beatrice but for her persistent "furie." He is a bit more coy than Petruchio and more wedded to his single blessedness. Don Pedro thinks that some day he will "look pale with loue," but he scoffs at the bare idea. He prefers Beatrice to the super-perfect Hero; but he swears and declares that he "would not marry her, tho she were indowed with all that *Adam* had left him before he transgrest." Indeed, he does protest too much; and, when she comes upon the scene, he pays her the compliment of running away. These are straws that point the direction of the wind: after all, choler of the sun was appropriate to "louers"; such were "Magnanimous," and so not likely to bear malice for a lady's hard words; and, unlike most choleric persons, they were regarded as fortunate,[40] and so the fit protagonists for comedy. Thus, given a little time for his martial choler to cool off, Benedick would quickly succumb; and, if he was by nature sanguine, he was all the more susceptible.

The Prince determines to play matchmaker. Benedick has retreated into an arbor to read himself a lengthy lecture against marriage—quite a needless task for a truly confirmed bachelor! Enter the Prince and Claudio and Leonato, supposedly without observing him; and they proceed to chide him in his hearing for not returning the love of Beatrice, who, they say is in an "extasie," and probably "wil die" as a result. They blame Benedick for wilful pride, the natural offspring of strong choler, and the cardinal sin of Christian dogma: could any "honorable" man fail to rise to such an occasion, especially when urged on by a Prince? Of course, poor Benedick's last barriers are down—even earlier, they had required the support of repeated self-assertion—and now he cries: "I wil be horribly in loue with her." Loving Beatrice has now become "the career of his humor"—a humor that can no longer be martial choler. In company, he seems "sadder," and says this "melancholy" comes from toothache. Indeed, his "humour" is to marry Beatrice; and he won't be flouted out of it, even by her vitriolic tongue or by the ridicule of his friends.

This happy conclusion came about in part by the natural decline in Benedick's martial feelings, in part, by the scheming of the Prince, but also in part, by the woman's wiles of Beatrice herself. She is "sun-burnt," that is a brunette, or "black" as the Elizabethans would say; and, therefore, her looks run counter to the current taste in beauty. Like Kate, moreover, she is "too curst" to attract marriageable youth, and so runs the risk of unregarded spinsterhood. She is "shrewd of tongue," and shows it in her speech. She is wild as a "haggard," a falcon caught when grown and so not fully tamed. Benedick declares her "possest with a furie." Having no lover nor much hope of one, she plays at "My Lady Disdain," [41] and declares she will be single. But she is neither as violent nor as wedded to celebacy as she makes believe: she has a "merry heart," was "born in a merry howre," and truly has by nature "little of the melancholy element in her": in short, she seems, like Benedick, to be either sanguine by nature or mildly choleric under the influence of the sun: this marks her off from Kate the Shrew as less violent and more witty and amenable.

The play opens with a messenger who tells the Governor, Leonato, that the Prince, having defeated his enemies, is about to pay a visit to the town. Beatrice interrupts the dialogue to enquire whether Benedick was killed; and, on being assured that he is back with his wits and witticisms unimpaired, she lets loose a flood of raillery against him that surprises and somewhat shocks the messenger. Shortly after, the young man himself enters in the Prince's train; and he speaks hardly two sentences before Beatrice acidly remarks: "I wonder that you will still [continually] be talking, Signior Benedicke, no body markes you." Surely, her original question as to his fate in the wars, and her opening shot in the canonade of wits that follows, show that she was concerned about the young soldier even before the curtain rose, and that she is determined not to be ignored. Indeed, she declares that she is "Courtesy itself" except in his presence. She seems a bit jealous of Hero whose modest exterior so readily wins her a spouse. Like Benedick, she insists profusely that she will never marry, though later she admits that she has always admired Benedick, and is in fact "sick" with love. The "merry war" between them is clearly part of her strategy. Choleric persons were warned to avoid those humored like themselves;[42] the marriage of two such was said to be a very hell,[43] "subject to Outrages and Anger";[44] and Beatrice, like Petruchio, assumes the humor if she has it not. Nevertheless, the Prince believes that Benedick and Beatrice would make an "excellent" match, though Leonato fears that "they would talke themselues madde." Contempt of others and scandalous speeches were recognized causes of choler,[45] and so their humor grew by what it fed on, and without some check would hardly have been resolved in wedlock.

Of course, when Hero and Ursula play the same trick on Beatrice that the Prince played on Benedick, she succumbs. They call her "too disdainful," and say that she will sacrifice anything to her wit; her "carping is not commendable"; and, truly, Benedick should be dissuaded from his love for her, even if this requires the floating of sundry scandals and slanders about her. Then the two pious frauds start a panegyric of Benedick that makes him "foremost in report through Italy." Beatrice is shocked to find herself "condemn'd for pride and scorne so much"; and she determines to reverse her mood and "requite" Benedick (as she says) "Taming my wilde heart to thy louing hand." The fruit is ripe to pluck, and certainly she will lose it if whispers of scandal reach his ears about her, for his jealous and suspicious nature would brook so such report. She must act and act at once. Thus shortly, both declare their love; but Beatrice must not let herself capitulate too quickly, and she is very much incensed at Claudio's public repudiation of her cousin; and so she demands that Benedick challenge his friend and kill him. The lover should endure any trial for his mistress,[46] and so Benedick reluctantly gives in; but luckily, the Hero-Claudio plot is resolved before any blood is shed. Even still, they are "too wise to wooe peaceably"; and, at the very end, they have a final—or perhaps not final—battle in which each declares that he loves the other only in "reason." One suspects that there is a bit of choler still in each, despite the purgings of the comedy; but finally all seems to come out well, and Burton, who was a shrewd physician in such matters, gives judgement on their case: sometimes those that "are harsh and ready to disagree, offended with each other's carriage, like Benedick and Beatrice in the comedy . . . by thus living together in a house . . . begin at least to dote insensibly one upon another."[47]

Since before the beginning of the play, Beatrice had set ser cap, wittingly or half-unwittingly, for the gay young Paduan philanderer: he had ignored her when he could—bitter insult!—and otherwise replied in kind to her sharp sallies. Then he had gone off to serve the Prince at war, and returned more choleric and less amenable than ever. She rallies and rails at him, for at least she will get his attention; and then he suddenly takes her onslaughts in good part; and, by a seeming accident, she hears that he is really in love with her: what a secret triumph must thrill her as she overhears the tale of his passion! She has succeeded. Portia and Olivia, being rich and beautiful and charming, spent their chief efforts in evading suitors; Beatrice, despite her being "black," and "curst" like Kate, at last has got one. But her choler is more persistent than Benedick's, and she cannot resist an occasional burst of witty petulance. At last the poem that he has tried to write to her, though poor poetry, is convincing proof of his affection; and the comedy reaches the happy conclusion of supposedly quiescent marriage. Critics have found this play, as many have found *Twelfth Night,* incoherent and insignificant as a whole; [48] but the Beatrice and Benedick plot at any rate progresses by stages at once logical and psychological to a reasonable comic end. Its theme might be phrased as the victory of Venus over Mars, or, as in *Love's Labour's,* the triumph of marriage over celebacy, or, in the words of Chaucer's Prioresse, *Amor vincit omnia.*

XXX

Dogberry's Due Process of Law

After Falstaff, Dogberry is perhaps Shakespeare's most famous comic figure. The sources of the play have nothing of him; but his part suggests that of the grandiloquent shepherd who acts as constable in *Selimus* (1594) ; and Shakespeare doubtless added him to *Much Ado,* partly because of the success of Constable Dull in *Love's Labour's* and of Shallow in *Merry Wives,* and partly because the genius of Will Kemp, who took the part,[1] particularly shone in such a role. The Prince and Count Leonato,[2] Governor of Messina, are arranging the marriage of the Lady Hero to young Claudio;[3] but the Prince's bastard brother, Don John,[4] determines to thwart them. He brings Claudio at night to Hero's window, and lets him overhear his "man"[5] Borachio make love to Hero's lady-in-waiting Margaret, whom Claudio mistakes for his mistress. Thus Hero seems faithless; and she is publicly dishonored. Don John, however, had paid Borachio "richly";[6] and Borachio tells this to his friend Conrade. Constable Dogberry's watchmen overhear the two, arrest them, and so bring all to light. A single scene, or even less, would have sufficed to accomplish this resolution of the comedy; but Shakespeare, in the prodigality of his realism, gives it three full scenes and part of a fourth:[7] he presents, moreover, not merely one constable but two, and also the watchmen and a "Sexton" or "Towne

268

Clerke." He prefaces the arrest with Dogberry's charge to the watch, and follows it with an examination of the prisoners and then a confession in a later scene. Most of this is inessential; but its rollicking low-life humor justifies its length. This humor largely derives from travesty, especially from Dogberry's travesty of legal parlance and procedure; and, to appreciate the full import of the fun, the official background of those concerned must be understood, and the legal significance of their words and actions should be clear; for the point of a travesty is lost unless the reader sees the comic disparity between the ideal and its all-too-human counterpart. Though critics have here and there illustrated the Dogberry scenes with happy comment, no detailed and systematic effort has been made to define the body of legal and social fact that underlies them. The present study, therefore, proposes first to sketch in this background and then to review the action of the scenes and so revivify their comedy.

The term *constable* refers to several offices, exalted and obscure. The great place of Lord High Constable of England, last held by the Duke of Buckingham whom Henry VIII beheaded,[8] is obviously irrelevant to Dogberry. As referring to two minor officers of law-enforcement, the term goes back to the thirteenth year of Edward I, if not to the Conqueror,[9] or even further in the remote antiquity of Common Law.[10] The hundred, which was the largest division of the shire, had one, or sometimes two, High, Chief, or Head, Constables;[11] but Dogberry cannot boast even this eminence. He is rather the Petty Constable[12] of the "town, parish or burrough," an office finally absorbed by the police in 1872.[13] In the reign of Elizabeth, the constable was the chief civil officer of the parish;[14] and his authority differed only in extent from that of the High Constable of the hundred.[15] He nominally held office for one year; but the position carried with it neither honor nor emolument; and, as one incumbent held over until his successor was appointed, many constables, like the notorious Elbow in *Measure for Measure,* were willing, for a consideration, to continue in office in the place of worthier citizens.[16] Constables, indeed, were expected to serve gratis,[17] and yet were so burdened with petty responsibilities[18] that the temptation to neglect their duties was very strong; and, moreover, their "long clinging black gowns" of office both impeded their movements, and made them obvious to thieves.[19] Thus the position

was thankless, unremunerative, and, even at best, sure to be inefficient. To make matters worse, "gentlemen of quality" were generally exempt from serving; [20] and thus, though every constable was
supposed to be *idoneous homo*,[21] the place was abandoned to
"artificers, labourers, and men of small abilitie," [22] who were
"either ignorant what to do, or dare not do what they should, or
are not able to spare the time to execute this office." [23] Many, like
Verges, were too old, or, like Dogberry, too ignorant, to command
respect; and the Elizabethan stage regularly portrayed them as
fools, or knaves, both. [24] They were accused of drunkenness,[25]
and, with their assistant watchmen, were charged with petty corruption.[26] Such in actual fact were the Elizabethan counterparts of
"The poore Dukes officers," [27] whose travesty of law and legal
procedure so amused Shakespeare's audience—amused it largely
because the travesty was so very close to life.

Dogberry is clearly a petty constable of the Burrough of Messina:
he is called "Master Constable," and "right master Constable," [28]
and he sets the nightly watch under the direct authority of Count
Leonato, the Governor of the town. Like most constables, he is of
low degree: not only does his name suggest a humble rustic
origin; [29] but also his exclamation, "God save the foundation," [30]
seems to imply that he was brought up in a home for foundlings and
so was probably base-born. In the passage of years, however, he has
climbed to the estate of "householder"; he boasts himself "a rich
enough fellow" and "as pretty a peece of flesh as any in Messina"—
perhaps because of ample girth. Moreover, he permits himself to
be called "learned," with special reference to the law. Though
younger than Verges, he delights in the accumulated dignities of his
"yeeres," [31] and waxes fittingly sententious, quoting snatches from
bourgeois manuals of elegant conversation and from current anthol-
ogies of moral aphorism.[32] Thus, like many another artisan of the
age, he has raised himself above his station, until, with all the fine
complacency of handbook self-assurance, he blossoms forth as legal
factotum of Messina, a Justice Shallow on a humbler scale, stupid,
pompous and none too honest, a perfect figure for low comedy.

Dogberry's associates are likewise realistic. "Good man Verges"
is his "neighbor," [33] and "compartner" in the office of constable;
but, since he is "an old man" and Dogberry considers his wits
"blunt," Verges is relegated to the background. The title of "Head-

borough" [34] might seem even to imply Verges' official precedence over his pushing colleague; but, as a matter of fact, it is merely another name for *constable*,[35] and indeed, "everie little Village hath commonly two Constables." [36] Dogberry and Verges' seem, therefore, to have been equals in office. Verges' name is probably a sly glance at his incompetence: as Steevens suggests,[37] it may, like Dogberry's, be derived from rustic botany, a dialect form of *verjuice;* or again it may possibly be an incongruous reference to the high and mighty Court of the Verge, which under the presidency of the Lord High Steward, might claim jurisdiction of trespasses *vi et armis* within twelve miles of the royal person, or of cases concerning members of the royal household such as Borachio; [38] or perhaps it sardonically alludes to the *verge,* or staff associated with the office of constable.[39] At all events, Verges seems to have been no better than Dogberry, except as his more modest silence brings his frailties less in evidence. Francis (or George) [40] Sea-coale understands the mystery of letters, and so is elevated to be Chief, or "Constable" of the watch to represent "the Princes owne person." [41] As such, he is solemnly invested with the lanthorn, his sign of office. He says little, and does little more; but his name implies to the initiate his lowly origins, whether it refer to the humble purlieus of Seacole Lane,[42] or to the hawkers of Newcastle "seacoals," whose grimy trade was beneath the common run of citizens.[43] That he is neighbor to Dogberry,[44] moreover, speaks little for him. Dogberry, Verges, Sea-coale—a characteristic trio of Elizabethan guardians of the peace. The common watchmen, who seem to glean their wisdom from Dogberry, are certainly no better. Indeed, the nameless "Sexton" or "Towne Clerk" is the only intelligent person of the lot; and it is lucky that in the end he elects to take Dogberry's maladroit examination of the prisoners to the Governor; for, without his explanations, the authorities could never have made head nor tail of it.

The two prisoners, Borachio and his friend Conrade, seem to be "servingmen," or gentlemen-in-waiting. At best, they were like Queen Elizabeth's bodyguard of "gentlemen pensioners" or Shakespeare's Fabyan in *Twelfth Night* [45] or the trusted Reynaldo of Polonius. [46] At worst, they might fall to menial labor, and end their days no better off than Adam in *As You Like It*. The Prince describes Conrade and Borachio as "my brothers men"; [47] and their position as servingmen to a mere younger son of the family might explain the dubious shifts to which they had recourse. Dogberry accepts Conrade upon his declaration, as a "Gentleman"; and Borachio, as the recognized suitor of Margaret, Hero's "gentle-woman," can hardly be less in rank. They are then, at once servants and gentlemen; and, as gentlemen, they object to being pinioned by the watch,[48] and do not hesitate to call Dogberry an "Asse." The place of servingmen, though not in theory menial, was far from re-munerative: they were usually younger sons of their master's vassals, and so could hope for no inheritance; and the financial decay of the nobility [49] reduced their largesse to mere food and clothing, and sometimes hardly that. Borachio, therefore, could not afford to be squeamish in any matter that promised a rich reward; and he certainly could not afford to risk his place by refusing to fall in with his master's plans, no matter how discreditable. The business done and paid for, he seems, like many another servant, to have taken his fling at the tavern, as his name, the Spanish for *drunkard,* would suggest. This doubtless explains his indiscreet garrulity to Conrade while the two are waiting under the penthouse for the rain to stop. They submit themselves to arrest; and Borachio con-fesses readily in the end, and seems to be detained more as state's evidence than for his part in the affair.[50] His chief concern is to exonerate Conrade and Margaret from complicity; and even Leon-ato half-forgives him. Borachio then is not a deep-dyed villain, but just a commonplace servingman caught, like Iago,[51] in a situation in which accepted convention led him to violate ethical ideals.

After this review of the characters concerned, a survey of the Dogberry episodes might be revealing. The first is the setting of the watch. According to a constable's oath, he was responsible for nightly "watch and ward"; [52] he might even "command his neigh-bors to assist him" [53] under pain of imprisonment in the stocks; [54] and he was supposed personally to see the "Watches duely set and kept,"[55] and is so presented in several Elizabethan plays.[56] Dog-berry, who apparently plans to go home peacefully to bed, at once proceeds to the appointment of a lieutenant for the night, and with a fine regard for learning, selects "neighbour Sea-coale" as "Consta-ble of the watch." [57] A petty constable was allowed to appoint a deputy,[58] though hardly, one suspects, for the discharge of his own ordinary official functions. At all events, Sea-coale is invested with

Dogberry's plentitude of powers, receives the lantern, and so comes to represent law and order and the very person of the "Prince." [59] Thereupon, Dogberry delivers the charge to the watch, or rather, his version of it. Lord Campbell says that charging a watch "has never been a law or a custom in England"; [60] but the archives of the Quarter Sessions do not seem to bear him out.[61] The charge that Dogberry gives is a pretty picture of the actual law-enforcement of the age: constables on duty, when possible, went to sleep,[62] and Dogberry declares that he "cannot see how sleeping should offend"; [63] Lord Burleigh bitterly complains of finding constables "under pentyces of ale-houses," [64] and Dogberry permits his man to frequent the local taverns; [65] in the face of actual crime, the constable was useless, and Dogberry gives the following instructions:

> If you meet a theefe, you may suspect him, by vertue of your office, to be no true man: and for such kinde of men, the lesse you meddle or make with them, why the more is for your honesty.
> *Watch.* If wee know him to be a thiefe, shall wee not lay hands on him.
> *Dogb.* Truly by your office you may, but I think they that touch pitch will be defil'd: the most peaceable way for you, if you do take a theefe, is, to let him shew himselfe what he is, and steale out of your company.[66]

Thus Dogberry, like Shylock, is condemned out of his own mouth. A constable was, to be sure, "indictable for neglecting Duty required by Common Law or Statute"; [67] but apparently, the statutes, as Lord Campbell suggests, were interpreted primarily "to save the constables from all trouble, danger, and responsibility, without any regard for the public safety." [68] The setting of the watch and Dogberry's charge take up almost a hundred lines; and the only passage in them that bears on the action of the play is his admonition to Sea-coale that he is to "comprehend [apprehend] all vagrom [vagrant] men": [69] undoubtedly, Shakespeare developed Dogberry for his own sweet, inimitable sake.

In view of this charge, the marvel is that the culprits were ever arrested; but so they were, if not according to strict form of law. Borachio and Conrade enter and start to discuss the plot against Hero; the whispering of the watch almost warns them; [70] and Borachio begins a diatribe against Fashion personified as a "deformed theefe"; and the watch take this "Fashion" as an actual malefactor: finally, Borachio comes to the point, and explains his wooing of Margaret under the guise of Hero. Thereupon the first Watchman interrupts with the legal formula, "We charge you in the Prince's name to stand"—the very words that Dogberry had bid them use.[71] Perhaps Shaksepeare meant this command to sound a trifle silly, for they had already been *standing* in the constricted area under the penthouse for some time; but the incantations of the law are supposed to mean more than meets the ear. At this point, the actor might well lay hold of the two prisoners to make the arrest legally complete.[72] No warrant needed to be shown.[73] The charge that Borachio tried to "slander the Ladie Hero" [74] was not proper cause for arresting him; for it was certainly not a breach of the peace committed in the presence of the constable; [75] and the watch, therefore, may well be vague as to the legal basis of their action. They call it "treason," a catch-all term for any important malefaction, and "lechery," which was certainly not a crime in Common Law. Though they do not say so, they were in reality arresting the men as vagrants according to Dogberry's injunction. The famous Statutum Wynton of 13 Edward I (1285) gave them their justification:

E si nul astraunge passe par eus arestu jeques au matin e si nule suspeciun ne feit trove aille quites. E si om trove suspeciun seit livere al viscunte maintenaunt e saunz daunger le receive et sauvement le garde jeques ataunt qe en due manere seit delivre.[76]

Sir Anthony Fitzherbarde, in his popular manual for justices, defines the duties of Elizabethan constables in these very words freely translated into modern English; [77] and the statute is reechoed by Bacon,[78] Lambard,[79] Coke,[80] Viner [81] and Ritson.[82] Since the office of constable was supposed to circulate among the commonality, everyone must have known what his duties were at least supposed to be, and so everyone could understand Shakespeare's travesty; and, since honest fellows who quaffed late at the taverns were likely to run afoul of him on the way home, his powers and his procedure were as widely understood as those of our modern state police upon the highways. Indeed, the Queen's own jester, Tarleton, was twice taken into custody for being on the streets after ten, and had to rely on his wit to save himself from jail.[83] The merest suspicion was enough for an arrest; and Conrade, moreover, had been seen to "keep suspicious company." [84] He tries to protest, and later claims his privilege status as a gentleman; [85] but his captors will not listen; and he wisely lets them have their way lest they should charge him with obstructing the enforcement of the law. So, with exchange of witticisms, they are led away. Perhaps the most comic part of the scene is this ironic outcome, that such a charge as Dogberry's should actually bring about the arrest of the conspirators.

Prisoners, properly speaking, should be haled before a Justice of the Peace [86] and then before the sheriff's court.[87] The procedure in *Much Ado* is slightly different, but not unreasonable. After an intervening scene, Dogberry and Verges come to Leonato the Governor of the town, to inform him of the arrest; but Dogberry is so anxious to show himself superior to his humble colleague that Leonato can make nothing of his pretentious mouthings; and it is the lowly Verges who finally explains that the watch have just taken "a couple of as arrant knaues as any in Messina." [88] As further talk seems to elicit no further information, Leonato begs to be excused, offers the constables some wine, and asks them to take the examination themselves. Dogberry, elated at the chance, promises to "spare for no witte," and sends for Sea-coale to fetch "his pen and inkehorne to the Goale." At last, Dogberry's legal attainments shall shine in their proper setting, on the judicial bench.

According to two statutes of Philip and Mary (1554), prisoners arrested for a felony should be examined before two justices; and the evidence against them put in writing.[89] In *Much Ado*, a person variously described as "Sexton" or "Towne Clerk" conducts the serious part of the trial, and makes the final decision that the prisoners be brought before Leonato; but Dogberry's legal light is not to be hid, and he takes unto himself the main part of the scene.[90] In defiance of the presumption that a man is innocent until proved guilty, Dogberry opens the examination by calling Borachio and Conrade "villaines." The whole "dissembly" has gathered at the jail; the Sexton is duly enthroned on stool and cushion; and Constable Dogberry takes on himself the glories of J. P. Conrade had protested that he is a "gentleman"; and His Lordship Dogberry has relaxed the decorum of the Bench sufficiently to call Borachio "friend"; and then with a fine judicial fervor, equal to Coke himself in the throes of a prosecution, he addresses the occupants of the improvised dock as "villaines." Thereupon to strengthen this assertion, he announces: "maisters, it is proued alreadie that you are little better than false knaues, and it will goe neere to be thought so shortly, how answer you for your selues?" This is a sort of Alice-through-the-looking-glass trial, with the verdict reserved for the beginning! Luckily, at least one of the prisoners was guilty; for, otherwise, like inmates in the Bastile, they could hardly have guessed their crime. They could not, moreover, let accusations under these circumstances go undenied; for silence might have seemed to give consent; and a confession before a J. P. was equal to a conviction.[91] Conrade declares that he is no false knave; whereupon Dogberry calls him with heavy sarcasm "a marvellous witty fellow." Borachio takes the same line of defense; and Dogberry suspiciously remarks that "they are both in a tale," that is, that they have pre-arranged their statements in collusion: he is treating their declaration of "not guility" as if it were perjured evidence.

So far the examination has proceeded by a standing still. The Sexton intervenes, explaining that Dogberry should "call forth the watch" to accuse the prisoners. That functionary accepts the notion with his own improvements, and in his most judicial voice commands the officers: "masters, I charge you in the Princes name, accuse these men." The word "charge" suggests the instructions of a constable to the watch: Dogberry cannot quite adapt his speech to his new eminence. The First Watchman, in obedience to this "charge," declares with the veracity of the average court-witness, that Borachio had called the Prince's brother a villain; and Dogberry orders Sea-coale: "Write down, Prince *John* a villaine: why this is flat periurie, to call a Prince's brother a villain." Borachio tries to interpose, but the court orders him silent. When there was no charge preferred against them, the prisoners are urged to speak; now, when there is one, they are not allowed. The Second Watchman depones that he heard Borachio admit having received a thousand ducats from Don John "for accusing the Lady Hero wrongfully"; and Dogberry declares this "flat Burglarie"—as if he had stolen the ducats—and one of the watchmen, much impressed, agrees, "Yea by th' masse that is so." Lechery, treason, perjury, burglary—no one ever mentions the prisoners' real crime, or even the pretext of vagrancy on which they were arrested. At last, the Sexton extracts the story from the watch; and Dogberry with his accustomed "nice derangement of epitaphs," dooms the culprits to "everlasting redemption"—a sentence more fit for an ecclesiastical than a civil court. Will Kemp's popular fooling, however, must not delay the plot forever; and the Sexton cuts this Gordian knot of legal ribbons and red tape by saying that Borachio and Conrade must "be bound" and brought before the Governor; and, to forestall misunderstanding, he will "goe before" and present the examination. He hurries off; but the conscientious Dogberry takes his suggestion that the men be "bound" in its literal rather than its legal sense: and the justice-constable concludes the trial be commanding: "Come, let them be opinion'd." The text of the following passage is obscure; but clearly the gorge of the two gentleman-servingmen rises at such indignity; and they call their captors "Coxcombe" and "asse." To Dogberry, this seems the very apogee of treason; and indeed any who used "opprobrious Words" or gave "a scornful Answer" to a constable was liable to arrest.[92] "Dost thou not suspect my place?" he cries, "dost thou not suspect my yeeres?" And in an oration vibrant with mortified vanity, he proceeds to justify his life and vindicate his learning. He especially regrets that the Sexton did not hear him called an ass, and that this major outrage was not included in the report of the examination; and, with the melancholy note, the scene concludes: "O that I had been writ down an asse!"

Pinioned despite their protests, Borachio and Conrade are haled before Governor Leonato, the father of the slandered Hero. Luckily for them, before they reached him, they chance into the presence of the Prince himself, who recognizes Borachio, and asks why they are bound. Dogberry, who still remembers the word "asse," has just called one of his prisoners "a cursing hypocrite," [93] and now accuses both in his best legal style:

> Marrie, sir, they have committed false report, moreouer they have spoken vntruths, secondly they are slanders, sixt and lastly, they have belyed a Ladie, thirdly, they haue verufied vniust things, and to conclude they are lying knaves.

The Prince keeps a serious face, and pursues the enquiry:

> First I aske thee what they haue done, thirdlie I aske thee vvhat's their offence, sixt and lastlie why they are committed, and to conclude, what you lay to their charge.

The misunderstandings of the examination-scene might here be all repeated, but Borachio wisely embraces the chance to confess and throw himself on the mercy of the Prince, who seems at the moment in a jovial frame of mind. The "learned Constable" has been "too learned" for his Prince; but luckily the prisoner himself helps out the prosecution and admits his malefaction. All are horrified at Don John's plot; and, just then, Leonato enters, fresh from his talk with the Sexton. The Dogberry scenes have served their purpose in the comedy: they have untangled the complication and lent a light touch to an almost-tragic episode. But to Dogberry, the main part of the proceedings have not yet begun; and he informs the august company how he was called an ass. Leonato tries to give him a quick *congé* with a tip.[94] Did Elizabethan governors generally tip policemen who brought in prisoners?—Then Dogberry takes his leave of us, and of the Prince, with all the ceremonious phrases he can think of, apt and inept, gleaned, one suspects, from some manual of manners:

> God keepe your vvorship, I wish your worship vvell, God restore you to health, I humblie giue you leaue to depart, and if a merrie meeting may be wisht, God prohibite it: come neighbor.

And so he leads Verges out. Whatever "merrie meeting" might have befallen is not vouchsafed to us; for Dogberry, unlike Shallow and Falstaff, does not re-appear in a later play: perhaps the Prince did not care to seek him further in his native haunts; perhaps Shakespeare felt that more contempt of court would savor dangerously of *lèse-majesté;* perhaps Kemp's retirement from the company [95] and Shakespeare's turning to more tragic themes precluded any sequel.

Since the suppression of the monasteries early in the century, the well-born youth of England had before it only two possible careers: the army with its background of Mediæval chivalry, and civil office, which centered in the law. The former of these careers, Shakespeare described and satirized in Falstaff; the latter, in Shallow. The young templars and courtiers of his audience knew both professions well, and would have seen at once any flaws in the realism of his treatment: indeed, many of them were at least perfunctory students of the law. Shakespeare's own legal knowledge may have been limited; [96] but he knew what justice was, and how it usually mis-carried; and he had seen the moods and motives of those who were supposed to enforce it. Dogberry is a Gargantua of arrogant stupidity; he unwittingly constitutes a sham of Swiftean magnitude. Indeed, he is more than a satire of constables, or even of all minor officialdom; he is the true descendant of Bottom and of the Artisans in *Julius Caesar*. He thinks in logical *non-sequitur* and speaks in Malapropisms fluent and rampant. He is the very incarnation of the lower *bourgeoisie:* their moral truisms slide off his tongue, so serious and so elevated and so inept; he boasts of his humility, and flaunts his wealth and learning, for he has no inkling what wealth or learning really are. He is a pillar of society, and yet would not arrest a thief. The "mechanicals" in *A Midsummer Night's Dream* are depicted in holiday guise in fairyland; but Dogberry vaunts himself in the actuality of Elizabethan life, a prudential middleclass Quixote with humble Sancho Panzas for assistants, the sort of persons officially described as "valued public servants." This growing realism of Shakespeare's legal scenes and characters leads to the political tragedies that shortly followed,[97] serious studies in the rise and fall of princes and governments. By degrees, Shakespeare's opportunities for observation progressed from the mere minions of the law to the seats of the high and mighty; and his psychological insight broadened from mere servants and artisans, whom he had known at Stratford, to courtiers and great nobles; and, in this evolution, Dogberry is a merry interlude, combining in himself the several comic types of pushing artisan and self-glorified petty officer—this Dogberry whom Shakespeare for future generations, once and for all, "writ down an asse."

Notes

NOTES FOR I

1. John Draper, "The Realism of Shakespeare's Roman Plays," *S.P.*, XXX, 225-242.
2. A. H. Thorndike, *The Influence of Beaumont and Fletcher on Shakespeare,* Worcester, Mass., 1901.
3. A. H. Gilbert, "Seneca and the Criticism of Elizabethan Tragedy," *P.Q.,* XIII, 370 ff.
4. John Draper, "La Vie Sociale Elizabéthaine dans les pieces de Shakespeare," *Rev. Ensig. Landg. Viv.,* LI, 392-402.
5. L. D. Frasure, "Shakespeare's Constables," *Anglia,* XLVI. 384 ff.
6. A. W. Ward, in *C. H. E. L.,* V, Chap. xiv, 390.
7. T. Lodge, *Alarvm* (1594), *Works,* ed. Hunt. Club, 1883, I, 13; Bacon, *Essays,* "Of Usury"; H. Hall, *Society in the Elizabethan Age,* London, 1886, p. 55 ff.
8. D. Lupton, *London and the Country Carbonadoed,* London, 1632.
9. F. L. Gent, *Characterismi,* London, 1631, Nos. 7 and 17. See also 12 and 14.
10. Sir T. Overbury, *Characters,* London, 1614.
11. J. Earle, *Micro-cosmographie,* London, 1628.
12. N. Breton, *Courtier and Country-man,* London, 1618.
13. "Cyuile and Vncyuile Life" in *Inedited Tracts,* Roxb. Lib., London, 1868, p. 87 ff. Country gentlemen consort with "Grasiers, Butchers" etc. *ibid.* p. 57.
14. *As You Like It,* ed. Furness var., p. 117.
15. Greek drama illustrates the theme in the *Archarnians* by Aristophanes, but Greek drama was not read by Elizabethan playwrights.
16. Lyly, *Euphues,* ed. Arber, Birmingham, 1868, pp. 113-4.
17. J. C. Jordan, *Robert Greene,* New York, 1915, p. 197.
18. This theme sometimes appears directly in the dialogue, as when the Prince contrasts the naturalness of a country girl with the "courtly coyness" of gently born ladies, which is "but foolery" (I, i, 76).
19. *Loves Labors,* ed. Furnivall and Monroe, New York, 1908, "Introduction," p. 13.
20. This attitude toward "old Verona" as a provincial town, "Where small experience grows," Shakespeare also expresses in *The Shrew,* I, ii.
21. A. H. Tolman, "Shakespeare's Part in *The Taming of the Shrew,*" *P. M. L. A.,* V, 201 ff.

22. E. P. Kuhl, *P. M. L. A.*, XL, 588 *passim*.
23. Cf. the Clown in *All's Well*, II, ii. Chambers takes *As You Like It* as a satire on court life (*Shakespeare's England*, Oxford, 1917, Chap. iii).
24. D. C. Boughner, "The Drinking Academy and Contemporary London," *Neophil.*, XIX, 272 ff.
25. John Draper, *The "Twelfth Night" of Shakespeare's Audience*, Stanford U. P. [copr., 1950].
26. _____"Shakespeare's *Coriolanus*," *W. Va. Phil. Stud.*, III (1939), 22–36.
27. _____*The "Hamlet" of Shakespeare's Audience*, Durham, N. C., 1938, p. 238 ff.
28. _____"*Macbeth* as a Compliment to James I," *Eng. Studien*, LXXII, 207–220.
29. _____"The Occasion of *King Lear*," *Stud. Phil.*, XXXIV, 176–185.
30. _____"*Timon*", *cit. sup.*

NOTES FOR II

1. See S. A. Small, *Shakespearean Character Interpretation*, Baltimore, 1927, p. 116.
2. In Udall's *Ralph Roister Doister* (1553–4?).
3. In Edwards' *Damon and Pithias* (1564).
4. In *Jacke Jugeler* (1563).
5. See O. J. Campbell, "Two Gentlemen of Verona and Italian Comedy," *Studies, Univ. of Mich.*, New York, 1925; and L. B. Wright, "Will Kemp and the Commedia dell'arte," *M.L.N.*, XLI, 516.
6. Campbell, *op. cit.*, p. 61.
7. O. M. Busbey, *Development of the Fool in Elizabethan Drama*, Oxford, 1923.
8. Earle, *Microcosmographie*, No. lix.
9. S. Rowlands, *Knave of Spades*, ed. Hunt. Club, XXII, 1874.
10. James I., "Basilikon Doron," in *Political Works*, ed. McIlwain, pp. 24-25.
11. Rowlands, *The Night-Rauen*, ed. Hunt., Club, IX; P. Stubbes, *Anatomy* (1583), ed. Furnivall, 1882, 39. Elizabeth revived the act of 21 Henry VIII. See D. Pickering, *Statutes at Large*, VI, 193.
12. Harrison, *Description of England*, London, 1587, Book II, Chap. xi.
13. M. Bacon, *New Abridgement*, Philadelphia, 1811, IV, *sub* "Master and Servant."
14. Harrison, *op. cit.*, II, xi.
15. Bacon, *op. cit.*, IV, 592.
16. *Ibid.*, IV, 557 and 593.
17. *Two Gentlemen*, IV, iv, 64 ff.
18. *Merchant of Venice*, II, ii.
19. *Batman upon Bartholome*, London, 1538, leaves 76-77; J. Fit John, *A Diamonde Most Precious*, London, 1577; W. Darell, *Short Discourse of the Life of Servingmen*, London, 1578; [G. Markham], *Profession of Servingmen*, London, 1598; W. Basse, *Sword and Buckler*, London, 1602.
20. *Comedy of Errors*, III, ii.
21. Cf. Desdemona. See John Draper, *Rev. Litt. Comp.*, XIII, 337 ff.
22. Basse, *op. cit.*, stanza 70.

23. See H. P. Pettigrew, "Bassanio, the Elizabethan Lover," *P. Q.*, XVI, 296 ff.

24. See John J. Draper, " 'This Poor Trash of Venice'," *J.E.G.P.*, XXX, 508 ff.

25. See John J. Draper, *The "Othello" of Shakespeare's Audience*, Paris, 1952.

26. See T. B. Stroup, "Launce and Launcelot," *J.E.G.P.*, XXX, 506–507.

27. See Basse, *op. cit.*, stanza 65 etc.

28. G. Markham (1598), in *Inedited Tracts*, Roxb. Lib., London, 1868, p. 157 etc.

29. Harrison, *op. cit.*, II, v; and *Cyuile and Vncyuile Life* (1579) in *Inedited Tracts, ed. cit.*, 30 *passim*.

30. Markham, *op. cit.*, 152. See also John Draper, "The Theme of 'Timon of Athens'," *M.L.R.*, XXIX, 20 ff.

31. Brathwait, *English Gentleman*, London, 1641, 88; and Markham, *op. cit.*, 127 ff.

32. Harrison, *op. cit.*, II, v and xi.

33. Basse, *op. cit.*, stanzas 10 and 11.

34. Fit John, *op. cit.*, sig. B ii.

35. Markham, *op. cit.*, 117.

36. *Ibid.*, 142; Harrison, *op. cit.*, II, xi.

37. J. Bodenham, *Wits Commonwealth*, London, 1640, 187 ff.; and Markham, *op. cit.*, pp. 146 and 157.

38. F. Moryson, *Itinerary* (1617), ed. Furnivall, New Shak. Soc., 271. See also Brathwait, *op. cit.*, 89; and [H. Peacham] *Coach and Sedan* (1636), London, 1925, sig. C.3.

39. Markham, *op. cit.*, p. 120 ff.; and Basse, *op. cit.*, stanza 45.

40. Markham, *op. cit.*, p. 131 ff.

41. Basse, *op. cit.*, stanza 18.

42. Markham, *op. cit.*, p. 103.

43. Basse, *op. cit.*, stanza 74.

44. S. Rowlands, *Doctor Merry-man* (1609), ed. Hunt. Club, 12; and *Knaue of Clubs* (1609), ed. Hunt. Club., 7; and Brathwait, *op. cit.*, p. 89.

45. Markham, *op. cit.*, pp. 123, 136 etc.; and Overbury, *Characters,* "Servingman."

46. Basse, *op. cit.*, stanzas 2, 46-47.

47. L. A. Fisher, *Shakespeare Assoc. Bulletin*, VII, 124.

48. S. A. Small, *op. cit.*, p. 66.

NOTES FOR IV

1. See John Draper, "This Poor Trash of Venice," *J.E.G.P.*, XXX, 508.

2. See John Draper, "Honest Iago," *P.M.L.A.*, XLVI, 726; and "Othello and Elizabethan Army Life," *R.A.-A.*, IX, 319.

3. See John Draper, "Desdemona, A Compound of Two Cultures," *Rev. Litt. Comp.*, XIII, 337; and "The Wooing of Olivia," *Neophil.*, XXIII, 37.

4. See John Draper, "Captain General Othello," *Anglia*, XLIII, 296.

5. See T. Dekker, "Seven Deadly Sins of London," *Non-dramatic Works,* II, 59-60. Cf. *Merchant of Venice*, I. ii.

6. See *Julius Caesar*, I, i.

7. See John Draper, *The "Twelfth Night" of Shakespeare's Audience*, Stanford U.P., [copr. 1950].

8. *Twelfth Night*, III, iv.

9. *Midsummer Night's Dream*, ed. Furnivall, London, 1908, 15-16.

NOTES FOR V

1. T. F. Crane, *Italian Social Customs of the Sixteenth Century,* New Haven, 1920, Chaps. ix and x.
2. *Ibid.,* 534.
3. M. A. Scott, *Elizabethan Translations from the Italian,* Boston, 1916.
4. Sir Edward Sullivan, "A Forgotten Volume in Shakespeare's Library," *Nineteenth Century,* Feb., 1904. See also his "Italian Book of Etiquette in Shakespeare's Day," *Ibid.,* June, 1913; and his introduction to his edition of *Guazzo's Civile Conversation,* London, 1925.
5. Crane, *op. cit.,* 278.
6. See John Draper, *The "Hamlet" of Shakespeare's Audience* Durham, N. C., 1938, Chap. iii.
7. See C. R. Sleeth, "Shakespeare's Counsellors of State," *Rev. Anglo-Amér.,* XIII, 97 ff.
8. *Twelfth Night,* ed. Aldis Wright, I, v., 122. Cf. *Love's Labour's,* IV, ii.
9. Cf. T. W. Baldwin, *Willian Shakespeare's Petty School,* Urbana, Ill., 1943. For like reason, the improving dialogues composed for bourgeois readers (L. B. Wright, *Middle-Class Culture in Elizabethan England,* Chapel Hill, N. C., 1935, 103 ff.) were probably of little influence: their effect might better be sought in certain passages of Dogberry and Sir Andrew Aguecheek.
10. S. Guazzo, *The Civile Conversation,* tr. Pettie and Young, ed. Sullivan, London, 1925, p. 119.
11. On the timely significance of his remarks, see D. G. Nuzum, "Shakespeare and the London Company," *W. Va. Phil. Bull.,* 1959.
12. The present writer and his friends have twice presented the conversazione. See E. F. Reed, *The West Va. Rev.,* XXII, 24-25.

NOTES FOR VI

1. Some 6 per cent of the population seem to have been illegitimate according to the narrow legal definition. In actual fact, the proportion must have been much larger. See C. L'Estrange Ewen, *Surnames of the British Isles,* London, 1931, 268. See also L. L. Schücking, *Eng. Studien,* LXII, 221-225.
2. *Troilus and Cressida,* V, vii.
3. *Ibid.,* V, v,; V, vii.
4. *Tempest,* V, i.
5. See M. Bacon, *New Abridgment,* Philadelphia, 1811, I, 512; and C. Viner, *General Abridgment,* Aldershot, n. d., IV, 213 *et seq.*
6. See D. Pickering, *Statutes at Large,* Cambridge, 1763, VI, 311; and Bacon, *op. cit.,* I, 520-521. The government tried to regulate such matters by a law, 18 Eliz., Cap. 3. The local J. P. was supposed to oblige the mother and reputed father to reimburse the parish for the child's care.
7. The Earl of Leicester disinherited his son by denying marriage with his mother.
8. Bacon, *op. cit,* I, 510 ff.; Viner, *op. cit.,* IV, 216. Common Law admitted a child born after spousals, i.e. bethothal, as legitimate; for a betrothal *in praesenti* if consummated, was regarded as a legal marriage. See L. C. Powell, *English Domestic Relations, 1487-1653,* New York, 1917, 6.
9. W. C. Bolland, *Publ. Selden Soc.,* XXXIII, xxi ff.

10. See John Draper, "Ophelia's Crime of *Felo de se*," *W. Va. Law Quart.*, XLII, 228 ff.

11. Viner, *op. cit.*, IV, 217-218.

12. See Grey, Davis and Verplanck in *King John*, ed. Furness var., 37-38; and John Lord Campbell, *Shakespeare's Legal Acquirements*, London, 1859, 61-62; and G. W. Keeton, *Shakespeare and his Legal Problems*, London, 1930.

13. In *The Troublesome Raigne*, King John's judicial procedure was hardly legal, for neither parent was a competent witness.

14. Shakespeare changes the six weeks' absence mentioned in *The Troublesome Raigne* to fourteen weeks.

15. Philip appeals to heaven and to his mother, apparently not knowing that her evidence was not admissible.

16. *Richard III*, III, v. See also III, vii.

17. *Ibid.*, IV, ii.

18. *Ibid.*, IV, iii.

19. *1 Henry VI*, III, i; *2 Henry VI*, IV, i; *King John*, I, i; *Richard III*, V, iii; *2 Henry IV*, II, i; *Henry V*, III, ii, and III, v; *Julius Caesar*, V, iv; *All's Well*, II, iii; *Coriolanus*, III, ii and IV, v; and *Cymbelino*, II, v.

20. *King Lear*, I, ii.

21. See Schmidt's *Lexicon* and *N. E. D., s. v.*

22. See John Draper, *Anglia*, XLIII, 304-305.

23. *Love's Labour's*, V, I.

24. See R. Lawson, "Lucio, in *Measure for Measure*," *Eng. Studies*, IX, 259-64.

25. *Measure for Measure*, III, ii.

26. *King Lear*, I, i ff.; cf. *Richard II*, V, ii.

27. King James I, *Workes*, London, 1616, 55.

28. See John Draper, "Honest Iago," *P. M. L. A.*, XLVI, 728-32.

29. *Winter's Tale*, II, iii.

30. *Pericles*, IV, ii.

31. *Merchant of Venice*, III, v.

32. *Troilus*, V, v; and V, vii.

33. *2 Henry IV*, III, ii.

34. See John Draper, "Ophelia and Laertes," *P. Q.*, XIV, 50-52.

35. See Ruth Kelso, *The Doctrine of the English Gentlemen in the Sixteenth Century*, Urbana, 1929, 31 ff.

36. J. [G.] B. Nenna, *Nennio*, tr. W. Jones, London, 1595, 16; cf. 76. The idea seems to have been a commonplace of the Italian Renaissance. It appears also in Castiglione, *Courtier*, ed. Rouse and Henderson, 32 ff.

37. H. Peacham, *Compleat Gentleman*, London, 1622, 1 ff.

38. J. Stephens, *Satyrical Essayes*, London, 1615, 35.

39. [J. Heywood?] *Of Gentleness and Nobility*, [1535?], sig. Ai ff.

40. [J. Bodenham], *Wits Common-wealth*, London, 1640, 102.

41. L. Bryskett, *Discourse of Civill Life*, London, 1603, 12.

42. James I, *Political Works*, ed. McIlwain, Cambridge [Mass.], 1918, 33.

43. *Shakespeare's England*, Oxford, 1917, I, 410.

44. *1 Henry IV*, III, ii.

45. *2 Henry VI*, IV, i.

46. *Hamlet*, IV, v. Intelligence also is imputed to heredity, *A. Y. L. I.*, III, II, 31-2.

47. *Julius Caesar*, II, i.

48. *King Lear,* I, iv.
49. *Ibid.,* IV, vi. Cf. *Richard II,* V, ii.
50. See John Draper, "Political Themes in Shakespeare's Later Plays," *J. E. G. P.,* XXXIV, 61 ff.
51. The semantic history of the word *villain,* which is derived from the Latin word for a farm-laborer, illustrates this association between bad conduct and the lower classes.
52. See Snider, quoted in *King John,* ed. Furness var., 592.
53. *Much Ado,* ed. Furness var., 49.
54. See John Draper, "Macbeth as a Compliment to James I," *Eng. Studien,* LXXII, 207.
55. See John Draper, "The Occasion of *King Lear,*" *Stud. Phil.,* XXXIV, 176 ff.

NOTES FOR VII

1. See Neilson and Thorndike, *Facts about Shakespeare,* pp. 71-72.
2. *Midsommer Nights Dreame,* ed. Furness var., pp. 250 ff. See also Stowe, *Annales* [London, 1605], pp. 1279 and 1281.
3. E. Rickert, "Political Propaganda and Satire in *A Midsommer Nights Dreame,*" MP., XXI, 53 ff. and 133 ff.
4. F. H. McCloskey, "The Date of *A Midsummer Nights Dream,*" MLN., XLVI, 389.
5. Cf. R. H. Darby, "The Date of Some of Shakespeare's Sonnets," *Sh. Jhb.,* LXXV (1939), 135-138.
6. Sir J. G. Frazer, *Golden Bough,* London, 1919, II, 65, 272-3; IX, 359.
7. The Gregorian calendar was not accepted in England until 1751.
8. There was a moon on June 27 O. S.; but this would be too late for June 11 and too early for July 6.
9. R. Harvey, *Astrological Discourse,* London, 1583, p. 56.
10. *Dreame,* Furness var. ed., p. 297.
11. T. von Oppolzer, *Canon der Finsternisse,* Vienna, 1887, p. 268 and plate 134.

NOTES FOR VIII

1. Cf. W. D. Briggs, ed. *Marlowe's Edward II,* London, 1914, "Introduction," and C. H. Herford, ed. *Richard II,* Arden ed. "Introduction."
2. See John Draper, "The 'Gracious Duncan'," *M.L.R.,* XXXVI, 495-499. For a fuller discussion of Elizabethan psychology, see John Draper, *The Humors and Shakespeare's Characters,* Durham, N.C., 1945.
3. T. Adams, *Diseases of the Sovle,* London, 1616, 7 ff.
4. C. Dariot, *Iudgement of the Starres,* tr. F. Wither, London, 1598, sig. D 1 r.
5. *Ibid.,* sig. D 4 v.
6. See John Draper, "Macbeth, 'Infirme of Purpose'," *Bull. Hist. Med.,* X, 16 ff.
7. Dariot, *op. cit.,* sig. D 4 r.
8. *Ibid.,* sig. D 4 v.
9. *Ibid.,* sig. D 4 v.
10. T. Hill, *Schoole for Skill,* London, 1599, leaf 50 v.
11. Adams, *op. cit.,* 9.
12. Dariot, *op. cit.,* sig. D 4 v.
13. *Ibid.,* sig. D 4 v.

14. See John Draper, *The "Hamlet" of Shakespeare's Audience,* Durham, 1938. Chap. xi.
15. Holinshed, *Chronicles,* III, 498.
16. *Ibid.,* III, 504.
17. *Ibid.,* III, 503.
18. *Ibid.,* III, 507-508.
19. Dariot, *op. cit.,* sig. D 2 r *passim.*
20. *Edward II,* I, iv.
21. Dariot, *op. cit.,* sig. D 4 r.
22. See John Draper, "Macbeth," *op. cit.*
23. See John Draper, "The Old Age of King Lear," *J. E. G. P.,* XXXIX, 527 ff.
24. See John Draper, "Political Themes in Shakespeare's Later Plays," *J. E. G. P.,* XXXV, 61 ff.

NOTES FOR IX

1. *Romeo and Juliet,* I, iii.
2. *Ibid.,* II, iv.
3. On this date, see *Romeo and Juliet,* orig. Rolfe ed., p. 12.
4. On the time-analysis, corrected from Daniel, see the orig. Rolfe ed., p. 219.
5. Schmidt's *Lexicon,* in accordance with the context of this passage, defines "odd" as "not even, not divisible into two equal whole numbers."
6. *Romeo and Juliet,* i, v.
7. Harvey, *Astronomical Discourse* (London, 1583), p. 56.
8. Von Oppolzer, *Canon* (Vienna, 1887), p. 268.
9. This seems improbable; for the play shows a correlation of tempo with character and humor in its text as a whole that suggests a date after *Richard II* (1595).

NOTES FOR X

1. *Romeo and Juliet,* ed. Furness var., p. 466.
2. *Ibid.,* pp. 451 ff.
3. J. Erskine, "Romeo and Juliet," in *Shakespearean Studies,* by members of the department of English in Columbia University, New York, 1916, p. 219.
4. See John Draper, "Political Themes in Shakespeare's Later Plays," *J.E.G.P.,* XXXV 61 ff.
5. *Romeo and Juliet,* III, i.
6. Dowden, *Shakespeare, a Critical Study,* London, 1876, pp. 106-7.
7. On the history of "fortune," see H. P. Patch, *The Goddess Fortune in Mediæval Literature,* Cambridge, Mass., 1927.
8. *Romeo and Juliet,* III, v; V. ii; and V, iii.
9. *Romeo and Juliet,* IV. i; V, iii; and V, iii.
10. See W. C. Curry, *Chaucer and the Mediæval Sciences,* New York, 1926.
11. Writers on Shakespeare and astrology barely refer to *Romeo and Juliet:* W. Wilson, *Shakespeare and Astrology,* Boston, 1903; *Shakespeare's England,* Oxford, 1917, 1, 444 ff.; and C. Camden, "Astrology in Shakespeare's Day," *Isis,* XIX, 1 ff.
12. The debate on the validity of astrology started at least as early as Pico della Mirandola just before 1500 (L. Thorndike, *History of Magic,* New York, 1934, Chap. lxi) and developed later in England (Camden, *op. cit.).*

13. L. B. Wright, *Middle-Class Culture in Elizabethan England,* Chapel Hill, N.C., 1935, pp. 593 ff.

14. L. Lemnius, *Touchstone,* London, 1581, leaf 79 r. Almanacks are said to have been of "readier money than Ale and cakes." See T. Nashe, "Have with You" (*Works,* ed. McKerrow, III. 72).

15. W. Warde, tr., *The Most Excellent Booke of Arcandam,* London, 1592. Most of these rare volumes are to be found in the Folger Shakespeare Library.

16. C. Dariot, F. Wither, tr. *Astrologicall Iudgement of the Starres,* London, 1598.

17. L. Lemnius, T. Newton, tr., *Touchstone of Complexions,* London, 1581.

18. T. Moulton, *Myrrour or Glass of Health, ed. princ.,* London, 1539.

19. R. Harvey, *Astrological Discourse,* London, 1582; supplement 1583.

20. T. Hill, *Schoole of Skill,* London, 1599, etc. On Hill and his writings see Wright, p. 565.

21. *Romeo and Juliet,* ed. Furness var., p. 456.

22. *Ibid.,* ed. Arden, p. xvi.

23. *Ibid.,* ed. Furness var., I, i, 102; III, i, 114; I, v., 87.

24. *Ibid.,* III, i, 150-151. Tybalt is "a gentleman of the very first house" (II, iv, 22-23); and this may refer to Aries, which governed the choleric type. His name signifies a cat; and perhaps this also is significant. See Lemnius, *op. cit.,* leaf 96^v ff.

25. Lemnius, *op. cit.,* leaf 138^r and 138^v. Cf. *N.E.D., s. spleen.*

26. Ptolemy, *Tetrabiblos,* tr. Ashmand, London, 1827, pp. 149, 198; Hill, *op. cit.,* leaf 8^v; and Lemnius, *op. cit.,* leaf 86^v.

27. *Arcandam, op. cit.,* sig. M2^r; and Lemnius, *op. cit.,* leaf 23^r.

28. L. Campbell, *Shakespeare's Tragic Heroes,* Cambridge, 1930, p. 60.

29. Hill, *op. cit.,* (leaf 8^v) imputes to this type thick, black, bushy hair; but Ptolemy (p. 149) thinks red hair of moderate growth; and *Arcandam* (sig. M^r) seems to agree.

30. *Cyuile and Vncyuile Life (ed. princ.,* 1579) in *Inedited Tracts,* ed. Hazlitt, Rox. Lib., London, 1868, p. 75; E. Tilney, *Flower of Friendship,* London, 1568, sig. Biiij^r; [?I.M.], *General Practise of Medicine,* London, 1634, sig. B2^v; L. Lemnius, *op. cit.,* leaf 29^v ff; and *Arcandam,* sig. M$_2$^{v}.

31. Cf. Falstaff. See Ruth Sims, *The Green Old Age of Falstaff, Bull. Hist. Medicine,* XIII (1943), 144-57.

32. *Romeo and Juliet,* III, i.

33. *Ibid.,* I, i. He is also fortunate in that he escapes the catastrophe.

34. *Batman upon Bartholome,* London, 1582, leaves 31^v and 32^r; *Arcandam,* sig. Mi^r and Mi^v; Lemnius, *op. cit.,* leaves 23^v, 86^v, 111^v; 122^r; 146^r; Hill, *op. cit.,* 16 and 26; and Dariot, *op. cit.,* sig. D4^r.

35. *Romeo and Juliet,* III, i.

36. Ibid., III, i.

37. *Ibid.,* III, i, *passim.*

38. *Ibid.,* I, i.

39. Campbell, *op. cit.,* p. 59.

40. Of course, he had used the humors earlier in *Love's Labor's.* On this whole problem, see John Draper, *The Humors and Shakespeare's Characters.,* Durham, N.C., 1945.

41. Dariot, *op. cit.,* sig. Di^r.

42. *Romeo and Juliet,* I, iv.

43. *N.E.D., s. mercury.*

44. *Romeo and Juliet,* I, iv.
45. *N.E.D., s. mercurial.* Mercury's influence, moreover, was supposed to make men ingenious. See Hill, *Schoole, ed., cit.,* leaf 50ᵛ.
46. *Romeo and Juliet,* I, iv.
47. *Ibid.,* II, iv.
48. *Ibid.,* II, iv.
49. *Ibid.,* I, iv.
50. *Ibid.,* II, iv.
51. *Ibid.,* II, iv. He talks bawdry to the Nurse, perhaps appropriately.
52. *Ibid.,* II, i.
53. See A. Guido, "The Humor of Juliet's Nurse," *Bull. Hist. Med.,* XVII, 297 ff.
54. Lammas-eve would be July 31 O.S., *i.e.* August 10 N.S. The sun is in the sign of Leo from July 21 to August 21.
55. Dariot, *op. cit.,* sig. Biiiʳ and Biiiᵛ. Venus and Leo were thought to incite lust. See Burton, *Anatomy of Melancholy,* III, 3, 2, 2, 1.
56. Dariot, *op. cit.,* sig. Diʳ.
57. Campbell, *op. cit.,* p. 59.
58. Lemnius, *op. cit.,* leaf 129ʳ and 129ᵛ. Many of these details could hardly apply to a young woman, and so are omitted.
59. Batman, *op. cit.,* leaf 32ᵛ.
60. Campbell, *op. cit.,* p. 59; and Dariot, *op. cit.,* sig. D₃ᵛ.
61. Of course the sun was a planet according to the generally accepted Ptolemaic system.
62. Dariot, *op. cit.,* sig. Civᵛ.
63. *Romeo and Juliet,* I, i. See John Cole, "Romeo and Rosaline," *Neophil.,* XXIV, 285 ff.
64. Hill, *Schoole, ed. cit.,* 25.
65. *Romeo and Juliet,* I, i,; I, iv.
66. See John Draper, *The "Hamlet" of Shakespeare's Audience,* Durham, N.C., 1938, pp. 175 ff.
67. Lemnius, *op. cit.,* prescribes "Moderate myrth and banqueting," leaf 154ʷ.
68. See John Draper, *The "Twelfth Night" of Shakespeare's Audience,* Stanford U.P., [copr. 1950] Chap. VI.
69. Lemnius, *op. cit.,* leaf 92ʳ and 92ᵛ.
70. *Romeo and Juliet,* II, iv. The sanguine type was supposed to be particularly susceptible to love. See Burton, *op. cit.,* III, 2, 2, 1; J. Ferrand, 'ἐρωτομανία, Oxford, 1640, p. 64; and N. Coeffeteau, *Table of Humane Passions,* London, 1621, p. 551.
71. Lemnius, *op. cit.,* leaf 86ᵛ.
72. *Ibid.,* leaf 45ᵛ.
73. Sir J. G. Frazer, *Golden Bough,* London, 1919, VI, 132 and 137.
74. *Romeo and Juliet,* II, v.
75. *Arcandam,* sig. M₂ʳ.
76. Lemnius, *op. cit.,* leaves 48ᵛ and 49ʳ.
77. *Ibid.,* leaf 86ᵛ; Batman, *op. cit.,* leaf 30ʳ; Campbell, *op. cit.,* p. 58; and Dariot, *op. cit.,* sig. D₂ᵛ.
78. *Romeo and Juliet,* II, iv.
79. Lemnius, *op. cit.,* leaf 101ᵛ.
80. *Ibid.*
81. Daniel ends the play Friday (*Trans. New Shak. Soc.,* 1877–79, 194); for a

discussion of his mistake, see old Rolfe ed., 202–19. See also Ferrand, Chap. xxi, who seems to feel that the stars had only a very limited influence over the human body; and P. Boaystuau, *Theatrum Mundi,* tr. Alday, London, 1574, pp. 202–3, who also seems to think the humours more important.

82. *Romeo and Juliet,* III, i. In Paynter, the marriage takes place on Saturday, and much time elapses before the catastrophe.
83. Juliet took the potion an hour or more after it was "near night" (IV, ii).
84. Dariot, *op. cit.,* sig. Di^v.
85. At the end of the scene, the Prince refers to "this morning" as if the sun were about to rise.
86. See A. H. Gilbert, "Seneca and the Criticism of Elizabethan Tragedy," *P.Q.,* XIII, 370; and Campbell, *op. cit.,* pp. 5 ff.
87. Wright, *op. cit.,* pp. 403 ff. See also W. Farnham, *The Medieval Heritage of Elizabethan Tragedy,* Berkeley, Calif., 1936.

NOTES FOR XI

1. John Draper, *The Tempo-Patterns of Shakespeare's Plays,* Heidelberg, 1957.
2. O. Jespersen, *Growth and Structure of the English Language,* Leipzig, 1919, Sec. 221.
3. J. Q. Adams, *Life of William Shakespeare,* Boston, 1925, 92 ff.
4. T. W. Baldwin, *Shakespeare's Small Latine,* Urbana, Ill., 1944, II, 378 ff.
5. Sister Meriam Joseph, *Shakespeare's Use of the Arts of Language,* New York, 1947.

NOTES FOR XIII

1. For a fuller explanation of the evidences of tempo, see John Draper, *The Tempo-Patterns of Shakespeare's Plays,* Heidelberg, 1957, Chap. i.
2. Psychologists today have reached similar conclusions. See F. R. Schreiber, "What to Do About Your Voice," *Reader's Digest,* July, 1959, p. 108.

NOTES FOR XIV

1. See E. E. Stoll, *Shakespeare Studies,* New York, 1927, p. 263; B. V. Wenger, "Shylocks Pfund Fleisch," *Shak. Jhrb.,* LXV, 92–174; and M. Schlauch, "The Pound of Flesh Story in the North," *J.E.G.P.,* XXX, 388 ff.
2. See John Foxe, *Sermon Preached at the Christening of a Certaine Jew,* London, 1578 (Harvard Library). This Jew was Spanish, as his "confession" subjoined to the sermon shows. Although Foxe still charges that the Jews "murdered Christ" (sig. E iii), and notes "Christenmens children here in Englande crucified by the Jewes Anno 1189," yet he declares the race not "altogether forsaken of God" (sig. A viii), and reminds his hearers that "the very first yssues of our Christian faith sprange out of that stocke" (sig. B v).
3. J. L. Cardozo, *The Contemporary Jew in Elizabethan Drama,* Amsterdam, 1925. The Jews had been banished from England in 1290; and unconverted Jews were still rigorously expelled as late as 1609 (pp. 36 ff.). But a few Jews lived in Elizabethan London generally under the guise of being Roman Catholics. See J. E. Bakeless, *Christopher Marlowe,* New York, 1937, p. 178; and C. J. Sisson in *Studies by Members of the English Association,* Oxford, 1938, pp. 38-51. The Spanish Jews had generally submitted to conversion in 1492, or else had fled to Morocco.

4. Cf. L. L. Schücking, *Character Problems,* London, 1922, p. 92. Lopez bears only slight relation to the Jews of Elizabethan drama. But two of them were physicians; and the tradition started before him, and ended long after (Cardozo, *op. cit.,* p. 195, etc.). Apparently, no one thought of Lopez as a Jew until his trial; and the tradition of Shylock's red wig, if trustworthy, suggests a relation to the Judas legend rather than to the Spanish Lopez.

5. Schücking, *op. cit.,* p. 92; Cardozo, *op. cit.,* pp. 53, 238-39, 329; R. Voldeba, "Over de Shylockfiguur," *Neophilologus,* XIV, 196 ff.; T. Gainsford, *The Glory of England* 1622, p. 268; and H. Smith (1550?- 91), *Examination of Vsury"* [London?], 1751, 7; Coryat (*Crudities* [London 1611], p. 234) distinguishes between the actual Venetian Jews and the English idea of them; and Shylock belongs in the latter category.

6. *Shakespeare's England,* Oxford, 1917, I, 217. See also Cecil Roth, "The Background of Shylock," *R.E.S.,* IX, 148 ff.; and P. Molmenti, *Venice,* tr. H. F. Brown, Chicago, 1906, Part I, Vol. I, 192 ff.

7. *The Merchant of Venice,* ed. Furness, III, i, 53 ff. For Venetian local color in Shylock, see C. Roth, "The Background of Shylock," *R.E.S.,* IX, 148 ff.

8. *Ibid.,* I, iii, 42 ff. The first italics are mine. This predominance of usury in Shylock was noted by Hunter and Lloyd (S. A. Small, *Shakespearean Character Interpretation* [Baltimore, 1927], p. 30), and by Stoll, *op. cit.,* p. 265.

9. *Ibid.,* III, i, 43 and 51.

10. *Ibid.,* I, iii, 117.

11. *Ibid.,* III, i, 121 ff.; iii. 4.

12. *Ibid.,* III, iii, 25 ff.

13. Even Jessica's elopement with a Christian was hardly as important to Shylock as the money she stole.

14. When the present study was almost completed, the writer came upon the similar suggestion of H. W. Farnam, *Shakespeare's Economics* (New Haven, 1931), pp. 4-5, reprinted from the *Yale Review,* April, 1913.

15. See *N.E.D., s.v.*

16. *Merchant of Venice,* I, iii, 61-62.

17. *Sonnets,* VI, 5.

18. *Lear,* III, ii, and IV, vi; *Timon,* II, ii; *Measure for Measure,* III, ii. Friar Lawrence refers to usurers' ill-gotten wealth (*Romeo,* III, iii); and Autoloycus pictures them as begrudging, like Shylock, their servants' food (*Winter's Tale,* IV, iv).

19. *Coriolanus,* I, i.

20. *Timon,* II, ii *passim.* See the present writer, "The Theme of 'Timon of Athens'," *M.L.R.,* XXIX (1934), 20 ff.

21. Stonex (*P.M.L.A.,* XXXI, 190) lists seventy-one plays, 1553-1637.

22. *Ibid.,* pp. 191-93; and W. Reinicke, *Der Wucherer im älteren eng. Drama,* Halle, 1907, p. 6.

23. See J. D. Rea, "Shylock and the Processus Belial," *P.Q.* VIII, 311 ff.

24. See Stoll, *op. cit.,* p. 255; and "Shylock," *J.E.G.P.,* X, 235 ff.

25. Schücking, *op. cit.,* p. 92.

26. Cardozo, *op. cit.,* p. 309. Of course, usury is incidental to Barabas.

27. R. H. Tawney, *The Agrarian Problem in the Sixteenth Century,* London, 1912, p. 193; and his "Introduction" to T. Wilson's, *Discourse upon Usury,* New York, 1925 (hereafter referred to as "Introduction"); K. L. Gregg, *Thomas Dekker, U. of Wash. Pub.* (Seattle, 1924), p. 55; E. P. Cheyney,

History of England from the Defeat of the Armada, New York, 1926, II, 35.
28. T. Dekker, *Works,* ed. Grosart, IV, 87: *Worke for Armorours* (1609?).
29. Tawney, "Introduction," pp. 155 ff. On the attitude of the merchant see G. de Malynes, *Englands View,* London, 1603 (Brit. Mus.), p. 162, and *Treatise of the Canker of Englands Commonwealth* (London, 1601) (Brit. Mus.), p. 120.
30. *Cyuile and Vncyuile Life* (1579). ed. Hazlitt, *Inedited Tracts,* Rox. Lib., 1868, p. 59; and Tawney, "Introduction," pp. 31 ff.
31. Marlowe's Barabas charged 100 per cent (*Jew of Malta,* IV, i 41 ff.). As the profits from trade might run from 150 to 250 per cent, the merchant could afford to pay 80 per cent on loans (W. Besant, *Tudor London* [London, 1904], p. 238). Sometimes Elizabeth paid 12 per cent, with bonuses for extension from 1 to 3 per cent (H. Hall, *Elizabethan Age* [London, 1886], p. 64); and, even as late as 1636, 15 and 20 per cent were common in England (Malynes, *Consuetudo* [London, 1636] (Huntington Lib.), p. 221). See also, F. P. Wilson, *The Plague in Shakespeare's London,* Oxford, 1927, pp. 107 ff.
32. *Shakespeare's England,* I, 332 ff.; Stubbes, *Anatomie* (New Shak. Soc. [1882]), Part II, pp. 21 ff.; Tawney, "Introduction," pp. 25 ff., 43 ff.
33. See Cunningham in *C.H.E.L.,* IV, 357; R. D. Richards, *Early Banking in England,* London, 1929, p. 2.
34. T. W. Baldwin, *Shakespearean Company,* Princeton, 1927, p. 16 ff.
35. Hall, *op. cit.,* p. 59 ff.
36. *Ibid.,* p. 52; Cardozo, *op. cit.,* p. 313; and *The English Usurer, or Usury Condemned by the Most Learned Divines,* ed. John Blaxton (Oxford, 1634) (Yale Lib.).
37. For texts see Cardozo, *op. cit.,* pp. 310-11, and Stonex, *Schelling Ann. Papers,* p. 263, etc.
38. Aristotle *Politics* i. 10. 4 and 11. 1; also Cato, Cicero, etc.
39. See Lodge, *Looking Glasse* London, 1617; also Tawney, "Introduction," p. 36 ff.
40. C. Viner, *General Abridgment,* Aldershot (1758), XXII, 291 ff.
41. Caesar, *Discourse Against Usurers,* London, 1578, (Huntington Lib.), p. 7 (*ed. princ.,* 1569).
42. Viner, *op. cit.,* XXII, 295-96; M. Bacon *New Abridgment,* Philadelphia, 1811, VII, 188 ff.; D. Pickering, *Statutes,* Cambridge, 1763, VI, 276.
43. Cunningham, *op. cit.,* p. 359; cf. Besant, *op. cit.,* p. 238.
44. See Stonex in *Schelling Ann. Papers.*
45. J. Marston, *Scourge of Villanie,* ed. Harrison, London, 1925, p. 41. Cf. Coke, *Institutes,* London, 1809, III, 151.
46. R. Barnfield, *Works,* ed. Grosart London, 1876, pp. 142, 179.
47. T. Overbury, *Characters,* London, 1856, p. 133.
48. W. Rowley, *Search for Money* "Percy Soc." (London, 1840), pp. 15 ff.
49. T. Adams, *The Deuills Banket,* London, 1614 (Huntington Lib.), p. 9. T. Nashe, *Works,* ed. McKerrow London, 1910, II, 162.
50. See Malynes, *op. cit.,* p. 217; Lodge, *op. cit., Alarvm,* ed. Hunt. Club, I, 44; and Henry Smith (1550?-91), *Examination of Usury* (London), 1751, p. 23.
51. P. Caesar, *op .cit.,* leaf 11.
52. *Ibid.,* leaf 21.
53. *Ibid.,* leaf 22.
54. *Ibid.,* leaf 6.
55. *Ibid.,* leaf 11.

56. [*John*] *Wharton's Dreame,* London, 1578 (Brit. Mus.).
57. Lodge, *Alarvm,* p. 49.
58. H. Smith, *Examination of Usury.*
59. M. Mosse, *The Arraignment and Conviction of Vsurie,* London, 1595.
60. N. Sanders, *Briefe Treatise of Vsvrie,* London, 1568 (Brit. Mus.).
61. *The Death of Vsury, or, the Disgrace of Vsvrers* (London, 1594) (Brit. Mus.).
62. T. Pie, *Usurers' Spright Coniured* London, 1604 (Brit. Mus.).
63. R. Fenton, *Treatise of Vsvrie* (London, 1611), p. 109.
64. D. Digges, *The Defence of Trade,* London, 1615 (Brit. Mus.), p. 2. See also L. B. Wright, *Middle-Class Culture in Elizabethan England,* Chapel Hill, 1935, p. 401.
65. Pie, *op. cit.,* p. 21 *passim;* Smith, *op. cit.,* pp. 5, 13 ff.; Fenton, *op. cit.,* pp. 33 ff.
66. Smith, *op. cit.,* title-page; Fenton, *op. cit.,* p. 60.
67. Smith, *op. cit.,* p. 13 ff.; Fenton, *op. cit.,* p. 33 ff.
68. Smith, *op. cit.,* p. 4, etc.; Fenton, *op. cit.,* p. 33 ff.
69. Fenton, *op. cit.,* p. 33 ff.
70. Smith, *op. cit.,* p. 13 ff.; Pie, *op. cit.,* p. 22 ff.; Fenton, *op. cit.,* p. 33 ff.
71. Smith, *op. cit.,* p. 13 ff.; Pie, *op. cit.,* p. 22 ff.
72. Smith, *op. cit.,* p. 13 ff. R. H. Tawney traces the history of this struggle in *Religion and the Rise of Capitalism,* New York, 1926.
73. Essay XLI. See also Essay XXVIII. How would Baconians explain this utter difference from Shakespeare's attitude?
74. Cf. Lodge, *Alarvm,* I, 13.
75. *Merchant of Venice,* I, iii, 74 ff.
76. *Ibid.,* I, iii, 74 ff.; cf. Cardozo, *op. cit.,* pp. 310 ff.
77. *Merchant of Venice,* I, iii, 117.
78. P. Caesar, *op. cit.,* p. 6.
79. *Merchant of Venice,* III, i, 41.
80. *Ibid.,* I, iii, 42.
81. *Ibid.,* IV, i, 238.
82. See John Draper, "The Theme of 'Timon of Athens'," *M.L.R.,* XXIX (1934), 20 ff.
83. If the present theory is correct, one need not suppose that Shylock represents the Huguenot and Dutch refugees in London (A. Tretiak, *R.E.S.,* V, 402). Why should a Machiavellian Jew stand for the Protestants to whom England had given hospitable refuge? How had they capital for moneylending; and, if they did, why do not those who attack the practice brand it as foreign rather than admit its being done by Londoners "of very good respect"? See Smith, *op. cit.,* p. 4; Fenton, *op. cit.,* p. 108; Stowe, *Survey* London, 1618, p. 233. Cf. Tawney, "Introduction."
84. Overbury, *op. cit.,* p. 134.
85. Hall, *op. cit.,* p. 53. England had notaries and Venice *memoriali* for such transactions. See Molmenti, I, 95.
86. *Merchant of Venice,* I, iii, 32, etc.: cf. Hall, *op. cit.,* p. 65.
87. See Lodge, *Alarvm;* Harrison, *Description,* London, 1587, Book II, chap. v. etc. Cf. J. U. Neff, *Rise of the British Coal Industry,* II, 33 ff.
88. Hall, *op. cit.,* p. 65.
89. *Merchant of Venice,* III, i, 43 ff.

90. *Ibid.,* I, ii, 50 ff. Apparently he preferred "usance" or "advantage"; cf. Smith, *op. cit.,* p. 22.

91. T. Adams, *Diseases of the Sovle,* London, 1616, p. 30; Overbury, *op. cit.,* pp. 134, 151-53.

92. *Merchant of Venice,* II, ii, 101, 152; II, v. 49.

93. *Ibid.,* III, iii, 5, 25, etc.

94. Tawney, "Introduction," pp. 125, 159.

95. R. H. Tawney and E. Power, *Tudor Economic Documents,* London, 1924, pp. 370 ff.

96. Tawney, "Introduction," pp. 126-27.

97. *Merchant of Venice,* IV, i, 33.

98. See Lodge, *Alarvm,* I, 13; Harrison, Book II, ch. v; and H. Peacham, *Coach and Sedan,* London, 1925 (*ed. princ.* 1636).

99. T. Gainsford, *The Glory of England* (London, 1622), p. 249. One must discount something for the obvious chauvinism of the author.

100. *Merchant of Venice,* ed. Furness, p. 444; cf. I, iii, 40.

101. *Ibid.,* p. 324.

102. *Merchant of Venice,* I, i, 48-49; cf. I, i, 187.

103. See John Draper, "Captain General Othello," *Anglia,* XLIII, 296 ff. See "Falstaff, an Elizabethan Soldier," No. XX.

104. The theory that Antonio is a prototype of Heraclitus seems to be supported only by his initial melancholy (G. C. Taylor, "Is Antonio the 'Weeping Philosopher'?" *M.P.,* XXVI, 161 ff.). *Is* Antonio a philosopher?

105. Cf. Schroer; W. Creizenach, *Shak. Jhrb.,* LI, 171 ff.; B. V. Wenger, *Shak. Jhrb.,* LXV, 92 ff. Cf. John Draper in the *Shak. Jhrb.,* LXII, 125 ff.

106. See W. W. Lawrence, *Shakespeare's Problem Comedies,* New York, 1931.

107. See John Draper, " 'This Poor Trash of Venice,' " *J.E.G.P.,* XXX, 508 ff., and " 'Honest Iago,' " *P.M.L.A.,* XLVI, 724 ff.

108. See John Draper, "The Realism of Shakespeare's Roman Plays," *S.P.,* XXX (1933), 225 ff.

109. See John Draper, "Desdemona: a Compound of Two Cultures," *R.L.C.,* XIII, 337 ff.

110. See John Draper, "Olivia's Household," *P.M.L.A.,* XLIX (1934), 797 ff.

NOTES FOR XV

1. Dariot, *Iudgement,* ed. 1598, sib. D 2 r.

2. L. Lemnius, *Touchstone of Complexions,* tr. T. Newton, London, 1576, leaf 146 r.

3. [T. Walkington], *Optick Glasse of Hvmors,* London, 1639, pp. 125-126.

4. Dariot, *loc. cit.;* and A. Laurentius, *Discourse of the Preservation of the Sight,* tr. Svrphlet, London, 1599, p. 82.

5. T. Elyot, *Castell of Helth,* London, 1541, leaf 3 r.

6. Laurentius, *op. cit.,* p. 98.

7. Lemnius, *op. cit.,* leaf 23 v.

8. Walkington, *op. cit.,* 129.

9. Dariot, *op. cit.,* sig. D 2 r; and Lemnius, *op. cit.,* leaf 146 r.

10. See Lemnius, *op. cit.,* leaf 96 v ff. T. Hyll, *Art of Phisiognomie,* appended to his *Contemplation of Mankind,* ed. 1571; *The Most Excellent Book of the famous Doctor Arcandam,* London, 1592; and G. B. Porta, *De Humana Physiognomonia,* 1586.

11. The dog was a flatterer according to Hyll, *op. cit.,* leaf 125 r.

12. Hyll, *op. cit.,* leaf 121 r; and Arcandam, see appended parallel columns.

13. Lemnius, *op. cit.,* leaf 147 r.

14. J. Downame, *Spiritual Physicke,* London, p. 1600, leaves 25 and 26; and T. W [right], *Passions of the Minde,* London, 1606, p. 308.

15. N. Coeffeteau, *Table of Humane Passions,* London, 1621, pp. 559-60, 568, 576.

16. *Merchant,* I, iii.

17. Elyot, *op. cit.,* leaf 3 r.

18. *Batman upon Bartholome,* London, 1582, leaf 32 r; Lemnius, *op. cit.,* leaves 131 v-132 r; Laurentius, *op. cit.,* p. 82; Nashe, Works, ed. McKerrow, I, 353 ff.

19. See John Draper, "The Jealousy of Iago," *Neophil.,* XXV, 50 ff.

20. *Ibid.,* II, v, 13.

21. T. Bright, *Treatise of Melancholy,* London, 1613 (*ed. princ.,* 1586), pp. 151, 122, 249.

22. Coeffeteau, *op. cit.,* pp. 627-628.

23. J. Huarte, *Examen de Ingenios,* tr. R. Carew, London, 1604, p. 147.

24. Coeffeteau, *op. cit.,* pp. 552, 582 *pass.*

25. See John Draper, "The Jealousy of Iago," *loc. cit.;* and " 'Honest Iago,' " *PMLA.,* XLVI, 724 ff.

26. See John Draper, "Shakespeare's Coriolanus," *West Va. Phil. Studies,* III, 22 ff.

27. See J. W. Cole, "Romeo and Rosaline," *Neophil.,* XXIV, 285 ff.

NOTES FOR XVI

1. A fuller discussion of the evidence of tempo appears in John Draper, *The Tempo-Patterns of Shakespeare's Plays,* Heidelberg, 1957, Chap. i.

2. O. Jespersen, *Growth and Structure of the English Language,* Chap. x.

3. T. W. Baldwin, *The Organization and Personnel of the Shakespearean Company,* Princeton, 1927, p. 246.

4. *Ibid.,* pp. 232-233.

5. *Henry IV, Part I,* II, iv.

NOTES FOR XVII

1. T. W. Baldwin, *Organization and Personnel of the Shakespearean Company,* Princeton, 1927, p. 261 ff.

NOTES FOR XVIII

1. See John Draper, "Desdemona," *Rev. Litt. Comp,* XIII, 337 ff.

2. *The Taming of A Shrew,* London, 1594, iv, 4. This "Pleasant Conceited Historie" is generally recognized as Shakespeare's source.

3. T. Elyot, *The Castel of Helth,* London, 1541, leaf 62 v. For a fuller discussion of the humors, see John Draper, *The Humors and Shakespeare's Characters,* Durham, N.C., 1945.

4. N. Coeffeteau, *Table of Humane Passions,* London, 1621, p. 551.

5. T. Walkington, *Optick Glasse of Humors,* London, 1598, p. 108.

6. L. Lemnius, *Touchstone of Complexions,* tr, Newton, London, 1581, leaf 129; and T. Hyll [Hill], *Art of Phisiognomy,* leaves 8 v and 21 v. (This is appended to his *Contemplation of Mankinde,* London, 1571.)

7. Walkington, *op. cit., p.* 109; and C. Dariot, *Judgement of the Starres,* tr. F. Wither, London, 1598, sig. D 4.

8. Hyll, *op. cit.,* leaf 8 v.

9. *The Most Excellent Booke of Arcandam,* London, 1592, sig. M 2 r.

10. *Ibid.,* sig. M 2 r.

11. Dariot, *op. cit.,* sig. D 3 r; and Coeffeteau, *op. cit.,* p. 602.

12. Lemnius, *op. cit.,* leaf 23 v.

13. Dariot, *op. cit.,* sig. D 3 r.

14. *Ibid.,* sig. C 3 v.

15. Coeffeteau, *op. cit.,* p. 544 ff.

16. P. de La Primaudaye, *The French Academy,* London, 1586, Chap. xxix.

17. Coeffeteau, *op. cit.,* p. 598 ff., and 617 ff.

18. *Ibid.,* p. 552.

19. *Ibid.,* pp. 613-14.

20. *Ibid.,* p. 572.

21. See W. S. Davis, *Life in Elizabethan Days,* New York, 1930; and C. L. Powell, *English Domestic Relations, 1487-1653,* New York, 1917, p. 14 *passim.*

22. Walkington, *op. cit.,* p. 109.

23. Coeffeteau, *op. cit.,* p. 623.

24. J. Ferrand, 'Ἐρωτομανία, or a *Treatise of Love,* Oxford, 1640, p. 93 (*ed. princ.,* Paris, 1624).

25. Cf. *Meeting of Gallants,* London, 1604, sig. B 4 v.

26. Coeffeteau, *op. cit.,* p. 547.

27. *The Shrew,* III, ii, 174; and *Shakespeare's England,* Oxford, 1917, II, 147.

28. Walkington, *op. cit.,* p. 104; and Coeffeteau, *op. cit.,* p. 612.

29. *The Shrew,* IV, i, 183. Cf. *A Shrew,* viii, 29.

30. Walkington, *op. cit.,* p. 104.

31. W. Bulleyn, *Gouernement of Healthe,* London, 1558, fol. ix.

32. Elyot, *op. cit.,* leaf 70.

33. *A Shrew,* xi, 13.

34. Walkington, *op. cit.,* p. 108.

35. The italics are mine.

36. Ferrand, *op. cit.,* p. 213.

37. Walkington, *op. cit.,* p. 104.

38. The speech reminds one of the material that made up the domestic-conduct books discussed in Powell.

39. See John Draper, "The Wooing of Olivia," *Neophil.,* XXIII, 37 ff.

NOTES FOR XIX

1. *Henry the Fourth,* the quarto of 1600, ed. H. A. Evans, p. iii.

2. *Henry IV, Part II,* Shaaber var. ed., p. 518.

3. J. Q. Adams, *Life of Shakespeare,* New York, 1925, pp. 225-226.

4. *Henry IV, Part I,* var. ed. II, i, and p. 352.

5. *Ibid.,* p. 354. The government tried to correct these abuses in September of that year.

6. *Ibid.,* 354-355.

7. *Henry IV, Part II,* V, ii, 46-49.

8. Richard Knolles, *Generall Historie of the Turkes* (*ed. princ.,* 1603), London, 1638, p. 1056. Modern histories of Turkey substantiate this account.

9. See John Draper, "Shakespeare and Abbas the Great," *Phil. Quart.*, XXX, 419 ff.
10. *Ibid.* and *Twelfth Night*, II, v, and III, iv.
11. See John Draper, "Shakespeare and Muscovy," *Slavonic Rev.*, XXXIII, 217 ff.
12. See John Draper, "Shakespeare and India." *Annales publiées par la Faculté des Lettres de Toulouse*, Nov., 1953.
13. Riche and Digges had published on the subject as early as 1578.
14. The brief reference to the high price of oats in *Part I* may well be a later addition, perhaps when the plays were revised for the excision of "Oldcastle."

NOTES FOR XX

1. See R. W. Babcock, *P.Q.*, XVI, 84-85; and G. T. Drury, *Some Seventeenth Century Allusions to Shakespeare*, 1920.
2. See E. E. Stoll, *Mod. Phil.*, XII, 197 ff; and A. H. Tolman, *P.M.L.A.*, XXIV, 1 ff; and E. C. Knowlton, *J.E.G.P.*, XXV, 193 ff.
3. A. C. Bradley, *Oxford Lectures*, New York, 1909, p. 264 ff (*ed. princ.*, 1902).
4. See Stoll, *op. cit.*, and Tolman's theory that Shakespeare introduced the seamy side of Falstaff's character as an afterthought in *Part II* is not satisfactory; for the Knight's shortcomings appear not only in his early actions but even in Hal's speech at his first appearance in *Part I*: and, according to stage-convention, such introductions were not misleading.
5. R. S. Forsythe, *Shirley's Plays*, New York, 1914, pp. 101-102, and p. 68 *passim*. T. W. Baldwin, *M.L.R.*, XXVI, 173 ff and G. P. Krapp, *Shakespeare Studies by Members of the Department of English in Columbia University*, New York, 1916, 291 ff would seem to agree. Stoll's contention of Falstaff's bad character is further supported by the similarity of his speech on honor (*Henry IV Part I* V, i, 137 ff) to the refusal of the worthless Liseo to take seriously the flight of his daughter, in Aretino's *Hipocrito*, V, vii, 273-4. See J. Lothian, "Shakespeare's Knowledge of Aretino's Plays," *M.L.R.*, XXV, 419.
6. See E. Legouis, in *Essays and Studies of the English Association*, XIII, Oxford, 1928, p. 74 ff.
7. Some would even go so far as to propose a definite person as Shakespeare's model, Cf. Stoll, *op. cit.*, p. 213.
8. W. J. Courthope, *History of English Poetry*, IV, 114 and Sir E. K. Chambers, *Shakespeare, A Survey*, New York, 1926, pp. 125-6 should perhaps be placed in this group; and more certainly L. L. Schücking, *Character Problems*, London [1922], 32 ff., and E. I. Fripp, *Shakespeare Studies*, Oxford, 1930, p. 146, both of whom take him as a study in drunkenness.
9. *Shakespeare's England*, Oxford, 1917, I, 112 ff.
10. Stoll and his followers of course agree in this matter with the present writer. Fripp, who would seem to make Falstaff "a study of alcoholism," seems to elevate an incidental matter to primary importance, and to read into Shakespeare a doubtful sociological purpose. On Falstaff's use of wine to maintain his youth and choler, see Ruth E. Sims, "The Green Old Age of Falstaff," *Bull. Hist. Med.*, XIII, 144 ff.
11. For further documentation, see John Draper, The *"Othello" of Shakespeare's Audience*, Paris, 1952, Chaps. VII-X; and Oman, *The History of the Art of War in the Sixteenth Century*, New York, 1937.

12. Officers received little or no salary, and seemingly were supposed to live on their private incomes or from ransoms of prisoners, as in feudal times.

13. T. Harmon, *Caveat for Common Cursetors* (1593), ed. Hindley, London, 1871, p. 15. See also More's *Utopia;* the anonymous *Life of Long Meg of Westminster,* London, 1635; and Sir John Smythe, *Certain Discourses,* London, 1590, sig. A.

14. See Sir Henry Knyvett, *Defense of the Realme,* London, 1596; and B. Riche, *Fruites of Long Experience,* London, 1604, pp. 33 and 72.

15. Complaints against such abuses begin as early as the reign of Henry VI (Major M. J. D. Cockle, *Bibliography,* London, 1900, p. 63).

16. See G. Gascoigne, "Dulce Bellum" in *Poems,* ed. Hazlitt, I, 166 ff; and Barret, *Theoricke and Practicke,* London, 1598, 7 ff.

17. See Fortescue, *op. cit.;* and Riche, *Farewell to the Militarie Profession* (1581), ed. Shak. Soc., London, 1846, p. 10.

18. *Henry IV, Part II,* II, iv.

19. B. Riche, *Allarme to England,* London, 1578.

20. Digges, *Arithmeticall Militare Treatise,* London, 1579, p. 81 etc.

21. Riche, *Fruites,* p. 51.

22. See *The Elizabethan Underworld,* ed. A. V. Judges, London, 1930, "Introduction."

23. *Henry IV, Part II,* III, ii; and *Part I,* IV, ii.

24. Riche, *Fruites,* p. 52.

25. *Ibid.,* p. 61 ff.

26. See Sutcliffe, *Lawes of Armes,* London, 1593, p. 316, Lawes 6 and 12.

27. *Ibid.,* 74 ff; Riche, *Fruites,* pp. 7-8; and Digges, *Foure Paradoxes,* London, 1604, 1 ff.

28. See Gascoigne, *op. cit.,* stanza cxlix; and Sutcliffe, "Epistle Dedicatorie."

29. Riche, *Fruites,* pp. 14 and 64.

30. Digges, *Treatise,* p. 123.

31. Digges, *Paradoxes,* pp. 19-20 and 48. Dekker, who had trailed a pike in Flanders, says that the captains in the Dutch Wars regularly lived on "dead pay" (God's Tokens," *Plague Pamphlets,* Oxford, 1924, p. 148). See also C. G. Cruickshank, "Dead Pays in the Elizabethan Army," *Eng. Hist. Rev.,* LII, 93-97. Shakespeare would seem to have gathered most of his knowledge of army life from returned soldiers from the Dutch Wars.

32. *Henry IV, Part I,* V, iii. Shakespeare is probably modelling King Henry's army with its "bands" of a hundred and fifty, on the English force in the St. Quentin campaign (Traill, *Social England,* III, 203, 453) rather than on the usual formation of sixteenth century armies, which consisted of bands of a hundred "centinels" (privates). See Sir J. Fortescue. *The Empire and the Army,* London [copr. 1928] p. 12.

33. *Henry IV, Part I,* V, iii.

34. Stoll would make Falstaff's going into battle a mere convention so that his cowardice might appear to the audience; but is not the financial motive obvious and more convincing?

35. See *King Lear,* III, ii. See also [G. Markham], *Health to the Gentlemanly Profession of Servingman* (*ed. princ.,* 1598), in *Inedited Tracts,* ed. Hazlitt, Roxb. Lib., London, 1868, p. 125; and "Deutie of a Servingman," ed. Wright, *S.P.,* XXXI, 122 ff.

36. Riche, *Fruites,* p. 53.

37. See *The Publicke and Militarie Discourses of the Lord de la Nowe,* tr. E.A., London, 1587, p. 115.

38. The list of Falstaff's dupes includes Shallow, Dame Quickly, Mistress Ursula (*Henry IV, Part II,* I, ii), and, had he succeeded, Prince Hal, Mistress Page, and Mistress Ford.

39. See S. Rowlands, *Doctor Merrie-man,* London, 1609, pp. 9-10. Cf. *Henry IV, Part I,* IV, iii.

40. *Henry IV, Part II,* I, iii. Lord Bardolph refers to Falstaff as "Harry Monmouth's brawn," *ibid.,* I, i. See Draper, *"Othello,"* Chap. vii.

41. See Greene, "Ned Browne," *Works,* ed. Grosart, XI, 11; Riche, *My Ladies Looking-glasse,* London, 1616, pp. 53-4; and of course a bully was necessary in the old "badger game." In the tradition of Paracelsus (*De Urinarum ac Pulsuum,* 1568), Falstaff sends his "water" to the doctor, who declares that he has "moe diseases than he knew for" (*Henry IV, Part II,* I, ii).

42. Riche, *Looking-glasse,* 65 ff. Cf. Sutcliffe, *op. cit.,* p. 67, and J. Earle, *Microcosmographie.* No. 55.

43. Brathwait, *English Gentleman,* London, 1633, 41.

44. B. H. Bronson, *P.M.L.A.,* XIV, 749 ff.

45. *Henry IV, Part I,* II, i.

46. Forsythe, *op. cit.,* pp. 87-88. See also the tavern scenes in Heywood's *Fortune by Land and Sea.*

47. See the introductory verses to Rowlands' *Looke to it for Ile Stabbe ye,* London, 1604. The nobility were no better (G. B. Harrison, *Elizabethan Journal,* London, 1928, pp. 6, 22, 71, 97 *passim;* Stephenson, *Elizabethan People,* New York, 1910, ii; and Judges, "Introduction").

48. Rowlands, *Night Raven,* London, 1620, p. 8. Of course, when on active service, Falstaff was beyond the reach of civil law.

49. Shakespeare apparently considered this a rather disreputable connection, if we are to accept Professor Hotson's identification of Shallow with William Gardiner (*Atl. Mon.,* Oct., 1931).

50. See W. W. Lawrence, *Shakespeare's Problem Comedies,* New York, 1930.

51. R. Brathwait, *Essaies,* London 1620, p. 120.

52. *Henry IV, Part I,* II, iv.

53. Digges, *Paradoxes,* p. 17.

54. T. Overbury, *Characters.*

55. The tradition of the Latin *miles gloriosus,* since its introduction into English comedy by Udall, had undoubtedly by Shakespeare's time undergone considerable assimilation to the actual boastful soldier of Elizabethan life.

56. He had been properly raised as a page in the household of the Duke of Norfolk (*Henry IV, Part II,* III, ii); he boasts himself a knight and a "gentleman" (*ibid.,* II, iv); and on occasion he promises himself to "live cleanly as a nobleman should do" (*Henry IV, Part I,* V, iv). The age furnished some notable examples of aristocratic decadence, as, for example, the Earl of Oxford.

57. See Tolman, *op. cit.,* p. 8.

NOTES FOR XXI

1. W. W. Fowler, *Social Life at Rome,* New York, 1909, p. 42 ff.

2. W. A. Becker, *Charicles,* 1874, I, 490 ff; Knorr, *Die Parasiten bei den Griechen,* Belgrade, 1875; and W. L. Walford, *Plautus and Terence,* Philadelphia, 1880, p. 32.

3. F. S. Boas in *The Cambridge History of English Literature*, Cambridge, 1910, V, 119.
4. E. Welsford, *The Fool*, London, 1935, pp. 24-25.
5. B. Riche, *My Ladies Looking-glasse*, London, 1616, pp. 49-50.
6. N. Breton, *The Courtier and the Country-Man*, London, 1618, p. 6; and *Characters*, No. 40.
7. J. E. Sandys in *Shakespeare's England*, Oxford, 1917, I, 225.
8. *Timon of Athens*, III, vi; *Coriolanus*, I, ix, 45; *Richard II*, II, ii; and *Winter's Tale*, I, ii. ed. W. A. Wright.
9. See J. Thümmel, "Der Miles Gloriosus bei Shakespeare," *Sh Jhb.*, XII, 1-12; H. Graf, *Der Miles Gloriosus im englischen Drama*, Rostock, 1892; E. E. Stoll, "Falstaff," *M.P.*, 197-240; and R. W. Withington, *P.M.L.A.*, XLIX, 743, 751.
10. *Stichus*, II, i.
11. *Menæchmi*, I, i.
12. *Persa*, I, iii.
13. *Asinaria*, IV, iii.
14. *Miles Gloriosus*, I, i.
15. *Captivi*, I, ii.
16. *Ibid.*, I, ii.
17. *1 Henry IV*, IV, ii.
18. *Ibid.*, III, v.
19. *2 Henry IV*, V, ii.
20. *Ibid.*, IV, iii.
21. *Ibid.*, V, i.
22. *Ibid.*, I, ii.
23. *Merry Wives*, I, iii.
24. *1 Henry IV*, II, ii.
25. *Ibid.*, I, ii.
26. Falstaff's board at the Garter Inn cost him ten pounds a week, the equivalent of over $500 in modern currency. See *Merry Wives*, I, iii.
27. *1 Henry IV*, II, iv.
28. *2 Henry IV*, II, i.
29. *Ibid.*, II, iv.
30. *1 Henry IV*, V, iii.
31. *2 Henry IV*, II, i.
32. *Ibid.*, II, i, and II, iv.
33. *Ibid.*, III, i.
34. *1 Henry IV*, II, iv.
35. *Stichus*, I, iii.
36. *Menæchmi*, I, ii.
37. *Persa*, I, iii.
38. Terence, *Eunuchus*, III, i and ii.
39. *Miles Gloriosus*, I, i.
40. *Captivi*, I, ii.
41. *2 Henry IV*, I, ii.
42. *1 Henry IV*, II, ii; II, iv; and *2 Henry IV*, II, iv.
43. *Stichus*, II, i.
44. *Captivi*, III, i
45. *Persa*, III, iii.

46. *2 Henry IV*, V, i.
47. *Captivi*, I, ii.
48. *Stichus*, III, ii, and IV, 2.
49. *Menæchmi*, IV, i.
50. *Captivi*, III, i.
51. *Ibid.*, IV, ii.
52. *Stichus*, II, ii.
53. *Ibid.*, IV, ii.
54. *1 Henry IV*, I, ii.
55. *Ibid.*, II, ii.
56. *2 Henry IV*, II, iv.
57. *Merry Wives*, I, i.
58. *Menæchmi*, I, iii.
59. *Miles Gloriosus*, I, i.
60. *Asinaria*, IV, i.
61. *Persa*, I, iii and III, i.
62. *2 Henry IV*, III, ii.
63. *1 Henry IV*, II, iv.
64. *Ibid.*, III, iii.
65. *2 Henry IV*, II, iv.
66. *1 Henry IV*, I, ii; and *2 Henry IV*, I, ii.
67. *2 Henry IV*, I, ii.
68. *Ibid.*, II, iv.
69. *1 Henry IV*, I, ii.
70. Terence, *Phormio*, II, i.
71. D. C. Boughner, "Don Armado as a Gallant," *Rev. Anglo-Am.*, XIII, 18-28.
72. See John Draper, "Olivia's Household," *P.M.L.A.*, XLIX, 797-806.
73. See John Draper, *The "Othello" of Shakespeare's Audience*, Paris, 1952, Chap. vii.
74. See John Draper, "The Theme of *Timon of Athens*," *M.L.R.*, XXIX, 20-31.
75. *1 Henry IV*, I, ii.
76. *2 Henry IV*, V, v.
77. A. C. Bradley, *Oxford Lectures*, London, 1909, pp. 226-75.
78. J. W. Cunliffe, in *Columbia Shakespeare Studies*, New York, 1916.
79. A. H. Tolman, *Falstaff*, New York, 1925, p. 4.
80. J. Monaghan, "Falstaff and his Forebears," *S. P.*, XVIII, 353-361.
81. E. E. Stoll, "Falstaff," *M.P.*, XII, 211 ff.
82. See John Draper, " 'Honest Iago,' " *P.M.L.A.*, XLVI, 724-737.

NOTES FOR XXII

1. See E. E. Stoll, "Falstaff," *M.P.*, XII, 197 ff.
2. See J. W. Shirley, "Falstaff an Elizabethan Glutton," *P.Q.*, XVII, 271 ff.
3. See R. J. E. Tiddy, *The Mummers Play*, 1923; and R. Withington, *Excursions*, New York, 1937, 46 ff.
4. See O. J. Campbell, in U. of Mich. Publ., 1932, 81 ff.
5. See John Draper, "Et in Illyria Feste," *Sh. Bull.*, XVI, 220 ff. and XVII, 25 ff.
6. See T. W. Baldwin, *M.L.N.*, XXXIX, 447 ff.
7. Olive Mary Busby, *The Development of the Fool in Elizabethan Drama*, Oxford, 1923, p. 13.

8. Barbara Swain, *Fools and Folly during the Middle Ages and the Renaissance,* New York, 1932, p. 176.
9. *Ibid.,* p. 78.
10. Busby, *op. cit.,* p. 29.
11. *Henry IV, Part II,* IV, iii.
12. *Ibid.,* IV, iii.
13. *Tarleton's Jests,* ed. Shakespeare Soc., London, 1844.
14. *Henry IV, Part II,* II, iv.
15. *Ibid.,* V, i.
16. F. Warde, *The Fools of Shakespeare,* New York, 1913.
17. Enid Welford, *The Fool, His Social and Literary History,* London, 1935, p. 25.
18. *Ibid.,* p. 52.
19. T. W. Baldwin, *The Organization and Personnel of the Shakespearean Company,* Princeton, 1927, Plate II, and pp. 232-233.
20. A. C. Bradley, *Oxford Lectures,* New York, 1909, 264 ff.
21. Busby, *op. cit.,* pp. 27 and 63.
22. *Merry Wives,* I, i, *passim.*
23. Busby, *op. cit.,* p. 64.
24. *Ibid.,* pp. 71-72.
25. *Ibid.,* pp. 54 and 65.
26. *Locrine,* ii. Cf. *Part II,* V, iv.
27. See A. F. Sieveking, in *Shakespeare's England,* ed. S. Lee, Oxford, 1917, II, 402-403.
28. See Busby, *op. cit.,* pp. 49-81 for the comparison that follows.
29. *Locrine,* I, iii.
30. Cf. L. B. Wright, *Middle Class Culture,* Chapel Hill, 1935, p. 257.
31. Busby, *op. cit.,* pp. 72-73; Welsford, *op. cit.,* pp. 280-281.
32. *Wit Without Money,* II, ii.
33. *Black Letter Ballads and Broadsides,* London, 1870, p. 88.
34. Busby, *op. cit.,* p. 44.
35. See R. E. Sims, "The Green Old Age of Falstaff," *Bull. Hist. Med.,* XIII, 144 ff.
36. J. W. Fortescue, in *Shakespeare's England,* ed. cit., I, 121 ff.
37. Welsford, *op. cit.,* pp. 25-26.

NOTES FOR XXIII

1. See S. Peller, "Studies in Mortality Since the Renaissance," *Bull. Hist. Med.,* XIII, 427-461, and XVI, 362-381.
2. See John Draper, *The "Hamlet" of Shakespeare's Audience,* Durham, N. C., 1938, p. 47 ff.
3. See A. Guido, "The Humor of Juliet's Nurse," *Bull. Hist. Med.,* XVII, 297 ff.
4. Ruth E. Sims, "The Green Old Age of Falstaff," *Bull. Hist. Med.,* XIII, 144 ff.
5. See John Draper, "Political Themes in Shakespeare's Later Plays," *Jour. Eng. Ger. Phil.,* XXXV, 61-94.
6. E. E. Stoll, "Falstaff," *Mod. Phil.,* XII, 197 ff.
7. See Draper, *"Hamlet,"* Chap. III.
8. C. R. Sleeth, "Shakespeare's Counsellors of State," *Rev. Anglo-Amér.,* XIII, 97-114.

9. *Batman uppon Bartholome,* London, 1582, fol. 70 v.
10. L. Lemnius, *Touchstone of Complexions,* tr. Newton, London, 1581, fol. 29 v. ff.
11. A. Laurentius, *Discourse of the Preservation of the Sight* (1599), ed. Larkey, Oxford, 1938, pp. 173-174.
12. *Booke of Arcandam,* London, 1592, sig, M 2v.
13. Henry Cuffe, *Differences of the Ages of Mans Life,* London, 1607, p. 116 ff.
14. Burton, *Anatomy of Melancholy,* I, ii, 3. See also John Draper, "The Old Age of King Leare," *Jour. Eng. Ger. Phil.,* XXXIX, 527-540.
15. Cf. Lemnius, *op. cit.,* fol. 75 v.
16. Cf. Cuffe, *op. cit.,* p. 132.
17. *Ibid.,* p. 121.
18. P. Barrough, *Method of Phisick,* London, 1591, p. 58; Walkington, *Optick Glasse of Humors,* London, 1639, Chap. xiii; Laurentius, *op. cit.,* p. 100 ff.
19. Laurentius, *op. cit.,* p. 104.
20. Lemnius, *op. cit.,* fol. 73; Cuffe, *op. cit.,* p. 102; Burton, *op. cit.,* II, iii, 1.
21. See John Draper, "The Occasion of *King Lear,*" *Stud. Phil.,* XXXV, 176-185.

NOTES FOR XXIV

1. *2 Henry IV,* III, ii; *Merry Wives,* I, 1.
2. See R. Kelso, *English Gentleman of the Sixteenth Century,* Urbana, Ill., 1929.
3. *2 Henry IV,* V, i, and V, iii.
4. *2 Henry IV,* III, ii; *Merry Wives,* I, i. He is also jocularly termed "Cavaliero-justice," II, i.
5. *2 Henry IV,* III, ii.
6. Sir William, of course, would be removable at the accession of Henry V. See Lord Campbell, *Shakespeare's Legal Acquirements,* London, 1859, 73.
7. *2 Henry IV,* V, iii.
8. *Ibid.,* V, iii.
9. On Shakespeare's legal limitations, see A. Underhill in *Shakespeare's England,* Oxford, 1917, I, 381.
10. See John Draper, "Ophelia's Crime of *Felo de Se,*" *West Va. Law Quart.,* XLII, 228 ff.
11. Statute 34-35, Henry VIII, 27, 53.
12. See also the statute, 1-2 Philip and Mary, 13.
13. See *2 Henry IV,* III, ii.
14. By the time of Elizabeth, it meant, in effect, "esquire." For a review of the term in the Middle Ages, see Du Cange, *Glossarium, sub armigeri.*
15. A J. P. had no power outside his shire. See Hawkins, *Pleas of the Crown,* London, 1795, III, 68.
16. Cf. affair between Lord Grey and John Fortescue, later Chancellor of the Exchequer, when the former poached on the latter's land *(Cal. State Papers Dom.,* 1547, 1580, 448 *pass.);* and according to the tradition of Shakespeare's poaching on the Lucy estate, Shakespeare found it advisable to flee at once to London.
17. *Merry Wives,* I, i.
18. W. S. Holdsworth, *History of English Law,* Boston, 1922, I, 290 ff.
19. Underhill, *op. cit.,* I, 384; and Lord Eustace Percy, *The Privy Council under the Tudors,* Oxford, 1907, 62-63.

20. Holdsworth, *op. cit.,* I, 285 ff.
21. *2 Henry IV,* V, iii.
22. See 12, Richard II, 10.
23. Sir T. Smith, *Common-wealth of England,* London, 1594, p. 89.
24. Holdsworth, *op. cit.,* I, 289; and statute of 2, Henry V, 2, 1.
25. See statute, 13, Richard II, 7.
26. Holdsworth, *op. cit.,* I, 290.
27. See statute, 1 Mary, Sess. 2, 8.
28. E. Coke, *Institutes,* IV, 170.
29. *2 Henry IV,* III, ii.
30. *Ibid.*
31. Underhill, *op. cit.,* I, 411.
32. Only J. P.'s learned in the law were supposed to be of the quorum. See Holdsworth, *op. cit.,* I, 290.
33. T. Nashe, *Works,* ed. Mc Kerrow, I, 207; and G. B. Harrison, *England,* London, 1928, p. 168, quoting W. Harrison, *Description of England.*
34. See E. J. Haller, "The Realism of the Merry Wives," *West Va. Phil. Bull.,* 1937, 32 ff.
35. See L. Hotson, *Shakespeare versus Shallow,* Boston, 1931.

NOTES FOR XXV

1. "Cyuile and Vncyuile Life" (1579), in *Inedited Tracts,* ed. Hazlitt, Roxb. Lib., London, 1868, p. 39.
2. See John Draper, "Lord Chamberlain Polonius," *Sh. Jhb.,* LXXI (1935), pp. 87-88.
3. C. R. Sleeth, "Shakespeare's Counsellors of State," *Rev. A-A.,* XIII, (1934), 97 ff.
4. This elaborate organization of the household came down into the Victorian Age. See the Marchioness of Bath, *Before the Sunset Fades,* Longleat Estate Co., 1951.
5. See John Draper, "Olivia's Household," *P.M.L.A.,* XLIX (1934), 797 ff.
6. E. E. Stoll, "Falstaff," *M.P.,* XII (1914), 197 ff; and R. J. E. Tiddy, *The Mummer's Play,* Oxford, 1923.
7. See John Draper, "The Realism of Shakespeare's Roman Plays," *S.P.,* XXX (1933), 225 ff.
8. John Newham, *Nightcrowe,* London, 1590, p. 2.
9. *Ibid.,* p. 3; and Bishop Andrews, *Pattern of Catechistical Doctrine,* London, 1675, p. 318 ff.
10. William Gouge, *Domesticall Duties,* London, 1634, p. 459.
11. R. S., *The Countryman and his Household,* London, 1920, p. 2 ff.
12. *A Relation of the Island of England* (c. 1500) Camden Soc., London, 1897, p. 24.
13. *Ibid.,* pp. 41 and 51.
14. G. Markham, "Health to the Gentlemanly Profession of Servingmen," (1598), in *Inedited Tracts,* ed. Hazlitt, London, 1868, p. 110.
15. "Cyuile Life," pp. 16-17.
16. See John Draper, "Captain General Othello," *Anglia,* XLIII (1931), 296 ff.
17. Ascham, *Scholemaster,* ed. Arber, p. 51.
18. H. Peacham, *Compleat Gentleman,* London, 1622, p. 31.

19. *Henry IV, Part I,* V, iv.
20. *Henry IV, Part II,* III, ii.
21. "Cyuile Life," pp. 14-15.
22. *Ibid.,* pp. 21, 68-69, 93.
23. Markham, *op. cit.,* pp. 114 ff and 164; and W. Darell, "The Duetie of a Servingman," ed. Wright, S.P., XXXI (1934), 123.
24. W. Basse, *Sword and Buckler,* London, 1602, stanza 73 *passim.*
25. Darell, *op. cit.,* p. 122.
26. "Cyuile Life," p. 20; and Markham, p. 141.
27. "Cyuile Life," p. 25.
28. Markham, *op. cit.,* p. 133.
29. Darell, *op. cit.,* p. 124.
30. Markham, *op. cit.,* pp. 125-6.
31. Ben Jonson, *Cynthia's Revels,* II, i.
32. James I, *Political Works,* ed. Mc Ilwain, p. 30.
33. James I, *Workes,* London 1616, pp. 167 and 168.
34. See J. W. Fortescue in *Shakespeare's England,* Oxford, 1917, I, 131 ff.
35. C. L. Draper, "Falstaff's Bardolph," *Neophil.,* XXXIII, 222 ff.
36. *Henry V,* II, i, and D. C. Boughner, "Pistol and the Roaring Boys," *Shak. Assoc. Bull.,* XI (1936), 226 ff.
37. See John Draper, " 'Honest Iago,' " *P.M.L.A.,* XLVI (1931), 724 ff.
38. See Sleeth, *op. cit.*
39. See C. White, "The Biography of Autolycus," *Shak. Assoc. Bull.,* XIV, 158 ff.
40. See John Draper, "Political Themes in Shakespeare's Later Plays," *J.E.G.P.,* XXXV (1936), 61 ff.
41. C. Spurgeon, *Shakespeare's Imagery,* New York, 1936, 137 ff.

NOTES FOR XXVI

1. C. Dariot, *Iudgement of the Starres,* tr. Wither, London, 1578, sig. d 2 v.
2. L. Lemnius, *Touchstone of Complexions,* tr. Newton, London, 1581, leaves 86 v and 87 v; *Batman upon Bartholome,* London, 1582, leaf 30 r.
3. Dariot, *op. cit.,* sig. D 2 v.
4. See E. E. Stoll, *M. P.,* III, 282 ff.
5. Dariot, *op. cit.,* sig. d 2 r; and C 4 v.
6. R. Burton, *Anatomy of Melancholy,* Part III, Sec. iv.
7. *Ibid.,* Part I, Sec. ii, 3.
8. See John Draper, "Hamlet's Melancholy," *Ann. Med. Hist.,* IX N. S., 142-147; and G. A. Bieber, *Der Melancholikertypus Shakespeares,* Heidelberg, 1913.
9. Lemnius, *op. cit.,* leaf 23 v.
10. *Most Excellent Booke of Arcandam,* tr. Warde, London, 1592, sig. M 2 r.
11. Dariot, *op. cit.,* sig. D 3 r.
12. L. B. Campbell, *Shakespeare's Tragic Heroes,* Cambridge, 1930, Chap. xiv.
13. Cf. [Jones], *Booke of Honor and Arms,* London, 1590, Bk. II, Chap. i.
14. *As You Like It,* II, ii. Cf. Digges, *Foure Paradoxes,* London, 1604, 17.
15. *Cyuile and Vncyuile Life (ed. princ., 1579) in Inedited Tracts,* ed. Hazlitt, Roxb. Lib., London, 1868, 26.
16. See D. C. Boughner, "Pistol and the Roaring Boys," *Shak. Assoc. Bull.,* XI, 226.

17. G. Sarrazin, "Nym und Ben Jonson," *Sh. Jb.*, XL, 213-22. Cf. G. L. Kittredge, *Complete Works of Shakespeare*, Boston [copr. 1936] 64.
18. Lemnius, *op. cit.*, leaf 23 v.
19. *Ibid.*, leaf 81 r.
20. *Ibid.*, leaf 80 r. The choleric type was lean and muscular, 129 r.
21. Batman, *op. cit.*, leaf 32 r.
22. Dariot, *op. cit.*, sig. D 4 r.
23. *Ibid.*, sig. E 1 r and v.

NOTES FOR XXVII

1. *The Shrew*, I, i.
2. See John Draper, *The "Othello" of Shakespeare's Audience*, Paris, 1953, p. 17, *passim.*
3. The reference to Ferrara in *Henry VIII*, III, ii, is omitted here because it is in the non-Shakespearean part of the play.
4. *Romeo and Juliet*, I, ii.
5. *The Shrew*, I, ii; and II, i.
6. *Othello*, II, i. The passage is difficult, but this seems the only consistent explanation.
7. *King John*, I, i.
8. Cf. Browning, "Up at a Villa—Down in the City."
9. *Works*, ed. A. Wright, I, 195 n. vii.
10. Pope and many later editors prefer Milan.
11. The Belmonte near Ancona seems too remote for Shakespeare's story, though one might take ship from it to Venice as Bassanio does (I, vi).
12. *King John*, III, i; and *The Tempest*, I, ii.
13. *Ibid.*, I, ii.
14. See John Draper, "Shakespeare and Florence and the Florentines," *Italica*, XXIII, 287 ff.
15. See John Draper, "The Realism of Shakespeare's Roman Plays," *S.P.*, XXX, 225 ff.

NOTES FOR XXVIII

1. See *A Relation of the Island of England* (c. 1500), Camden Soc., London, 1897, 24-35. W. Gouge declared that "children under their parents are as servants," *Domesticall Duties*, London, 1634, p. 459.
2. *Relations*, pp. 41, 51.
3. Sir W. Besant, *Stuart London*, London, 1903, p. 173 ff.
4. G. Markham, *Health to the Gentlemanly Profession of Servingmen* (1598), *Inedited Tracts*, Roxb. Lib., ed. Hazlitt, London, 1868, pp. 109-110. See also John Draper, "Captain General Othello," *Anglia*, XLIII, 296 ff.; and " 'This Poor Trash of Venice,' " *J.E.G.P.*, XXX, 508 ff.
5. *Cyuile and Vncyuile Life, Inedited Tracts*, pp. 26-27.
6. Markham suggests this as a solution, pp. 107-109.
7. See H. H. Tawney, *Introduction* to Wilson's *Discourse upon Usurye*, New York 1925, 31 ff.; and John Draper, "Olivia's Household," *P.M.L.A.*, XLIX, 797-806; and "The Theme of *Timon of Athens*," *M.L.R.*, XXIX, 20 ff.
8. [H. Peacham] *Coach and Sedan* (1636), London, 1925, sig. C. 3.
9. R. Brathwait, *English Gentleman* (1630), London, 1641, p. 89.
10. H. Peachman, *Compleat Gentleman*, London, 1622, p. 31 ff.; *Cyuile and*

Vncyuile Life, pp. 20 and 29; W. Powell, *Tom of all Trades*, London, 1631; and R. Kelso, *The English Gentleman in the Sixteenth Century*, Urbana, Ill., 1929, p. 122.

11. Kelso, *op. cit.*, p. 66.
12. W. Gouge, *op. cit.*, p. 585, quoting Deut. 21.17.
13. J. Earle, *Characters*, "A Younger Brother" (1628).
14. Perhaps this explains why, during the life-time of the elder Hamlet, the courtiers "would make mows" at Claudius (*Hamlet*, II, ii).
15. Cf. Horatio as discussed by John Draper, *The "Hamlet" of Shakespeare's Audience*, Durham [N.C.], 1938, Chap. ii. See also J. B. Nenna, *Nennio*, tr. W. Jones, London, 1595, 76.
16. See *Cyuile and Vncyuile Life*, 23 and 25. The Earl of Leicester, who, though the fifth son in an impecunious and attainted family, the Dukes of Northumberland, made his fortune by three marriages.
17. Hist. MSS. Commission, *MSS. of Marquis of Salisbury*, Pt. IV, 4-5.
18. *Cyuile and Vncyuile Life*, p. 25. See also S. Rowlands, *Runnagetes Race*, ed. Hunt. Club, No. XIX.
19. *Cyuile and Vncyuile Life*, p. 25.
20. Cf. C. R. Baskerville, "Bassanio as an Ideal Lover," *Manly Ann. Papers*, Chicago, 1923; and H. P. Pettigrew, "Bassanio, the Elizabethan Lover," *P.Q.*, XVI, 296 ff.
21. A comparison with the *Gamelyn*, perhaps a supplementary source, shows even more striking changes in the same directions.
22. Markham, *op. cit.*, p. 108 ff.
23. This presumption is basic in W. W. Lawrence, *Shakespeare's Problem Comedies*, New York, 1930.
24. Cf. a similar change from *The Taming of a Shrew* to *The Taming of the Shrew*.
25. See Draper, "Olivia's Household."
26. See Lawrence, *op. cit.*; and in *P.M.L.A.*, XXVII, 418 ff.
27. See Draper, "The Theme of *Timon of Athens*."
28. See John Draper, " 'Honest Iago,' " *P.M.L.A.*, XLVI, 274 ff.
29. See Madeleine Doran, "Elements in the Composition of *King Lear*," *S.P.*, XXX, 34 ff.
30. On the exact date, see T. W. Baldwin, *M.L.N.*, XLVII, 901 ff.
31. See A. H. Thorndike, "The Relation of *As You Like It* to the Robin Hood Plays," *J.E.G.P.*, IV, 59 ff.
32. In *Twelfth Night*, also, the sub-title "What you Will" seems similarly addressed to the courtiers and the young benchers of the Middle Temple before whom the play seems to have been performed. See John Draper, "The Wooing of Olivia," *Neophil.*, XXIII, 37 ff.
33. See H. P. Pettigrew, "Bassanio, the Elizabethan Lover," *P.Q.*, XVI, 296 ff.
34. *Batman uppon Bartholome*, London, 1582, leaf 30 r.
35. C. Dariot, *Iudgement of the Starres*, tr. F. Wither, London, 1598, sig. D 2 v.
36. Sir T. Elyot, *Castel of Helth*, London, 1541, leaf 8.
37. H. Cuffe, *The Differences of the Ages of Mans Life*, London, 1608, 97-98.
38. Dariot, *op. cit.*, sig. D 2 v.
39. W. Vaughan, *Directions for Health*, London, 1633, 121.
40. Cuffe, *op. cit.*, pp. 118-119.
41. L. Lemnius, *Touchstone of Complexions*, tr. T. Newton, London, 1581, leaf 86, v ff. Cf. leaf 29 v.

42. T. W[alkington], *Optick Glasse of Humors,* London (1631 ?), 115.
43. Dariot, *op. cit.,* sig. D 2 v.
44. Vicary, *Anatomie, E.E.T.S.,* Ex. Ser. LIII, 1888, 41.
45. Vaughan, *op. cit.,* p. 127.
46. T. Hill, *Schoole of Skill,* London, 1599, leaf 7 v.
47. Vicary, *op. cit.,* p. 41; Dariot, *op. cit.,* sig. D 2 v; *Most Excellent Booke of Arcandam,* tr. W. Warde, London, 1592, sig. M 2 r.
48. Dariot, *op. cit.,* sig. D 2 v.
49. Arcandam, sig. M 2 r.
50. Walkington, *op. cit.,* p. 114.
51. *Ibid.,* p. 111.
52. *Ibid.,* p. 116.
53. See J. W. Cole, "Romeo and Rosaline," *Neophil.,* XXIV, 285 ff.
54. See John Draper, "The Melancholy Duke Orsino," *Bull. Hist. Med.,* VI, 1020 ff.
55. T. Cogan, *Haven of Health,* London, 1589, sig. Hh 2 v.
56. Lemnius, ed. 1576, leaf 23 v; Walkington, *op. cit.,* p. 117.
57. J. Ferrand, *'Ερωτομανία, or a Treatise of Love,* Oxford, 1640, 11-12, 41-42, 124; R. Burton, *Anatomy of Melancholy,* Part III, Sec. 2 Memb. 2, Subs. 2; and N. Breton, *Melancholicke Humours,* London, 1600, No. 21.
58. *Twelfth Night,* V, ii.
59. N. Coeffeteau, *Table of Humane Passions,* London, 1621, p. 238.
60. Dariot, *op. cit.,* sig. D 2 v.
61. Walkington, *op. cit.,* 116.
62. Dariot, *op. cit.,* sig. D 2 v.
63. Lemnius, *op. cit.,* leaf 89 v.
64. Ferrand, *op. cit.,* 67-68; A Laurentius, *Discourse of the Preservation of the sight,* tr. Svrphlet, London, 1599, 118; P. Boaystuau, *Theatrum Mundi,* tr. Alday, London, 1574, pp. 202-203.
65. Burton, *op. cit.,* III, 2, 2, 1; Coeffeteau, p. 551.
66. See John Draper, *The "Twelfth Night" of Shakespeare's Audience,* Stanford U.P., Chap. V.
67. Ferrand, ed. 1645, 93.
68. Dariot, *op. cit.,* sig. C v 4: Lemnius, *op. cit.,* leaves 86 v and 87 v.
69. R. Boyce, *N. and Q.,* May 26, 1928.
70. A. Ransford, *N. and Q.,* June 30, 1928, and September 1, 1928.
71. J. Q. Adams, *Life of William Shakespeare,* Boston, 1926, p. 450.
72. This common joke on "horns" as a symbol of cuckoldry is reiterated in the play, *e.g.* III, iii, 45 ff.; IV, i, 59 ff.; IV, ii, 15 ff. Of course, the Elizabethans could not fail to grasp the double entendre, and interpret the song accordingly.
73. C. J. Sisson, *Thomas Lodge and Other Elizabethans,* Cambridge [Mass.], 1933.
74. *As You Like It,* ed. Furness var., p. 2.
75. On the life of Lord William Howard, see his *Household Books,* ed. Ornsby, Surtees Soc., lxviii., 1878.
76. See *D.N.B.,* sub Lord William Howard.
77. See T. W. Baldwin, *M.L.N.,* xxxix. 447 ff.
78. Ornsby, *op. cit.,* pp. xxxi.
79. *Ibid.,* pp. xxxv. and xxxviii.
80. *Ibid.,* pp. ix., xxii., xl., xlix., lvii.

81. *Ibid.*, p. 1.
82. *Ibid.*, pp. liii ff.
83. C. J. Sisson, *Lost Plays,* Cambridge, 1936, p. 58 ff.
84. In just this fashion, Hamlet defends the play presented before the King and Queen; he points out that it is an Italian story and so cannot have any application to affairs in Denmark, and outwardly the King accepts this defence.
85. See John Draper, "The Theme of *Timon of Athens,*" *M.L.R.*, XXIX, 20 ff.

NOTES FOR XXIX

1. Even Claudio's later repudiation of Hero is conventional. See N. Page, "The Public Repudiation of Hero," *P.M.L.A.*, L, 743-744.
2. See John Draper, "Desdemona," *R.L.C.*, XIII, 340 ff.
3. C. Dariot, *Iudgement of the Starres,* tr. F. Wither, London, 1598, sig. D 3 v.
4. Dariot, *op. cit.,* sig D 3; and Lemnius, *Touchstone of Complexions,* tr. Newton, London, 1581, leaf 23.
5. *Twelfth Night,* ed. Furness var. p. 329.
6. T. Elyot, *Castel of Helth,* London, 1541, leaf 9.
7. Dariot, *op. cit.,* Sig. D.
8. Dariot, *op. cit.,* D 3 v.
   Much Ado, II, iii, 53 *passim.*
9. J. Downame, *Spiritual Physicke,* London, 1600, Leaf 25 ff.
10. L. B. Campbell, *Shakespeare's Tragic Heroes,* Cambridge, 1930, p. 182.
11. See John Draper, "Coriolanus," *W. V. U. Philological Studies,* 1939, p. 22 ff.
12. Elyot, *op. cit.,* Leaf 2 v.
13. J. Huarte, *Examen,* tr. Carew, London, 1594, 26, 57, 73, 120, 203-204.
14. T. Bright, *Treatise of Melancholy,* London, 1613, (1586), 115.
15. *The Most Excellent Booke of Dr. Arcandam,* tr. W. Warde, London, 1592, sig. M 2 r.
16. T. Wright, *Passions of the Minde,* London, 1604, 212-213 etc.
17. Dariot, *op. cit.,* sig. D 3 v.
18. Huarte, *op. cit.,* p. 280.
19. T. Adams, *Diseases of the Sovle,* London, 1616, p. 40; P. de la Primaudaye, *French Academy,* London, 1586, pp. 313-314.
20. B. Varchi, *Blazon of Jealousie,* tr. R. Tofte, London, 1615, p. 29; N. Coeffeteau, *Table of Humane Passions,* pp. 627-628.
21. W. Vaughan, *Directions for Health,* London, 1633, p. 136.
22. See John Draper, "The Jealousy of Iago," *Neophil.,* XXV, 50 ff.
23. Coeffeteau, *op. cit.,* p. 571.
24. Dariot, *op. cit.,* sig. D 3 r and v.
25. T. Walkington, *Optick Glasse,* London (1631?), 107.
26. Elyot, *op. cit.,* leaf 8 v.
27. Lemnius, *op. cit.,* leaves 86 v and 87 v; *Batman upon Bartholome,* London, 1582, leaf 30 r; Walkington, *op. cit.,* p. 111.
28. Lemnius, *op cit.,* leaf 86 v. Cf. H. Cuffe, *Differences of the Ages of Mans Life,* London, 1607, pp. 118-119.
29. Dariot, *op. cit.,* sig. D 2v.
30. *Arcandam,* sig. M 2 r.
31. *Much Ado,* II, i. This type of harmless wit fits the sanguine rather than the choleric humor. See Lemnius, *op cit.,* leaves 99 v and 100 r.

32. T. Cogan, *Haven of Health,* London, 1589, sig. Hh 2v; Coeffeteau, *op. cit.,* p. 551.
33. T. W[alkington], *Optick Glasse of Humors,* London (?1631), 117.
34. Ptolemy, *Tetrabiblos,* tr. Ashmand, London, 1822, p. 149.
35. Dariot, *op. cit.,* sig. D 3 v. It was proper to "louers."
36. *Arcandam,* sig. M 2 r; Dariot, *op. cit.,* sig. D 2 v; Walkington, *op. cit.,* p. 115.
37. Dariot, *op. cit.,* sig. D 2 r.
38. *Arcandam,* sig. M 2 r. Her remark (I, i, 127-129) that she and Benedick have "cold blood" seems to be ironic.
39. See John Draper, *The "Hamlet" of Shakespeare's Audience,* Durham, 1938, pp. 201-202; and *The Humors and Shakespeare's Characters,* Durham, 1945, Chap. viii.
40. Dariot, *op. cit.,* sig. D 3 v.
41. See N. Page, "Beatrice: 'My Lady Disdain'," *M. L. N.,* L. 494 ff.
42. Coeffeteau, *op. cit.,* p. 623.
43. A. Niccholes, *Discourse of Marriage,* London, 1615, 14.
44. J. Ferrand, 'ἔρωτομανία, or a *Treatise of Love,* Oxford, 1640, 93.
45. Coeffeteau, *op. cit.,* pp. 568 *passim.*
46. R. Burton, *Anatomy of Melancholy,* III, 2, 3.
47. *Ibid.,* III, 2, 2, 4.
48. E. K. Chambers, *Shakespeare,* New York, 1926, p. 128; and W. W. Lawrence, *Shakespeare's Problem Comedies,* New York 1931, pp. 69 and 72.

NOTES FOR XXX

1. See the First Folio, iv, ii, where the name of Kemp is substituted for Dogberry. Kemp probably played Shallow also. See T. W. Baldwin, *Shakespearean Company,* Princeton, 1927, Plate II.
2. *Much Ado,* ed. Furness var., v, i.
3. See N. Page, "Repudiation of Hero," *P.M.L.A.* (1935), L, 739 ff.
4. Bastards were supposed to act from base motives.
5. *Much Ado,* v. i.
6. *Ibid.,* v, i; and III, iii.
7. *Ibid.,* III, iii, III, v; IV, ii; and V, i.
8. J. Ritson, *Office of Constable,* London, 1791, pp. xv-xvi.
9. *Ibid.,* xvii ff;and F. Bacon, *Works,* ed. Spedding, Boston, 1861, XIV, 376.
10. F. Bacon, *op. cit.,* XIV, 375. See also XV, 339 ff.
11. C. Viner, *General Abridgment,* Aldershot, (1742-56), v, 427-428.
12. F. Bacon, *op. cit.,* XIV, 379; and XV, 339 and 264; M. Dalton, *The Country Justice,* London, 1682, p. 57; and W. Lambard, *The Dvties of Constables,* London, 1602, pp. 32-33.
13. See *N. E. D.,* s.v.
14. Webb, *English Local Government,* London, 1906-13, I, 26.
15. F. Bacon, *op. cit.,* XV, 346.
16. Webb, *op. cit.,* I, 19.
17. F. Bacon, *op. cit.,* XV, 342.
18. See L. D. Frasure, "Shakespeare's Constables," *Anglia,* XLVI (1934), 384 ff.
19. G. Latham, *Sh. Jhb.,* XXXII (1896) 140. According to the stage-directions, they appear "in gownes," iv, ii. Dogberry boasted of "two gownes" (iv, ii).
20. M. Bacon, *New Abridgment,* Philadelphia, 1811, I, 686.

21. Dalton, *op. cit.*, p. 58; and Ritson, *op. cit.*, p. 3.
22. Sir Thomas Smith, *Common-wealth of England*, London, 1594, p. 97; and Webb, I, 15 ff.
23. Dalton, *op. cit.*, p. 58.
24. See citations from Gifford *et al. Much Ado*, ed. Furness var., 160-61.
25. See William Hornby, *Scourge of Drunkenness*, London, 1618.
26. The statute of 27 Elizabeth, cap. xii, referred to "grievous complaints" against "evil behaviour of under-sheriffs." See D. Pickering, *Statutes at Large*, Cambridge, 1762-68, VI, 393.
27. *Much Ado*, III, v; III, iii; IV, ii.
28. *Ibid.*, III, iii.
29. The dogberry was the wild cornel, or corn tree, a common shrub. See Turner, *Herbal*, London, 1551, I Mjb.
30. *Much Ado*, IV, ii.
31. *Ibid.*, IV, ii.
32. See L. B. Wright, *Middle-Class Culture in Elizabethan England*, Chapel Hill, 1935, 146 ff. Dogberry had evidently memorized from conversation-manuals several expressions of polite withdrawal; and he favors the Prince with one that the Prince might more fitly have used to him. See *Much Ado*, v, i. Cf. Wright, 146 ff.
33. *Much Ado*, III, iii.
34. *Ibid.*, III, v, 1.
35. See *Conductor Generalis*, Philadelphia, 1722, p. 59; Smith, *op. cit.*, pp. 97-98; William Lambard, *Dvties of Constables*, London, 1602, p. 4 *passim;* Webb, I, 58 etc.; and Shakespeare, *Taming of the Shrew*, Induct., I, 11.
36. Smith, *op. cit.*, p. 97; and Ritson, *op. cit.*, pp. xx-xxi.
37. *Much Ado*, ed. Furness var., 2 n.
38. W. S. Holdsworth, *History of English Law*, Boston, 1922, I, 208 ff.; W. Lambard, *Archaion*, London, 1635, p. 38. Possibly there is a reference to Burleigh's "Acte for Westmynster," *Statutes of the Realme*, London, 1819, IV, 763.
39. See *N E D.*, *s. v.;* and Webb, *op. cit.*, p. 27.
40. *Much Ado*, III, iii. Cf. III, v.
41. *Ibid.*, III, iii.
42. J. R. Moore, *N. and Q.*, CLXXIV, 60-61.
43. See *Romeo and Juliet*, ed. Rolfe, 140. Dogberry calls attention to his "good name," as if it were significant (III, iii).
44. *Much Ado*, III, iii.
45. See John Draper, *The "Twelfth Night" of Shakespeare's Audience*, Stanford U. P., 1950, pp. 160-164.
46. See John Draper, *The "Hamlet" of Shakespeare's Audience*, Durham, N. C., 1938, 45.
47. *Much Ado*, v. i.
48. *Ibid.*, IV, ii, 66 ff.
49. See John Draper, "The Theme of '*Timon of Athens*'," *M.L.R.*, (1934), XXIX, 20 ff.
50. *Much Ado*, v, i.
51. See John Draper, *The "Othello" of Shakespeare's Audience*, Paris, 1952, Chap. IX.
52. The constable "ought to be in company with them [the watch] in their walk and march." Ritson, *op. cit.*, pp. 11 and 14.

53. *Ibid.,* p. 13; Dalton, *op. cit.,* p. 449.
54. Viner, *op. cit.,* v. 437.
55. Lambard, ed. 1602, 13; and *Conductor Generalis,* v, 60.
56. See *Much Ado,* ed. Furness var., pp. 161-162; and especially T. May, *The Heir,* v.
57. *Much Ado,* III, iii.
58. F. Bacon, *op. cit.,* XV, 346; and Ritson, *op. cit.,* p. 13.
59. *Much Ado,* III, iii.
60. Lord Campbell, *Shakespeare's Legal Acquirements,* London, 1859, p. 53.
61. Webb, *op. cit.,* I, 469.
62. Parkes, *Curtaine-Drawer of the World (ed. princ.,* 1612) ed. Grosart, p. 52.
63. *Much Ado,* III, iii.
64. *Ibid.*
65. *Ibid.,* III, iii.
66. *Ibid.,* III, iii.
67. Viner, *op. cit.,* v, 435.
68. Lord Campbell, *op. cit.,* p. 55. Persons of importance, of course, had their own retainers to guard them; and, in that homicidal age, other people hardly counted.
69. *Much Ado,* III, iii.
70. *Ibid.,* III, iii.
71. *Ibid.,* III, iii.
72. J. Parker, *Conductor,* New York, 1788, p. 29.
73. F. Bacon, *op. cit.,* I, 678; Viner, xv, 14.
74. *Much Ado,* v, i.
75. Viner, *op. cit.,* v, 438.
76. Pickering, *op. cit.,* I, 233.
77. A. Fitzherbarde, *New Bok of Justices,* London, 1560, sig. AA iiiir.
78. F. Bacon, *op. cit.,* XIV, 375; xv, 345.
79. W. Lambard, *Dvties of Constables,* London, 1619, p. 12.
80. E. Coke, *Fourth Institute,* Cap. XXV.
81. Viner, *op. cit.,* v, 436-37.
82. Ritson, *op. cit.,* pp. 11 and 12.
83. J. Doran, *History of Court Fools,* London, 1858, pp. 177-78.
84. Viner, *op. cit.,* v, 437.
85. *Much Ado,* IV, ii.
86. Viner, *op. cit.,* v, 437.
87. F. Bacon, *op. cit.,* XIV, 378; Smith, *op. cit.,* pp. 94 and 97.
88. *Much Ado,* III, v.
89. W. S. Holdsworth, *History of English Law,* Boston, 1922, I, 285 ff.
90. *Much Ado,* IV, ii, *passim.*
91. *The Compleat Justice,* London, 1661, p. 13.
92. Viner, *op. cit.,* v, 437-38; Ritson, *op. cit.,* p. 12.
93. *Much Ado,* v, i.
94. *Ibid.,* v, i.
95. See T. W. Baldwin, "Shakespeare's Jester," *MLN.,* XXXIX, 447 *et seq.*
96. See A. Underhill in *Shakespeare's England,* Oxford, 1917, I, 381 ff.
97. See John Draper, "Political Themes in Shakespeare's Later Plays," *J.E.G.P.,* (1936), XXXV, 61 ff.

INDEX

The more important page-references are set in italics.

Abbott, E. A., 117
Achilles, 69-70
Acolastus, 179
Adam (in *A.Y.L.I.*), 12, 14, 17 *pass.,* 35, 202 *pass.,* 231, 248 *pass.,* 271
Adams, C., 132
Adams, J. Q., 113
Addison, J., 214
Adriana, 201-2
Ægeon, 201-2
Ajax, 69
Akbar, Emperor, 167
Albany, 68
All's Well that Ends Well, 8, 21, 46, 52, 55, 135, 153, 154, 202, 204, 231, 250
Amurath (Murad) III, 166, 168
Aguecheek, Sir Andrew, 35, 36, 175, 185, 190, 204, 231
Antecedent action, *24 ff*
Antonio (in *Temp.*), 57
Antonio (in *M. of V.*), 32, 33, 37, 38, 52, 57, *128 pass.,* 138 *pass.,* 145 *pass.,* 203
Antony, 175
Antony and Cleopatra, 107, 155, 244
Apolonius and Silla, 261
Arcadia, 67
"Arcandam, Dr.", 207, 262
Arden of Feversham, 13, 26
Ariel, 18, 207, 221, 232
Aristotle, 89, 132, 133, 159, 207, 253, 263
Armado, Don, 6, 27, 50 *pass.,* 185, 191, 221
Armin, R., 189, 198
Army, *170 ff,* 237
Arnold, M., 10
Arthur, Prince, 29
Ascham, R., 49
Asinaria, 180
Astrology, *88 ff,* 158-9. See Aristotle, Humors, Galen
As You Like It, 5, 6, *7-8,* 9, 12, 16, 17, 20, *34-35,* 38, 44, ⁴5, 50, 52, *54-55,* 56, 57, 152-3, 202, 204, 224, 231, 248 *pass.,* 271
Audrey, 7
Aumerle. 77

Austen, Jane, 214
Autolycus, 46, 231

Bacon, F., 19, 133, 171, 224, 245, 274
Bagot, 76
Baldwin, T. W., 148 *pass.,* 156
Balthasar, 112, 231
Balzac, H. de, 175
Bandello, M., 65
Banquo, 175
Bardolph, 171, 176, 195, 229 *pass.*
Barnfield, R., 132
Bartholomæus Ang., 207, 238
Basilikon Doron, 225
Bassanio, 14, 18, 19, 32, 33, 37, 44, 57, *128 pass.,* 220, 249, 251
Basse, W., 15, 18, 225
Bastard of Orleans, 60 *pass.*
Batista, 243
Beatrice, 34, 47, *260 ff*
Belarius, 8
Belch, Sir Toby, 7, 20, 35, 36, 149, 175, 185, 191
Bellario, 44, 242-3
Bembo, P., 50
Benedick, 34, 47, 293, *260 ff*
Bentivoglio, Cardinal, 244
Bentivoglio, G., 244
Benvolio, 31, 90 *pass.,* 97, 102 *pass.,* 116
Bergamo, 240, 244, 245
Bianca, 29, 43, 260
Biondello, 16
Biron, 27, 52 *pass.,* 56
Blind Beggar, 192
Bodenham, J., 65
Bodenstedt, F., 86
Bolingbroke, 30, 38, 75 *pass.*
Bologna, 244
Borachio, 44, *268 ff*
Boris, Tsar, 167
Bottom, 6, 279
Boult, 21, 22
Bovary, Madame, 216
Boy (in *R. and J.*), 222

313

DATE DUE

APR 29 '75			